GUADALCANAL

Books by Eric Hammel

76 Hours: The Invasion of Tarawa (with John E. Lane)
Chosin: Heroic Ordeal of the Korean War
The Root: The Marines in Beirut
Ace: A Marine Night-Fighter Pilot in World War II
(with R. Bruce Porter)
Duel for the Golan: The 100-Hour Battle That Saved Israel
(with Jerry Asher)

GUADALCANAL
Starvation Island

ERIC HAMMEL

CROWN PUBLISHERS, INC

New York

In Memory of
DONALD KNOX

Published by Crown Publishers, Inc.,
225 Park Avenue South,
New York, New York 10003 and represented in
Canada by the Canadian MANDA Group

CROWN is a trademark of Crown Publishers, Inc.

Manufactured in the United States of America

Library of Congress Cataloging-in-Publication Data

Hammel, Eric M.
Guadalcanal: starvation island.

Includes index.
1. World War, 1939-1945—Campaigns—Solomon Islands—
Guadalcanal Island.   2. Guadalcanal Island (Solomon
Islands)—History.   I. Title.
D767.98.H33 1987   940.54'26   86-16586
ISBN 0-517-56417-3

10 9 8 7 6 5 4 3 2 1

First Edition

GUIDE TO ABBREVIATIONS
AND TERMS

Adm	Admiral
Air Ops	Air Operations
AP1	Aviation Pilot 1st Class
Avenger	Grumman TBF Torpedo Bomber
B-17	Boeing Flying Fortress Heavy Bomber
B-24	Consolidated Liberator Heavy Bomber
B-26	Martin Marauder Medium Bomber
BAR	Browning Automatic Rifle
Betty	Mitsubishi G4M Medium Bomber
BGen	Brigadier General
Butai	Unit
C-47	Douglas DC-3 Skytrain Transport
Cactus	Code Name for Guadalcanal
Capt	Captain
Catalina	Consolidated PBY Patrol Bomber
Cdr	Commander
'Chutes	Parachute Battalion
cm	Centimeter
CO	Commanding Officer
Col	Colonel

CP	Command Post
Cpl	Corporal
CUB	Construction Unit, Base
Dauntless	Douglas SBD Dive-Bomber
Ens	Ensign
Exec	Executive Officer
F4F	Grumman Wildcat Fighter
1stLt	First Lieutenant
1stSgt	First Sergeant
Gen	General
GI	Government Issue; i.e., Soldier
GySgt	Gunnery Sergeant
HIJMS	His Imperial Japanese Majesty's Ship
Kate	Nakajima B5N Torpedo Bomber
KIA	Killed in Action
kg	Kilogram
LCdr	Lieutenant Commander
Lt	Lieutenant
Lt(jg)	Lieutenant (junior grade)
LtCol	Lieutenant Colonel
LtGen	Lieutenant General
M1	Garand Rifle
MAG	Marine Air Group
Maj	Major
MG	Marine Gunner (Warrant Officer)
MGen	Major General
MGySgt	Master Gunnery Sergeant

MIA	Missing in Action
mm	Millimeter
NCO	Noncommissioned Officer
P-38	Lockheed Lightning Fighter
P-39	Bell Airacobra Fighter
P-40	Curtiss Warhawk Fighter
P-400	Bell Airacobra Export Fighter
PBY	Consolidated Catalina Patrol Bomber
Pfc	Private First Class
PlSgt	Platoon Sergeant
PT	Patrol Torpedo Boat
Pvt	Private
RAAF	Royal Australian Air Force
RAdm	Rear Admiral
R4D	Douglas Skytrain Transport
Rikusentai	Japanese Infantry-trained Bluejackets
SBD	Douglas Dauntless Dive-Bomber
Seabee	Navy Construction Battalion Engineer (i.e., CB)
2ndLt	Second Lieutenant
Sgt	Sergeant
SgtMaj	Sergeant Major
Skytrain	Douglas DC-3/R4D/C-47 Transport
TBF	Grumman Avenger Torpedo Bomber
TSgt	Technical Sergeant
USA	U.S. Army
USMC	U.S. Marine Corps
USN	U.S. Navy
USS	United States Ship
VAdm	Vice Admiral

GUIDE TO ABBREVIATIONS

Val	Aichi D3A Dive-Bomber
VMF	Marine Fighter Squadron
VMJ	Marine Utility (Transport) Squadron
VMO	Marine Observation Squadron
VMSB	Marine Scout-Bomber Squadron
WIA	Wounded in Action
Wildcat	Grumman F4F Fighter
Zero	Mitsubishi A6M2 Fighter

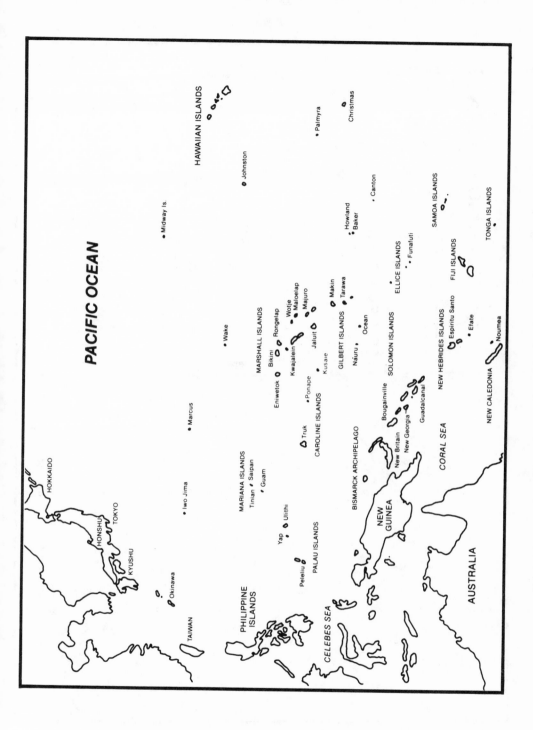

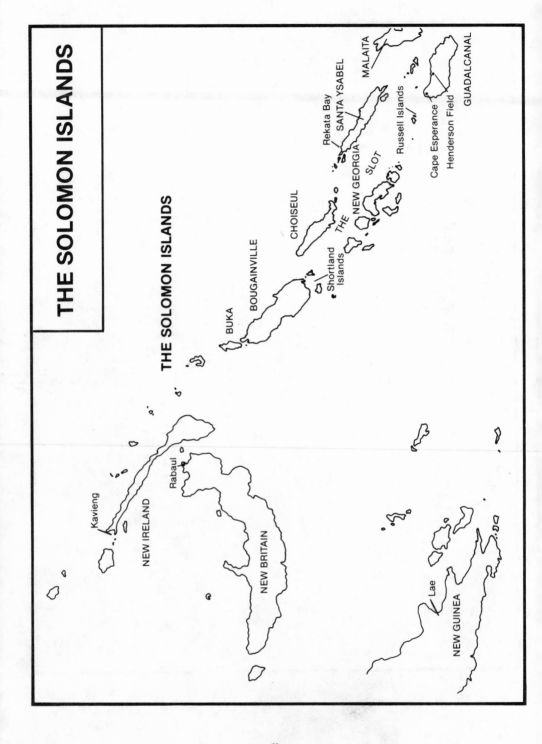

THE SOLOMON ISLANDS

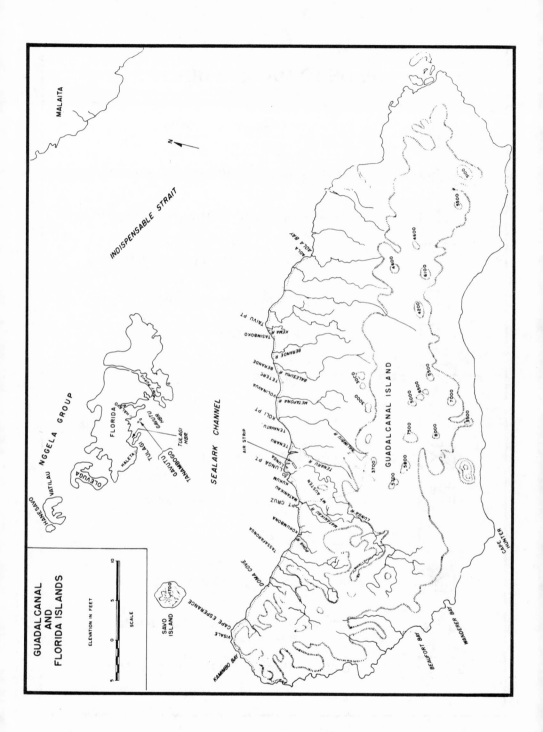

GUADALCANAL
AND
FLORIDA ISLANDS

ELEVATION IN FEET

SCALE

MALAITA

N

INDISPENSABLE STRAIT

NGGELA GROUP

FLORIDA

MARAVOVO
VATILAU
OLEVUGA

HALETA
TULAGI
GAVUTU HBR
GAVUTU
TULAGI HBR
TANAMBOGO

SEALARK CHANNEL

SAVO
ISLAND

CAPE ESPERANCE
VISALE
KAMIMBO BAY

DOMA COVE
TASSAFARONGA
BONA
YOKUMBONA
MATANIKAU R
KOKUM
LUNGA PT
MT AUSTEN
PT CRUZ
AIR STRIP
TENARU
TENARU R
TENAVATU
KOLI PT
METAPONA R
VOLINAVUA
TETERE
BALESUMA R
BERANDE R
BERANDE R
TASIMBOKO
KEMA
TAIVU PT
AOLA
AOLA BAY

MALIMBU R
ILU R
KUKUM

GUADALCANAL ISLAND

5700
3500
3000
5000
5500
6500
6500
7500
8000
5900
7000
5500
6100
8000
5500
4600
4200
9800
5500

BEAUFORT BAY
WANDERER BAY
CAPE HUNTER

xi

GUIDE TO MAP SYMBOLS

1st Marine Division Headquarters

Marine or Infantry Regiment (7th Marines)

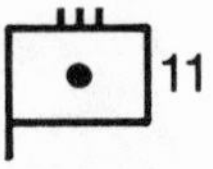

11th Marine Regiment (Artillery) Headquarters

Infantry Battalion (1st Battalion, 5th Marines)

1st Amphibian Tractor Battalion

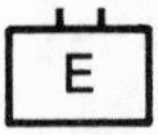

1st Engineer Battalion

1st Parachute Battalion

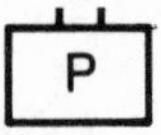

1st Pioneer Battalion

1st Raider Battalion

1st Tank Battalion (minus detachments)

3rd Defense Battalion

Infantry Company (E Company, 5th Marines)

Infantry Outpost (2nd Battalion, 1st Marines)

Battalion Bivouac (3rd Battalion, 5th Marines)

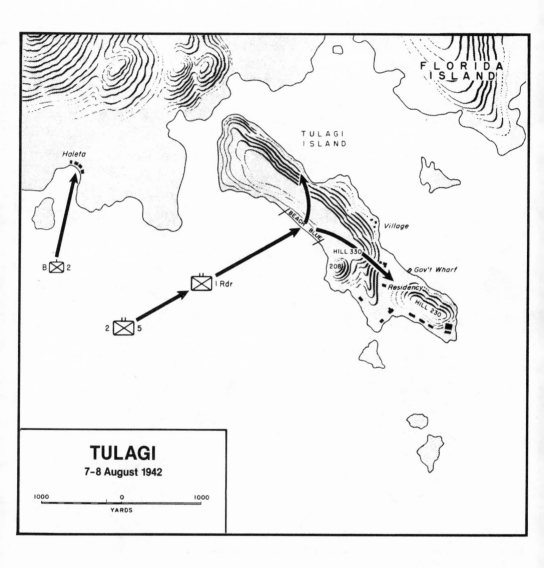

FLORIDA
ISLAND

TULAGI
ISLAND

Haleta

B ⊠ 2

2 ⊠ 5

I Rdr

BEACH BLUE

Village

HILL 330

208

Residency

Gov't Wharf

HILL 230

TULAGI

7–8 August 1942

1000   0   1000

YARDS

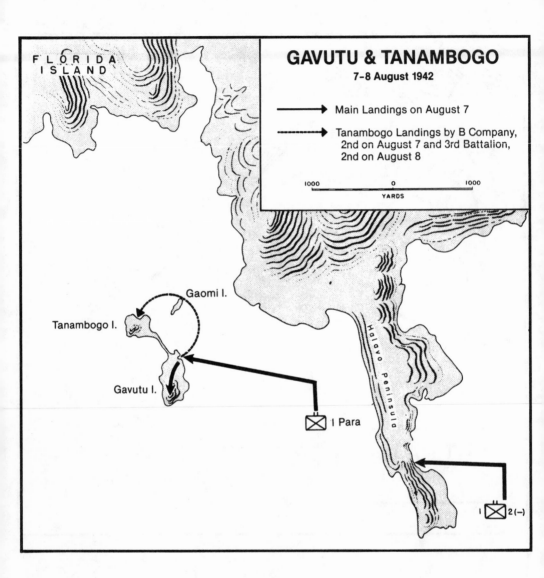

GAVUTU & TANAMBOGO

7–8 August 1942

→ Main Landings on August 7

┈┈→ Tanambogo Landings by B Company, 2nd on August 7 and 3rd Battalion, 2nd on August 8

1000   0   1000
YARDS

FLORIDA ISLAND

Gaomi I.

Tanambogo I.

Gavutu I.

I Para

Halavo Peninsula

1 ⊠ 2(−)

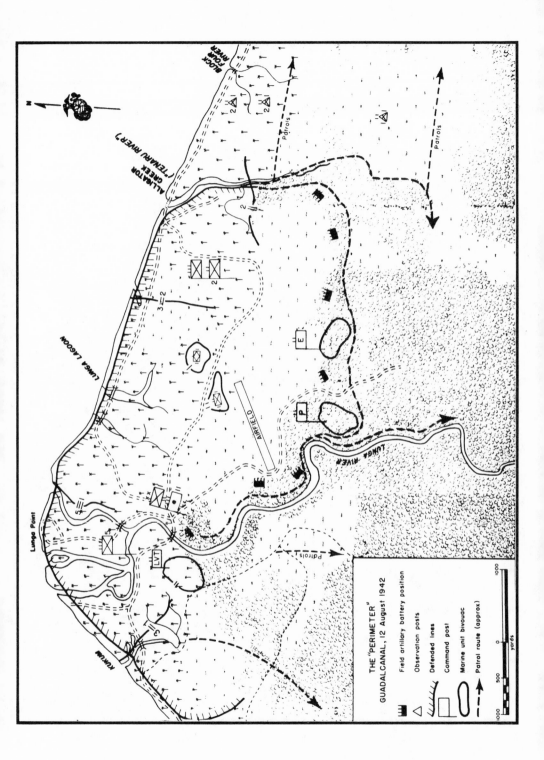

THE "PERIMETER"
GUADALCANAL, 12 August 1942

△ Field artillery battery position

△ Observation posts

⊏⊐ Defended lines

▭ Command post

▬▬▬➤ Marine unit bivouac

- - -➤ Patrol route (approx)

1000   500   0   1000
yards

AIRFIELD

Lunga Point

LUNGA LAGOON

ALLIGATOR CREEK
("TENARU RIVER")

BLOCK FOUR RIVER

LUNGA RIVER

KUKUM

Patrols

N

XV

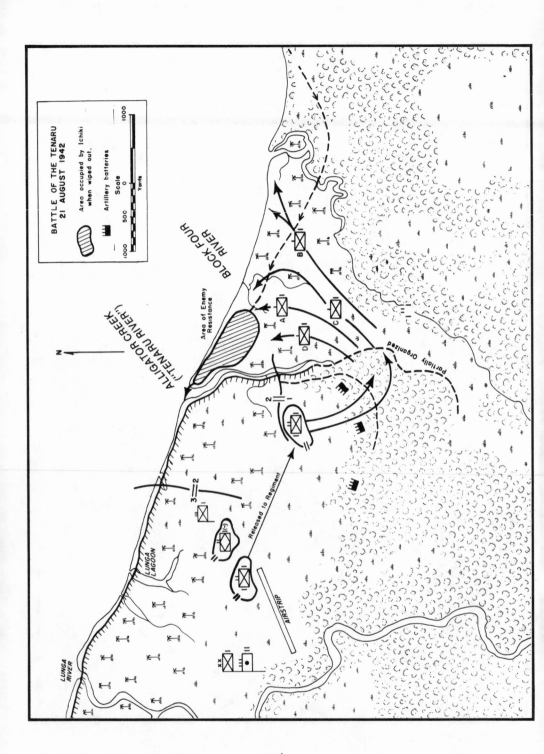

BATTLE OF THE TENARU
21 AUGUST 1942

Area occupied by Ichiki
when wiped out.

Artillery batteries

Scale

1000   500   0   1000

Yards

BLOCK FOUR

BLOCK RIVER

ALLIGATOR CREEK
("TENARU RIVER")

N

Area of Enemy
Resistance

Partially Organized

Released to Regiment

LUNGA LAGOON

LUNGA RIVER

AIRSTRIP

xvi

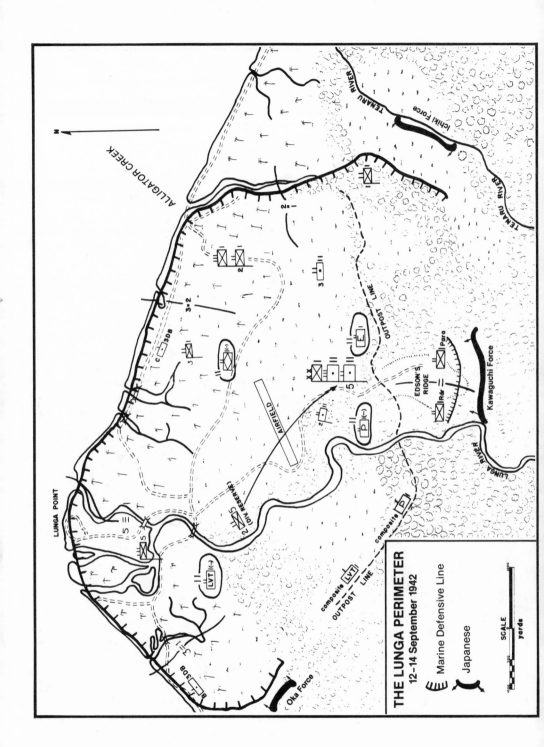

THE LUNGA PERIMETER
12–14 September 1942

Marine Defensive Line

Japanese

SCALE
yards

xvii

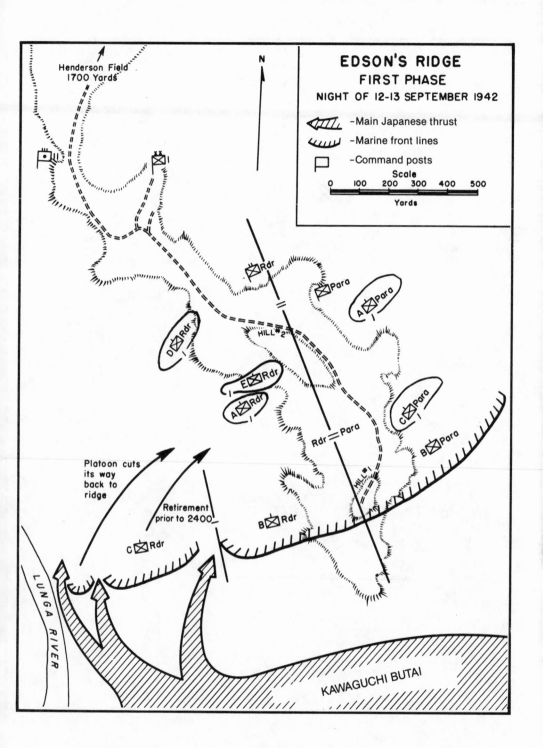

EDSON'S RIDGE
FIRST PHASE
NIGHT OF 12-13 SEPTEMBER 1942

- Main Japanese thrust
- Marine front lines
- Command posts

Scale

0   100   200   300   400   500

Yards

Henderson Field
1700 Yards

N

Rdr

Para

A Para

D Rdr

HILL #2

E Rdr

A Rdr

C Para

B Para

Rdr ≡ Para

HILL #1

Platoon cuts
its way
back to
ridge

Retirement
prior to 2400

B Rdr

C Rdr

L U N G A   R I V E R

KAWAGUCHI BUTAI

xviii

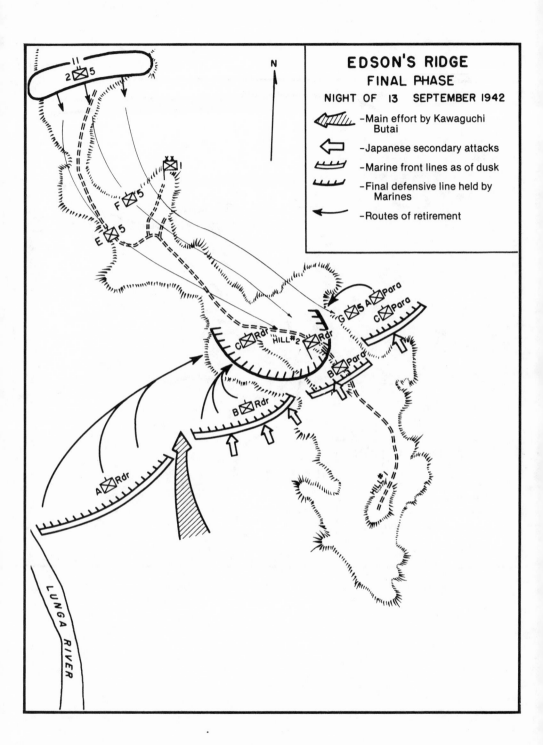

N

EDSON'S RIDGE
FINAL PHASE
NIGHT OF 13 SEPTEMBER 1942

- Main effort by Kawaguchi Butai
- Japanese secondary attacks
- Marine front lines as of dusk
- Final defensive line held by Marines
- Routes of retirement

2 ⊠ 5

X 1

F ⊠ 5

E ⊠ 5

G ⊠ 5 A ⊠ Para

C ⊠ Para

C ⊠ Rdr   HILL #2 ⊠ Rdr

B ⊠ Para

B ⊠ Rdr

A ⊠ Rdr

HILL #1

LUNGA RIVER

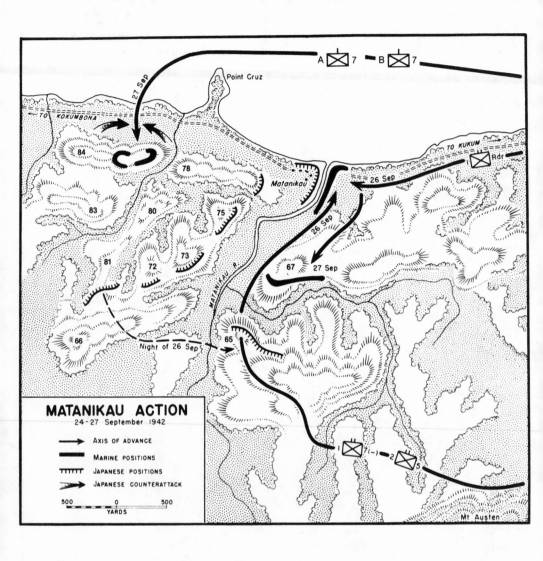

A 7 — B 7

Point Cruz

27 Sep

TO KOKUMBONA

TO KUKUM

Rdr

84

78

Matanikau

26 Sep

83

80

75

26 Sep

67 27 Sep

81

72

73

MATANIKAU R

66

Night of 26 Sep

65

1 7(-) — 2 5

MATANIKAU ACTION
24–27 September 1942

→ AXIS OF ADVANCE

▬ MARINE POSITIONS

ⅢⅢⅢ JAPANESE POSITIONS

▶ JAPANESE COUNTERATTACK

500   0   500
YARDS

Mt Austen

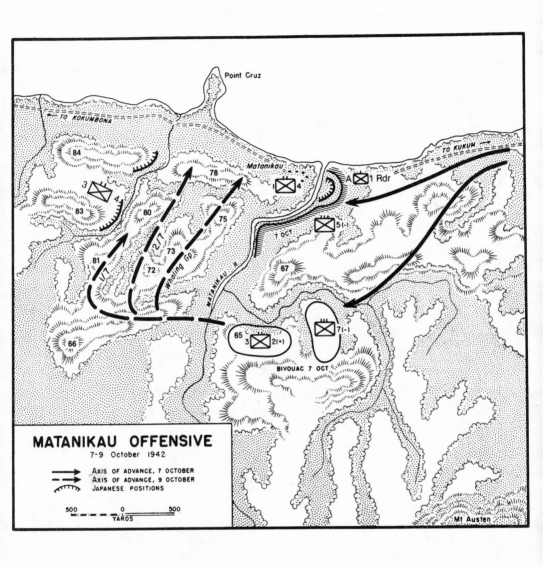

Point Cruz

TO KOKUMBONA

TO KUKUM

84

Matanikau

3 [X] 4

A [X] 1 Rdr

83

78

80

75

[X] 4

[X] 5(-)

7 OCT

2/7

73

67

81

72

Whaling Gp

MATANIKAU R.

1/7

66

65 3 [X] 2(+)

[X] 7(-)

BIVOUAC 7 OCT

Mt Austen

MATANIKAU OFFENSIVE
7-9 October 1942

→ AXIS OF ADVANCE, 7 OCTOBER
⇢ AXIS OF ADVANCE, 9 OCTOBER
⌒⌒ JAPANESE POSITIONS

500   0   500
YARDS

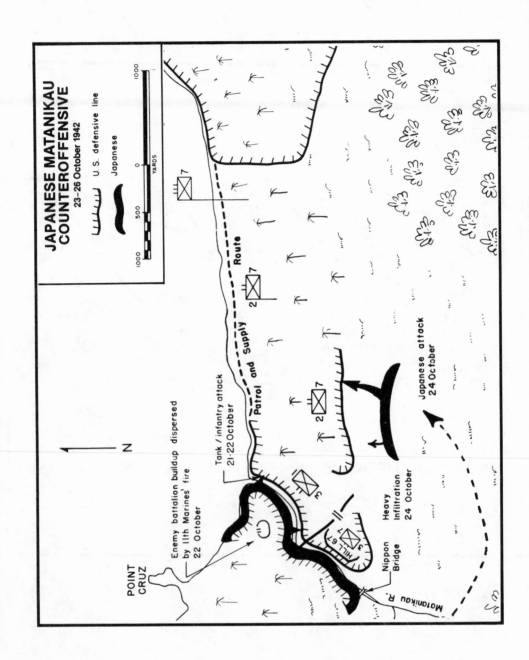

JAPANESE MATANIKAU
COUNTEROFFENSIVE

23–26 October 1942

U. S. defensive line
Japanese

YARDS

POINT CRUZ

Enemy battalion buildup dispersed by 11th Marines' fire 22 October

Tank / infantry attack 21-22 October

Patrol and Supply Route

Japanese attack 24 October

Heavy Infiltration 24 October

Nippon Bridge

HILL 67

Matanikau R.

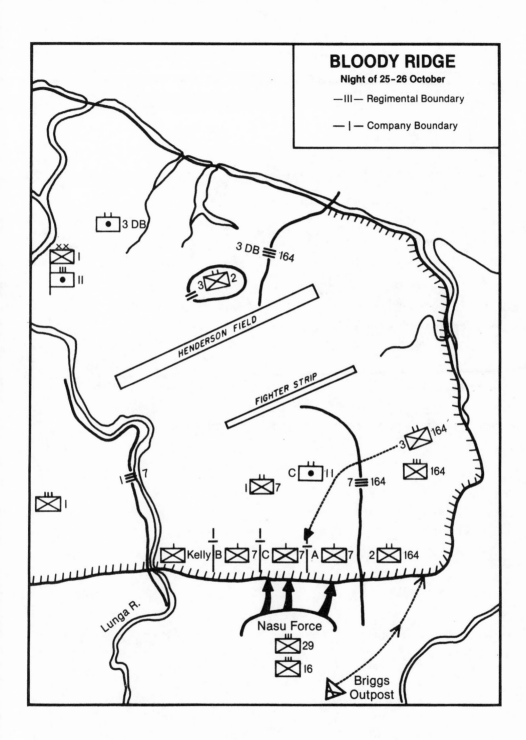

BLOODY RIDGE

Night of 25–26 October

—III— Regimental Boundary

— I — Company Boundary

3 DB

3 DB ≡ 164

3 ⊠ 2

HENDERSON FIELD

FIGHTER STRIP

3 ⊠ 164

164 ⊠ 164

I ≡ 7

C ⊡ 11

I ⊠ 7

7 ≡ 164

⊠ I

⊠ Kelly | B | ⊠ 7 | C | ⊠ 7 | A | ⊠ 7 | 2 ⊠ 164

Nasu Force

⊠ 29

⊠ 16

Briggs Outpost

Lunga R.

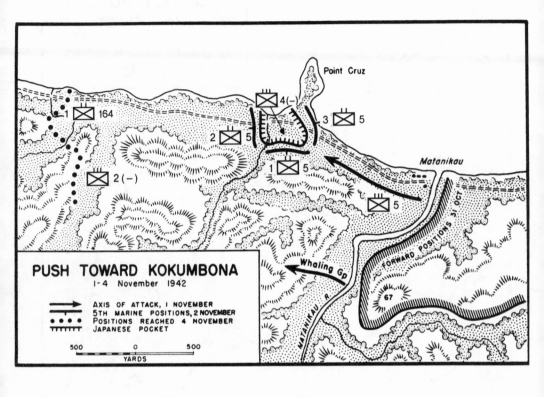

PUSH TOWARD KOKUMBONA
1-4 November 1942

AXIS OF ATTACK, 1 NOVEMBER
5TH MARINE POSITIONS, 2 NOVEMBER
POSITIONS REACHED 4 NOVEMBER
JAPANESE POCKET

500   0   500
YARDS

Point Cruz

4(−)

164

3   5

2   5

2(−)

1   5

5

Matanikau

Whaling Gp

FORWARD POSITIONS 31 OCT

MATANIKAU R.

67

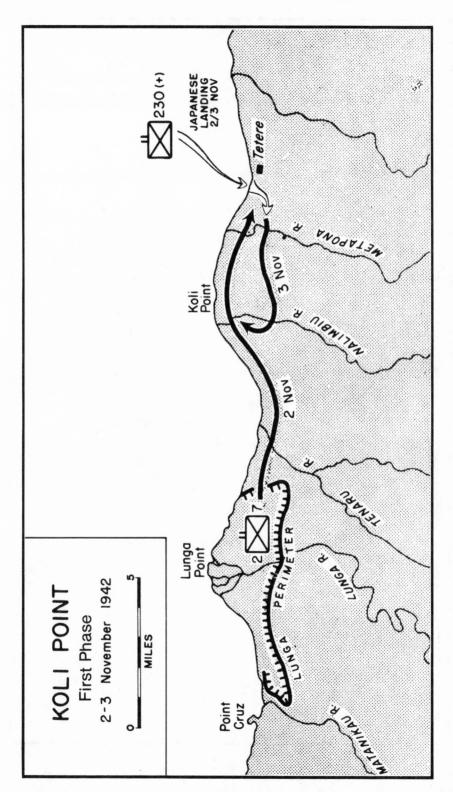

KOLI POINT
First Phase
2-3 November 1942

0 MILES 5

230 (+)

JAPANESE LANDING 2/3 NOV

Tetere

METAPONA R.

3 NOV

NALIMBIU R.

Koli Point

2 NOV

TENARU R.

7

2

LUNGA PERIMETER

Lunga Point

LUNGA R.

Point Cruz

MATANIKAU R.

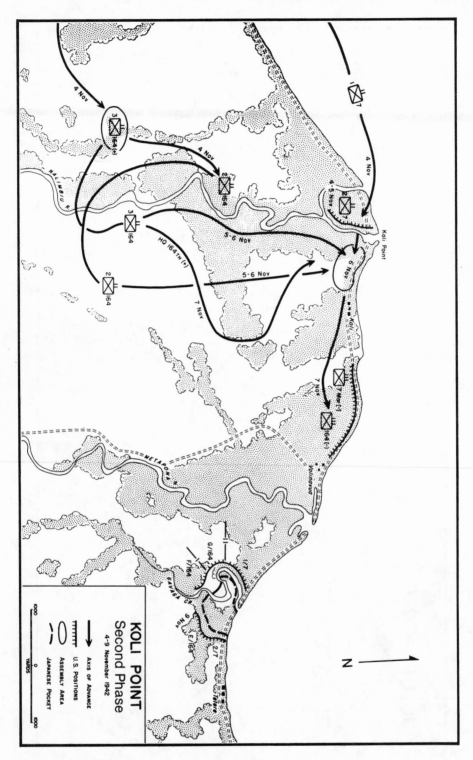

KOLI POINT
Second Phase
4-9 November 1942

Axis of Advance
U.S. Positions
Assembly Area
Japanese Pocket

YARDS

PROLOGUE

The Empire of Japan opened the Pacific War on December 7, 1941, with a dizzying array of bold, far-ranging strikes, mainly from the air, against the fleets and airbases of the United States and Great Britain, the nations that posed the greatest threats to its program of imperial expansion.

By December 11, the remnants of the armies, navies, and air forces of Japan's chosen enemies were in total disarray. English-speaking nations with war-making potentials far greater than Japan's were on the defensive, demoralized and overcome by fear and defeat. Within the last month of 1941, Japan met or exceeded every single one of her early objectives. Within three months of the sudden onset of the Pacific War, Japanese divisions defeated larger Commonwealth land-based forces on mainland Asia, and Japanese aircraft carriers staged daring, unchallenged, utterly demoralizing raids against British, Dutch, and American bases and warships.

There was the odd glimmer of hope, at Wake Island for a few weeks, and in the Philippines for a few months. But the end of resistance in those places was assured by the inability of the United

States to resupply or reinforce its far-flung garrisons. The English-speaking allies had not the resources to stem this rising Japanese tide as it washed across increasingly vast expanses to engulf holding after holding.

Almost unperceived, however, was a growing Japanese recklessness: The more Japanese arms won, the more Japanese arms sought to win. The Japanese charged blindly from island to island in the Pacific. After attaining economically and strategically necessary victories in Southeast Asia and the East Indies, the push was redirected south and east, toward the ripe "South Seas" islands, with their underdeveloped mineral and agricultural potentials, along stepping-stones radiating across the shipping lanes that connected Australia and New Zealand with the rest of the English-speaking world. Unable to muster any military resources, the Commonwealth nations in the Pacific gave ground, allowing the Japanese to charge headlong across still more islands.

It was unintentional, but the very impotence that forced the Allies to give ground—combined with the progressively more-pronounced Japanese proclivity for expansion—was leading Japan into a potential trap. As Japanese garrisons were placed upon beach after successive beach, the ability of the Imperial Navy to protect and provision them adequately diminished. It was not noticeable at all to the Japanese, but they eventually were winning easy victories at the expense of a defensible perimeter.

In territorial expansions that range across vast distances, balances must shift. As one side advances, its lines of supply become longer, its periphery becomes larger, its manpower requirements increasingly shift from aggressive to protective. At the same time, a once-extended adversary, now back-pedaling, inevitably finds itself operating along shorter lines of supply, with a shrinking periphery to defend, and attempting to draw reinforcements toward the center of the conflict from outlying areas it can no longer afford to defend. That nation—if its leadership is alert and courageous—might, in desperation, find the resolve to stand firm, to seize the fleeting, historical moment in which the other, attacking side takes a breather or finds itself off balance. Napoleon was defeated far inside Russia by such a confluence of events in 1812. So was Hitler in the winter of 1941–42.

And so was Japan in the second half of 1942.

The confluence of events that defeated Japan in the Pacific War occurred in the eastern Solomon Islands, on and around a large but largely unheard of island called Guadalcanal. It had been named in the mid-sixteenth century by the first white men to venture into the area, a boatload of Spanish fortune-hunters. Neither the Spaniards, nor the Frenchmen, the Englishmen, nor any other Europeans who followed in the next 300 years saw any value in claiming the Solomon Islands for their sovereigns. In the late-nineteenth century, the late-blooming German Empire was eager to send missionaries and traders to any unclaimed backwater. Thus a brief race arose in 1884, when Germany proclaimed the protectorate of Kaiser-Wilhelmsland, comprising northeastern New Guinea, the Bismarck Archipelago, and the Northern Solomon Islands. Britain was moved to establish a protectorate in the adjacent Southern Solomon Islands (also called the Lower or Eastern Solomons) and to annex the remainder of New Guinea. The British territories were turned over to Australia in 1905 and renamed the Territory of Papua, with its capital at Port Moresby. In 1914, at the outbreak of the Great War, Australia seized the German protectorate, then administered it after the war as a League of Nations mandate, with its capital in Rabaul, on the island of New Britain, in the Bismarck Archipelago.

Politically, the Australian territories were divided into several government districts: Northeast New Guinea, New Britain, New Ireland, Manus (incorporating the Admiralty Islands and the Northwest Islands), and Kieta (incorporating Buka and Bougainville, the so-called Northern Solomons). Not under Australian control were the British Solomon Islands Protectorate (incorporating the Santa Cruz Islands, Choiseul, Santa Ysabel, New Georgia, Malaita, Guadalcanal, San Cristobal, and numerous other islands, which were all under British administration) with its capital at Tulagi.

Not much happened between the wars. Missionaries came and went, traders came and went, government officials came and went, goldminers came and stayed. Mainly, the islanders, missionaries, storekeepers, traders, and bureaucrats lived near the water, where cooling sea breezes make life tolerable. The miners ranged farther inland in search of gold.

The Bismarcks and Solomons are not tropical paradises, but merely tropical. Most of the islands are mountainous, with peaks rising in some places to over 13,000 feet. They are volcanic, but many of the smaller islands are coral, and the waters throughout are filled with treacherous coral obstacles. It rains a great deal in the Solomons and Bismarcks, more than 200 inches per year upland, and well over 100 inches per year along the coasts. Indeed, the evaporation in these islands is greater over land than over water. The temperature stays at 75–90 degrees year-round; the climate is extremely humid and conducive to a wide range of tropical diseases.

In 1941, the islanders numbered about a quarter-million, and were of mixed Melanesian and Polynesian stock. They were tribal and primitive, living in small villages and subsisting upon jungle gardens of taro, yams, and sweet potatoes supplemented with fish and gathered fruit.

Christianity had gotten the attention, if not the undevoted allegiance or total comprehension, of many of the islanders by 1941, but the basic belief system was animistic. The only common language among the linguistically diverse islanders was a polyglot tongue known as Pidgin, which itself varied from place to place. Most government functions were carried out in this simple sing-song.

There was nothing to defend in the Bismarcks and Solomons in late 1941 and early 1942, and the Australians and British did not seriously attempt to do so. Also, there was nothing really worth taking. Japanese planners certainly did not envision a massive incursion into the area. Rather, they occupied the vacuum left by those who had fled. They took Rabaul without a fight in January, then waited until March to move from there.

Inadvertently, each step beyond Rabaul brought the Japanese nearer the range of the very few aircraft the Allies had deployed in the region. And each step took the Japanese a bit farther from their own secure bases.

There was no reason inherent in the value of the Bismarcks and Solomons that made them worth a fight. Only a confluence of events would make them a focal point for a desperate gamble.

PART I

Before

I

Morinda hove into view an hour before noon, trailing a great plume of thick black smoke from her ancient coal-fired boiler. She was an old inter-island steamer owned by the Burns-Philp Company, the great Pacific copra conglomerate, and her mission on February 8, 1942, was to evacuate European and Asian planters, miners, businessmen, and missionaries from Gavutu Island, the seat of the Burns-Philp operation in the British Solomon Islands.

The wharf at Gavutu, a tiny coral-sand islet dominated by a single, sparsely wooded hill set against the lush backdrop of larger jungle-shrouded islands and a picture-book sea, was an incongruous, cacophonous hubbub of stolid, patient Europeans and near-panicked Chinese shopkeepers jockeying for better positions nearer the wharfside.

As *Morinda* labored up the channel, the low, ominous drone of aircraft engines could be heard over the soothing seashell sound of the surging surf and the gabble of anxious voices. Fearful eyes scanned the bright blue sky and picked out the shape of a large, four-engined reconnaissance bomber.

The Japanese had arrived!

As the lumbering bomber grew fearsomely larger, *Morinda* chugged gracelessly into a tree-shrouded estuary formed by a minor river debouching from the uneven shoreline of neighboring Florida Island, her telltale plume of thick coal smoke marking her progress for the Japanese aircrew.

Four tiny objects detached themselves from the gigantic bomber and plummeted earthward: Two blew up harmlessly ahead of the steamer's bows, while the other two missed well astern. Then the Japanese bomber lazily turned for home amidst the cheers of the men, women, and children who moments earlier had awaited disaster. *Morinda* chugged into sight once again and completed her docking without further incident.

Nearly 700 Europeans, mainly Britons and Australians, lived in the Solomon Islands. Although the British Empire and Commonwealth had been at war since 1939, woefully little had been done to defend the Solomons; the islands were far from any of the places anyone thought of fighting over. A Royal Marines commando brigade earmarked for the area had been sent, instead, to Malaya, and would be lost there.

Still, the war *had* come, and something had to be done. Stopping the Japanese was out of the question, so stinging them a bit here and there seemed to be the only solution. No one doubted but that the Solomons would be lost and, one day, won back; work proceeded to facilitate the coming of that day.

Australian military officers had long feared an incursion into their part of the Pacific by the expansionist Japanese, but lack of popular interest and severely limited financial resources had prevented them from implementing any of the makeshift plans they had proposed following World War I.

As a result of rumors circulating through the area in late 1939 concerning the presence of the German commerce raider, *Europa*, a number of British and Australian government district officers had been outfitted with wireless radios and told to watch out for trouble. The German raider had not materialized and the "Coastwatching" network soon lapsed into routine operation. However, the wireless sets remained in the hands of many of the district officers, and they could serve as the basis for an effort to impede the Japanese.

Rabaul, the administrative center of the Australian-mandated Bismarck and Northern Solomon Island groups, and one of the largest commercial centers in the entire South Pacific region, was taken by the Japanese without a struggle on January 23, 1942. Within days, a stream of refugees—Europeans, Chinese, Fijians, islanders—snowballed along the projected Japanese route of conquest. As the stream ebbed and swelled, the district officers spent more time working on their coastwatching network. Most of them faced little immediate danger, so they remained at their stations, carrying out their governmental duties. As the Japanese moved through the Bismarcks in early 1942, however, many of the local district officers and other Europeans took to the bush to report what little they could see of Japanese movements.

The Japanese did not move beyond the Bismarcks for nearly six weeks following the seizure of Rabaul, but refugees nonetheless poured southeastward along the 600-mile-long Solomons chain, toward Tulagi, seat of the British Solomon Islands government, only a few hundred yards from the Burns-Philp complex at Gavutu. It had been rumored that *Morinda*, the Burns-Philp trading vessel, was to dock at Gavutu on February 8, during her final voyage to Australia.

As the thoroughly alarmed evacuees fought their way aboard the rescue ship—many arguing with the inappropriately officious captain, who insisted for a time upon collecting tickets from each of them—a lone figure fought through from the deck to the wharf. He was a burly twenty-five-year-old with a sandy moustache and the fluid movements of an athlete, and he had about him for the moment an undisguised air of confusion. After running up and down the wharf several times, he fought his way back aboard the steamer to fetch a few useful items from his luggage. Then he made his way back through the throng and on down to a small-boat slip, where he begged a ride over to nearby Tulagi.

Sometime later, Warren Frederick Martin Clemens climbed the hill to the Resident Commissioner's office, wondering a bit at his own aplomb. Having arrived in the Solomons in 1938 as a colonial service cadet, the former Cambridge oarsman was just returning from leave in Sydney to duty he-knew-not-where. A high-ranking colonial officer had welcomed him only minutes before in a bone-chilling sort of way: "Why did you come back, you ass?"

As *Morinda* cast off from Gavutu with nearly the whole of his luggage, Martin Clemens found himself embroiled in a debate with William Marchant, the elderly, peevish resident commissioner, who wanted Clemens to travel northwestward, to assume responsibility for Gizo Island, in the Central Solomons. Clemens had traded advice with several of the other young district officers gathered near Marchant's office, including the former Gizo district officer. They had warned him to steer clear of the island at all costs. So, when Marchant uttered Gizo's name, Clemens pointed out that that place was close to the Japanese, and that he doubted he would have time to establish himself there before it was overrun. Marchant gave in to Clemens, who was ordered to Guadalcanal, the largest of the British Solomon Islands, just twenty miles south of Tulagi. Far from satisfied, the young district officer went off to try to salvage the few possessions he had stored on Tulagi before going on leave.

Clemens packed what little of his personal gear he could find, scrounged what little there was to scrounge, and crossed from Tulagi to Aola, on Guadalcanal's northern coast, on February 11 to take up his duties there as the assistant district officer. Accompanying him was Royal Australian Navy Paymaster-Lt Donald Mac-Farlan, who moved some days later to Berande, where a planter named Kenneth Hay had set up a camp at the homestead on the Burns-Philp plantation.

Resident Commissioner Marchant endeavored to do what he could, but he was terribly confused by the high excitement of the time. His duty, as he saw it, was to salvage what he might from the abandoned stores of many of the local plantations and make his way, under orders, to Auki, on nearby Malaita Island, to establish a new residency. In the little time between *Morinda*'s last trip and their own departure, Marchant and the few of his assistants who had not already fled toured the villages to move important stores to prevent looting, and to collect and repatriate scores of Malaitans who had been left in the lurch with neither food nor pay when their European employers had sailed away.

The lot of the men who were to stay behind—Clemens, Mac-Farlan, Hay, and others—could be seriously affected by the attitude of the locals. Getting a plausible positive message across to the islanders was no mean feat in the face of objective reality. The British, whom the islanders saw as being immensely powerful, were fleeing. An even stronger people must be at the root of the problem, a people with whom the islanders might well throw in. Such a shift in the popular sentiment would doom any effort by the stay-behinds—the Coastwatchers—to establish a viable observing network. It was a sobering thought that influenced their every action.

On March 8, 1942, six Japanese auxiliary cruiser-transports and two destroyers dropped anchor near Buka, off the northern tip of Bougainville, the northernmost and largest of the Solomon Islands. A stream of armor-plated landing craft deposited a force of infantry-trained bluejackets—*rikusentai*—on the beach, to establish a permanent base. The occupation of Buka Passage was monitored by the local Australian district officer and Coastwatcher, Jack Read, who flashed word to Port Moresby, New Guinea, the closest secure Allied base. During the next several weeks, Imperial Navy landing forces spread southeastward through the Solomons with such success that even they were surprised. Ships and aircraft were sent from Rabaul, and detachments of *rikusentai* were landed at various points around Bougainville in order to inspect or occupy likely looking base sites. European planters and traders, and a few missionaries, were detained. Most had no interest in the war and were released following interrogations and stern warnings. However,

Percy Goode, an Australian planter, was arrested on Buka, suspected of relaying one of Jack Read's covert messages to Port Moresby. Goode was executed on March 16, though he was totally innocent of any wrongdoing. At about the same time, an American Catholic priest manning a lonely mission disappeared without a trace.

The Japanese mounted several light air raids and frequent reconnaissance flights over Tulagi and neighboring bases in March. The action picked up through April.

The object of attention was the potentially important fleet anchorage at Tulagi, and the Royal Australian Air Force (RAAF) refueling and wireless stations at nearby Tanambogo Island. However, except for an Australian commando platoon, a detachment of RAAF technicians, and a pair of RAAF twin-engined American-made PBY Catalina patrol bombers, the base was undefended.

Martin Clemens received a message on April 29 from Donald Kennedy, the district officer in northern Santa Ysabel: "A large Japanese flotilla has been sighted making towards the Eastern Solomons."

A particularly vicious Japanese air strike hit the RAAF base at Tanambogo on May 1. Both Martin Clemens and Don MacFarlan spotted the aircraft from their observation posts on Guadalcanal, and both flashed warning messages to the base, but the radio there was routinely tuned in to RAAF headquarters in Port Moresby for the day's orders, and the twin warnings could not be heard.

Both Catalinas were damaged. One scooted out to sea, where it was intercepted by a Japanese transport; the aircrew was never seen again. The Tanambogo base was put to the torch by the commandos and groundcrewmen, who then sailed to Aola and from there to the New Hebrides.

But for several hardbitten goldminers who refused to leave their digs in the mountains, and several planters plagued with inertia, the only Europeans left in the Guadalcanal area were the Coastwatchers and their assistants, and numerous Catholic and Anglican missionaries and nuns.

The Japanese flotilla that Donald Kennedy had seen off Santa Ysabel on April 29 arrived in the Tulagi anchorage on May 4. *Riku-sentai* from the Kure 3rd Special Naval Landing Force, 800 infantry-trained bluejackets, moved against the former British holdings at Tulagi and Gavutu. No one had any reason to suspect that the quiet arrival of those ships would represent the high-water mark of Japan's program of conquest in the Pacific.

Two days later, on the morning of May 6, the skies filled with, of all things, American carrier-based bombers and fighters.

The U.S. Navy had committed two of its precious fleet aircraft carriers to the Coral Sea to stop a Japanese invasion force bound for Port Moresby, at the eastern tip of New Guinea. The ultimate aim of the Japanese operation was to sever the supply line between mainland America and Australasia. The seizure of Tulagi and Gavutu was a side operation. Basing its plan upon radio intercepts, the U.S. Pacific Fleet was gambling upon achieving a surprise victory over a substantial portion of the Imperial Navy's Combined Fleet.

The aircraft that struck the Tulagi anchorage on May 5 were from a battle force commanded by RAdm Frank Jack Fletcher that had come to within relatively few miles of Guadalcanal's southern coast. The aggressive American aircrews sank four small craft and a small cargo ship. In addition, one Japanese destroyer had to be beached, a total loss, and another was sent limping toward Rabaul; it was sunk several days later by an American submarine. An estimated 200 Japanese were killed ashore by bombs and strafing. Many of the wounded died for lack of adequate medical care.

Admiral Fletcher was forced to leave late in the day to take on the more formidable Port Moresby invasion force and its covering group of Japanese carriers.

This bolt from the blue caused European morale to soar, and it provided a timely object lesson for the impressionable islanders, whose previous sight of large numbers of Europeans had been the backs of fleeing men. But the blessing was mixed. Japanese sailors washed ashore on Savo Island were treated by a native medical practitioner who had been working with a local resident named Leif Schroeder, a civilian loosely involved with the Coastwatcher organization. Schroeder fled to the islands north of Tulagi, but the practitioner was detained and interrogated until he revealed the names and approximate whereabouts of many of the Europeans still in the area.

Don MacFarlan left Berande Plantation and moved with Ken Hay to Gold Ridge, an eyrie well away from any serious danger. Martin Clemens, at Aola, did not hear of the defection for some time, and was not seriously affected by it.

The Port Moresby invasion force was turned back (at the cost of American carrier *Lexington*) and Japanese initiative in the region was somewhat blunted. However, while Martin Clemens traveled to Lavoro Plantation to establish a coastwatching outstation for the plantation manager, Snowy Rhoades, the Japanese consolidated and expanded their gains. The Tulagi garrison was reinforced and *rikusentai* were sent to occupy many of the islets in the vicinity. Two 1,000-man labor battalions composed largely of Korean and Okinawan conscripts arrived to construct port facilities, for Tulagi was to be transformed into a major base from which further thrusts were to be mounted and supported. Gavutu and Tanambogo were joined by a crushed-coral causeway, and the vacated RAAF base was restored and expanded. Within weeks, a complete air group of Japanese seaplane fighters and amphibian patrol bombers moved in from Rabaul.

The building boom helped Martin Clemens's intelligence-gathering efforts. When a call for local laborers went out, picked men infiltrated the work force and reported the position and size of every gun in the area. The data was transmitted to the control station at Auki, Malaita, and then sent to Australia.

卐

Clemens felt a bit exposed in the Aola Bay residency, so he moved into the bush, to Paripao Village, on May 19 to establish a lookout station and residency.

Despite the press of war-making, it was the district officer's desire to carry out his governmental duties on a "business-as-usual" basis. Organization of the Crown presence continued apace with the establishment of substations, observation posts, and dispensaries in the bush. Records were kept in meticulous order. Clemens even found time to hold public court, and defendants were detained under police guard in a jail built chiefly from ivory nut palm leaves. Gardens were planted all over the government station at Aola Bay, and a variety of fruits and vegetables found their way to Clemens and his defense force volunteers.

Rumors about Japanese patrols on Guadalcanal began reaching Paripao at the very end of May. The activity seemed to be centered around Lunga Point, halfway between Aola Bay and Cape Esperance, the western end of Guadalcanal. One scout told Clemens on June 8 that the Japanese had established a camp on the plain directly behind Lunga Point. On June 20, Clemens learned that a wharf was being built near the Lunga encampment. No one had any idea why the Japanese had chosen to occupy any part of Guadalcanal in force, though Clemens hoped that they were merely after a source of lumber for the growing Tulagi installations.

Martin Clemens had by then recruited a sizeable following. Eighteen full-time native policemen and clerks were on the payroll, and forty-odd islanders served as part-time scouts and runners. There were twenty-two serviceable rifles of various calibers and vintages in the hands of the Coastwatchers and their native auxiliaries, but only about 300 rounds of ammunition, total. Soon, six more rifles and 2,500 rounds were taken from an abandoned police station on Florida. Though his job was to watch and wait—and to avoid direct contact with the enemy—Clemens felt that he might eventually be forced to fight.

With the increased Japanese presence came increased pressure upon the Coastwatcher stations. Snowy Rhoades moved into the bush west of Lavoro Plantation, and Don MacFarlan seemed to be having some sort of morale problem, though he and Ken Hay appeared to be the best-situated of all the Guadalcanal Coastwatchers.

There was little doubt, however, but that the Japanese were on to them. Natives reported that very pointed questions concerning the whereabouts of the Europeans were being asked by members of Japanese patrols and foraging details.

Martin Clemens was beginning to feel that he ought to be moving farther into the bush as well. Weeks earlier, he had had a disturbing interview with a rather sanctimonious mission-trained local priest who said that, if asked after the district officer's whereabouts, he would have no choice but to tell all; the tenets of his religion forbade him to lie. Clemens heatedly responded that the priest would not know where he was, for he planned to keep himself concealed from all but a few of his most-trusted employees. If the Japanese asked where the district officer was, Clemens instructed, the priest was to answer, truthfully, "He is gone."

The Coastwatchers had speculated for some time about the purpose of the Japanese encampment near Lunga Point; it was revealed on July 6, when a dozen small ships dropped anchor in Lunga Roads and began ferrying supplies, men, and earth-moving equipment to the newly constructed wharf. An airstrip was to be constructed on the Lunga Plain.

Clemens had by then felt compelled to leave Paripao, so great was the chance of his being discovered by a Japanese combat patrol or one of the many foraging parties that regularly scoured the area for food. He hid his records and, with only a very few trusted workers, headed upland to Vungana Village.

Life at Vungana was spartan. The Japanese had been visiting the Aola Bay gardens every Tuesday and Thursday, while Clemens's workers dug for food there every Monday, Wednesday, and Friday. The miserable hill villages of the region could barely support their own populations, so Clemens was on his own when it came to feeding himself and his workers. Sugar was refined from the tops of coconut palms, which had to be cut and dragged up to Vungana from lower down, where they grew. A typical day's fare, which might or might not include a cheering cup of sweetened tea, consisted of taro and yams.

For all the hardship, Vungana offered a breathtaking and

useful view. Captain Clemens, as he was now officially styled, could see everything from west of Savo to a point about fifteen miles east of Lunga Point, and about seventeen miles due north from the coast below his lookout to Tulagi Harbor. There was no tree high enough for the radio antenna, so Clemens had to erect a mast of collapsible bamboo poles for transmissions. The isolation was fine for confounding the Japanese, but it added considerably to the problems of collecting intelligence.

Vulnerable to inaccurate reporting and mysterious rumors, the Coastwatchers were becoming severely depressed by the time the Japanese started preparing the airstrip on the Lunga Plain. Hunted, isolated from friends, facing an uncertain future, and unable to determine the value of their reports, each man suffered from black images brought on mainly from not knowing how long he would have to remain behind enemy lines. Only by maintaining themselves in something approaching a vacuum—which did their intelligence-gathering mission not one bit of good—were the Coastwatchers able to evade capture.

Events did not bode well for the future.

2

Histore's first two carrier-air battles determined the course of
the Pacific War. The Coral Sea Battle, in early May 1942,
stunned free-wheeling Japan as it reached southeastward to
block vital shipping lanes between Australasia and America; the
Midway Battle, in early June, dashed the Imperial Navy's best
hope to establish itself in the eastern Central Pacific before a rearm-
ing America could recover from the shock of her humiliations at
Pearl Harbor, Guam, Wake, and the Philippines. Japan's war of
colonial expansion ended at Midway, where the Combined Fleet,
the strong sinew of Japan's maritime might, lost *four* aircraft carriers. Japan was no longer unbeatable. But she was hardly
vanquished.

Strategy for the Pacific War was based upon the ranges of land-
based fighter aircraft. Land bases—island bases—could not survive
if they were vulnerable to attacking aircraft. The key to winning
air superiority was the fighter. In the event of closure of a
local airfield, a land defense with any hope of success would have

to be supported by a combination of fighters and bombers (and enough of them to attain continuous local air superiority) from bases to which they could successfully return to rearm and refuel between sorties.

The best range of any Allied fighter operational in the spring of 1942 was about 1,000 miles; Allied airbases had to be within 450 miles of one another to be mutually supporting. The best average range of the Japanese Zero fighter in the spring of 1942 was about 1,300 miles; Japanese bases could be as far apart as 600 miles and still be mutually supporting. Put another way, at less extreme ranges, Japanese fighters could remain aloft over a friendly base or an enemy target many minutes longer than could Allied fighters sent from a similar distance to attack that base or defend that target.

Aircraft carriers were the wild cards, for they could bring fighters and bombers quite close to enemy bases, or friendly bases under enemy attack. On December 7, 1941, six Japanese carriers actually continued sailing at high speed *toward* Pearl Harbor after launching air strikes; that gave the attacking aircraft a shorter leg home than they had had going in. More time could be spent over the target area. In mid 1942, the Japanese had more carriers than the Americans, and they had many more longer-ranged carrier fighters, dive-bombers, and torpedo bombers. But the carriers of both sides were equally vulnerable to attack by aircraft and sub-marines, and both sides determined early in the war to use these precious capital ships with caution.

The Japanese lost five carriers at the Coral Sea and Midway, but they still had seven operational carriers on June 7, 1942, and several more were well under construction. The Americans lost two fleet carriers, one each at the Coral Sea and Midway, but had only four fleet carriers available on June 7, 1942. Thus, the Americans were forced to make cautious use of carriers, while the Japanese had some leeway in the many critical decisions that would mark this new, fast-moving type of warfare. Carrier-based air would be a bonus, however, and not a factor that could be counted upon absolutely in the strategies and tactics that would mark the second phase of the Pacific War. That phase would be characterized by the strategic and tactical use of air power, which would remain a factor of the effective operational ranges of *land-based* fighter aircraft.

Beyond the circumference of the Greater East Asia Co-Prosperity Sphere, as Japanese propagandists styled their colonial empire, a very few Allied soldiers and airmen strove against incredible adversity to prepare to meet the Japanese.

At the end of the first week of May 1942, the opposing sides lay too far apart to threaten one another seriously from the air. The Allies had insufficient four-engine bombers to do more than harass the forwardmost Japanese bases, and the few Japanese four-engine amphibious patrol bombers were far too vulnerable to be risked on even harassing the Allied bases.

While the Japanese consolidated for a push south and east from the Lower Solomons, the Allies—chiefly Americans—sought to screen their vital, vulnerable anchorages with a ring of fighter bases from which attacks upon the expected Japanese invasion fleet could be mounted. In mid March, 500 U.S. Army National Guardsmen landed at Efate Island, in the New Hebrides. On March 29, as the Japanese tide swept over the Northern and Central Solomons and into northern New Guinea, the Efate garrison was bolstered by the 4th U.S. Marine Defense Battalion and the ground echelon of one Marine Corps fighter squadron. During April, every American on Efate alternated shifts at guarding the beaches and gouging out a crude runway. At length, a U.S. Navy base force and eighteen obsolescent Marine fighters arrived to put Vila Field to use.

The soldiers and Marines serving on Efate at the time felt sacrificial.

They were.

On February 18, 1942, Adm Ernest King, commander in chief of the U.S. Fleet, said that he wanted Rabaul returned to Allied hands at the earliest possible date. King's desire did not coincide with objective reality. Coral Sea and Midway lay months in the future. The Allies were losing land—and, more importantly, men and materiel—throughout Asia and the Pacific, and Japan kept expanding with what appeared to be inexhaustible reserves of energy and manpower. The move through the Solomons took place with stunning speed, given the distances involved, and Rabaul quickly became the nexus of a bustling network of bases, near and far.

The Japanese had long preferred an expansion from Rabaul toward Port Moresby, New Guinea, over an occupation of the Solomons, but the outcome of the Coral Sea Battle turned them from the preferred course. The Lower Solomons had been breached, the ample anchorage at Tulagi had been taken, and the sea-lanes to the southeast were clear of Allied warships. Absent new airbases in southeastern New Guinea, the Japanese had only to choose from among dozens of adequate sites in the Solomons in order to prepare a base from which land-based fighters and bombers could cover an advance into the New Hebrides. They chose a spot closest to the objective, for they were limited by the range of their fighters.

Japan did not contemplate the annexation of Australia or New Zealand, but the physical isolation of those nations from the rest of the Allied world would be useful in the shaping of an eventual peace settlement that would leave Japan in control of the mineral-rich Solomons, New Guinea, and the New Hebrides.

The two Commonwealth nations had been at war against Hitler for over two years, and the bulk of their forces had been drawn into the fighting in North Africa or captured in Southeast Asia. Only very limited forces were available to defend the two nations, and virtually none was available for the defense of the periphery.

The most important intermediate concern of the Imperial Navy, which was responsible for the conduct of the Pacific War, was the destruction of the American aircraft carriers. That would remain the chief goal of the Combined Fleet through 1942.

If the Japanese were attempting to force the conditions of defeat upon Australasia while simultaneously destroying the American carrier fleet, the Allies were doing everything in their power to win a respite, however brief, in order to marshal their forces and put a stop, however slight, to Japanese expansion. No act was too desperate, and no force was not ultimately expendable—except for the precious carriers. It was America's goal simply to conserve her four remaining fleet carriers while retaining her new, sparsely defended air, fleet, and logistics bases in the New Hebrides, the Samoas, the Tongas, and the Fijis.

It is remarkable that the Americans managed to place men of just the right temperaments in the jobs for which they were most suited. While it was then a good thing for the nature of a carrier admiral to be on the conservative (as in "conservation") side, it was most important that the men who would be shaping strategic policies be of an aggressive disposition. No man involved in Pacific strategy-making was more aggressive than the commander in chief of the U.S. Fleet, Adm Ernest King, who announced an offensive strategy at a time when there was little hope of a successful *defense* of American bases in the Pacific. King was able to look beyond the daily news of defeat heaped upon ignominious defeat to a time, not far distant, he said, when an American offensive would take the war to the Japanese. Equally as farsighted as King were Gen Douglas MacArthur and Adm Chester Nimitz, the top Army and Navy commanders in the Pacific.

A refugee from the American embarrassment in the Philippines, Gen Douglas MacArthur was ordered upon his evacuation from Corregidor in mid March to oversee the Allied defense of Australia and New Zealand, and what little was left of Allied holdings in the Southwest Pacific. He quickly fabricated the basic strategy that would take his "cause" from the defensive to the offensive. While there was little of material good that he could do at the outset, MacArthur quickly launched a propaganda effort as the first step in reinvigorating the defeat-weary peoples of Australia, New Zealand, and the United States. It was a crucial first step, and a shrewd one.

Following a brief period in which MacArthur received conflicting mission directives from a confused War Department, he was named Supreme Commander of Allied forces in the Southwest Pacific Area, which encompassed Australia, New Zealand, New

Guinea, the Solomons, the Bismarcks, and the Philippines. Half of that area, and more, had already been forcibly seized by Japan.

Adm Chester Nimitz, who assumed command of the ravaged U.S. Pacific Fleet on the last day of 1941, was named commander in chief of the Pacific Ocean Area, which comprised everything in the Pacific that was not MacArthur's. Nimitz was a brilliant innovator, a product of thirty-five years of naval service. He had designed and implemented the Naval Reserve Officer Training Corps in the late 1930s, and had effectively seen to the acceptance of hundreds, then thousands, and ultimately tens of thousands of wartime reserve officers by the tiny, cliquish career naval establishment. He would prove to be the perfect officer to oversee the military hardware that would soon be bursting forth from American shipyards, aircraft plants, and armaments factories, and the men who would be graduating from American training camps and flight schools.

With Ernest King overseeing the Pacific War from Washington, it would be up to MacArthur and Nimitz to find a way to stop the Japanese, to discover the "main chance," and to take it. Both men were as aggressive as King, but the realities they faced on the scene were wholly different than the ones King saw on maps and in reports. While neither of the area commanders despaired of losing the Pacific War, they had yet to attain the physical means for winning it.

MacArthur announced in May that he agreed with King's desire to regain Rabaul. He next articulated *his* ultimate imperative, a desire to launch an invasion of the Philippines from the Bismarcks, and he even ordered his staff to draw up a concrete plan.

Nimitz did not agree. Midway had yet to be fought, though it was in the offing, and Nimitz's command was all that stood between the Combined Fleet and Hawaii; he was having too much trouble establishing a meaningful defense to be concerned with a premature and, to his mind, ill-advised offensive. The admiral proposed that a Marine raider battalion, then training in Samoa, launch hit-and-run raids against Tulagi and other Solomons bases to force the Japanese to proceed with caution. The offensive would come, Nimitz knew, but he hoped it would come when he was better equipped to mount it.

MacArthur took umbrage at the suggestion, for Nimitz had unveiled a plan that was to take place within the general's domain. Admiral King, who was ultimately responsible for the conduct of the Pacific War, shifted the area boundary one degree to the west, giving Nimitz control over the Eastern Solomons.

In simple truth, the Allies lacked the *means* for going over to the offensive. So, fortunately, did the Japanese lack the immediate means for continuing their program of conquest south and east of Tulagi. Restricted, as were their enemies, by the range of their fighter aircraft, they halted in place to build an airfield at the limit of the Zero fighter's operational range. There would be no moves south and east from Tulagi until an airstrip could be completed in late August or early September.

3

Even before the Coral Sea Battle had been fought, Adm Chester Nimitz had been contemplating the professional merits of various flag officers who might be named to oversee the South Pacific Area, the sub-department of his own vast Pacific Ocean Area, which incorporated the Lower Solomons, a region he felt would be at the center of the conflict during much of 1942. Nimitz's choice for the job was Adm William Pye, who had been interim Pacific Fleet commander before Nimitz took the assignment. Pye, a conservative battleship admiral, did not meet with the approval of Admiral King, though the two were Naval Academy classmates. King had a nominee of his own, an intelligent organizer who could pull together the forces and resources of several branches of service and of several nations.

King's choice was VAdm Robert Ghormley, who had been the American naval observer in London until his arrival in Washington on April 17, 1942. On that date, Ghormley was named by King as commander of the South Pacific Area and, concurrently, as commander of the South Pacific Force, with orders to proceed via Pearl

Harbor to Auckland, New Zealand, to establish a headquarters. Additional orders required him to mount an expedition to the Tonga Islands to prepare a forward base to support a late-summer offensive against an as-yet-undisclosed Japanese base.

The appointment went well with Admiral Nimitz, who knew Ghormley from their days together at Annapolis.

There were a few things that Bob Ghormley would have to overcome if he were to be successful at his new job. He had no troops with whom he might garrison the Tongas and none, certainly, with whom he might mount an offensive. He had no staff. He had not even been given adequate charts of the vast realm he was to oversee and organize. The general mobilization of American manpower and the foresight of Admiral Nimitz had put hundreds of able reserve and retired officers with solid staff experience into uniform, and battle-area commanders were able to choose from the best of these as well as from the regular officers. It took Ghormley two weeks to assemble his staff from among the best men available.

RAdm Richmond Kelly Turner, a prickly intellectual just promoted and released from prestigious duty as head of the Naval War Plans Staff, was given the vital task of organizing and commanding the South Pacific Force's transport and logistics, should any of either turn up. Aircraft in the South Pacific went to a peppery Alabamian named John Sidney McCain, who, like Turner, had studied at the Naval Academy at the same time as Ghormley and Nimitz. Many important appointments were made during Ghormley's brief stay in Washington, and others were made after he left, for the area commander was urgently needed in the Pacific.

Ghormley arrived in Auckland in early May 1942 just as the Coral Sea Battle opened, and he set about undertaking the tasks assigned to him. He still had no offensive target, no place for meeting the Japanese, and no means for meeting them had he wanted to do so. He built his force and took small steps forward to occupy hitherto unoccupied and uncontested islands and groups along the vast periphery of what would undoubtedly be the area of confrontation. Everyone in the know was certain that Tulagi would be an early target, but no one had a clue as to what the Japanese might do to upset the plan that was being formulated.

By the end of the Midway Battle, in early June, the decision to strike at Tulagi was just about assured.

When the time came, and barring unforeseeable events, the South Pacific Force would have two or three fleet carriers on loan to help. Each carrier boasted a complement of about 90 short-range aircraft of three major types: fighters, dive-bombers, and torpedo bombers. In addition, RAdm Slew McCain, Ghormley's air chief, would have under his control 166 Navy and Marine land-based aircraft of all types, including unarmed models. The U.S. Army Air Forces had deployed about 95 aircraft of all types in McCain's area, but fewer than 30 were operational long-range bombers, and the single fighter squadron was even shorter-legged than the single Marine land-based fighter squadron. Thirty-odd New Zealand and Australian aircraft were nominally under McCain's control.

Five hundred U.S. Army National Guardsmen advanced 150 miles from Efate on May 28 to occupy Espiritu Santo. Elements of the 4th Marine Defense Battalion and construction engineers followed the Guardsmen to build a new fighter strip, which would be lengthened and widened to accommodate long-range bombers as soon as possible. The indescribably crude new field was not expected to accommodate its first fighters until early July.

The move to Espiritu Santo had no immediate practical effect, for that island and Tulagi were mutually beyond the operational ranges of every type of fighter each side then boasted. Any thrust forward from Espiritu Santo, once its fighter complement was in place, would have to be gingerly handled. The only possible acquisitions were the Santa Cruz Islands or Rennell Island, and these were well within the operational range of fighters the Japanese expected to deploy in the Tulagi area by late August or early September, which was about as soon as the Americans could have a base up and running forward of Espiritu Santo. An eventual thrust at Tulagi, assuming it was successful, would place the Americans within range of the Japanese air establishment around Rabaul.

But all the prognosticating about who would be in range of which base and when was begging the issue, for the Allies had no ground force of reasonable size to commit to the seizure or subsequent defense of a base at or near Tulagi. Not, that is, until June 25, when Admiral Ghormley learned that the advance echelon of a division of U.S. Marines had arrived in Auckland on June 14. Further investigation revealed that the bulk of the division, still at sea, was due to arrive by July 11.

Even as Ghormley was learning of the arrival and pending arrival of Marines and more Marines, the final moves were being played out in the command controversy between MacArthur and Nimitz. Nimitz was in San Francisco awaiting the arrival of Admiral King, with whom he was to hammer out various aspects of the Pacific War strategy, including the conduct of the Eastern Solomons offensive. RAdm Kelly Turner, Ghormley's transport chief, was on hand to act as his admiral's representative.

It was firmly decided that the occupation of the Santa Cruz Islands, north of the New Hebrides, and the seizure of Tulagi would be the opening phase of the Pacific offensive. After submitting a detailed plan for the operation, Admiral Turner left on July 4 to catch a flight to Pearl Harbor to begin actively assembling his amphibious force.

On July 5, general plans for the seizure of the remainder of the Solomons, and of Rabaul, were worked out. Late in the day, just as the meeting was winding down, blockbuster news was brought to the conference table: A radio intercept revealed that the Japanese were landing troops at Guadalcanal, and that an airfield was to be constructed there. The Santa Cruz offensive was stricken from the plan; the seizure of Guadalcanal was given the highest priority. It would have to be mounted before the airfield could be completed. The admirals set D-Day for August 1, 1942.

Just as things seemed blackest, as food became all but unobtainable, as the ennui of solitary living among the islanders pressed upon the innate fears of several of the European Coastwatchers, and as the Japanese seemed to grow dramatically in strength, a glimmer of hope was rekindled.

The long weeks of July 1942 passed slowly, with no sign of hope except for inquiries from Port Moresby, and the occasional overflight by an Allied bomber. Then, on July 31, the largest single Allied bombing mission of the period took place. Nine American B-17 bombers equipped with bomb-bay and radio-compartment auxiliary fuel cells flew the 710 miles from Efate, in the New Hebrides. Though the auxiliary fuel cells restricted bomb loads, the heavy bombers of the U.S. Army Air Forces' 11th Heavy Bombardment Group succeeded in striking a major blow at the timetable of the engineering troops responsible for building the airfield on the Lunga Plain. Zero floatplane fighters based at Gavutu were unable to get airborne in time to catch the bombers as they passed over the target area at 14,000 feet, and the American aircrews, who were largely drawn from among survivors of aerial combat at Pearl Harbor and Midway, suffered no losses. However, little permanent damage was inflicted.

A smaller B-17 raid on August 1 did a little damage, and the heavily armed bombers destroyed two Gavutu-based floatplane fighters with machine-gun fire. Five Zero floatplane fighters intercepted three B-17s on August 4. One of the fighters, severely damaged by the heavy American machine-gun fire, rammed the engine of a B-17, and both aircraft hurtled, burning, to the ground. A second B-17 was downed by the Japanese on August 5, when a strike was sent to hit port facilities at Tulagi and Kukum, a coastal village near Lunga Point.

Despite the growing activity in the air over Guadalcanal and Tulagi, Capt Martin Clemens was unaware that the burgeoning Japanese facilities were being harried from the outside. Port Moresby had been asking for more and more detailed information concerning the uncompleted airstrip on the Lunga Plain since the end of July, but Clemens was unable to make any connection between the rising interest and air raids he could neither see nor hear. The rising interest, however, did keep his hopes alive.

PART II

The Division

4

First Marine Division was something less than half trained and understrength by one of its three infantry regiments when it arrived at Wellington, New Zealand.

Activated at New River, North Carolina, in February as the largest unit of U.S. Marines ever assembled under one command, the division immediately became a manpower pool from which cadres for even newer units were drawn. The hard core of experienced, blooded "old salts" had been built up and whittled down over the months of training, replaced by rapidly promoted green kids with experience in neither leadership nor combat.

The loss of valuable cadres was bad enough, but spring saw the loss of some of the best staff noncommissioned officers (NCOs), the solid substrata of any military organization bound for combat. Seventh Marine Regiment (7th Marines), one of the division's three infantry components, was ordered to Samoa to defend against an impending invasion, and many of the division's ranking NCOs, along with many fine officers, had claimed the privilege of being the first to fight. Harried troop commanders reluctantly granted the perks of rank and posted some of their best men to the 7th Marines.

As MGen Alexander Archer Vandegrift battled mightily to bring his new division to order, he was suddenly informed that the remainder of his command was to be moved part and parcel to Wellington. If that was not shock enough—for the division was by no means ready to enter a combat zone—word came down that the two remaining infantry regiments, 1st and 5th Marines, with their supports, were to be split up for lack of transport. Fifth Marines was to sail from Norfolk while 1st Marines was to be shipped by rail to California and then by troop transport to Wellington. General Vandegrift sent out a small advance party, took ship with 5th Marines, and wondered what was to become of him and his abused command.

The troops left New River lean and hard, but 5th Marines arrived in Wellington somewhat softer after weeks of enforced idleness at sea. On finding that the striking New Zealand dockworkers union would not unload the Marines' equipment, the forthright Archer Vandegrift created something of a sensation in the socialized nation by putting his troops to the task, as much to toughen them as to get the job done.

As the troops labored in the winter rains at Aotea Quay, Wellington, Vandegrift was called to Auckland by VAdm Bob Ghormley. He made the trip on June 26 with key senior staffers. Upon his arrival, Vandegrift was escorted alone to the area commander's office. He and Ghormley knew each other slightly, so the general was merely expecting a courtesy call with a superior officer, a standard enough affair; he was not prepared to meet with the harassed, brusque individual the usually affable Ghormley had become after only a few weeks on the job.

The two flag officers had only just shaken hands when the admiral said, "Vandegrift, I have some very disconcerting news."

"I'm sorry to hear that, Admiral."

"You'll be more sorry," Ghormley predicted, handing Vandegrift a top-secret dispatch, "when you read this."

The document Vandegrift sat down to read was a directive ordering Ghormley to confer with Gen Douglas MacArthur about an amphibious operation against the Japanese base at Tulagi. First Marine Division was to land on August 1, just five weeks hence.

Vandegrift, who was known for his characteristic optimism, was speechless. Ghormley silently took back the sheet of paper, tapped it idly with his fingers, and asked "Well?"

Well! It was going to be a close-run thing. Of that, all concerned could be certain. Fifth Marines had five weeks in which to turn it around, but 1st Marines was not due in Wellington for at least two more weeks. And what was Archer Vandegrift to do about replacing 7th Marines, which could not be released in time from garrison duty in Samoa?

The matter of replacing 7th Marines was covered by the temporary transfer of 2nd Marines from 2nd Marine Division to Vandegrift's command; that regiment would proceed independently to the South Pacific from San Diego, where it was to be fully combat-loaded. On the minus side, however, 2nd Marines was only to "support" the landings before proceeding on an independent mission out of the area.

The planning was well under way when, early in the second week of July, Ghormley's headquarters informed Vandegrift's that 1st Marine Division would also have to seize the airfield near Guadalcanal's Lunga Point. (This, more than a month following the discovery of the runway construction!)

Further augmentations to 1st Marine Division were hurriedly effected: First Raider Battalion was training in Samoa and would be used as an assault force; 3rd Defense Battalion, a coast artillery and antiaircraft unit, was to be transferred from Hawaii to defend the airfield on Guadalcanal, once it was captured; and the small, finely honed 1st Parachute Battalion would draw an amphibious assault role.

In addition to his infantry and the Raiders and 'Chutes, General Vandegrift would employ several battalions of his artillery regiment—11th Marines—and his tanks, amphibious tractors, engineers, shore party, medical personnel, and communicators. The complete landing force, including 2nd Marines and its supports, comprised 25,000 men.

Assembling an adequate combat force had been a problem, but the obstacles placed in the way of that force as it struggled to mount an operation out of Wellington were formidable. In just a month's time, 1st Marine Division, such as it was, had to unload thousands of half-trained Marines and hundreds of tons of their equipment, supplies, armaments, and munitions from the transports that had carried them all from the United States, then combat-load everything onto transports and cargo ships. Archer Vandegrift's first imperative was haggling with his superiors for an extension, which he won: First Marine Division would mount its twin assaults against Tulagi and Guadalcanal on August 7 instead of August 1.

ॡ

Despite several decades of planning, and frequent landing exercises involving U.S. Fleet units and many of the Marines assembled in Wellington, the job facing 1st Marine Division and its naval supports was largely experimental. A modern combat assault had never once been run *in combat* by any of the men assembled in Wellington in June and July 1942. Many of the transports were converted civilian liners, commandeered, leased, or purchased by the Navy and manned by inexperienced junior officers and enlisted sailors. Much of the specialized equipment vital to sound combat-landing procedures had yet to be invented. Just getting the division away from Wellington involved a mass learning experience for men at all levels of command.

With feverish haste, and ingenious improvisation born of necessity, 5th Marines—and 1st, when it arrived—completely unloaded every pound of cargo as soon as its transports docked at Aotea Quay. This was done for two reasons: None of the gear had been combat-loaded, which meant that it could not be combat-*un*loaded in anything resembling the order in which it would be needed to support Marines attacking across a hostile beach; and most of the ships involved in ferrying the Marines to New Zealand had to depart in order to undertake operations elsewhere, to which they had already been assigned and from which they could not be released.

After it had been unloaded, all that gear had to be sorted and, where possible, reloaded by Marines. While the shortage of civilian labor meant grueling 'round-the-clock toil, often in the winter rains that plagued New Zealand in June and July, the physical work had the positive effect of whipping the troops into top condition following the inactivity of long weeks at sea. In the end, however, New Zealand militia units had to be called out to help the Marines meet their impossible deadline.

Aotea Quay became an impenetrable jumble of every conceivable type of gear, haphazardly strewn in every available square inch of free space. The incessant drizzly rains turned the light cardboard boxes bearing medical supplies and food into gooey mounds of slippery, slushy waste.

There was not sufficient space aboard the available ships for all the division's equipment and arms. Heavy trucks had to be left behind for shipment later—along with the division's entire twelve-gun 155mm heavy artillery battalion.

There were times when Navy officers exhibited an appalling lack of sympathy for the plight of the Marines, though that was often as not inadvertent, brought on by inconsistent efforts to maintain secrecy. The captain of transport *Heywood*, for example, steadfastly refused to allow his passengers to combat-load their ammunition; he demanded that the Marines adhere strictly to stowage regulations meant for the peacetime shipment of such dangerous cargos. The commander of 1st Parachute Battalion, Maj Bob Williams, who knew only too well that his small unit was to be at the forefront of the assault, was unable to tell the Navy captain of the need to dispense with the peacetime regulations. So the naval officer, who had not been taken into anyone's confidence regarding the importance of the mission, which had been advertised as a training exercise in the Fijis, stuck to the rules despite repeated and varied—but less-than-accurate—explanations and requests. In the end, a thoroughly outmaneuvered Major Williams had to ask the division chief of staff to quietly leak the word to the transport's master: The ammunition had to be combat-loaded because it was to be used in combat. The flabbergasted transport captain immediately and wholeheartedly complied amid a storm of profuse apologies.

The division's gear was packed and, after a fashion, ready to go by July 22, a truly remarkable accomplishment. When the convoy left Wellington, it carried enough supplies to see the division through sixty days, and ammunition enough for ten days of heavy fighting.

⇋

The objective was a mystery. When Archer Vandegrift received his first briefing on June 26, no one—not his staff, nor Ghormley's, nor even the Australian and New Zealand authorities—had much more than a vague notion as to what the physical appearance of the Eastern Solomons might be. The task of gathering pertinent data fell to the 1st Marine Division's Intelligence Officer, LtCol Frank Goettge. And all Frank Goettge could do was ask the local authorities for a list of people who had lived, or might have lived, in the Eastern Solomons at one time or another and with whom he might be able to speak. Very few people filled the bill, but on July 2 Goettge flew to Australia to conduct interviews. While its chief was gone, the division intelligence section, in Wellington, sifted through the very small amount of data that the New Zealand government had been able to unearth.

Frank Goettge spent eleven days in Australia, tracking down miners, traders, government workers, seamen, and missionaries— many of whom had passed through but had never actually set foot in the objective area. He returned to the division headquarters in Wellington on July 13 to begin making some sense of his discouragingly small grab-bag of data.

Following a week's frantic effort, Goettge's staff produced a nine-page written description and a very rough map detailing the northern coast of Guadalcanal from Lunga Point to Aola Bay. It was a crude showing, and it left most questions unanswered. It also contained crucial errors, and these would jeopardize lives.

While Frank Goettge and his staff worked overtime to collect and assess intelligence matter, LtCol Bill Twining and Maj Bill McKean were dispatched to try to eyeball the objective area so that a reasonable plan could be fabricated. Twining and McKean spent days traversing the air routes from Wellington to Noumea to Australia before eventually securing the use of an Army Air Forces B-17 based at Milne Bay, New Guinea.

Following a six-hour flight, during which Major McKean tried his hand at flying the B-17 while fretting over what he considered to be the slapdash methods of the bomber's navigator, the two Marine passengers spotted their objective, only forty miles from where it should have been on the navigator's charts.

While the navigator uttered course corrections to the pilot, McKean crawled into the bomber's perspex nose compartment to direct the photographer-gunner.

As the photographer snapped his photos, McKean and Twining peered at the reefs around Florida Island and concluded that they could not be breached by light landing craft.

The B-17 was at 10,000 feet, skirting Tulagi, Gavutu, and Tanambogo, which were known to mount antiaircraft guns. McKean shifted to the starboard side of the bomber to get a good look at Tulagi and saw white feathers of spume forming near Gavutu: Floatplane fighters were scrambling to attack the lone bomber!

The Marine major tapped the navigator's shoulder and wordlessly pointed to the rising aircraft.

"Navigator to pilot. Three float Zeros taking off about two o'clock, close in." There was a pause, then the young lieutenant turned to Bill McKean. "Pilot says we've reached the turnaround point on fuel. He wants to know what to do."

McKean relayed the news to Bill Twining, who was senior man aboard the B-17. "Tell him he's skipper. We're just passengers.

We've seen enough if it's necessary to turn back," Lieutenant Colonel Twining replied.

After a brief interval, the navigator replied, "Pilot wants to know if you still want to look at Guadalcanal."

"That's in the contract," Twining shot back from the bombardier's seat, "but we won't sue if he skips it."

The aircraft veered southwestward toward Aola Bay. Twining asked the pilot to fly closer to Lunga Point. The shift was made, and Twining directed the photographer to shoot more photos.

The photo session broke up when the navigator crawled forward from his compartment and yelled, "We're jumped! There's one at five o'clock." Twining armed the machine gun by the bombardier's seat as crew gunners opened fire on the floatplane fighters. The pilot glided for the nearest cloud while the navigator asked how low it was safe to fly without hitting a mountain. "Four thousand feet," McKean advised.

While Major McKean balanced on a longitudinal frame, protected only by the bomber's thin metal hide, the pilot reversed course in the heavy cloud cover. The machine-gun fire ceased for only a moment, then burst anew as the tail gunner downed a Zero through a rift in the cloud. And then it was over. The flight home was a bit nerve-wracking because the navigator lost his position fix in the cloud, but the crew managed to find Port Moresby and land safely.

That was on July 18. It took until July 26 for Australian and New Zealand commercial airline schedules and the vagaries of thinly spread military air transport to carry Twining and McKean and their precious photographs to Suva, Fiji, which was within range of 1st Marine Division's final stop on the way to the Solomons. The data, gained at so much risk, was about the best the division ever received, but it arrived too late to have much impact upon the plan the operations staff had been able to cobble together.

Another request for long-range photo-reconnaissance was fulfilled by General MacArthur's headquarters, which sent another B-17 from New Guinea. The photo coverage was nearly perfect and would have been invaluable had not the photo composites been *mailed* to an incorrect address. The parcel was delivered to 1st Marine Division in early 1943.

⁂

The plan, coded WATCHTOWER in official channels (and SHOESTRING everywhere else), was simple. It had to be, predicated as it was upon the questionable, inadequate data uncovered by LtCol Frank Goettge, and upon the inexperience of the troops and troop leaders who would be facing Japanese defenders in the war's first offensive amphibious assault.

The landing force was to be divided into two major components—one to attack Guadalcanal itself, the other to seize the smaller islands and islets twenty miles to the north, across Sealark and Lengo channels.

The units landing on the north side of the channels, against Florida, Tulagi, Gavutu, and Tanambogo, were designated Force Yoke and placed under BGen William Rupertus, the Marine division assistant commander. This force comprised 1st Raider Battalion and 2nd Battalion, 5th Marines, which were to seize heavily defended Tulagi; 1st Parachute Battalion, which was to seize Gavutu and Tanambogo Islets; and the reinforced 2nd Marines, which was to provide a battalion to reconnoiter portions of Florida Island and serve as a pool from which reinforcements could be drawn in the event of stiffer-than-expected opposition anywhere in the area, including Guadalcanal.

Force X-Ray comprised two battalions and headquarters of 5th Marines, which were to assault a beach several miles east of Lunga Point and advance along the coast to the Point and beyond; the reinforced 1st Marines, which was to sweep the high ground dominating the airfield; most of two light 75mm pack howitzer and one medium 105mm howitzer battalions of 11th Marines, whose guns were to leapfrog forward from the landing beach to support the rifle battalions; and the bulk of the division's service and support units, which were to carry out a variety of tasks, including the unloading and movement of supplies at the beach and the provision of a reserve combat force. It was to be by far the largest amphibious assault ever undertaken by U.S. forces. No one knew quite what would happen.

The task force from Wellington dropped anchor at Koro, in the Fijis, to allow the combat elements of the reinforced division to undertake practice landings. Other convoys brought 2nd Marines from the West Coast and 1st Raider Battalion from New Caledonia, and warships arrived from around the world.

The practice landings were an unrelieved disaster, an embarrassment of the first magnitude. The components of the division, and those of the fleet, had not operated with one another before Koro, and the disorganization was simply astounding. Tall, courtly Archer Vandegrift, whose Virginia manner was usually amiable, exploded time and again as the troops he had painstakingly trained looked increasingly inept. He blamed the failure upon the ill-chosen landing site and the relative softness of the troops, who had not yet recovered from their long sea journeys.

Many of the division's junior troop leaders were satisfied with the rehearsal at Koro. It is true that many of the lessons were negative, but any amount of practice was seen as beneficial by men who would be facing combat at the water's edge.

The poor showing by his troops between July 28 and 31 proved to be among the least of Archer Vandegrift's troubles.

𒀭

On July 26, a month to the day after first meeting with VAdm Bob Ghormley, Archer Vandegrift attended a meeting aboard fleet carrier *Saratoga*, VAdm Frank Jack Fletcher's flagship. Also attending were RAdm Kelly Turner, the amphibious-force commander; RAdm Dan Callaghan, Ghormley's chief of staff; RAdm Slew McCain, the South Pacific aircraft commander; and Col Blondie Saunders, commander of 11th Heavy Bombardment Group, the B-17 force that was to "soften" the beaches.

The *Saratoga* meeting was a singularly cold confrontation in which Fletcher revealed that he had no intention of exposing his precious carriers to Japanese reprisals. Vandegrift had the distinct impression that Fletcher neither knew very much about the upcoming offensive, nor cared.

Fletcher had a reputation as an amphibious warfare expert, for, as a young line officer, he had been awarded a Medal of Honor for being on the beach at Vera Cruz. (So had all but two officers on that beach.) But that had been in 1916, and much had changed—both in the art of amphibious warfare, and in the heart of Frank Jack Fletcher, who was neither a professional carrier admiral nor a particularly aggressive one. He had lost a carrier both at the Coral Sea and Midway, and that weighed heavily upon his already very conservative approach to meeting the enemy.

While RAdm Dan Callaghan, who could have invoked the authority of the area commander, silently took notes, Fletcher ignored the arguments and pleas of the ground and amphibious force commanders, Vandegrift and Turner. He said that he was leaving the Lower Solomons on the morning of the third day, though Turner said that he would require at least five days to unload the transports with his inexperienced bluejackets and Vandegrift's inexperienced shore party. In the end, faced with an immovable Fletcher, Turner was forced to make his stand: lacking carrier-based air cover, the transports would be obliged to retire on the third morning with whatever supplies remained in their holds.

Thrown into an operation for which his command was barely prepared, fresh from evolving a plan based on almost zero information, informed that 2nd Marines—a third of his combat force—would be withdrawn early, and faced with the early retirement of his naval supports, Archer Vandegrift managed to leave *Saratoga* with his optimism shaken but intact.

5

There were 25,000 of them that first week in August 1942. They came from nearly as many neighborhoods and towns, and from every one of the forty-eight states. They had been trained to do a hundred different jobs, and could do them with 25,000 varying degrees of proficiency.

They were of dozens of nationalities and religions. They had parents who, among them, spoke over a hundred different languages and dialects. Their families had been American families for nearly four hundred years, or a few months, or were yet to become Americans. They had been raised in New Haven, Brooklyn, Boston, Bangor, Baltimore, Atlanta, Gary, Perth Amboy, Mine Ridge. Their names were Casamento, Kosanovich, Moran, Jachym, Hernandez, Weiss, Jones, Smith. . . .

A few had been to Shanghai, Culbera, Manila, London, Santo Domingo, Port Au Prince, Managua. Others had spent their lives within fifty miles of home, except for brief visits to such places as Parris Island, Quantico, New River, San Diego, San Francisco, Norfolk, and, most recently, Auckland and Wellington.

They had received the best training their technocracy could then offer. They were not, however, armed with the best weapons and equipment their nation could then produce.

They had little in common, but they were, most of them, U.S. Marines. They were proud; proud to be Americans, and proud to be Marines. They were too proud to admit fear. They were young men growing up or grown men growing old. Some had been Marines for as many as forty-five years, others for just three months. They were 1st Marine Division and they were on their way to battle.

There may never again be an American military organization quite like the one that was 1st Marine Division that summer of 1942. The division, the Marine Corps, the nation itself, were all in a state of transition, about to become the instruments of change in a world that would never again be the same as it was during that summer of uncertainty.

The mission that lay before the division, the Marine Corps, the nation, would change each, irrevocably.

For its part, 1st Marine Division was an unalloyed mixture of several distinct types of Marines—officers and enlisted. There were lifetime career professionals ("old salts"), career-minded youngsters, and a vast majority of wartime officers and enlisted Marines.

The older career officers, and many of their younger colleagues, had divided themselves into two camps. The one was a grizzled, oft-blooded core of war lovers, men who sought other men on fields of battle. Many of the older members of this group had struggled up through the ranks. Typically these were men who had enlisted in the Marine Corps in 1917 and 1918 to serve in France, though many did not so serve. A large number had been temporarily commissioned for the Great War, then had taken reductions to enlisted rank simply to remain on active duty with the tiny peacetime establishment. They had fought in Haiti, in Nicaragua, and in Asia. These men had earned commissions in the 1930s, and had been rapidly promoted under the gathering clouds of war. They moved into meaningful positions of authority as the Marine Corps prepared itself for the new war. Their enlisted contemporaries—men who had either disdained commissioned rank or who had not yet been offered commissions—provided the solid substrata of experience that would sustain the division until the untested wartime volunteers saw combat. Increasingly, however, enlisted old salts had accepted junior commissions, and they had not yet risen to positions of meaningful influence.

The second group of professional officers, young and old, modeled itself upon the British career-officer pattern. These men spent the interwar years sharpening their theoretical and social skills. These officers were staff oriented, usually better educated, and of a more intellectual bent than their hell-for-leather contemporaries. Most, though by no means all, had never served as enlisted Marines, and some had little or no effective troop leadership experience. Many of the colonels and lieutenant colonels had been junior combat officers in France. These men, and the younger career and wartime officers who gravitated into their orbit, rose the fastest to important staff and command duties.

There was an often unbridgeable gap between the two groups of career Marine officers. Each group, however, would produce its share of successful commanders and staffmen, as well as its share of incompetents.

The young wartime officers were very much a "new breed." By and large, they were the cream of the nation's finest colleges and universities. They came to the Marine Corps as early as 1939, but typically in 1940 and 1941. They were eager and, in most cases, exceedingly bright. They earned the grudging respect (or the enmity) of the old salts by learning the lessons of decades in a few short months of intense training. They were highly motivated young men eager to get on with the war in order to get on with the peace that would follow. By July 1942, the most senior of this group commanded the companies and staffed the battalions and regiments of 1st Marine Division.

Of the mass of enlisted Marines composing the division, it is revealing that the most junior found the rank of Private First Class to be exalted. Most of the privates, and even a fair number of junior NCOs, had enlisted after December 7, 1941. The great majority comprised adventure-seeking youths whose concepts of patriotism would be formed during the wartime service that would separate them forever from their roots in the Great Depression. The brightest of these young men, or the bravest, would earn commissions in the field, or between battles. Many would find a home in the Marine Corps, as had the earlier generation of old salts who had been drawn into the Great War.

Of all the officers in the division, not one had ever commanded or controlled a division in combat, nor even a regiment. Only a handful had ever commanded as much as a battalion in combat. Very few officers had commanded even a *company* in combat. Textbook and field training exercises notwithstanding, very few even knew how. Of the entire establishment, it is doubtful that as many as 2,000—ten percent—had ever *seen* combat.

Everything that lay before the division was new and untried.

On the night before they left their ships, the men and boys of 1st Marine Division and the fleet did what hundreds of thousands of men and boys would do on eves of battle throughout the long war. Their acts and feelings were unique only in that they were the first and their futures were the most obscure. At some point or another, most listened to what their leaders had to say. Otherwise they talked or slept or listened to each other and groused about this and that or played cards or shot craps or wrote home or made final preparations or prayed. Inevitably, they considered the unknown and wondered at mortality. The chaplains did a thriving business.

Here is Col Clifton Cates, the dapper commander of 1st Marines, who has been to the wars, who has been gassed in the trenches in France, and who has had honors bestowed upon him for being among the bravest of the brave at Belleau Wood. His words are in a sober, sobering vein: "We're fighting for a just cause, there is no doubt about that. It is for right and freedom. We have enjoyed the many advantages given us under our form of government and, with the help of God, we will guarantee that same liberty and freedom to our loved ones and the people of America for generations to come."

Here is Col Roy Hunt, Cates's colleague, commanding 5th Marines, which will be leading the assault on Guadalcanal come dawn. Hunt is in a different frame of mind. He helps while away the time entertaining his staff with an impromptu dance, described variously as a clog and a buck-and-wing, while accompanying himself with a so-so bass medley of standard songs and ditties.

Here is LtCol Merritt Edson, a grim, thin-smiled, redheaded Vermonter with an incongruously soft voice. Edson tells his 1st Raider Battalion—which is to lead the assault on Tulagi—of a Japanese propaganda broadcast of the previous evening: "Where are the United States Marines hiding," Red Mike Edson quotes with deep sarcasm, "The Marines are supposed to be the finest soldiers in the world, but no one has seen them yet." The Raiders' response is predictably profane.

Here is Capt Gordon Gayle, operations officer of 1st Battalion, 5th Marines. Three years out of the Naval Academy and one of the new breed of professional career officers, Gayle is still appalled by the wholesale embarrassment of the Koro rehearsal. He has spent every available moment since the Fiji exercise holding school for Navy and Marine officers in the mechanics of amphibious operations, with particular emphasis upon the Navy's role in the ship-to-shore phase. Given the results of Koro, Gayle and fellow Marine officers are gratified to see that the interest of their Navy colleagues is much enhanced.

Here is Capt Bill Hawkins, commander of B Company, 5th, which is slated to lead its regiment and its division ashore on Beach Red in the morning. A short, burly, balding former New England school teacher, twenty-seven-year-old Bill Hawkins loses his night's sleep overseeing the fabrication of a set of special steel grappling hooks, the better to negotiate a deep trench expected to be just behind the beach, in the path of B Company. A reservist with nearly two years' active duty behind him, Captain Hawkins is buoyed by the memory of a brief reunion at Koro with his brother,

Bob, a Marine major serving as quartermaster of one of the cruisers that will blast clear the morning's beaches for Hawkins's company. The war will keep the brothers apart, killing one of them.

Here is Pvt Jobert Williams, who, at age sixteen, is perhaps the youngest of Bill Hawkins's brood. Young Williams has run away from school and lied about his age to enlist in the Marine Corps, and his greatest fear is that he will be found out and sent home, unblooded. The prospect of dying in the morning has not yet fazed the young company runner. In that respect, Jobert Williams is like most of his older peers. The fear will come, but not this long night.

Here is 1stLt Nikolai Stevenson, the twenty-three-year-old New Yorker, who will lead C Company, 1st, in support of 5th Marines. As anxious as are his young troops about the future, Nick Stevenson blurts out the grim news that division headquarters expects 50-percent casualties on the beach. (There is a collective intake of breath.) "But don't worry," he ad-libs, "that means the guys on either side of you will be hit; you'll be okay."

Here is Pvt Austin Wortley, one of Stevenson's runners, who, like everyone else in C Company, glances surreptitiously from side to side to have a last look at two doomed Marines.

Here is Cpl Frank Blakely, chief of Colonel Cates's command radio team, who gave up three stripes in the National Guard to become a Marine private exactly two years ago. This long night's reveries bring to mind the possibility that the girl he married during a leave in April might be widowed in the morning. It is the first time he has ever thought he might die in the war. Frank Blakely tries to unwind as a quartet from the 1st Marines intelligence section serenades the headquarters troops late into the night.

Here is MG Bill Rust, of the 5th Marines operations section. The tall, lanky, gregarious athlete has been tabbed to lead the regiment's advance from the beach to the airfield. This honor is a legacy of what Rust secretly believes to be an unearned reputation as a fearsome veteran of jungle warfare in Nicaragua.

Here is Pfc Jack Lyons, a member of that quartet. His haunting solo rendition of "Riding Down the Canyon" will echo across the years. However, young, popular Jack Lyons will be dead within the week.

Here is Pfc Johnny Smolka, a communicator with 2nd Battalion, 5th, which is headed to Tulagi to support the Raiders. A former hobo, Smolka dreams of becoming a Big League baseball umpire. But the dream is a world war away, and there are deadlier games to survive.

Here is Maj Bob Williams, a former presidential aide-de-camp, very junior in grade, and the Marine Corps' senior parachutist. Along with a few Army officers with whom he has trained, Williams has written the American version of the book on combat parachute assault. His half-size 1st Parachute Battalion has brought its parachute packs to the Solomons but will be carried to Gavutu by landing craft.

Here is Ens Galen Brown, whose father had been in destroyers in the Atlantic during the Great War, and whose idyllic boyhood on Catalina Island taught him a reverence and a calling for the sea. Just over a year in the Navy, which he yearns to make his life's work, has placed Brown at the leading edge of the emerging amphibious warfare technology. The direction that new specialty takes will be largely decided in the morning by Galen Brown and his peers.

Here is Lt(jg) Smokey Stover, of *Saratoga's* Fighting Squadron 5, less than two years a naval aviator and, though a participant at Midway, still unblooded. Stover is twenty-two, and he dreams of venturing outward to the stars. But first he must survive tomorrow's promise of flaming death, and a war of unknowable duration and danger. Stover spends a quiet evening hour writing his parents and brother of his love for them, of his hopes for the future, of the "Great Adventure" that is still ahead. This he seals in an envelope addressed to his parents, which he places in another envelope inscribed, "To whoever is unlucky enough to have to inventory my effects. Open only in case of death."

Here is 1st Marine Division, the South Pacific Amphibious Force, aircrews from three American aircraft carriers, and the crews of several dozen American and Australian warships, transports, and merchantmen. In the morning, they will lead their nations into the offensive, into the teeth of an enemy feared for his cunning, respected for his prowess in the attack, unassessed in his skills as a defender of ill-gotten gains.

In truth, neither side is at all prepared for the confrontation that will shape the popular image of the modern U.S. Marine Corps and decide the course of the Pacific War.

PART III

Invasion

6

Friday, August 7, 1942. 0310.

The Allied invasion fleet was directly west of Cape Esperance, the western tip of Guadalcanal Island. The Marines of the landing force had been shaken from their bunks at 0300. Most were awake before reveille had sounded. The morning was clear, dark, hot. Six miles of sea separated the Guadalcanal force from the Tulagi force as they came up on Cape Esperance at a speed of twelve knots. A rugged silhouette of tree-clad hills was vaguely visible to starboard.

As the leading vessels neared Savo Island, at the confluence of Sealark and Lengo channels, Task Group Yoke, the Tulagi force, detached itself from the main body and rounded the northern shore of the small island before coming west, bound for Florida and Tulagi. Task Group X-Ray swung north and east to parallel Guadalcanal's northern beaches, dropping off picket destroyers to guard the entrances to the channels.

Lt(jg) Smokey Stover, of *Saratoga's* Fighting Squadron 5, was awakened at 0400 and sent off to eat an unenjoyable breakfast before manning his F4F Wildcat fighter in the dark at 0500. Three four-plane fighter divisions led by the squadron commander, LCdr Roy Simpler, were launched from *Saratoga* at precisely 0530. Their target was the airstrip on the Lunga Plain. In the confusion of the pre-dawn launch, Smokey Stover's wingman went astray.

The eleven *Saratoga* fighter pilots headed north from the carriers, flipped off their running lights forty miles from Cape Esperance, turned west between Savo and Guadalcanal, and followed Guadalcanal's north coast toward Kukum.

It was about 0610.

As the transports made for their stations, cruisers and destroyers turned toward the beaches around and east of Lunga Point, training out their main batteries, waiting for the command to commence firing.

Cpl Frank Blakely, the 1st Marines' command-radio team chief, stared in awe as heavy cruiser *Quincy* turned parallel to the beach, all aglow as she belched smoke through her great guns. An instant later, other cruisers, and destroyers closer in, joined in the bombardment. It was 0614. The battle for Guadalcanal had begun.

Lt(jg) Smokey Stover grew wary of possible antiaircraft resistance as he neared Kukum, the tiny coastal village just north of the runway. There! Yellow-red flashes below! Stover tensed, then realized that he was witnessing the first friendly naval gunfire probing the dark, hostile shore. Twenty minutes remained until sunrise; it was still so dark that Stover could see little more than the dark silhouette of the island beneath his Wildcat's wings.

The *Saratoga* fighters, which had been gliding earthward from 5,000 feet since passing Cape Esperance, had quite a bit of speed built up as LCdr Roy Simpler's leading division opened with machine guns on the unseen runway and an unfinished hangar. Yellow ricochets bounding from steel girders beneath the hangar's thatched roof into the darkened sky convinced Smokey Stover that the Japanese were returning the fire. He opened with his four outboard .50-caliber machine guns as soon as his division leader fired, blurping out short bursts, then correcting his aim as he concentrated intently upon the fall of his tracers. The *Saratoga* fighters went round, and round again, stitching streams of bullets into buildings and revetments that could be seen more and more distinctly as the sun rose. Stover made one pass at less than fifty feet—low enough to look beneath the roofs of several tin sheds—but saw no living thing on or near the airstrip.

The fighters left at 0650 to make way for a squadron of *Saratoga* SBD dive-bombers, which struck targets along the shoreline. Cpl Frank Blakely saw the first of them swoop toward the dark, uneven stands of trees fronting the beach, then pull up in graceful arcs as their 1,000-lb bombs plummeted to earth. One of the first bombs, or perhaps a salvo from one of the warships, found a fuel dump near Kukum. Oily smoke pillared into the deep blue dawn. Then a cry, thin and reedy at first, rose in waves above the crescendo of bombing and shelling as the troops vented emotions pent up through the last long night of waiting.

The miserable garrison at Vungana was awakened by a terrible din. Capt Martin Clemens, who was by then living like a nomad, with neither bed nor a decent pair of shoes, rolled out of his blankets: He had no doubt as to what it meant, could hardly believe that help had come at long last, yet instinctively knew it had. A scout rushed down and breathlessly gave out that "the whole Jap fleet" was at anchor between Lunga and Tulagi. Clemens's heart stood still. He turned on his wireless receiver and madly spun the dial until he picked up the wavelength of the landing force. Clemens was ecstatic.

0909, Friday, August 7, 1942.
The warships offshore cease fire so three flimsy fabric spotter planes from one of the heavy cruisers can safely buzz Beach Red and deliver a last-minute report on enemy activity.
Pvt Jobert Williams, the sixteen-year-old high school runaway, stares at the broad back of his company commander, Capt Bill Hawkins, the twenty-seven-year-old high school teacher. Worlds apart, the two are being hurtled into the teeth of history, for their

53

*landing boat is leading the pack into Beach Red. The bond between
the two unblooded Marines is more in Williams's mind than in
Hawkins's, for the captain has been the young private's only real
authority figure, and he has unknowingly earned the utter devotion
of the unformed youth. Jobert Williams will follow Bill Hawkins
anywhere, even to the early and violent death he is certain they will
share in the unknown, unknowable struggle on Beach Red. Both
Marines are having thoughts about individual mortality; so is everyone else in every other boat.*

*The three spotter planes drop clusters of small smoke bombs to
mark the extremities of Beach Red for the leading wave, four reinforced rifle platoons of A and B companies, 5th Marines.*

*Jobert Williams, who is hunkered down beside the boat engine,
is unable to hear a thing. When the action starts, he will simply
have to keep an eye on Captain Hawkins, and follow. Bill Hawkins
has no one to keep an eye on. His command group, his company, his
battalion, his regiment, his division are all behind him.*

*After dropping their smoke bombs, the puttering spotter planes
dip over the jungle right behind the beach, then swing across the
wide, open Lunga Plain in the direction of the unfinished Japanese
runway. One reports "many enemy troops" moving toward Beach
Red. These are really only scrawny cattle running to escape the noise
of the naval bombardment. The report, correct or not, is valueless,
for there is no way to get word to the troops, who are only a minute
from the beach.*

0913.

"Okay! Let's go!"

*The words shake Jobert Williams from wherever his mind has
led him. The boat is on the beach, stopped. The adrenaline coursing
through his arteries induces a drugged response. Williams watches a
slow-motion procession as he tightens his left-handed grip on his
Springfield '03 rifle and vaults the gunwale of the rampless plywood
landing boat. Out ahead, automatic pistol raised in the traditional
"Follow me!" attitude of combat infantry leaders, Bill Hawkins
races across the sand; he is the first American Marine to set foot on
Guadalcanal.*

The balance of B Company, all of A Company, and two machine-gun platoons from D Company landed along a 1,600-yard front within a moment of Capt Bill Hawkins's arrival on Beach Red.

Given a moment to reflect upon the events of the past minutes as he passed into the first line of dense foliage, Hawkins was amazed at how close the boats had been able to get to the beach. The landing was not particularly dry, but it was bloodless.

The evolution of the leading companies from amphibious to land organizations was virtually unmarred. Despite expectations that he had only moments left to live, Pvt Jobert Williams reacted to his months of training by keeping his eyes on Captain Hawkins's radioman, who trailed a long whip antenna through the thickening undergrowth just inland from the beach; Williams was determined to be where he could do the most good when Captain Hawkins's first demand for a runner was sounded. Bill Hawkins expertly guided B Company, 5th, into the dense growth, exposing himself frequently, but for brief intervals, to pass traditional infantry hand signals to his troop leaders.

The landing was anticlimactic for troops so well trained, so keyed up. Not a shot was fired as A and B companies, 5th, moved inland to form a security screen for the remainder of 1st Battalion, 5th, and all of 3rd Battalion.

Capt Bill Hawkins encountered his first disappointment of the day as the point moved deeper into the bush. He had conferred at great length with an Australian who had once managed a plantation near Lunga. The man had assured everyone who would listen that the way inland was barred by a ditch, ten or fifteen feet wide, eight or ten feet deep, paralleling the shoreline for a distance of 250 yards. No end of discussion had gone on in rather high circles with respect to this potentially perfect defensive barrier and how it might be breached. In the end, Hawkins had been robbed of a crucial night's sleep to oversee the fabrication of a set of grappling hooks designed to assist his heavily encumbered company across the ditch. The barrier never materialized. More glaring intelligence gaffes would soon emerge. For the moment, however, the most glaring error was a solid bonus: There was no opposition—there were no losses—at all!

Once the beach was securely screened by a strong defensive perimeter and the leading elements of 1st Marines had been landed, Col Roy Hunt brought in his 5th Marines command group to plan and oversee continued advances.

First Battalion, 5th, was to reform and proceed directly along the beach to Lunga Point. However, the battalion vanguard was blocked a short distance in back of Beach Red by the standing water of Ilu Creek. Engineers attached to the regiment commandeered a pair of amphibian tractors and had them driven into the water near the mouth of the sluggish stream. The two cargo-carrying vehicles were scuttled end to end and decked over with lumber "acquired" from a nearby transport.

It was 1330 before 1st Battalion, 5th, turned its line along Ilu Creek over to a support unit and resumed its advance westward along the coastal track toward Lunga Point. Ramrodding the advance, which was planned as a rapid sweep into the Japanese command compound, was LtCol Bill Whaling, executive officer of 5th Marines. Whaling, the division's best woodsman, was dissatisfied with the progress. The bush on either side of the road was fearsome, but there was no enemy action and, to Whaling's mind, no reason for the extreme caution exhibited by the men in his care. Somehow, Whaling contrived to prod the advance to more speed without ever revealing his general dismay.

Still keyed up, Pvt Jobert Williams received his first big shock when he passed the shattered corpse of an Asian man killed in the morning's bombardment. As far as Williams and every man in that column was concerned, the war had been taken to the enemy and, in at least one case, was a thoroughgoing success.

When Col Clifton Cates's 1st Marines headquarters boat grated into the sand fronting Beach Red, Cpl Frank Blakely heaved the weight of his pack and the heavy transceiver unit of the command radio up the beach right on the heels of the radio team's generator man. Blakely expected to be hit by fire from hostile defenders, so he quickly crossed the crowded beach and hit the deck face down behind the first clump of trees he encountered. As the communicator lifted his head, the first thing he saw was a grinning Marine picking at a coconut.

As five rifle battalions—two from 5th Marines and all three from 1st Marines—were being shaken out along the expanding front, several 75mm light and 105mm medium artillery batteries of 11th Marines arrived ashore. Unfortunately, their arrival marred the smooth landing operation, for the gunners brought in far too much gear far too soon. Due to a shortage of ramped boats, there were no trucks for the twelve 105mm howitzers of 5th Battalion, 11th. One-ton reconnaissance cars were offered by infantry units, but these were far too light. In the end, the 105s were moved by amphibian tractors, whose steel-cleated treads ground communications wire to bits, and that reduced control over and between infantry units fanning outward from the beach.

For a time, until 1st Marines was released from its reserve status at 1115, the beachhead was overcrowded, and becoming more so as thousands of eager Marines piled ashore. Opposition remained nil. Most Marines were let down, but everyone continued to anticipate enemy resistance.

First Marines advanced in the general direction of a high, open piece of dominating ground identified as "Grassy Knoll" on hand-drawn maps. Foul-ups and misunderstandings occurred. When it came time to strip down the regimental command radio, Cpl Frank Blakely found that the two Marines who normally carried the bulky switchboard components had been assigned to a rear echelon that had not yet landed. So, in addition to his personal gear and heavy transceiver, Blakely had to hump one of the bulky switchboard pieces while the regimental communicator, a young captain, hauled the other. It was a man-sized job, made more exhausting by the burden of fear that permeated the extraordinarily hot rain forest. The command group trudged through high grass and trees for what seemed like miles until a scout spotted a lone man ahead. Col Clifton Cates, who had earned a Navy Cross while commanding a rifle company in France, calmly ordered all hands to hit the deck and prepare for action. The intruder, however, turned out to be a fellow Marine who had become separated from his unit. Such encounters were typical by that hour.

For all the often frantic human activity, the troops were singularly impressed with the overriding silence of the strange and beautiful surroundings. The heat was oppressive, and unnecessary burdens, particularly gas masks, soon marked the routes of the scattering infantry columns.

As they blundered through the trees and dense brush, the troops came upon signs of the Japanese occupation. C Company, 1st, stumbled into a small work camp that seemed to have been hurriedly abandoned only minutes earlier. Scavenging riflemen uncovered a cache of green *sake* bottles, and a number of the troops became temporary casualties as they hit upon a simple, effective expedient for disposing of the contraband.

Colonel Cates became certain that his regimental objective, Grassy Knoll, was much farther from the beach than indicated on his crude map. LtCol Frank Goettge, the division intelligence officer, had been assured during his whirlwind fact-finding journey to Australia that the knoll was a mere 1,000 yards south and west of Beach Red. Cates's battalions became increasingly disoriented as they moved deeper into the bush without being able to see the objective; high stands of triple-canopy rain forest obscured vistas in all directions, forcing infantry vanguards to move slowly, by dead reckoning.

Grassy Knoll was really eight miles from the beach, well beyond the Lunga Plain. None of the civilians interviewed in Australia had ever actually set foot on the mountain—named Mount Austen by the British, and Mambulu by the islanders.

The march inland was grueling in the extreme for men whose muscles had been softened by weeks of idleness. Moreover, the troops were encumbered by too much gear. Water and salt tablets were in short supply, and the heat was utterly oppressive. After advancing only a mile, Cates's battalions were ordered by the division headquarters to stop, reorient themselves, and regain internal contact. The thoroughly exhausted 1st Marines established battalion-size defensive cordons for the night: 2nd Battalion on the east bank of the Tenaru River; 1st Battalion slightly to the north, on the Tenaru's west bank; and 3rd Battalion west of 1st, about two miles inland from the mouth of Alligator Creek. First Battalion, 5th, got as far as the mouth of Alligator Creek and halted in a coconut grove on the east bank.

In contrast to the many rather minor difficulties encountered by the advancing infantry columns, the task of getting adequate supplies and equipment to Beach Red simply overtaxed the skill and experience of the Navy and Marines.

First Marine Division's logistical situation had been deteriorating since the New Zealand winter rains had caught 5th Marines working in the open at Aotea Quay. Bad enough were the losses incurred by the rains, by misplacement of equipment and supplies, and by the voluntary abandonment of heavy artillery and heavy equipment for delivery later, but the tragic loss of precious, essential goods continued right onto Beach Red.

Moving supplies from ships' holds into lighters was easy in the calm waters of Lengo Channel, but the very instant the first supply-laden craft nosed into Beach Red the situation went downhill with appalling swiftness.

The facilities ashore were completely inadequate to meet the problems. The beach-labor party was too small and inexperienced to cope with the deluge of material mounting at the water's edge. The efficiency of boat groups in getting the gear as far as the beach far outstripped the ability of the slim beach parties to get it moved to burgeoning inland dumps. Small craft were soon stacked four- and five-deep awaiting frontage on the beach. Apart from the narrow coastal track, there was nothing that could be called a "road." The few trails in the vicinity could not withstand the churning of wheels bearing heavy loads. All the Marines' vehicles were too light for efficient hauling, and there were not enough of them in any event. The muggy heat quickly sapped the energy of the relatively soft beach laborers.

RAdm Kelly Turner fixed the blame for the mess on the Marines, claiming that they had failed to provide adequate manpower. The Marines, however, had ample cause to believe that every available combat-trained individual would be needed to help fight off Japanese counterattacks. General Vandegrift had asked the Navy to provide details of bluejackets for work on the beach, but his request had been ignored.

In truth, the Marines were overcautious. For example, over 300 members of 1st Pioneer Battalion—the only trained beach-labor pool—were committed to the division combat reserve, and not to shore labor. An urgent appeal by the transport commodore for the release of combat troops from the (unengaged) defensive line was refused by the wary division staff, which claimed the riflemen were too tired to help. At length, seventy-five artillerymen from the transport-poor 5th Battalion, 11th, were sent to the beach as a first, token offering.

At 2200, August 7, Archer Vandegrift issued the first revision of his division's operational plan—a change made possible by the total lack of opposition anywhere on Guadalcanal. First and 5th Marines were ordered to establish a joint perimeter defense around the uncompleted Japanese airstrip on the Lunga Plain, the seizure of which seemed inevitable. The entire landing force would move from Beach Red to the new perimeter once all supplies and equipment had been landed and transferred.

The new plan represented Vandegrift's first great compromise; while Beach Red was the only suitable beach in the vicinity of Lunga, it could not be held with the available force if the airfield was to be adequately defended against Japanese reprisals. The beaches were to be abandoned by August 12, the day the transports were scheduled to depart.

The first night was scary. Itchy because of the new and threatening surroundings, inculcated with stories of Japanese combat prowess, frustrated by their inability to vent pent-up hostility during the day, the troops were easily rattled.

The 1st Marines command group was camped beside the Tenaru River, but forbidden to replenish their depleted canteens by LtCol Bull Frisbie, the regimental executive officer, who felt the scummy water might have been poisoned by the retreating Japanese defenders. The dark silence was shattered by the booming voice of the hulking exec, no doubt stirred by thirsty men blundering into trees during clandestine trips to the waterway: "The next son of a bitch that I hear," Frisbie warned, "I will personally blow his goddamned head off."

Several drunk machine gunners spent part of the night vying with a group of restive fellow Marines who insisted upon moving noisily across 1st Battalion, 5th's compound. No one was harmed, but no one slept either.

A sergeant was shot dead by a rattled sentry within the lines of L Company, 5th, the battalion's first fatality.

First Battalion, 5th, crossed Alligator Creek, a sluggish lagoon halfway between Beach Red and Lunga Point, at 0930, August 8. Prodded by an impatient LtCol Bill Whaling, the column undertook a cautious, deliberate advance from the creek all the way to Kukum Village, just west of Lunga Point.

First Battalion, 1st, waded Alligator Creek about 500 yards inland. The steep, densely overgrown banks of the creek severely hampered the crossing. Second and 3rd Battalions, 1st, skirted the headwaters of Alligator Creek and drove into the overgrown ridge country just south of the 3,600-foot runway. The going was tedious, and components of both battalions became entangled in the undergrowth and with one another. Col Clifton Cates, initially jubilant, became increasingly suspicious that he was being led into a trap.

Elements of 3rd Battalion, 5th, were stepping onto the eastern end of the runway at about noon when screams of "Japs!" and "Down!" were hurled across the open area. All hands tried to bury themselves in the packed coral-and-earth surface as a Japanese Zero fighter made a low pass but did not fire. The Japanese aviator pulled up to avoid trees and shaken Marines headed for the nearest cover.

All the advancing battalions ran into sporadic sniper fire and, at first, the troops killed every Asian they could root out of the brush. In time, information began passing from the pockets and packs of dead Japanese and Koreans to the care of various intelligence sections. Prisoners eventually began making their way safely to the rear, where they underwent rudimentary interrogation before being transferred to the Navy's custody for transportation to New Zealand. Nearly all of the prisoners were laborers, mainly Koreans, and none was privy to any important information. Minor details, however, soon began to fill in a puzzle reasonably fathomable to the intelligence specialists.

First Battalion, 1st, contracted its front at 1430 and crossed the Lunga River bridge immediately north of the runway, then advanced directly on the Kukum River, a minor stream in the western fan of the Lunga River delta. The ground was densely overgrown with tall, sharp kunai grass, but not defended.

Scouts from D Company, 1st, a weapons unit, led the way into the main Japanese encampment at about 1500. There were no occupants, but abandoned cooked food throughout the area attested to a hurried, recent evacuation.

Early in the afternoon, just as 1st Battalion, 5th, was moving into Kukum, Capt Gordon Gayle, the battalion operations officer, put his head through the door of a large wooden building and found a large radio set. Gayle immediately reported the find to his battalion commander who, in accordance with standing policy, ordered the radio station destroyed. As Gayle prepared to call out a work detail, it occurred to him that the impressive array of equipment might be of use to the division. It simply went against the captain's grain to destroy such gorgeous equipment when Marines were struggling with ancient, unreliable communications devices of their own. He detailed two men to guard the radio station and passed word to 1st Signal Company, the division communications unit. Then, pressed by other business, Gayle simply forgot about the radio station. His decision was crucial.

Of considerably less importance was the acquisition by many riflemen of quantities of large green bottles and small brown bottles—*sake* and beer. Prodigious quantities of foodstuffs and equipment fell into American hands through the day, including nearly 100 trucks, which were put to immediate use. Captured bicycles were soon careering along picturesque jungle paths, barely controlled by Americans unfamiliar with handlebar brakes.

Marines wrecked many potentially valuable stores and much equipment, but sober-thinking individuals like Gordon Gayle soon took control. Exotic delicacies such as tinned crabmeat and pickled plums, however, advanced westward in the packs, pockets, and bellies of Depression-deprived American youngsters.

Among other things, Marines took possession of a functioning ice plant and a nearly completed twin-generator electrical station. Tractors and a narrow-gauge railway were passed along to the engineers, who were glad to receive anything to replace what they had had to leave in New Zealand.

All in all, August 7 and 8 on Guadalcanal had been a propitious beginning for an effort that had been hastily organized and poorly planned. The Japanese had eased the burden considerably by keeping to themselves for the two crucial days it took the Marines to find their land legs and get used to the notion of actually participating in a war with an enemy that had yet to be seriously tested on land.

The same could not be said for events to the north.

7

The approach of Task Force Yoke on the north side of Sealark Channel was uneventful, and Marines were climbing down into their landing craft by 0600. Though several of the transports lost formation, all elements of Yoke were in position by 0630. The commodore informed BGen Bill Rupertus that the landings would commence at 0800.

On receiving news that unidentified aircraft were approaching Tulagi, the transports suddenly weighed anchor and pulled *away* from the objective while Marines were in the early stages of disembarking. Boats in the water were left to their own devices. The run to find sea room was repeated almost as soon as some order had been regained from the chaos that followed the first alert. This time, frantic bluejackets threw much valuable equipment overboard when the transports attempted to recover some of the largely unseaworthy little landing craft.

Fifteen fighters and fifteen dive-bombers from carrier *Wasp* streaked out of the morning sky to attack shoreline emplacements on Tulagi at 0614. Airmen observed fires throughout the target area, mainly from nine Zero floatplane fighters and eight four-engine amphibian patrol bombers that had been caught at their moorings off neighboring Gavutu.

Destroyer *Monssen* broke away from the main covering force at 0727 to blanket a hill on Florida Island with 5-inch shells. The promontory dominated by the hill was the objective of a reinforced company of 2nd Marines, which was to lead off in the sector. *Monssen*'s guns were joined by those of another destroyer and light antiaircraft cruiser *San Juan*, each of which poured about 200 rounds into Haleta Village and other possible areas from which the landings might be opposed.

The task of securing the promontory, the hill, and Haleta Village fell to Capt Ed Crane's B Company, 2nd Marines.

The first shots of the campaign—and of the American offensive in the Pacific—were fired by Pvt Russell Miller, who raked the beach with his 1918-vintage Lewis machine gun moments before his boat slid up onto the sand. At 0740, 1stLt Maxie Williams became the first American officer to land on Japanese-occupied ground in the Pacific.

Eager, fearful Marines gawked at the imposing rain forest for a bit, then ventured inland. A thorough search produced nothing of interest, so B Company, 2nd, returned to its boats—an inauspicious beginning to the American Pacific offensive.

The remainder of 1st Battalion, 2nd, drew small-arms fire as it passed Gavutu and landed on Florida Island's Halavo Peninsula at 0845. Once again, there was no sign of any Japanese. The battalion returned to its ship later in the day.

Other objectives in the area were far less easy to secure.

At 0800, precisely, the leading elements of 1st Raider Battalion moved on Beach Blue, a narrow sandy shelf on Tulagi's west coast, some 2,000 yards from the northwest tip of the island.

Tulagi's rugged coastline had presented the planners with some interesting compromises. The only really suitable beaches were on the eastern and southeastern coasts, but these were dominated by high ground close to Florida, from which obstructing fires could be directed. The remainder of Tulagi was protected by a coral reef. After weighing the odds, the planners decided to mount the assault force over the reef against a beach from which it could best deploy to sweep the island. This, despite the effect the jagged coral might have upon plywood landing craft. Any Japanese machine guns on the heights overlooking the beach could do serious harm to the landing force.

The two lead Raider companies, under the command of the battalion exec, LtCol Sam Griffith, did get hung up on the coral. The troops were forced to pick their way carefully across thirty to one hundred yards of pitted bottom in armpit-deep breakers. It was a fearful, fearsome plunge into the unknown, even by troops as finely trained as the attack-minded Raiders.

Beach Blue was undefended; the Japanese were concentrated around the former British administration buildings on the southeastern one-third of the narrow island. In fact, the *rikusentai* holding Tulagi had no inkling that a hostile force had landed until long after a thankful LtCol Sam Griffith emerged from the surf to direct his leading platoons.

Griffith, a 1929 Naval Academy graduate who had learned the art of shock assault as an exchange officer with the Royal Marines commandos, was efficiently expanding his holdings while the Japanese commander of the Tulagi communications center was informing his superiors in Rabaul that the island was under attack and would be defended to the last man.

As B and D companies formed a defensive cordon around Beach Blue, A and C companies stormed into the reef. Unable to push his assault, and with half the battalion still foundering in the surf, Griffith experienced long minutes of uncertainty. When the follow-up units finally straggled onto the beach, Griffith left them to sort themselves out while he started the lead companies into the dense undergrowth in an expanding line of battle.

Behind the Raiders, 2nd Battalion, 5th, which was to sweep the northwestern third of Tulagi, ran into difficulties on the reef at 0830. The battalion had been trained as a "rubber-boat assault" unit early in the war, but it had been broken up for cadres so often that its expertise lay more in a dimly recollected reputation than in fact.

B and D companies were soon confronted with a steep 340-foot-high coral spine running the length of the island. B Company, in the vanguard, pushed over the summit and on down to Sesapi Village, on the eastern shore. Not a shot was fired. D Company moved partway down the slope, tied its left flank to B Company's right, and opened a deliberate southeastward advance.

While the lead companies were crossing Tulagi's spine, the remainder of the battalion reorganized on Beach Blue. A Company swung rightward and tied in with D Company while C Company followed partway up the slope before pivoting into line, its right flank echeloned to the rear along the water's edge. The bulk of E Company's medium machine guns and all its 81mm mortars remained on the beach, in reserve.

The advance, which got off to a slow, cautious start, encountered no opposition. The finely honed Raiders were disappointed as they slowly continued forward without incident until B Company, on the far left, reached Carpenter's Wharf and found itself face-to-face with a line of hurriedly manned outposts. At 1120, just as the Americans came abreast their first objective line, mortar rounds dropping in among the closed ranks severely wounded the D Company commander in the head.

Just then, the battalion commander, LtCol Red Mike Edson, caught up with the advancing line and took over from Sam Griffith; he had had the infuriating and humiliating experience of being in a boat caught at an odd angle on the coral, unable to get into the water for precious hours. Thus, the sanguinary, carrot-topped Vermonter was among the last of the Raiders to approach the Japanese.

In front of Edson's rambling line lay the settled, sparsely wooded portion of Tulagi. The Raiders' immediate objective lay in a saddle between two ridges. The larger of the heights, to the northwest, was secured in the face of very light opposition. On the second ridge and in the open ground around and behind it was the main body of Kure 3rd Special Naval Landing Force, which in early May had seized Tulagi.

Red Mike issued a lip-curling, whisper-voiced order to clear the front with automatic-weapons' fire before advancing. As the leading Raiders stepped out of the dense underbrush to mount their sweep, C Company, on the extreme right, was hit immediately by fire from emplacements on Hill 208, on the extreme left and in front of the main Japanese line. Gunfire, from emplacements gouged into the seaward face of the knob, struck portions of C Company as they passed between the hill and the surf. While C Company turned to launch reactive assaults, A Company quickly bypassed the hotspot.

Assault teams from C Company mounted the slope, carefully employing the cunning infiltration tactics Red Mike had pounded into them during months of brutal training. Several Raiders intent upon hurling hand grenades into the Japanese burrows were injured in the intense close-quarters first combat, and one was killed when a Japanese officer interrupted surrender negotiations to hurl a defiant grenade of his own. The C Company commander, Maj Ken Bailey, one of the Marine Corps' most gifted troop leaders, made his way alone to a precarious purchase atop the entrance of a particularly troublesome emplacement and attempted to kick through the earthen roof. A Japanese peered from within and, before anyone could act, shot Bailey through the leg.

Hill 208 and the 200-yard gap between it and the surf were secured by 1230. Only one Japanese naval rating was extricated alive, stunned by the concussion of a mortar shell.

Meantime, Raiders farther to the west met vicious opposition based around Hill 281, a steep knob protruding from the southeastern end of the island's jagged spine. Antiaircraft cruiser *San Juan* moved precipitously toward Tulagi when plotters in the fire-direction center manning a direct link with Red Mike Edson heard him say he needed help fast. The light cruiser ripped out 280 5-inch rounds, blanketing the hill in a seven-minute precision bombardment that killed many defenders. Suddenly, a 5-inch round exploded in its super-hot breech before it could be fired. Five gunners died, including one who was blown overboard from inside the turret. *San Juan*'s rapid, accurate fire allowed the Raiders to approach the defenses while the defenders had their heads down. But the advance pretty much bogged down.

After hours of persistent communications difficulties, Lieutenant Colonel Edson was able to speak at 1625 directly with his superior, BGen Bill Rupertus. He told the assistant division commander that about 500 *rikusentai* had broken contact and withdrawn toward a ravine on his southeastern flank.

At the end of the action, D Company was situated on the extreme left of the line; it had run into the least opposition and had been slowed only by the requirement that it keep pace with the remainder of the battalion. The company turned its dangling left flank and dug in for the night near the beach. B Company, holding the left center position, had met only light opposition during the day. It, too, had had to slow its pace to remain in contact with adjacent A Company, which was strung out across the crest of the island's central spine. Although both units tried mightily, B and D companies were unable to maintain contact across a deep ravine. A and C companies had borne the brunt of the afternoon's fighting, but both had weathered the ordeal in good condition.

After withdrawing from the facing slope of the hill, the Japanese occupied the deep ravine bordering the old cricket pitch between Hill 280 and Hill 281. The area was honeycombed with coral caves from which Marines attempting to advance through the ravine could be subjected to withering crossfires. The Japanese no longer held much ground, but they were well concentrated and clearly full of fight.

Fearful of a night attack, mindful of the many gaps in his line where the terrain prevented firm contact between units, and in need of troops to commit to the anticipated renewal of the Marine assault in the morning, Red Mike called forward elements of 2nd Battalion, 5th, which had uneventfully seized the northwestern portion of the island. Two companies were deployed in defensive cordons in the vicinity of D Company, Raiders, while the third company was held in reserve close to Beach Blue.

The first Japanese assault burst out of the darkness after several hours of inactivity and attained a lodgment at the juncture of A and C companies, pushing outposts back upon the main line and isolating C Company from the remainder of the battalion.

The weight of the attack next shifted toward the left, against the A Company right platoon, which was struggling to re-fuse the connection with C Company. Maj Lew Walt, the A Company commander, ordered his left platoon to fill in on the company right, where the attack was strongest. First Lieutenant Myles Fox was severely wounded in the arm during the move across the company rear, but he refused relief until he had seen the Japanese driven back. He soon succumbed to loss of blood.

The Japanese next brought up several Nambu light 7.7mm machine guns and poured a dangerous flanking fire into Walt's company. Without asking for permission or support, PlSgt Clifford Hills crawled forward to within twenty yards of the nearest Nambu and picked off the entire crew with his .45-caliber automatic pistol.

Partly as a result of training and largely because of a cultural trait, Americans were generally uncommunicative in combat. Japanese were not. Once the need for secrecy had passed, the *rikusentai* on A Company's front loudly encouraged and warned one another. Raiders fired at the voices, and the Japanese pinpointed Marines by muzzle flashes, then guided one another by voice command. Slowly, with infinite patience, the Japanese worked their way uphill toward the British Residency, where Red Mike had established his forward command post.

As the first Japanese neared the crest of Residency Hill, they came within range of an observation post manned by the battalion's intelligence section and the battalion's 81mm mortar platoon leader and several gunners, who were ordered to withdraw just as dark silhouettes appeared against the lighter night sky. The Raiders silently hurled the leading *rikusentai* from the cliff, then withdrew.

B Company Raiders who were sent from the left center to help A Company had to fight through pockets of infiltrators.

The initial lodgment and subsequent infiltrations were the only successful efforts by large groups of Japanese to disrupt the Raider defenses. Individuals and small groups spent the predawn hours trying to kill Raiders, particularly those near the ravine by the cricket pitch. Several Marines were killed and injured during the night, but the Japanese gained little.

At daybreak, August 8, E and F companies, 5th, passed through D Company, Raiders, to sweep the northwest slope of Hill 281. The fresh riflemen scoured the objective, then pivoted to pocket most of the surviving Japanese in the ravine below the cricket pitch. When the Japanese were firmly hemmed in on three sides, the Marines fired 60mm and 81mm mortars into the ravine.

The Japanese front collapsed around 1500 and the Marines rapidly pushed across the ravine and ground up against the last tough remnant, which clearly had no intention of giving up or giving in. In one place, three Japanese holed up in a tiny coral burrow with one pistol and one magazine of bullets among them were able to hold a Marine squad at bay by firing one infrequent round at a time, then took their own lives with the last three rounds. Most of the caves fell to dynamite and hand grenades hurled by lone Marines supported by heavy suppressive fire.

At length, Red Mike informed General Rupertus that Tulagi was secure and that surviving defenders would be hunted down. Of 500 *rikusentai* manning Tulagi's defenses on August 7, three were taken alive.

8

Gavutu and Tanambogo, two unremarkable coral-and-sand humps nestled between Florida's Halavo Peninsula and southeastern Tulagi, were the objective of Maj Bob Williams's 1st Parachute Battalion. Gavutu had been the regional headquarters of the Burns-Philp Company, and Tanambogo had been developed early in the war by the Royal Australian Air Force as a seaplane base. Both islets boasted machine shops, jetties, permanent buildings, and a radio station apiece, all of which had been expanded and improved by the Japanese since they seized the area in early May.

The 351-man parachute battalion, disappointed to a man because it was going into first combat by boat, was to land on Gavutu at 1200 in three company-sized waves. Following a rapid reduction of the expected small labor and base operating forces, the 'Chutes were to sweep Tanambogo by crossing the narrow causeway the Japanese had built between the two islets.

A shortage of naval gunfire support vessels, air cover, and small boats prevented the 'Chutes from mounting a dawn assault alongside Marine battalions going into Guadalcanal, Florida, and Tulagi, but no one was overly concerned about losing four hours of daylight and any chance of surprising the Japanese garrison. The seizure of the twin objectives was billed as a milk run. In fact, the battalion commander took the optimistic view that four additional hours of bombardment—even sporadic bombardment—was at least as desirable as achieving tactical surprise.

Capt Bill McKennan's 102-man A Company was the first wave. No one had formally assigned the company to the leading position. Rather, McKennan had won a toss of the coin with the B Company commander; C Company, weighing in at only seventy-seven effectives, had not been considered for the lead position, but would be coming in last, with the battalion headquarters.

The 'Chutes went over the sides of transport *Heywood* at about 1000. Before setting out, the spirited Marines whistled and cheered in a final gesture of defiance against *Heywood*'s master, a stiff-necked man who had made his distaste for whistling and cheering—and Marines in general—a memorable part of that trip to first combat.

Ens Galen Brown, the young Navy boat officer in charge of shepherding the 'Chutes third wave to the beach, was as concerned as he could be about the choppy sea, stiff breeze, and seven-mile run that still lay ahead. The 'Chutes themselves only dimly perceived that Brown and his fellow boat officers and bluejackets were as new to their jobs as the rawest 'Chutes were to theirs. The Gavutu landings were rated little higher than a live-fire exercise, an opportunity to learn about what the new war would really be like while, almost as an afterthought, seizing some ground from the Japanese.

Before starting for the distant objective, Galen Brown had to bring his ramp boat alongside another boat to pass instructions to the crew, which was on loan from another transport. The two plywood craft bumped into each other rather heavily in the strong chop. No serious damage was then perceived, but halfway to Gavutu, puking, wet, thoroughly miserable Marines passed word to Brown that a good deal of water was spraying through a smashed plank six inches below the waterline. After watching the water in the bilges for a few moments, Brown determined that his craft was not about to sink, so he turned his attention back to navigating through the choppy swells and maintaining his third-wave position in the formation.

Pfc Bill Keller, a Browning Automatic Rifleman (BAR-man) with A Company, was awed by the impact of the day's journey. The Ohio farm boy found himself reciting the Twenty-third Psalm over and over as his first-wave boat plowed toward the fireswept waters around Tulagi.

Capt Dick Johnson, the B Company weapons-platoon leader, was moved beyond words when a destroyer passed his boat, a huge white bone in her teeth, decks littered with spent shell casings, the Stars-and-Stripes standing stiffly out from her mast.

As the three four-boat waves steadied themselves and plowed past Tulagi, which had stood between the transports and the 'Chutes objective, light antiaircraft cruiser *San Juan* pounded the landing beach centered around the main seaplane ramp, her fourteen 5-inch guns spewing out a round apiece every twelve seconds for four minutes. The cruiser seemed to erupt in a cloud of yellowish grey smoke at each salvo. At the same time, dive-bombers from carrier *Wasp* attacked defilade positions and attempted to suppress possible fire from neighboring Tanambogo.

The 'Chutes nearly pulled it off.

Capt Bill McKennan was one of the first men ashore. His A Company came in precisely as planned, the four boats grounding in soft mud just to the left of the boat pier and concrete seaplane ramp. The 'Chutes charged across the beach under the lightest fire necessary to rate as opposition.

The only first-wave casualty was Capt Kermit Mason, the battalion intelligence officer, who was shot dead as he stood to ascertain the quantity and location of points of resistance.

Pfc Bill Keller's squad advanced into the open without drawing fire. Suddenly, Keller saw puffs of dust beside his feet, but it was not until his squad leader told him so that he believed he was under hostile fire. He immediately took cover behind a coconut tree and asked his sergeant to tell him from where the fire was coming. The sergeant said he thought it was coming from the hill, but no one was able to spot any targets.

Pfc Larry Moran, a B Company rifleman who had been one of the first to join the then-experimental battalion in 1940, was nearly to the beach when he saw gunfire wink from the summit of Hill 148. Before Moran could duck, he felt rather than saw Navy fighters pass close overhead, and 5-inch shells from a destroyer behind the boat waves blanketed the hill.

B Company was only four minutes behind A, but might have been involved in another war, so different was its reception.

The boat wave had gotten marginally out of line, which resulted in a collision between Pfc Larry Moran's boat and a cement wall that had been part of the small-boat pier at the right extremity of the beach. The boat was pushed up at a forty-five-degree angle, causing its human cargo to tumble every which way but out. Struggling to order, the heavily laden Marines were taken under brutal, heavy fire. Others dropped around him, but Larry Moran broke free from the confused mass and tumbled into a shell crater to inventory his vital parts.

Two Marines in Capt Dick Johnson's boat were killed by gunfire from Hill 148 just as the second wave plowed into the rubble of the concrete pier and seaplane ramp. Johnson got out as fast as he could, breasting a heavy burst of machine-gun fire. Greeted by the spectre of several dead and wounded Marines on the beach, Johnson turned to see how his troops were faring, but found only one, a corporal. His boat's coxswain had panicked. The bluejacket had reversed engines within an instant of dropping the ramp and headed for the demolished seaplane ramp. However, the rubble prevented the boat from getting close to shore, so the troops had to drop into chest-deep water. As Dick Johnson helplessly looked on from shore, an ammunition carrier wearing a vest laden with six 60mm mortar rounds stumbled beneath the surface; he would have drowned had not another Marine fished him out.

Dumped into waist-deep water yards from the beach, Dr. Harold Schwartz, the battalion surgeon, reflexively reached out to a mortally wounded sergeant, but felt himself flinch under the impact of slugs in the head, left shoulder, and left hand. He was pulled ashore by one of his corpsmen and dropped on a beach littered with incongruous broken brown beer bottles. A Marine seated beneath a nearby palm tree was nursing his wounded jaw.

Ens Galen Brown's four landing craft were racing flat out for the beach. As Brown stared through his binoculars, he could see that several landmarks upon which he had been counting had been rearranged by the naval and air bombardment. Marines were wading through the fire-swept water.

It was impossible for Brown to control the final approach by all four of his boats; it was difficult for him to convey instructions to his own coxswain. Bullets seemed to be whizzing by from all directions, smacking against the boat's plywood sides. When Brown raised his binoculars for a final fix, his vision blurred. He took the glasses from his eyes to see what the trouble was. The right lens and prism were shattered; on the metal bridge between the two lenses was a new quarter-inch hole.

When the four-boat wave hit the beach, Cpl Ernie DeFazio, a C Company squad leader, was huddled below the command boat's gunwale, ears ringing with the deafening roar of gunfire. Towering over the troops, Capt Dick Heurth, the C Company commander, roared, "Clear the boat!" and went down immediately, dead from a round through the head. Ernie DeFazio crawled into waist-deep water, heading right, away from the heaviest gunfire.

The ramp of Ens Galen Brown's boat dropped the instant forward motion ceased, but it took two or three heartbeats before even one Marine in the troop compartment moved a muscle. Then a parachute officer shouted "Let's go!" and the boat was vacant within a minute. Only then did Brown see that his coxswain had chosen a spot of beach between two other boats. Men in the boat to the right were unloading gasoline and water over the side to Marines in the water, though the boat officers had told all hands to retract from the beach as soon as the troops were landed, that supplies could be brought in when the risk had abated. Ensign Brown shouted to get the nearby coxswain's attention as the crewman stooped to pick up another jerrycan. The man popped up again a second later to hand the can to a waiting Marine, but the Marine had by then been felled by gunfire. The coxswain looked right at Galen Brown through wide eyes, then ran to the boat's wheel and pulled out. Brown's boat followed, stopping 100 yards from the beach so one of the crewmen could crank the ramp up. That job was delayed when, each time the man tried to fit the crank into the winch, a bullet would ping into the boat. This dance with death went on for several moments before the crewman yelled, "Sir, is there any hurry about getting the ramp up?"

The entire 1st Parachute Battalion was ashore within twenty minutes of the first man.

A Company moved to the flanks and directly ahead, toward Hill 148, to secure the beachhead. B Company was to have re-formed behind A Company to mount a sweep of the hill, and C Company was to be held in reserve. Once the island was secure, the battalion was to move to Tanambogo via the causeway, secure its 121-foot hill, and scour the island for the dazed, demoralized survivors of the naval and air bombardments.

When Capt George Stallings, the battalion operations officer, clambered over the pier and made his way to the spot where he and Maj Bob Williams had agreed to meet to establish the battalion command post (CP), he was subjected to heavy small-arms fire. Stallings made little progress before receiving numerous conflicting reports concerning events ashore; the first stated that Major Williams had already led a small force to Tanambogo. Stallings got all the troops he could find under cover and moved to establish the CP in a wooden building nearby.

Pfc Bill Keller, of A Company, had just taken cover with the rest of his squad, unable to find targets for his BAR, when Maj Bob Williams appeared from nowhere to rally the troops for an attack on Hill 148. Keller was left behind to deliver supporting fire with his BAR.

Major Williams was immediately shot through the lung and used as bait by Japanese on the heights, who casually fired on 'Chutes trying to get him to safety. Two Marines were wounded before the major coughed orders for everyone to leave him be. Williams settled down for a painful, hot, breathless day in the sun while command of the battalion fell to Maj Tony Miller.

Capt Dick Johnson, the B Company weapons officer, could do little to help the battalion's progress. His machine guns were quickly doled out to the line, and his 60mm mortar crews were having difficulties bearing on targets because equipment shortages early in the war had stripped the unit of its mortar sights; the weapons could be fired, but not with accuracy.

Fighting was fierce in the center, where B Company was trying to pass through A Company, but the A Company platoon closest to Tanambogo was virtually untouched by enemy fire.

Capt Bill McKennan, the A Company commander, spent the greater part of the afternoon passing messages back and forth to the battalion CP and B Company, all aimed at sorting out the two leading companies and effecting a concerted effort against the stubborn defenders of Hill 148.

Capt Harry Torgerson, a supernumerary, noted early that the 'Chutes took ground rather than lives, that many caves and dugouts on and about Hill 148 were being ignored and bypassed. Part of the difficulty arose from the individualistic natures of many of these elite troops. Trained to fend for themselves, many 'Chutes insisted upon going their own way, often to the sound of the firing despite the wisdom of remaining where they were placed by their officers.

Steady, if slow, gains were eked out against stubborn opposition. Everyone had been wrong about the number and quality of the defenders, nor had anyone anticipated finding them in relatively bomb-proof coral caves. Still, by 1430, the 'Chutes were in possession of the greater portion of Gavutu; elements of B Company, in fact, had secured the eastern and southeastern slopes of Hill 148 and a few Marines had topped the hill.

Several of the B Company 'Chutes were traversing a captured 3-inch dual-purpose gun to fire on Tanambogo Hill when a Navy dive-bomber pilot, who thought his plane was being tracked by a hostile guncrew, dived on the emplacement. Two 'Chutes were killed and several others severely injured.

Further gains, particularly on the enfiladed north side of the island, were impossible. Naval gunfire could not be brought to bear on this area for lack of sea room. However, a pair of destroyers stood offshore and fired over Hill 148 into the portions of Tanambogo Hill that they could reach.

It was a stalemate.

Although his 'Chutes continued to press home daring attacks upon the caves within their reach, Major Miller decided that he could not secure Gavutu without first reducing the caves on Tanambogo Hill. Miller's operations officer, Capt George Stallings, recommended that a platoon each from A and C companies be sent across the causeway, but Miller said the battalion needed reinforcements. While higher authorities weighed the request against other needs, the 'Chutes did what they could on Hill 148.

Capt Harry Torgerson devised a method for blowing caves after the Japanese repeatedly returned live hand grenades and TNT blocks the 'Chutes hurled into their burrows. Torgerson used communications wire to strap TNT to long wooden boards salvaged from the wreckage of the seaplane base. Covered by several riflemen, he approached each newly discovered cave from a blind side, speared the explosives through the entrance, and bent his end of the long board back against one side of the opening to counter efforts by the occupants to eject the sputtering charge. This method was over-perfected on one cave when Torgerson added some aviation gasoline to the mix. His pants and wristwatch were blown off, but the enhanced charge took care of the objective. In all, Torgerson alone expended the contents of twenty cases of TNT during the afternoon, as well as serving as an example for other 'Chutes, who blew other caves on their own. In time, however, the 'Chutes ran out of targets that could be reduced at reasonable risk.

The only unit that was available to reinforce the 'Chutes on Gavutu and which could be mounted out rapidly was Capt Ed Crane's B Company, 2nd, which had earlier landed at Florida's Haleta Village. The company was just reboarding its landing craft when Crane was directed to report to Major Miller on Gavutu.

As soon as the reinforced rifle company arrived at Gavutu's damaged seaplane ramp at about 1800, Major Miller ordered Captain Crane to seize Tanambogo. When asked about opposition, Miller said that the islet was held by "a few snipers."

The six boats bearing B Company and its attached machine-gun platoon pulled off the beach, reformed, and chugged past tiny Gaomi Islet, bound for a night landing on a small pier on Tanambogo's north shore. One platoon was prevented from landing when its boat ran into a coral outcropping.

The first boat beached without drawing fire. The company executive officer, 1stLt John Smith, jumped to the pier, yelled, "Follow me!" and headed inland without a look back. No one followed because the moment Smith stepped from the boat a friendly 5-inch round set a fuel dump ablaze, and that bathed the pier area in the light of a glaring fireball. As soon as Lieutenant Smith realized he was alone, he dropped into a shell crater, but only until he heard a faint rustle nearby. Hoping a fellow Marine had found him, Smith whispered a challenge. A Japanese rifleman stood up. Smith fired his .45-caliber automatic pistol at the looming shadow and ran back to the pier.

The burning gasoline doomed the landing. Every Japanese gun that could be brought to bear was fired, and serious casualties were inflicted. An entire boat crew was felled and the boat slowly drifted away from the beach until a Marine took the helm and ran for safer waters. The machine-gun platoon managed to reach the pier, but plunging fire from Tanambogo Hill hit many gunners. Two other boats tried to touch down, but they were sent packing before more than a handful of Marines could leap to the pier.

Only thirty Marines got from the pier to the beach. Captain Crane snapped an order to get the injured back aboard the boats, then sent most of the able-bodied out. Covered by Crane, Lieutenant Smith, and a dozen riflemen, the boats scattered toward Gavutu and their transport.

Crane's covering party cautiously worked to the left, along the beach, and reached the packed-coral causeway connecting Tanambogo with Gavutu. Two of the riflemen elected to row to Gavutu aboard a boat they found on the beach. They arrived safely at about 2200, just as Captain Crane and the rest of the party, which had crawled across the causeway in a driving downpour, was reporting the repulse of B Company to Maj Tony Miller. All hands were accounted for by midnight.

A steady trickle of Japanese reinforcements arriving from Tulagi and Florida passed at least an equal number of outbound refugees from Gavutu. Alert 'Chutes on the beach managed to kill a number of arriving and departing Japanese as they passed one another in the dark. At length, the withdrawal stopped, though new arrivals continued to emerge from the rainswept surf.

Several groups of defenders sacrificed themselves during the night by launching futile assaults against the Marine line. Several Japanese who managed to penetrate the American line to stake out some buildings near the beach accounted for several Marines before they were hunted down and killed.

When higher authority learned that Crane's company had been repulsed at Tanambogo, it was decided to commit a battalion of 2nd Marines, part of the invasion fleet's floating reserve.

At 0330, August 8, two fleet transports upped anchor and moved to a safe spot off Tulagi. While 2nd Battalion, 2nd, stood by awaiting developments ashore, LtCol Robert Hunt's 3rd Battalion was landed without mishap.

The first thing that twenty-seven-year-old Pvt George Lundberg, of I Company, 2nd, saw was three pairs of jump boots sticking out past the end of a canvas shroud.

Pvt Bob Libby, an 81mm mortar ammunition carrier, dashed through sporadic gunfire to a corrugated-iron building which was being used as a sickbay despite the bullets that were clanking against the metal walls. The mortarman immediately felt out of place. The 'Chutes in the vicinity of the sickbay were a haggard, filthy lot in torn dungarees. One 'Chute was kneeling in the surf rinsing sand out of his submachine gun. Libby was deeply impressed by the casual élan of the one-day combat veterans he encountered. Private Libby saw his first dead Japanese when he ventured inland, a bluejacket with a big chunk of shrapnel imbedded in his head.

The island was a mess. Palm trees were skewed at odd angles, and tents and makeshift shelters were holed and strewn about in unnerving disarray. All sorts of exotic powder and perfume concoctions in broken jars and bottles added a strange tang to the prevailing scent of putrefaction and destruction.

Lieutenant Colonel Hunt assumed overall command of the operation from Major Miller. Capt Bill McKennan, the commander of A Company, 'Chutes, was just back from a lone dawn reconnaissance of Hill 148 and recommended that the sparsely held hill be ignored in favor of an immediate assault by Hunt's battalion and the 'Chutes against Tanambogo. Nevertheless, Hunt decided to commit his fresh K Company to sweeping the hill before moving on Tanambogo. As foreseen by Bill McKennan, the K Company sweep was a walk-through, and Gavutu was declared secure at 1330, August 8. Seven Japanese were taken alive.

As the fighting on Gavutu was winding down, I Company, 2nd, was reembarked in two large tank lighters and sent to Tanambogo in the company of two other lighters, each bearing a light tank. As the four craft resolutely chugged toward the islet, a destroyer moved to a station from which its fantail gun could flail a path across the beach for the tanks and riflemen. A .30-caliber medium machine-gun platoon deployed at the Gavutu end of the causeway opened fire to keep defenders' heads down.

The light tanks hit the beach first, at 1615. One swiveled on its tracks and moved to cover the south side of the hill while the other moved against the east slope.

Most of the ragtag defenders occupied a crude bomb shelter set through the day as the Marines sealed caves wherever they could be found. Tanambogo was declared secure at nightfall, August 9.

When calm was restored, it was found that twenty-seven 'Chutes had been killed and forty-seven wounded. Most of the losses had been incurred during the landings. Second Marines lost far fewer men in all.

against the southern slope of Tanambogo Hill or hid behind a rude earthen bulwark running for about forty feet between the shelter and a roadway from the causeway to the hill. Several Japanese apparently had lashed themselves into the tops of palm trees. When the leading squads of Marine riflemen passed those trees, the snipers accounted for several of them.

The tank-platoon leader, who was peering over the lip of his turret hatch as his vehicle bucked forward toward the bomb shelter, was shot through the head. The driver, however, continued to advance, though he was far ahead of his infantry support, which was only just landing.

A Japanese shoved a length of steel pipe into the tank's wheel assembly, and the vehicle stopped. Then, though a Marine rifle company was forming on the nearby beach, several dozen Japanese broke from cover and attempted to set the tank ablaze with oily rags. Several nearby Marine riflemen fought off the crazed assailants, who by then had pried open the hatches, dragged the screaming crewmen from their places and battered their heads against the steel hull of the tank. Three of the tankers were killed and one was critically injured before forty-two dead Japanese were piled around the disabled armored vehicle.

Once it was ashore and reformed, I Company split i groups; one worked toward the southern face of the hil other veered right and inland to assault the eastern sl

The Japanese manning the bombproof and th were killed or dispersed in short order, but tackl and small groups holed up in hillside caves w work. Several snipers on Gaomi, only 10 to the backs of Marines on the east slo mpeded progress until a destro the able to secure the entire The in anticipation of a fightir se survivors mo vainly, d through th

I C rate the v moved a

PART IV

Reaction

9

Moments before Allied cruisers opened fire on August 7, Tulagi Island's radio station transmitted a brief, perplexing message: "Large force of ships, unknown number or types, entering the sound. What can they be?"

RAdm Sadayoshi Yamada, commanding the Imperial Navy's land-based 25th Air Flotilla, presumed that Tulagi was being raided, so he sent out a long-range reconnaissance bomber to investigate.

Before the reconnaissance could be completed, Tulagi sent a second—final—message: "Enemy forces overwhelming. We will defend our posts to the death, praying for eternal victory."

Bomber and fighter squadron leaders and air staff officers were summoned to Yamada's headquarters for a briefing. A raid scheduled against an Allied base in New Guinea was cancelled so that every available airplane could be sent south.

LCdr Tadashi Nakajima, flight leader of the crack Tainan Air Group, perhaps the finest fighter unit Japan ever put into the air, protested vigorously that the 1,200-mile round trip to Tulagi and back was at the extreme range of his Zero fighters and could lead to the loss of half his command. A fierce argument ensued, but a compromise was achieved: Twenty-seven twin-engine Betty medium bombers would be sent with eighteen fighter escorts against the mysterious invaders.

Tainan Air Group had been based at Lae, in northern New Guinea, for some months following its transfer from Formosa. There, the land-based naval aviators had honed their predatory skills against obsolete American fighters and bombers and their outclassed pilots, and had moved to Rabaul only days earlier.

Nakajima led his fighters down the dust-shrouded strip—an active volcano brooded nearby—on what was to be the longest round-trip fighter mission to that time.

The fleet in the Lower Solomons was amply forewarned. Paul Mason, a planter-turned-Coastwatcher, spotted the Japanese formation from his hideout in southern Bougainville and radioed the news on a priority frequency: "Twenty-seven bombers headed southeast." The message was picked up at Port Moresby and relayed to Townville, Australia, which boasted the strongest transmitter in the region. The news was next flashed to Pearl Harbor and, finally, to the fleet off Guadalcanal.

Seventeen Japanese fighters (one had aborted with engine trouble) and twenty-seven bombers came within range of American radars shortly after 1300, dead on time. While one "challenge" section of five Zeros led by Lt Shiro Kawai went in early to draw off the American fighter combat air patrol, the two remaining sections, under Lieutenant Commander Nakajima and Lt(jg) Junzo Sasai, remained tethered to the slower Bettys, which were to execute high-level attacks on shipping with the 250-kg bombs meant for Allied ground targets in New Guinea.

Two four-plane divisions of Fighting-5 were launched from *Saratoga* under the direction of Lt Pug Southerland at 1215 to relieve eight F4F Wildcat fighters patrolling over the fleet anchorage between Guadalcanal and Tulagi. While Southerland was en route, four *Enterprise* Wildcats under Lt Lou Bauer were ordered by the fleet fighter direction officer to intercept "bogies" to the northwest at an altitude of 8,000 feet. Bauer did not know that the four F4Fs he left on station pending relief by Southerland were critically low on fuel and had to depart immediately. Other fighters were then being launched, but they were thirty minutes away.

Bauer's division was nearing Savo Island—and heading toward the incoming Japanese—when it was ordered south, back toward the carriers. Bauer requested a confirmation, which he did not receive. Though puzzled, he had no choice but to comply.

Pug Southerland's eight Wildcats arrived over the anchorage at about 1300 and at 12,000 feet. The sky above was overcast, all but precluding the visual sighting of the approaching Japanese, who were at between 15,000 and 18,000 feet.

Minutes after reporting in to the fighter direction officer, Southerland's own four-plane division was ordered to the northwest. Minutes later, the second division, under Lt Pete Brown, was ordered to follow.

Shortly after 1300, the Japanese bomber leader began a gentle descent through the clouds from 15,000 feet. He had been unable to see the transports, so decided to attack warships he and his bombardier could see near Savo Island. All twenty-seven bombers bellied through the clouds into clear daylight at about 1315. They were at 12,000 feet and only 500 yards from an astonished Pug Southerland, also at 12,000 feet and on a reciprocal heading.

"Horizontal bombers, three divisions, nine planes each, over Savo, headed for transports, Angels 12 (12,000 feet)," Southerland rattled off through his throat mike. "This division from Pug: Drop belly tanks, put gun switches and sight lamps on.

"Let's go get 'em, boys!"

The Bettys had opened their bomb-bays. Southerland dropped his fighter into a low-side run from the left and fired several bursts from his six .50-caliber wing guns at the leading bomber squadron. As he hurtled by, he aimed at the right-hand nine-plane squadron and fleetingly fired from longer range. He was soon able to fix his aim upon a bomber in the rear squadron, to the left again, and saw his bullets start a fire in the fuselage just forward of the open bomb-bay. Japanese bullets cracked the bulletproof glass windscreen in front of Southerland, and an incendiary round started a fire behind his cockpit. Southerland banked around to execute a low-side attack upon the trailing division. He used up all his remaining ammunition smoking another Betty, but he could not finish it off, nor could he hang around in his smoking F4F to see what happened to the Japanese.

The other three F4Fs in Southerland's division were jumped by Lieutenant Kawai's five challenge fighters before they could attack the bombers. Kawai had missed seeing them as he passed over Savo at 15,000 feet, but he retraced his route just in time to catch them as they followed Pug Southerland against the Bettys. Ens Don Innis saw Kawai coming and managed to shake his assailants in the clouds after suffering some damage.

Lt Pete Brown's Fighting-5 division was moving to aid Southerland's two remaining F4Fs when Brown spotted the bombers, which were his primary targets. He was turning into a favorable attack position when his division was beset by at least five Zeros from Lieutenant Commander Nakajima's section, and possibly two from Lieutenant(jg) Sasai's. Meantime, however, Southerland's two remaining Wildcats were downed, their pilots lost.

While Brown and Ens Foster Blair parried the Zeros, Brown's second element pressed on after the Bettys. After being separated from Blair, Brown claimed two Zeros before damage to his Wildcat and a painful hip wound forced him from the sky. He barely made it home to *Saratoga*. Blair ran for cover in the clouds.

The Bettys released their bombs at 1320. As they did, Lt(jg) William Holt and Ens Joseph Daly, of Brown's division, roared through the Zeros and delivered a diving high-side attack upon the bombers, then pulled up to attack again. The Zeros, just barely under Lieutenant Commander Nakajima's control, regrouped and went after Holt and Daly. As they did, Ensign Blair rejoined the fight by attacking the bombers. Holt and Daly destroyed two of the

Bettys and Blair severely damaged another, but Holt and Daly were both downed by Zeros, and Blair was forced to run for home. (Daly, with nine bullet holes in his leg and second-degree facial burns, was rescued by cruiser *Chicago*, and Holt was picked up by destroyer *Jarvis*.)

The combination of the fighter attack, the altitude, and the number of moving targets below threw off the Japanese bombardiers. No real damage was done.

Lt Pug Southerland was diving through 11,500 feet on his way out of the fight when he was attacked by a lone Zero. As the Japanese pilot executed repeated firing passes, Southerland cranked his seat down and hunched behind the armor plate at his back. Then he went to work on his guns, which he thought were empty but which he hoped had merely jammed during his last firing pass on the Bettys.

By this time, the Zero was attacking from Southerland's starboard quarter, so he pushed over as though diving to escape him, then immediately pulled out, cracked his landing flaps, and pulled his throttle to low power. When the Zero overran the suddenly slowing Wildcat, as Southerland had hoped it would, the Japanese pilot made a climbing turn to the left. Southerland easily turned inside the Zero and saw that an aviator's dream had come true; he had a Zero at close range and perfectly lined up in his gunsight for an easy quarter-deflection shot. However, when Southerland pressed the gun-button knob, nothing happened. He would have to fight the rest of the battle unarmed.

Then two fresh Zeros joined the attack on Southerland. The three Japanese repeatedly dived at Southerland in changing pairs, firing first from one side and then from the other.

Pug Southerland's job now merely consisted of determining which of the rotating pairs of Zeros attacking almost simultaneously on either quarter was about to open fire first and then sharply turning toward him as he opened up. This gave the firing Zero a full deflection shot so that he invariably underled the Wildcat. Countless bullets struck the Wildcat's fuselage from cockpit to tail but did little serious damage. The Wildcat's quick evasive turns also placed the second Zero directly behind the Wildcat so that Southerland was adequately protected by the armored back of his seat. When the Zeros' runs were not quite simultaneous, Southerland would rely on his armor, placing the attackers directly aft in succession as they made their runs.

AP1 Saburo Sakai was one of Japan's three top-scoring aces. It was Sakai who had shot down the B-17 of U.S. Army Air Forces Capt Colin Kelly months earlier in the Philippines, giving America her first war martyr. This day, he was leading Lt(jg) Junzo Sasai's second three-plane element above the Bettys.

As Sakai joined Sasai at 12,000 feet, he noted that his two brash, young wingmen were gone, no doubt drawn to the action against Holt, Daly, and Blair. As Sakai scanned the sky in the hope of spotting the errant pilots, he saw that three Zeros were trying to down a lone American Wildcat. Sakai spotted the melee just as two of the swift Zeros overtook and passed the slower Wildcat. It seemed to the ace that the Wildcat was winning the fight, so he flew up alongside Lieutenant(jg) Sasai and motioned for permission to join the action. Sasai nodded.

Saburo Sakai fired his Zero's two 7.7mm cowl-mounted machine guns and two 20mm wing-mounted automatic cannon from over 600 yards, more to distract Pug Southerland than in the hope of destroying him. Southerland countered with a mock attack, snapping into a tight left turn to disrupt Sakai's firing run.

Where the other three Japanese had hunted Pug Southerland with superior firepower, Saburo Sakai hunted with his Zero's superior maneuverability. Two superb airmen were pitted against each other, but the battle was unequal, for Sakai was armed and Southerland was not.

This was Sakai's first encounter with the F4F Wildcat. He had routinely been shooting down Chinese, Dutch, and American Army Air Forces pilots for five years—fifty-six kills thus far—but he had yet to meet anything like the rugged Grumman carrier fighter he was taking on this day. He repeatedly maneuvered into superior attack positions only to find himself outmaneuvered by the slower but deftly handled Wildcat. Sakai pushed five separate attacks against Southerland but did not fire a round because he knew his bullets would not down the American. Since Sakai did not know that Southerland had no bullets left, he remained cautious lest he fall under the Grumman's mangling .50-caliber guns.

When Southerland tried to pull out of the fight after Sakai's fifth abortive attack, the Japanese pilot realized that the Grumman was not in fighting condition.

All Southerland wanted to do was get over friendly territory and bail out of his stricken fighter.

Sakai withheld his killing pass long enough to snap a photo of the Grumman with his Leica camera. Then he took careful aim and fired 200 7.7mm rounds from only fifty yards. Amazingly, though few of the bullets could have missed, and the Grumman seemed tattered and ripped to shreds, Southerland doggedly continued to fly toward Guadalcanal. Even more amazing, Sakai found himself hurtling over the suddenly slowing Grumman; Southerland was dead on Sakai's tail and could have destroyed the flimsier Zero if he had had bullets.

The riddled Wildcat was in bad shape but was still performing to Southerland's satisfaction. The F4F's landing flaps and radio had been put out of commission, a large part of its fuselage was like a sieve, and it was smoking from incendiary hits, though it was not on fire. All of the ammunition box covers on Southerland's left wing had been blown off, and 20mm explosive rounds had torn several gaping holes in the upper left wing surface. The instrument panel was badly shot up, the goggles on Southerland's forehead were shattered, the rearview mirror was broken, the bulletproof windshield was riddled, tiny drops of fuel were leaking onto the cockpit floor, and oil from the punctured oil tank was pouring down Southerland's right leg and foot.

At length, curiosity, along with his esteem for his dogged enemy, got the better of Sakai. He pulled up beside the American, whose rudder and tail were so much scrap. The two stared at each other as they flew straight and level, then Sakai surged ahead and signaled the American to come and fight if he dared. Pug Southerland shifted his joystick from his right to his left hand and made what looked to Sakai like a plea for mercy. It was not. Southerland was preparing to bail out, and he needed his right hand to free his legs and body from his seat harness. Sakai chopped his throttle, dropped behind the American, and switched on the pair of 20mm cannon in his Zero's wings. Sakai's finger lightly rested on the gun button, then pressed down.

The 20mm burst from Southerland's port quarter struck just under the Wildcat's left wing root. The fighter finally exploded, no doubt because of the gasoline vapor that had been collecting in the cockpit and fuselage. When Southerland felt and saw the flash below and forward of his left foot, he was ready for it. He dived headfirst over the right side of the cockpit, just aft of the starboard wing root. The holster of his .45-caliber automatic pistol caught on the hood track, but he immediately got rid of it without quite knowing how.

Saburo Sakai saw Pug Southerland fall away, trailing a huge silken canopy as he drifted toward the water.

Seconds later, Southerland thudded to earth on Guadalcanal, several miles from the coast and many miles west of friendly lines. (He reached Marine lines with the help of an islander on August 10.)

Lt(jg) Dick Gay, a former enlisted pilot with many years of military flying experience, was leading his division of *Enterprise*'s Fighting-6 from the south when he was ordered to investigate antiaircraft bursts over the Tulagi anchorage. Gay's division was at 16,000 feet and just over Guadalcanal's northern coast when all four pilots saw the telltale black puffs about ten miles ahead and at about 13,000 feet.

Gay's wingman, Lt Vince DePoix, a sharp-eyed 1939 Naval Academy graduate only a few months out of flight school, was the first to spot the riddled Japanese bomber formation over Florida as it was turning northwest for Rabaul. After trying unsuccessfully to attract the attention of his division leader, DePoix dived at several

Zero escorts and the Bettys, which were at 12,000 feet. The interception was made over the center of Florida.

DePoix hurtled in at a relative speed of nearly 500 knots, fired a single burst while in range, then sharply pulled up beneath the bombers and pitched over to attack from astern. Another good burst caught one of the Bettys, which rolled away out of formation and crashed in the water north of Florida.

Meantime, Dick Gay and Warrant Machinist Howell Sumrall swept through the disintegrating bomber formation, firing as they were diving. They crossed over, climbed, and pitched in again from either side. Gay smoked a Betty despite distraction from a pair of Zeros, which went after Sumrall's wingman, Machinist Julius Achten. Achten got a good burst into one of the Zeros from behind, but was prevented from seeing what happened because his airplane's wings and fuselage took solid hits from another Zero's 20mm cannon. He shook his assailant by diving for the thick cumulus clouds over Florida, but eventually had to land his unflyable Wildcat in the water, from which he was plucked by a Navy transport. Sumrall tangled with four Zeros at once, and his Wildcat took several 20mm hits. Gay's F4F was also shot up as he and Sumrall fled into the clouds. DePoix was wounded by a 7.7mm slug and his instrument panel was shattered as he, too, was driven into the clouds by swarming Zeros. All three later landed safely: Gay and Sumrall aboard *Enterprise* and DePoix aboard *Wasp*.

The next American aircraft to tangle with the Japanese were five *Wasp* SBD Dauntless dive-bombers that happened to be orbiting beneath the clouds above Tulagi Harbor. Ordered to top the clouds, see what was going on and, if possible, break up the Japanese bomber wave, LCdr John Eldridge, commander of Scouting Squadron 71, pulled up. The mixed formation of Bettys and Zeros was climbing past 15,000 feet when Lt Dudley Adams, at the controls of the first Dauntless to top the clouds, fired on a three-plane fighter section from their left rear with the pair of .50-caliber machine guns mounted on his bomber's engine cowling.

The section leader was AP1 Saburo Sakai, just returned from his triumph over Lt Pug Southerland. Sakai, whose fighter's glass canopy was punctured by one of Adam's rounds, whipped after the lone assailant and sent him down out of control. The Dauntless crashed into the waves. Adams was rescued by a nearby destroyer, but his radioman-gunner was killed. Lieutenant Commander Eldridge and the remainder of his flight withdrew back into the clouds before suffering further loss.

Shortly after downing Adams, Saburo Sakai spotted eight *Enterprise* SBDs stationed over Tulagi to provide on-call air support for Marine Raiders and 'Chutes. However, Sakai and one of his wingmen mistook the distant dive-bombers for fighters, and they launched a beam attack, never suspecting that their quarry was armed with twin rear-firing .30-caliber machine guns.

Aviation Machinist's Mate 2nd Class Herman Caruthers was the first to see Sakai's approach, and he alerted Aviation Ordnanceman 2nd Class Harold Jones, another rear-seatman. Jones saw Sakai's wingman approach the formation from underneath, then saw Sakai close to within 300 yards. By then, Sakai knew of his error, but he was committed to the attack. At least four of the American gunners opened fire, their bullets converging on Sakai's cockpit. Sakai got 232 rounds into Jones's aircraft, but neither Jones nor the pilot was hurt.

Sakai's Zero began a vertical plunge toward the water. By incredible good fortune, Sakai overcame his severe head wounds and gravity to pull out at wavetop height and lurch for home.

Sakai's wingman broke off some distance from the Americans, but bullets damaged the elevator of one Dauntless and distorted the vane of a 500-lb bomb slung beneath the belly of another.

Six Fighting-6 fighters led by Lt Gordon Firebaugh, a former enlisted pilot with ten years in fighters, had been launched from *Enterprise* at 1300, just as the Japanese formation was approaching Tulagi. Firebaugh's flight found the retiring brown-green bombers as they passed over the southwest tip of Santa Ysabel Island, about thirty-five miles north of Savo. Firebaugh split his force into two three-plane sections to mount simultaneous attacks on the bombers from the left and right.

Warrant Radio Electrician Thomas Rhodes, Ens Bob Disque, and AP1 Paul Mankin attacked the Bettys from out of the sun, releasing their thirty-gallon belly tanks as they approached. However, when Mankin discovered at the last moment that his vulnerable belly tank was still affixed to his fighter, he stayed high to cover Disque and Rhodes.

Disque made two runs, and he spotted solid hits on two Bettys. Both bombers dropped out of the formation, but neither burned. A third run produced flames, however, when Disque hit an engine or fuel line on one of the twin-engine bombers. To Disque's chagrin, the bomber maintained its station, trailing bright orange flames and black smoke. The young ensign was so exhilarated that he drew up alongside the burning bomber for a good look, oblivious to gunners who might be firing at him. He was pulling away to attack another bomber when Mankin warned, "There's a Zero on your tail." Disque twisted into evasive action and maneuvered into a head-on run. Neither fighter scored a hit, the Zero dived away, and Disque joined Mankin to nurse their limited fuel back to the carriers. They found *Wasp* first, and Disque landed; his Wildcat had used the last drops of gasoline as it stopped in the arresting gear. Mankin barely made it aboard *Enterprise* on the last of his fuel.

Radio Electrician Rhodes made one pass at the bombers, then continued through the formation to help Lieutenant Firebaugh and his two wingmen. The problem was that there was no sign of Firebaugh's element. Rhodes shot down one Zero in the course of some extremely frantic aerobatics, and escaped with his thoroughly riddled Wildcat into a friendly cloud until the heat died down. He later landed safely aboard *Enterprise*.

While the other three Wildcats had gone after the Bettys, Firebaugh and his wingmen, AP1 William Stephenson and Machinist William Warden, had taken on three Zeros in a head-on attack. Firebaugh saw hits on one Zero's engine, then recovered to port in time to fire at a Zero which was chasing Stephenson. The Zero rolled away and Firebaugh was recovering in a near-vertical turn to the right when another, unseen, Zero put several rounds through his cockpit canopy and obliged him to pull away. As he did, he saw Stephenson crash into the sea. Suddenly, five new Zeros joined from starboard, and the Zero leader got onto Firebaugh's tail and scored repeatedly with bursts of 7.7mm and 20mm rounds. Three more of the five new fighters attacked Firebaugh, and he returned fire in a wild melee, later claiming two kills. However, Firebaugh was burned when his cockpit was set ablaze, and he dived head-first out of the airplane. His spine was injured when his parachute deployed, and he landed in the water.

Machinist Warden tried to follow Firebaugh through the initial attack, but his F4F sustained hits in the oil-cooling system, and was soon ablaze. Warden ran, diving to wave-top height, but at least one Zero gave chase. The American emptied his guns at the Zero, but his engine seized and he was obliged to land in the sea.

Firebaugh and Warden eventually reached safety, but nothing was ever heard from Stephenson.

Nine of the eighteen Wildcat fighters engaged and one Dauntless dive-bomber were downed. A number of the Japanese aircraft that had been damaged but managed to get clear of the Lower Solomons went down along the 600-mile return track. AP1 Saburo Sakai, who lost the sight of an eye in his fight with the American dive-bombers, survived the flight home only through unusually skillful flying.

A second attack developed at about 1430, when ten Rabaul-based Val carrier-type dive-bombers went after the fleet. Four Fighting-6 fighters led by Lt Scoop Vorse caught three Vals on the way in. Though Vorse's wingmen were thrown off when the Vals dived, he locked onto the tail of one and followed it down until it knifed straight into the channel.

Six other *Enterprise* fighters led by Chief Warrant Machinist

Gene Runyon were on the way to Savo to take over the combat air patrol when black puffs from exploding antiaircraft rounds drew them toward Guadalcanal. As they flew through the friendly fire, Runyon and AP1 Howard Packard opened fire on a Val, which dived. Runyon missed, but Packard blew the dive-bomber apart in mid air.

Runyon leveled off immediately after passing the first Val and spotted another Japanese dive-bomber coming right at him. He fired as he pulled up his Wildcat's nose. At the same time, Runyon's wingman, Ens Dutch Shoemaker, launched a beam attack into the same target. The Val fell away, cartwheeled into the water, and brightly exploded on impact. Runyon next spotted a pair of Vals breaking into the clear at wave-top level. He got one, Shoemaker and Ens Earl Cook downed the second, and Ens Harry March nailed the third Val east of Savo.

Two additional Vals were downed by antiaircraft fire from ships in the channel. Thus, seven of ten Vals were downed over the anchorage. The three damaged survivors headed north, but all were too badly damaged or too low on fuel to save themselves.

The only air strike on August 8 involved all of Rear Admiral Yamada's twenty-three remaining Bettys, nine Vals, and a strong Zero escort. The Japanese medium bombers, all armed with torpedoes, came in low and fast at 1156, evading American radar by dodging between high mountain ridges north of the target area.

A three-plane *Enterprise* fighter section led by Chief Machinist Gene Runyon picked up the first flight of Bettys as it crossed the eastern tip of Florida so low that the propwash foamed the flat sea. Runyon dived on one Betty, which he missed, then pulled up and over to drop another of the nimble bombers neatly into the water. Ens Bill Rouse got the Betty that Runyon had first missed, but was bounced by a Zero as he went after a second target. The Zero on Rouse's tail was itself chased by Ens Dutch Shoemaker. When the Zero veered to escape Shoemaker's guns, it flew directly into Runyon's sights and was hammered into the sea. Shoemaker immediately banked toward another Betty and downed it, bringing the score for the three Americans to five kills.

Warned that the Japanese were closing on the anchorage, four *Wasp* dive-bomber pilots prepared to meet them. However, a call for ground support left only one of them, Ens R. L. Howard, in a position to intercept. He dived through the Betty formation, but forgot to turn on his gun switches, so could do no damage. When Howard turned back into the fight, his slow Dauntless was jumped by several Zero fighters. The Dauntless's radioman-gunner had a lively time keeping the Zeros from his tail while Ensign Howard ran for cover. The remaining Bettys evaded fighter interception and pressed their attacks upon the shipping.

The crew of light antiaircraft cruiser *San Juan* at first mistook the Bettys for friendly planes, but gunners aboard *Canberra*, an Australian heavy cruiser, knew better and opened fire on them. Soon all the ships in the channel opened fire as the Bettys roared at them low over the water. The initial surprise was more than offset by the fact that the Bettys attacked the American fleet bunched up in one formation instead of from different angles.

For Gunner's Mate 2nd Class Jim O'Neill, aboard *San Juan*, the noise of the firing was almost overwhelming. From O'Neill's vantagepoint, the Japanese medium bombers were being shot down like ducks in a shooting gallery. *San Juan*, a modern antiaircraft cruiser, accounted for five of the Japanese warplanes. O'Neill's own Oerlikon 1.1-inch pom-pom gun got one for sure. O'Neill clearly saw rounds from his gun stitch a pattern across the Betty's fuselage, and then he saw the Betty explode.

At least thirteen Bettys and Vals were downed by the fleet before they could launch torpedoes. However, destroyer *Jarvis* was hit well forward by a torpedo, and a Zero damaged in the melee dived into transport *George F. Elliott*, setting her ablaze and causing her to drift aground.

In all, eighteen of twenty-three Bettys and at least two Zeros were downed without American loss. *Jarvis* was ordered to sail to safety alone under her own power, but she was never seen or heard from again. *Elliott*'s crew was evacuated to a nearby transport and the ship was left to burn herself out.

The bomber strength of 25th Naval Air Flotilla—the only Japanese combat air unit in range of Guadalcanal—had been gutted in only two days of fighting. Senior American air officers were proud of the showing; their aggressive fighter pilots, however, were generally dismayed over allowing so many Zeros to escape, though the Wildcat was no match for the Zero and the Japanese fighter pilots were the best in the business.

10

VAdm Gunichi Mikawa was commander of the newly
formed 8th Fleet, a mixed cruiser and destroyer force
based at Rabaul. It was his job to defend the Solomon Islands against Allied incursions and to prepare to spearhead a new
drive southeastward, toward the New Hebrides.

The fragmentary reports from Tulagi on August 7 caused an
immediate division of opinion between Admiral Mikawa and his
Imperial Army counterpart, LtGen Harukichi Hyakutake, commander of the newly formed 17th Army, a corps-sized infantry
force headquartered in Rabaul but charged with securing New
Guinea.

The Imperial Army had no responsibility for events in the
Solomon Islands, which were under the control of the Imperial
Navy, so perhaps Hyakutake was serving his own interests when he
rated the incursion at Tulagi as a mere raid. He refused to provide
Admiral Mikawa with troops for an immediate counterblow.

Though Mikawa was operating in a virtual information vacuum, he nevertheless divined the enormity of the challenge. At the very least, he reasoned, duty demanded that he strike swiftly, and in force. If his estimate of enemy intentions proved to be overblown, little harm would have been done. He ordered every available bluejacket in Rabaul to be armed with infantry weapons and formed into a provisional battalion. In the end, only 410 such troops could be found, and not as many rifles. The minuscule force was sent south aboard a small cargo ship while Mikawa redoubled his efforts to mount a more meaningful response.

An urgent message was dispatched to the Naval General Staff, in Tokyo, requesting permission to mount a surface attack upon the Allied fleet the following night, August 8.

The Imperial Navy's chief of staff, Adm Osami Nagano, considered a night surface attack too audacious; Mikawa had few warships while the Allies seemed to have many, and the transports were certain to be closely guarded. Still, Nagano deferred to Adm Isoroku Yamamoto, commander in chief of the Combined Fleet, the Navy's operational arm. Yamamoto knew Mikawa to be a cautious man, and respected his judgment. He radioed his approval: "Wish your fleet success."

Mikawa, who had been admonished to oversee the foray from Rabaul, boarded his flagship, heavy cruiser *Chokai*, on the afternoon of August 7 and ordered the remainder of 8th Fleet to stand south through St. George Channel. The force comprised five heavy cruisers, two light cruisers, and one fleet destroyer.

The waters were poorly charted, and the going was slow. Though Mikawa and his staff navigator spent long hours poring over the few charts they had at their disposal, the day was lost. Mikawa feared discovery by Allied reconnaissance aircraft, so he decided to remain north of Bougainville until the late afternoon of August 8, when he would steam at all possible speed through St. George Channel, between the double chain of islands—soon to be known as "the Slot"—and launch his attack after rounding Savo. The Slot, narrow and restricted, presented the surest means for arriving off Savo at a favorable hour. The risk of discovery was great, but speed was of the essence.

RAdm Kelly Turner received a message from the north late on the afternoon of August 7: "Two destroyers and three larger ships of unknown type heading [southeast] at high speed eight miles west of Cape St. George."

The source of the message was an American submarine charged with guarding the waters around the Slot. The boat had had barely enough time to avoid being run down by the Japanese column, much less launch a torpedo attack.

Eighth Fleet reached Bougainville by dawn, August 8, and launched four float reconnaissance planes to probe the Allied anchorage. The Japanese warships then scattered to confound routine Allied reconnaissance flights in the area.

Chokai was spotted at 1020 by an RAAF patrol bomber, which circled overhead for a time while Admiral Mikawa reversed course until the Australian left, hopefully convinced that the Japanese cruiser was heading back to Rabaul. However, when a second RAAF bomber appeared, Mikawa felt he had little to lose, so he ordered his force to reform and head through the Slot toward Savo.

Meantime, one of the Japanese floatplanes returned to report that eighteen transports, six cruisers, nineteen destroyers, and a battleship were arrayed around Tulagi, Savo, and the northern coast of Guadalcanal. It seemed to Mikawa that he was outnumbered, twenty-six warships to eight. However, the reconnaissance pilot added that the Allied warships were split into three groups, and that gave the Japanese admiral hope that he could destroy at least one battle force before the others could join. Eighth Fleet steamed on, entering the Slot itself late in the afternoon. The fleet navigator estimated that the cruiser column would arrive off Savo at midnight.

Eighth Fleet had been formed only a week earlier, and never before operated as a unit, so the simplest of battle plans had to be promulgated. *Chokai's* signal lamp blinked Admiral Mikawa's orders to the other vessels at 1630: "We will proceed from south of Savo Island and torpedo the enemy main force in front of the Guadalcanal anchorage, after which we will turn toward the Tulagi forward area to shell and torpedo the enemy. We will withdraw north of Savo." The warships were ordered to stream white sleeves from both wings of their bridges for identification.

Minutes before dusk, just as the danger of discovery was nearly past, one of *Chokai's* lookouts spotted a masthead to starboard. The fleet sprang to action, sirens wailing, guns tracking the target, which was identified as a friendly seaplane tender bound for New Georgia, a bit farther to starboard.

Just as 8th Fleet left the friendly ship astern, MGen Archer Vandergrift, on Beach Red, was asked to join RAdm Kelly Turner and RAdm Victor Crutchley, the British commander of the screen warships, aboard Turner's flagship for urgent consultations.

Turner had heard from VAdm Frank Jack Fletcher only minutes earlier: "Fighter plane strength reduced from ninety-nine to seventy-eight. In view of the large number of enemy torpedo planes and bombers in the area, I recommend the immediate withdrawal of my carriers. Request tankers sent forward immediately as fuel is running low." Fletcher was pulling out even earlier than he had threatened during the Koro rendezvous!

Though he had no inkling as to its purpose, Admiral Crutchley sensed a note of urgency in Kelly Turner's summons. The giant, red-bearded Briton ordered his flagship, heavy cruiser *Australia*, to leave the screening force south of Savo and follow Guadalcanal's northern coastline to the anchorage.

The Allied screen had been informally divided into three groups. Southern Force, with which *Australia* had been on station, was reduced to two cruisers and two destroyers. Its patrol sector lay between Savo and Cape Esperance at the southern entrance to the channel. Another group, Northern Force, comprising three cruisers and several destroyers, patrolled the northern entrance, be-

tween Savo and Florida. The third group, Eastern Force, comprised a pair each of light cruisers and destroyers patrolling the
eastern extremity of the anchorage. Crutchley exercised direct tactical control over all three groups and had designated no subordinate commanders. His departure without word to Northern or
Eastern forces left two-thirds of his command leaderless to all practical purposes. He did inform his senior Southern Force captain
that he was leaving, but did not actually leave him in control. That
officer did not even think to move his own heavy cruiser, *Chicago*, to
the head of the patrol column, as convention dictated, nor did he
inform any of the other captains. Capt Frederick Reifkohl, whose
heavy cruiser *Vincennes* was in Northern Force and who was senior
captain in the screening force, should have been left with the overall command, but he did not even know that Crutchley had left the
patrol area with the flagship. The cruiser screen was left leaderless
and without a plan.

Turner's meeting was late getting started. Admiral Crutchley
had pulled *Australia* out of the screen in haste, but it still took two
hours of poking around in the gloom to find Turner's flagship.
Archer Vandegrift, embarked in a small boat, did not find the
flagship until 2300.

While waiting for Vandegrift, the two admirals discussed a
message that had just been relayed from the airbase at Milne Bay,
New Guinea. An RAAF aircrew had spotted a Japanese naval force
heading southeast from northern Bougainville. The message had
arrived following an eight-hour delay because the pilot had waited
to land before making his report. The message indicated that the
Japanese force comprised three cruisers, three destroyers, and a
pair of seaplane tenders.

Turner and Crutchley agreed that the presence of the tenders
might indicate a morning air attack. The fact that only three
cruisers had been sighted was reassuring; the Japanese would not
dream of launching a surface attack, particularly at night, with a
force of only three escorted cruisers.

Turner knew that the Japanese would feel obliged to make

some sort of gesture against his fleet, and he suspected that the Slot would be used to make an approach. Accordingly, he had requested a Navy long-range patrol bomber to search the channel that day. There was, as yet, no report, which the admirals took to be a good omen. In fact, the mission had not been undertaken.

When Archer Vandegrift entered Kelly Turner's compartment, he noted that the two admirals seemed about to pass out from the oppressive heat. He accepted Turner's offer of a cup of coffee, then sat down to hear the bad news.

Turner told him of Fletcher's decision to leave early. Vandegrift grew livid: The carrier admiral had promised to give him at least twelve hours more than he now proposed. Even then, he had had no hope of getting his division's supplies ashore. Turner repeated the news about the seaplane tenders, and indicated that, lacking air cover, he too was obliged to retire at dawn; his transports were highly vulnerable to air attack.

The amphibious-force commander asked the Marine division commander for his opinion, and the general replied that 1st Marine Division was in fair shape on Guadalcanal; he doubted that Tulagi could be adequately defended, though he admitted having no direct knowledge in that regard. Turner nodded and mentioned that he had foreseen the response, and that a fast minesweeper was standing by to carry Vandegrift to Tulagi.

Crutchley offered to take the general to the minesweeper on his way back to *Australia*. Vandegrift declined, but the Briton insisted: "Your mission is much more important than mine." The two boarded Crutchley's gig minutes before midnight. A heavy rain squall was blustering to port, separating Northern and Southern forces. To starboard, a red glow marked the spot where transport *Elliott* lay grounded and burning. As Vandegrift mounted the minesweeper's ladder, Crutchley shook his hand and said that he knew what losing the fleet meant to the Marines. "I don't know as I can blame Turner for what he's doing."

Gunichi Mikawa was moving in for the kill. The Japanese had any number of advantages, not the least being their ability to control events. But they lacked radar, and that, Mikawa feared, might be their undoing.

Rigorously selected and keenly trained lookouts, the finest in any navy, were capable of spotting mere shadows at eight miles, and they were equipped with the finest night binoculars in the world. In addition, three three-place spotter planes had been launched to track the Allied fleet. When Mikawa engaged Southern Force, they were to launch parachute flares to assist Japanese guncrews.

American picket destroyers near Savo heard the sound of aircraft engines as the Japanese floatplanes traversed the anchorage. Several duty officers queried higher authorities, and several issued warnings. A few did nothing. It was finally agreed that the aircraft were Fletcher's, though no one could explain what carrier aircraft might be doing over Savo in the dead of night, nor why no one had been told to expect them.

It was 2345. Admiral Crutchley was unavailable, somewhere amidst the shipping, ferrying Archer Vandegrift to his minesweeper. *Australia* was routinely notified of the aircraft contact, but no one aboard felt compelled to take charge.

Eighth Fleet was approaching Savo at 0010. The conical island was ahead to port and Cape Esperance loomed to starboard when lookouts spotted a low form moving dead ahead. Guncrews swung out their batteries to cover the dark silhouette; fifty naval rifles were brought to bear in a trice.

Blue, an aging picket destroyer, routinely changed course at 0040 from roughly northeast to roughly southwest, maintaining her speed at twelve knots. Visibility was good. No unusual contacts had been made by radio, radar, sonar, or sight since 2345. The crew was at General Quarters, the highest state of alert. Lookouts had been concentrating on navigation landmarks to the east for several minutes before and during the turn, which happened to be away from the path of 8th Fleet. *Blue* made no movement of recognition and continued blithely on her way. It was 0043.

Blue's failure to react worried the Japanese admiral nearly to distraction. He had no idea what the American skipper's game might be, though it was easy to imagine him trying to bluff his way out of certain destruction while filling the airwaves with alarms. Mikawa chose to assume that he had not been sighted. To make certain, he dispatched his lone destroyer, *Yunagi*, to keep tabs on the seemingly blind picket. Ironically, *Blue* had been moving toward the projected Japanese track from 0010 to 0040. Even more ironic is the fact that *Ralph Talbot*, the picket destroyer north of Savo, also had her stern to the Japanese as they squeezed through the passage.

Japanese lookouts perched in the masts poured down a torrent of data to fire control stations as their ships approached the Allied force. Mikawa ordered speed increased to twenty-six knots and released his captains to commence independent firing at any time. Torpedoes hissed into the water an instant later.

It was 0136. Southern Force had been firmly fixed, coming up from the southeast.

At 0143, just as the Japanese spotter aircraft were preparing to release their flares, lookouts aboard destroyer *Patterson* sighted a shadow in their ship's path. "Warning! Warning! Strange ships entering harbor."

It was an instant late. The parachute flares blossoming overhead silhouetted *Chicago* in Japanese gunsights. Then Australian cruiser *Canberra* appeared. *Chokai*, only 4,500 yards distant, opened with her main batteries, *Aoba* fired from 5,500 yards, and *Furutaka* opened from 9,000 yards.

Before *Canberra*'s crew even spotted the enemy, before the Australians could train out their guns, Japanese torpedoes had blasted a great hole in the side of their ship, followed closely by the first 4.7- and 8-inch salvoes. *Canberra*'s captain fell, mortally wounded. The ship's gunnery officer died in the first blast, along with many of his shipmates. *Canberra* launched two torpedoes and got off a few 4.7-inch rounds. Then she was out of the fight, her power out, dead in the water.

Patterson surged after the enemy cruiser column while Japanese gunners put out a few disdainful salvoes in her direction. The after gun–mount was hit, and ready ammunition and powder exploded and burned. *Patterson* came on, firing at the tail cruiser, *Yubari*. Suddenly it was quiet. The Japanese were beyond sight. *Patterson's* torpedoes were still in their tubes despite the captain's order to launch them.

Destroyer *Bagley* was up next, but she had no luck. The spread of torpedoes she launched sped off uselessly to the north.

Chicago got off easier than *Canberra* by pure chance and because her lookouts had seen orange flashes at 0142—the Japanese launching torpedoes—and aircraft flares over the transports a minute later. *Canberra's* sudden wheel to starboard from dead ahead clinched the matter. Lookouts passed word that two shadows were in sight nearby. The captain was just awakening from a nap and ordered his 5-inch secondary batteries to prepare to illuminate with star shells. A lookout spotted a torpedo wake to starboard at 0146, and *Chicago* was hit a minute later, her bows blown clear off. Gunners staggered under the impact, then fired star shells off both bows to try to pinpoint a target—*any* target. The damaged cruiser tried for two minutes to range in on a pair of mysterious lighted targets ahead. One must have been destroyer *Yunagi*, which Admiral Mikawa had detached to look after *Blue*. The second target might have been *Jarvis*, the destroyer damaged by a Japanese aerial torpedo that afternoon.

Preoccupied with licking their own wounds or coming to the aid of cripples, no one in Southern Force thought to issue an alert. The Japanese had sustained zero damage in the course of crippling a pair of cruisers and a destroyer.

Admiral Mikawa was already on the scent of the Northern cruisers, which were maintaining a box-like patrol pattern north and east of Savo. American lookouts had no idea that a battle had been fought to the south because Savo's silhouette and a line of squalls between the two Allied forces obscured the view.

On glimpsing Northern Force through a break in the squall line, Mikawa ordered a course shift to east-northeast at 0144.

Chokai, in the van, made the prescribed move, as did the three heavy cruisers immediately astern. But *Furutaka,* the last of the heavies, found herself on collision course with the cruiser ahead and veered to port, her bows aimed directly at the American cruiser line to the north. She settled on a more northerly heading at 0147, the two light cruisers in her wake. By pure chance, the two Japanese columns were on parallel courses with the Northern Force column between them.

Patterson's voice-radio warning at 0143 and the string of parachute flares to the south had alerted Northern Force to danger, but no one knew from where it might emerge nor, in fact, that it was approaching at all. Without hard facts, the line of cruisers maintained its ten-knot patrol speed, the helmsmen taking care to turn a square corner to the northeast at the end of the southwestern leg of the box.

Tenryu's lookouts spotted the American column at 0146, just as their ship was turning to follow *Furutaka* to form the inadvertent second column. Word was flashed at 0148 to Admiral Mikawa, who ordered torpedoes launched immediately; seventeen were away within moments. Eighth Fleet majestically charged against the unknowing Americans, batteries swiftly swinging outboard to track targets.

Astoria, at the tail of the American column, was maintaining a routine watch. Her skipper, Capt William Greenman, was sleeping off the accumulated strain of two days on the conn. The officer-of-the-deck, LCdr Jim Topper, noted slight tremors from the south, but assumed that destroyermen were relieving their anxieties by dropping depth charges upon phantom submarines. The tremors were *Chokai's* torpedoes harmlessly detonating after missing *Chicago.*

A lookout reported seeing a star shell far to port, and Jim Topper looked up in time to see a string of aircraft flares. Someone else pointed to a searchlight beam (*Chokai's*) at 0150. That did it! Topper called *Astoria's* crew to General Quarters only a minute before a shell exploded just off her bows.

The main-battery spotter announced that three enemy cruisers were off the port quarter and closing, but it was ninety seconds before *Astoria*'s 8-inch guns could be trained out to port and fired at *Chokai*.

As Lieutenant Commander Topper was passing the order to commence firing, Captain Greenman, who had been routed out of his bunk moments earlier, stepped onto the control bridge and hurriedly assessed events to that moment. "Topper," he cautioned, "I think we're firing on our own ships. Let's not get excited and act too hasty. Cease firing."

The ship's gunnery officer remained convinced that the targets were hostile, and pleaded to be allowed to resume firing. Captain Greenman assented at 0154.

Meanwhile, *Chokai* had had time to fire four full salvoes at *Astoria*, but none had yet scored. The misses might have given the American gunners time to strike back, but the debate on *Astoria*'s bridge and the cease-fire order benefitted the Japanese flagship. The fifth 8-inch salvo ripped through the American cruiser's superstructure, and *Astoria*'s midships section burst into flames. *Chokai* blazed away as Captain Greenman firmly ordered all his guns into action.

It was too late for *Astoria*. Her communications had been destroyed, and her deck was disintegrating under the impact of repeated hits. The guncrews were severely hampered by the heat and smoke of fires; in all, *Astoria* managed to get off eleven partial 8-inch salvoes. Captain Greenman had to order an abrupt course correction to avoid ramming *Quincy*, which was in line dead ahead. The move was unfortunate, for it brought Greenman's ship between *Quincy* and more menacing Japanese batteries.

Then the worst blow of all fell: A shell burst directly on *Astoria*'s bridge, cutting down most of the bridge watch. The helmsman managed to regain his feet and bring the cripple back on course to the northwest. Scores of sailors below decks were ravaged by searing flames, billowing smoke, and superheated steam. The cruiser slowed to barely seven knots. Fires were raging down her entire length, but her crew continued to fight; Turret-2's last salvo caught *Chokai*'s forward turret. But then *Astoria* was left behind.

Quincy was already getting hit. The watch had had warnings and hints identical to those registered aboard *Astoria*, but they too had helped little. On receiving *Patterson*'s warning, the officer-of-the-deck had called Capt Samuel Moore from his emergency cabin, abaft the bridge, where he was resting. Just as Moore appeared on the bridge, the second cruiser in the Japanese starboard column, *Aoba*, fixed his ship in her main searchlight battery and pumped several rounds into the water beside *Quincy*'s bows. Moore ordered his gunners to "fire at the ships with the searchlights on."

When the guns did not bear on the targets quickly enough, Moore again ordered, "Fire the main battery!" But nothing happened for long seconds, though the cruiser's 5-inchers had been trained out for minutes. "Hurry up," the captain fumed. "What's taking so long?" Immediately, a full nine-gun salvo was loosed. "Full speed ahead," Moore ordered.

After the second salvo, Moore decided that he was firing on friendly ships, so he ordered recognition signals lighted.

The officer-of-the-deck felt that *Quincy* was on a collision course with *Vincennes*, dead ahead, so he ordered course shifted slightly to starboard, a move that masked the forward guns.

Quincy was struck in the stern aircraft hangar, and the volatile contents of the structure erupted in a furious blaze. The captain ordered the burning observation plane to be pushed over the side, but crewmen could not get close enough.

"Hard a-starboard," Moore ordered. The ship turned directly into the beam of a Japanese searchlight.

"Fire at the searchlight!"

Turret-1 traversed and fired, and the Japanese ship went dark.

Lighted better than she could have been by searchlights, *Quincy* caught numerous rounds from both Japanese columns. The next incoming salvo was 100 yards short, and the next was seventy-five yards over. Everyone on the bridge pulled in their heads; they knew a straddle when they saw one. Nearly all the starboard 5-inch guncrewmen were felled by the next salvo. Two torpedoes struck the port bow and breached the forward magazine, which blew up.

Moments after Turret-2 received a direct hit and exploded, Captain Moore berated his surviving gunners to "Give 'em hell," then was felled by a direct hit on the pilothouse, which took out most of the bridge watch.

The galley was ablaze, as were all the boats on the boat deck, the hangar area, the well deck, and the fantail. The ship was listing to port. A Japanese cruiser passed by at high speed, about 200 yards to port, and fired salvo after salvo into the cripple. One of *Quincy's* firerooms was opened to the sea by a torpedo, and communications to that point were lost, dooming the black gang, which was sealed off. A 5-inch gun was destroyed when another hit sparked its ready ammunition.

Captain Moore said with his dying breath, "Beach the ship." The bridge phone talker, a lieutenant commander, staggered out of the pilothouse and mumbled through a face that had been half shot away, "Everything will be okay. The ship will go down fighting."

Quincy's senior surviving officer made his way to the bridge, where, stunned by the carnage, he immediately ordered, "Abandon ship!" The survivors made it into the water by the slimmest of margins. At 0235, the heavy cruiser capsized to port, furiously twisted, and slid away beneath the waves—the first of numerous warships to inhabit the floor of what would soon be called Ironbottom Sound.

The leading cruiser—the last the Japanese overtook—was *Vincennes*, and she had had more warning than her dying sisters. Capt Frederick Reifkohl was awakened after the deck watch first spotted flares and after men on deck felt two distinct underwater explosions and spotted flashes of gunfire away to the south. Reifkohl felt that *Chicago, Canberra, Australia*, and their escorts were firing on aircraft. He ordered speed increased to fifteen knots.

Aviation Machinist's Mate 3rd Class Rusty Campbell, a member of the port aft 20mm guncrew, distinctly saw illumination burst over *Astoria*, then saw Japanese shells strike the trailing cruiser from the waterline to the bridge. Fires flared and died.

A Japanese cruiser abaft the port beam illuminated *Vincennes* at 0150, but Captain Reifkohl thought that the lights were those of Southern Force, and sent an urgent radio appeal for the lights to be doused. However, the gunnery officer ordered his guns trained out to port to track the nearest silhouette.

Rusty Campbell spoke rapidly into the sound-powered phone resting on his chest, asking permission to open with his aft 20mm gun to try to douse the lights. Permission to fire was denied because, a disembodied voice said in his ear, "They might be our friends out there."

The 8-inchers and most of the lighter weapons were tracking targets, but *Kako*, the third cruiser in the eastern Japanese column, got off the first rounds. A violent explosion engulfed *Vincennes* well forward on the port side. Rusty Campbell's sound-powered phone went dead.

Vincennes's 8-inchers returned fire at 0153 over a distance of five miles. Their second salvo hit the last of the Japanese eastern cruisers, *Kinugasa*, but incoming struck Battle-2, the secondary command center, right over Rusty Campbell's head.

Campbell slipped out of his harness and crouched behind his gun's splinter shield. Another salvo hurtled him over the splinter shield and onto the deck, burying him under a pile of 20mm ammunition cans. A helping hand pulled the temporarily blinded gunner from beneath the cans.

The Japanese had succeeded in setting the American cruiser's aircraft hangar aflame, so they switched off their searchlights and fired at the burning target.

Rusty Campbell regained his sight as he was crawling inboard past the motor launches. A chief petty officer grabbed him and ordered him to run out some hose to try to fight the fire raging around the spotter plane on the port catapult, Campbell's primary work station. Campbell did as he was told, clamping the hose to the nearest hydrant on the boat deck and turning the valve. All he got was an ample shot of live steam.

The deck was growing hot beneath Campbell's feet, so he was only too glad to obey instructions to get down to the fantail; a storage locker only ten feet beneath Campbell's gun was filled with bombs and depth charges, and Campbell wanted to be as far away as he could get from that blast when it occurred.

As Captain Reifkohl ordered a turn to port so he could close on the Japanese, a hit on the port side of the bridge cut down many of the men standing around him, but Reifkohl remained on his feet, untouched. All around, guns were being demolished and communications throughout the ship were disrupted as more of the Japanese cruisers found the range. *Vincennes's* main battery fire had to be maintained under local control.

Reifkohl next ordered a starboard turn to bring his ship out of the crossfire. Just then, however, several of *Chokai's* torpedoes exploded on the port side by Fireroom-4.

It was 0155, and *Vincennes* was doomed. One fireroom was off line, its crew smothered to a man. A torpedo from *Yubari*, in the western Japanese column, burst beside a starboard fireroom at 0203, killing the entire complement.

Emerging from the cover of the starboard aft 20mm gun, Rusty Campbell and the gunners around him peeked down at the well deck, where they saw the port 5-inch batteries and the bridge take repeated hits. There were fires everywhere. Campbell shouted down to a shipmate to learn what was going on, and the man shouted back that "Abandon ship" had been passed.

In fact, though the cruiser was slowly losing way and listing heavily to port, Captain Reifkohl was only just beginning to think about ordering the crew into the water.

Rusty Campbell felt it was time to make a decision. He told the two guncrews, "We'd better get our asses out of here."

Twenty frightened sailors moved for the ladder at the same instant, jostling one another for position, dropping heavily to the deck below. They had to pass through the main superstructure aft, down three decks in all, to get to the fantail, from which they could enter the water. The ship's power was gone, so it was stone dark inside. Shells burst through the port bulkhead, sending everyone sprawling to the deck in a great heap. Rusty Campbell fell face-up, another man's shoes in his face. He saw holes appear in both bulkheads as another shell went right through the compartment without detonating. There was a good deal of shouting. A third shell exploded when it hit the starboard bulkhead. The man on top of Rusty Campbell went limp while Campbell took a piece of shrapnel in the foot.

The roiling mass of men slowly sorted itself out and dribbled down the ladder to the next deck, where a secured manhole cover barred the way. It seemed to take ages before eager hands undogged the hatch. Rusty Campbell was the first man through, and he was terrorized. It was pitch dark, so he could not see if a hatch directly beneath his feet was open. If it was, Campbell could plunge 20 feet to a steel deck. If not, the drop was a few inches. He hung for long moments by his fingertips, until a pair of feet hit him in the head, and he plunged into the abyss. The fall was a four-incher. Campbell shouted to the men above that it was safe to come ahead.

A dilemma arose. Campbell's berthing space was directly beneath his feet. He pondered the merits of making a quick side trip to winkle out the $60 in cash he had hidden among his skivvies and the new $55 gabardine dress blues he had worn only twice. Suddenly, the connecting hatch opened and ammunition handlers from below boiled toward the adjacent fantail. Rusty Campbell followed them into the open, wondering at his stupidity.

Campbell stepped onto the fantail and walked forward until stopped by thick flames and smoke. He turned back aft just as Japanese shells hit the bulkhead over his head. He ran. Another shell sent a piece of shrapnel into his left leg and hit the kapok life jacket covering his stomach so hard he doubled over. He smelled something burning, reached down to where he had been hit, and scorched his fingers on a white-hot piece of shrapnel imbedded in the life jacket.

The firing abruptly stopped at 0215.

Only destroyer *Ralph Talbot* stood between 8th Fleet and freedom, and her skipper ordered her in after the Japanese. *Furutaka*,

Tenryu, and *Yubari*, the western Japanese column, fired a total of seven salvoes at the oncoming American destroyer, but she was hit only once, in the torpedo tubes. Then *Yubari* fired one last time, holing *Ralph Talbot*'s charthouse, knocking out part of the automatic gun-control system, and striking a 5-inch mount. The destroyer countered with an unsuccessful four-torpedo spread, and ended the fight by entering a rain squall near Savo.

Ens Tuny Moffat, a destroyer-squadron supply officer, was asleep in his stateroom aboard *Ellett*, a new destroyer, one of the fastest in the U.S. Fleet, when he was awakened by the general-quarters klaxon. On waking, Moffat could hear the sound of gun-fire from the west and could feel the ship storm away from its sta-tion off Tulagi. When Tuny Moffat came topside and headed for his battle station, the forward machine-gun battery, he could see flashes of gunfire to the west. By then, *Ellett* was steaming toward the battle at full speed.

By the time the fast destroyer arrived off Savo, the Japanese were gone. Though mindful that his primary mission was getting at the transports, Admiral Mikawa elected to forego his advantage be-cause he expected the American carriers to mount search-and-strike missions. He need not have worried, for Fletcher's task force had already steamed out of range. The foray had been a clear victory, but the Japanese warships had seriously depleted their magazines, and Mikawa was convinced that he had tackled a far larger battle force than the Allies actually had in the vicinity. He chose discre-tion and left.

Ellett's captain, LCdr Francis Gardner, conned his ship di-rectly to the aid of *Quincy* and *Vincennes*, which were aflame and in imminent danger of sinking. When Gardner heard cries for help from the water, he took an unprecedented and incredibly dan-gerous step. At his order, *Ellett* went dead in the water, fully illumi-nated by the burning cruisers. Rescue operations immediately commenced.

Ens Tuny Moffat was the first man into the water, the one who tested rumors about schools of predatory sharks being loose in the channel. There were no sharks, but there were more castaways than Moffat could begin to help. He got a firm grip on one swimmer and helped him back to *Ellett*, at which point he was ordered to reboard because he was not secured to the ship with a lifeline, as were dozens of other destroyermen who had followed him into the inky water.

Vincennes was listing heavily to port, and there was a wide divergence of thought on the subject of abandoning ship. Some gunners had remained at their stations with secondary batteries, but crewmen were also drifting astern in life rafts. As Rusty Campbell stood by the rail trying to make up his mind, watching seawater reach the port scuppers, he reached into his pocket, pulled out a cigarette, and lit up. He had taken only a few drags when a young officer snarled from by his elbow, "Sailor, put that cigarette out! Don't you know the smoking lamp is out?" The seaman stared at the officer in disbelief. *Vincennes* was aflame from stem to stern, and here was a character who was worried about a burning cigarette. Shock deepened when the officer repeated his order: "You heard what I said! Put that cigarette *out!*" Campbell flipped the butt into the water and glared back at the officer, convinced the man was about to ask for his name, rate, and service number.

Then it was time to go. Campbell took off his shoes and placed them neatly in line with forty or fifty other pairs, then stepped off the deck into the water and swam about 100 feet to the nearest raft. A strange sound behind Campbell brought him around. He floated on his back just in time to see *Vincennes* roll over, her four screws right on the surface. People were standing on her keel, between the screws. She hung there for a few minutes, then gently slid beneath the light swell.

Twenty-year-old Rusty Campbell, who had been at home aboard *Vincennes* since before the war, felt warm tears in his eyes as he pulled for the nearby raft and was helped out of the water.

Hundreds of refugees boarded *Ellett* and moved into every available space below decks to receive medical care or rest, as required. A bluejacket whose lower jaw had been shot away died in Ens Tuny Moffat's bunk. Moffat was sickened when the open deck behind his machine-gun battery was used to store the dead, who were neatly stacked—like cordwood—to conserve space.

Quincy and *Vincennes* went down during the night. *Canberra's* crew fought to extinguish the flames that were ravaging its ship, but the Australian cruiser was too badly mauled for quick salvage. A message from RAdm Kelly Turner clinched her doom; she was to be scuttled if she could not retire with the fleet at 0630. Her executive officer reluctantly ordered his crew to abandon ship, and hundreds of pajama-clad Aussies transferred to *Patterson*, where spare clothing was broken out of the crew's lockers and unselfishly passed around. *Blue* moved to assist *Canberra's* crew at 0600, and she and *Patterson* took off the last of 608 Australian officers and sailors shortly after 0615.

Ens Tuny Moffat, of destroyer *Ellett*, watched as a dark form loomed out of the semi-darkness several thousand yards out. Was a Japanese cruiser returning to sink rescue vessels? Moffat watched and waited as the barrel of *Ellett's* forward 5-inch gun depressed and tracked the target. Shell after shell was pumped into the silhouette, frightening men in the water and aboard *Ellett*. The target was *Canberra*! Unbeknown to Tuny Moffat, *Ellett* had been ordered to scuttle the Australian cruiser with gunfire, but could not. *Canberra* did not sink until torpedoed by another destroyer at 0800.

Chicago's befuddled captain was looking for game, and he settled 'on *Patterson* in the half-light of the new day. No hits were scored before *Chicago* ceased firing.

Astoria was still afloat, and her crew wanted her to stay that way. Prodigious efforts by Captain Greenman and 300 volunteers who reboarded her following rescue proved fruitless. A minesweeper tried to pass a tow, but that effort failed and a cargo ship finally came alongside to evacuate the salvage crew. *Astoria* heeled over to port at 1235 and sank.

Hundreds of men remained in the water for hours. Shortly after getting aboard a life raft, Rusty Campbell went back over the side to make room for an injured man. Somehow, he wound up alone and adrift on the wide sea, fearful that his limited prowess as a swimmer would kill him. He was treading water, getting panicky, when something nudged him in the side. A shark? No. It was an empty 5-inch powder can, which he grabbed for dear life. Minutes later, several more powder cans floated by, and Campbell put one apiece beneath each armpit and behind his knees. Out of the darkness came the sound of singing. It was a shipmate, who was repeating the lyric of a popular song: "Hold tight, hold tight. I want some seafood, Mama." The two exchanged tales and scuttlebutt, then drifted apart. The tide carried Campbell toward the burning and grounded transport, *Elliott*.

In time, Campbell saw ships stopping to take on survivors. His prayers seemed about to be answered when he saw a destroyer (*Ellett*) heading right for him. She was only 100 yards away when she began dropping depth charges at an imagined submarine in the channel. The concussion nearly bilged Rusty Campbell, but he desperately clung to his ammunition cans until another destroyer, *Helm*, came up beside him. Campbell was dragged to the deck, where he asked the time. It was 0900. His watch had stopped when he went into the water; it read 0240.

The unprecedented loss of four first-line cruisers in a single action in which the enemy had been but superficially damaged was catastrophic. The defeat was mitigated somewhat on August 10 when an American submarine put a pair of torpedoes into *Kako's* hull and left her sinking off New Ireland. That put the score in the Solomons at four heavy cruisers and one transport sunk and one destroyer missing to one Japanese heavy cruiser sunk.

Kelly Turner's amphibious force and its surviving escorts retired early in the morning, as promised. It carried in its holds a vast amount of equipment and stores belonging to 1st Marine Division.

PART V

Interlude

I I

The precipitous withdrawal of its naval supports left 1st Marine Division in dire straits. The bottlenecks encountered in getting food and equipment ashore had cut anticipated limited supply levels to the bone. There were rations enough for thirty-seven days, and sufficient munitions for about four days of heavy fighting. The troops and their officers were simply stunned by the retirement of the fleet, and, when news arrived, by the defeat at Savo.

MGen Archer Vandegrift's first priority was the establishment of strong defensive positions on either side of Sealark and Lengo channels, and the completion and development of the airbase on the northern coast of Guadalcanal, near Lunga Point.

The Tulagi area was fortified and manned by 1st Raider Battalion, 1st Parachute Battalion, 2nd Battalion, 5th, the three battalions of 2nd Marines, and a mixed bag of service, headquarters, and artillery troops, about 6,000 Marines in all.

The strategic offensive in the Solomons had bogged down. First Marine Division had occupied all of its viable objectives in the area, and at very little cost, but it could only sit on them. Everyone expected the Japanese to mount a swift, brutal challenge on land. Steps taken during the first days ashore were in response to that expectation.

The first priority was defending miles of beaches around Lunga Point, which, the amphibious-minded division staff assumed, the Japanese would strike first. Limited resources in the form of the coast artillery batteries of 3rd Defense Battalion, a self-contained unit specially designed to defend beaches and airbases, were augmented by temporary attachments of from one to three infantry battalions, pioneers, engineers, tankers, and special-weapons troops. There was no way to defend the entire beach in depth, but efforts were made to securely defend about two miles of coastline between Alligator Creek and Kukum Village, the area fronting the uncompleted airfield.

Sgt Ben Selvitelle, the L Company, 5th, light-machine-gun-section leader, was put in charge of a short stretch of beach line between a coconut grove on one flank and thick woods on the other. The sector was covered only by Selvitelle's two light machine guns and a dozen Marines armed with rifles and pistols until someone higher up thought that a narrow dirt track in the rear of the position might be used by enemy tanks. Selvitelle was given a pair of .50-caliber heavy machine guns to be manned by his ammunition carriers, who knew as well as anyone that they would be useless against armor. The line was further bolstered on one flank by two M Company .30-caliber medium machine guns and, to the rear, by L Company's two 60mm mortars and a 37mm antitank gun. The battalion's four 81mm mortars and a four-gun 75mm pack howitzer battery were registered on Selvitelle's sector, and a halftrack mounting a 75mm antitank gun was placed on call. The light-machine gunners strung some barbed wire along the front, dug shallow foxholes, and settled in to wait.

A battery of 75mm halftracks and two companies of light tanks mounting 37mm guns were to have been deployed in fixed emplacements along the beach, but it was quickly decided to provide only the empty pits, leaving the light armored vehicles to be used as a mobile reserve in the event the line was breached, or in case the expected counteroffensive took an unexpected form from an unexpected direction.

Five 75mm light batteries and three 105mm medium batteries of 2nd, 3rd, and 5th Battalions, 11th,—thirty-two guns in all— were grouped south of the runway in such a way as to bring their massed fires to bear upon any given sector anywhere within range. The guns were concealed in the forest and several pits were dug for each gun so that just about any azimuth could be covered. Obstructions, particularly high stands of timber, had to be painstakingly hacked down to clear lines of fire.

Machine-gun emplacements were hastily constructed and manned along the stretch of Alligator Creek nearest the beach, particularly in front of a sandbar at the creek's mouth which, at low tide, might provide attackers with easy access to the rear.

Only the beach and the eastern flank of the perimeter were defended by infantry lines. The western flank and most of the interior offered no defensive advantages and required other forms of security.

West of the Lunga delta is a sweeping re-entrant arc curving four miles toward the Matanikau River. About midway between the rivers is the Lunga Plain, a lozenge-shaped bowl formed by the first line of sharply rising ridges, which curve away to the southeast. Nearest the coast, the ridges are high, jumbled, and covered with thick head-high stands of sharp kunai grass. As the line of ridges sweeps inland, the interior rain forest impinges upon the coastal savannah. East of the Lunga River, the heavily forested ridges give way to heavily forested lowlands which, in turn, give way nearer the coast to grassy lowlands. It was decided to anchor the division left flank on the forested high ground west of the Lunga River. While this ground could be approached under the concealment of the rain forest, the defenders had the advantage in height and, in some cases, vista.

There were not sufficient troops on the island to establish a continuous defensive line across the ridges, so each of several rifle battalions was assigned an interior sector, which it was to hold from an all-around defensive cordon augmented by a network of observation and listening posts and from which it was to mount daily aggressive patrols. An attacking force could sweep past individual strongholds, but such a force would either have to contain the Marine battalions it bypassed or face aggressive assaults from the rear. Early encounters by Marine patrols with the incredibly dense rain forest convinced planners that the Japanese would probably never be able to mount a significant assault from the inland flank.

The defensive establishment was by no means static. A full schedule of patrols was mounted in all directions anywhere from several hundred yards to several miles.

The nights were extremely unsettled during the first week. Pfc Tom Crean, a communicator with 3rd Battalion, 5th, fired at a shadow that had been flitting in and out of view behind a tree. The battalion commander, a tough old salt, bellowed, "Who fired that shot? Give them cold steel. Take them with the bayonet!" No one went quite that far, and the battalion settled itself down. Tom Crean learned in the morning that his intruder had been a wind-whipped hawser.

On the night of August 10, a 1st Marines clerk crawled out of his tent to relieve himself. On returning, he inadvertently jostled his tentmate, a Navy corpsman, who reflexively grabbed a rifle and shot the Marine dead in his tracks.

The green gunners of 11th Marines were even more prone than green riflemen to becoming jittery during eerie night watches. As a means for restoring order, Col Pete del Valle, the artillery regiment's commander, asked division headquarters for a fair share of patrol assignments into the bush. Each of the artillery battalions sent out three daily patrols on identical compass headings, each group maintaining lateral contact with the others and with those of flanking battalions. They left at dawn and advanced for only so long as they could be sure of returning to friendly lines by nightfall.

Few patrols during the first week made any "hard" contacts. The inexperienced, often sleepless Marines were overcautious. As the gunners—and all Marines—spent more time in the rain forest,

Above: RAdm Richmond Kelly Turner (*left*) and MGen Alexander Archer Vandegrift plan the landings at Beach Red.

(*Official USN Photo*)

Left: Capt Bill Hawkins, of B Company, 5th Marines.

(*Courtesy of W.L. Hawkins*)

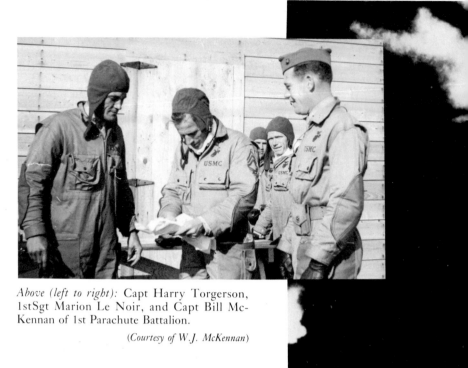

Above (left to right): Capt Harry Torgerson, 1stSgt Marion Le Noir, and Capt Bill Mc-Kennan of 1st Parachute Battalion.

(*Courtesy of W.J. McKennan*)

Right: USS *Quincy* as seen during the Savo Island Naval Battle in a searchlight beam from Japanese cruiser *Aoba.*

(*Official USN Photo*)

Above: Aviation Machinist's Mate 3rd Class William "Rusty" Campbell, of USS *Vincennes.*

(*Courtesy of William Campbell*)

Right: Japanese Betty medium bombers streak by at wavetop height to deliver a torpedo attack against the Guadalcanal invasion fleet on August 8.

(*Official USMC Photo by Cpl Gerald Koepplinger, USMC*)

VAdm Gunichi Mikawa

(Official USN Photo)

Capt Martin Clemens on August 15, the day
he arrived at the Lunga Perimeter.

(Courtesy of W.F.M. Clemens)

Marine Gunner Bill Rust, of 5th Marines.

(Courtesy of E.S. Rust)

A Marine patrol near the Lunga Perimeter in August 1942.
(Official USMC Photo)

2ndLt John Jachym, of A Company, 1st Marines.
(Courtesy of J.J. Jachym)

Above: Henderson Field in late August 1942. Note planes dispersed in the open as well as numerous shells and bomb craters.

(*Official USN Photo*)

Above left: A Marine F4F-4 Wild-cat scrambles from Fighter-1.

(Official USMC Photo by L.M. Asham)

Left: A Marine SDB Dauntless dive-bomber with 500-lb bomb aboard.

(Official USMC Photo by Sgt Bill Brunk)

Below: Sixty-seventh Pursuit Squadron P-400 fighter-bombers.

(Official USMC Photo)

Above (left to right): Maj John L. Smith, LtCol Richard
C. Mangrum, and Capt Marion E. Carl.

(Official USMC Photo)

Below left: 2ndLt Hank Hise, of VMSB-232.

(Courtesy of H.W. Hise)

Below: Capt Dale Brannon, of 67th Pursuit Squadron.

(Courtesy of D.D. Brannon)

they became surer of themselves. In time, when patrols were able
to penetrate deep into the forest, they began capturing Japanese
and Koreans who had run from the invasion force on D-Day. That
enormously increased their confidence. Nocturnal shootings at
shadows subsided, the troops became better rested, and generally
more alert and more aggressive.

The sum of the data gleaned from patrol reports indicated that
the Japanese were strongest to the west, and that virtually no laborers nor combat troops were to the east nor within patrol range to
the south. No one could say how many Japanese were on the island, but it was felt that Rabaul had not had time to mount a significant effort. (The small provisional battalion of bluejackets sent
south on D-Day by VAdm Gunichi Mikawa had been torpedoed
by an American submarine.) It was felt that all of the contacts that
first week were with members of the original Lunga garrison and
labor force. Most of the prisoners were laborers.

The Japanese at Rabaul lacked the means for mounting an immediate ground offensive, and they were restricted in the amount
and type of aggressive action they could take against the American
castaways in the Lower Solomons.

Until the very heavy bomber losses of the first two days could
be made good, Japanese aerial operations were largely restricted to
harrassment and reconnaissance flights by lone Betty bombers from
Rabaul or floatplane fighters operating from a seaplane tender anchored at Rekata Bay, Santa Ysabel.

Third Defense Battalion had batteries of 90mm and light automatic antiaircraft weapons which, though often inaccurate, kept
the bombers at great altitude. But it was psychologically devastating for Marines to hear the *carumph* of bombs, to feel the ground jar,
while knowing that they had no air cover and, thus, little chance of
turning the tide.

Other Japanese forays reinforced that sense of isolation. Sgt
Ben Selvitelle was marching briskly westward along the coastal
road for the third time in as many days when a Japanese submarine—one of the most vulnerable of surface targets—appeared a

short distance out in the channel and directly opposite the Marine patrol. That was nothing new; these Marines had spent a few days manning beach defenses, and they had seen Japanese submarine lookouts scanning the defenses. No one was concerned until one of the Marines said the submariners were manning the deck gun. All hands merely turned to look. Then someone yelled, "It's aimed at *us!*" Everyone headed into the adjacent coconut grove. When Ben Selvitelle heard the deck gun fire, he dived for cover. He heard the shell coming, and heard it plow through the foliage. It did not detonate. The Marines were rooted to their places. Not a sound could be heard for several seconds. Then someone suggested, "Let's get the hell out of here." All hands headed back to camp. It was an utterly humiliating experience.

The feelings of isolation and desperation were driven home yet again the next day. Sergeant Selvitelle's unit, L Company, 5th, was fed rice for breakfast, raisins with rice for lunch, and rice with raisins for supper. The cooks strained the weevils from the rice for at least one of those meals, thus depriving the troops of needed extra protein. That same day, M Company, 5th, enjoyed captured oatmeal for breakfast, captured oatmeal for lunch, and captured oatmeal for supper.

12

The acute need for precise information regarding the strength and deployment of Japanese forces near or beyond the Matanikau River impelled the 1st Marine Division intelligence section to plan a systematic penetration and reconnaissance of the area. It was evident that a force of *rikusentai* was in the area, and it had become vital to learn if this force was comprised of the remnants of the Lunga garrison or of fresh troops.

The original concept for a patrol to be undertaken by the 5th Marines intelligence section was 1stSgt Stephen Custer's. It was a comprehensive plan, calling for a trip by boat from Kukum in the early morning of August 12 by a well-armed force of Marines. The patrol was to land on any of a number of beaches close to a tiny peninsula known as Point Cruz and march inland along the left bank of the Matanikau before bivouacking as far into the bush as it could penetrate by nightfall. On the second day, the patrol was to march to Lunga. This was to be a heavily armed, highly mobile combat force capable of holding its own in a fire fight.

LtCol Frank Goettge, the division intelligence officer, was

planning to accompany a patrol mounted by 1st Marines to the Tetere area, but he decided to join the Matanikau patrol when he heard of 1st Sergeant Custer's plan. It is doubtful that Goettge had any desire to change Custer's plan, but events seemed to dictate changes.

The first was the capture of a hungry, haggard Japanese naval warrant officer in the rear of 1st Battalion, 5th. Interrogators asked a series of routine questions, which the Japanese answered in a surly tone. The interrogators persisted, and the man finally revealed that there was a large number of *rikusentai*, naval base troops, and laborers wandering through the bush west of the Matanikau. All, he said, were nearly starved. He added that, given proper conditions, many of these men might be induced to peaceably surrender. The interrogators found no reason to doubt the man's sincerity.

Next, a captured Japanese naval rating in much the same physical condition as the warrant officer freely admitted that a large, disorganized group of Japanese was in the vicinity of Point Cruz and the mouth of the Matanikau. He, too, said that a large number were ready to surrender.

Frank Goettge was under something of a cloud because of the poor maps and limited intelligence he had produced in New Zealand and was producing on Guadalcanal. The prisoner interrogations presented him with an opportunity to gather an abundance of fresh data. Furthermore, it seemed possible to save a number of human beings from the ravages of disease and slow starvation.

Drastic changes in the composition of the patrol took place. Goettge became convinced that the Japanese navy men were telling the truth, so he ordered the inclusion in the patrol of a number of division intelligence clerks and scouts. The 5th Marines' regimental surgeon, Dr. Malcolm Pratt, volunteered to go along. (Pratt told a fellow officer that afternoon that he had contracted tuberculosis, was in failing health, and that the patrol might be his last opportunity to see some action.) In the end, the group, which could consist of no more than twenty-five, bore little resemblance to a heavily armed combat patrol.

Capt Bill Ringer, the 5th Marines' intelligence officer, was driven nearly to distraction by Goettge's changes. Ringer, a 1937 Tufts College graduate and top man in his Basic School class at Quantico in 1938, was one of the brilliant new breed of officers populating the division, and he expressed some resentment—not to mention foreboding—over Frank Goettge's meddling. His remonstrances were ignored.

The inclusion of 1stLt Ralph Cory, the 5th Marines' language officer, who replaced a rifleman, bordered on the delinquent. Cory had joined the Marine Corps in April after working as a civilian employee for the Navy's communications-intelligence section in Washington. If captured in a combat situation, he might have been forced to reveal the nature of his highly classified civilian work and thus expose the fact that U.S. Naval Intelligence was capable of eavesdropping on Japan's most delicate communications.

Even the Japanese warrant officer whose capture had set the ball rolling was included in the patrol—at the expense of yet another Marine rifleman. By the time Frank Goettge was done turning the information-gathering patrol into a rescue mission, 1st Sergeant Custer's requirement for an early start was totally compromised. In all, twelve hours were lost.

The object of travel was speed and mobility. Each man carried only the barest essentials: poncho, a can of C-Rations, a canteen, a can of fish, some ammunition, and whatever personal items he could cram into his pockets or a small ditty bag. There were no heavy-caliber automatic weapons along, not even an automatic rifle, because, it was felt, their weight and the weight of their ammunition might impede the group's progress.

Shortly before departing from the 5th Marines CP, Frank Goettge and Bill Ringer had a brief conversation with the regimental exec, LtCol Bill Whaling, who had spent some days overseeing and participating in patrols west of the Matanikau. Whaling explicitly warned Goettge and Ringer to stay clear of the area between Point Cruz and the river because of the number and aggressive traits of the Japanese there.

The patrol left Kukum at 1800, August 12, aboard a ramp boat provided by the Lunga Boat Pool, an improvised unit manned by Navy and Coast Guard crews left behind by the fleet. It would be dark in a few hours, far too late to travel, land, and hike a safe distance into the bush, as the Custer plan stipulated. The boat turned for shore after dark and headed for a spot about 200 yards west of the Matanikau River, precisely the area Bill Whaling had told Frank Goettge to avoid.

Suddenly, the boat stuck fast on a sandbar, its ramp jammed in the up position. Several Marines vaulted the gunwales and attempted to rock the boat free, but it was decided after a few moments that everyone should drop over the side and wade to the beach, as much to lighten the craft as to keep moving. Several Marines continued to rock the boat while Lieutenant Colonel Goettge led the rest ashore to form a cordon defense.

The effort to free the boat created quite a racket in the still night air. When it floated free at length, the coxswain backed it off the sandbar and turned eastward for Kukum.

The entire group moved to the first row of giant banyan trees backing the beach and deployed in a rough, shallow line while Frank Goettge held a council of war on the sand with his officers. At the water's edge, PlSgt Denzil Caltrider held his rifle at the head of the Japanese warrant officer.

The talking was over in minutes, a course of action agreed to. Frank Goettge rose and started walking through the perimeter line to lead the troops through a coconut grove to find a suitable bivouac. Several men, including 1st Sergeant Custer, rose to follow the huge, solidly built former football star.

The stillness was shattered by gunfire. Frank Goettge fell first, then Custer. Dr. Malcolm Pratt rushed to the aid of the fallen men, but found Goettge in the sand with most of his face shot away. Custer was also dead. Platoon Sergeant Caltrider blew off the top of the Japanese warrant officer's head.

The Japanese poured a torrent of fire from the underbrush, catching the small knot of surprised Marines at close quarters. A corporal ran into the surf and fired his rifle into the air to attract the attention of the departing boat crew. Dr. Pratt fell under the hail of bullets, solidly hit in the chest and buttocks as he worked over a wounded Marine. In the extreme confusion of the moment, stunned survivors burrowed into the soft sand in the hope of escaping the furious, deadly crossfire. There was no cover whatsoever on the flat beach, and very little among the coconut palms.

Command fell to Capt Bill Ringer, who ordered Cpl William Bainbridge to head down the beach to get help. An hour later, Sgt Monk Arndt, a small, wiry Mississippian who had served two hitches in the Corps, volunteered to swim back to the Lunga Perimeter for help. Captain Ringer nodded his assent.

Arndt stripped and headed for the water, taking only his helmet, boondockers (combat boots, which he could not get off), and a pistol. Sergeant Arndt was forced to stay close to the beach because the weight of the boondockers threatened to pull him under, and the coral along the shore badly cut him. He was threatened at one point by an armed Japanese, but he killed the man in a brief scuffle. Arndt eventually found a bullet-riddled dugout canoe, which he laboriously paddled toward friendly lines. When he was just off Kukum, however, he realized he stood a good chance of being shot as he approached the beach. He paddled out to a landing boat he knew was moored offshore, and convinced the crew to take him to the beach. He finally reported in at the 5th Marines CP at about 0530, after at least six hours in the water. There had been no word from Corporal Bainbridge.

When Monk Arndt reported that the whole patrol might have been wiped out, MG Bill Rust, Bill Whaling's protégé and a member of the 5th Marines operations staff, volunteered to lead a patrol to the Matanikau to rescue any survivors. Col Roy Hunt vetoed the idea; if Arndt's story was accurate, he felt nothing would be gained by sending more men out into the dark. Hunt ordered A Company, 5th, alerted, then sent it off by boat at first light to try to find the ambush site and survivors.

At 0730, A Company was hailed to the beach by Cpl Joseph Spaulding, who had started back for help shortly after Sergeant

Arndt. Then PlSgt Frank Few emerged from the underbrush, covered by a mass of cuts. He told of coming through a round of hand-to-hand combat with a bayonet-wielding Japanese, whom he had to disarm and stab to death with his own weapon. Few told of watching the Japanese wield knives among the bodies on the beach, of seeing swords flashing in the morning sun. He was certain he was the last man to leave.

None of the survivors could pinpoint the site of the ambush, so the boats carrying A Company, 5th, turned in at Point Cruz, which is where the Goettge Patrol had been slated to land.

Two platoons of L Company, 5th, and a medium-machine-gun platoon—about 100 Marines—were sent to assist A Company in what became a futile search. In time, A Company started for home along the Government Track and arrived late in the evening of August 13. The L Company force took a far tougher route across the first line of ridges south of the beach and had to bivouac in the open that night. It arrived safely around noon on August 14. Neither group found a trace of the Goettge Patrol, nor of any concentrations of Japanese.

13

First Marine Division's first offensive began on August 19, 1942, a week after the annihilation of the Goettge Patrol. The action was designed to sweep the coastal area from the mouth of the Matanikau River to Kokumbona Village of the last remnants of the dispersed Japanese Lunga garrison, an estimated 400 poorly armed *rikusentai*, naval base personnel, and unarmed laborers who had been without food for nearly two weeks.

Information gleaned from patrol reports during the week following the Goettge massacre indicated that the Japanese had landed no fresh troops west of the Perimeter. However, unbeknown to the Marines, who had not been able to effectively penetrate the Japanese area, an advance detachment of the fresh Yokosuka 5th Special Naval Landing Force had been landed near Kokumbona on the night of August 17. While not large, the force was composed of well-armed *rikusentai* whose officers organized the combatant elements of the stragglers into makeshift combat units.

Given the breadth of the new war, the first Matanikau offensive was small potatoes. Given the backgrounds of the men who planned it, and particularly their limited combat experiences during the manpower-starved interwar years, it was about the biggest land operation undertaken by Marines since 1918.

Capt Bill Hawkins's B Company, 5th, was to cross the mouth of the Matanikau at dawn, August 19, while L Company, 5th, which would cross the river downstream on the evening of August 18, pushed northward along the west bank in order to compress the Japanese in the area between itself and Hawkins's company. In a strangely unconnected maneuver, I Company, 5th, was to land from small boats to seize and hold Kokumbona Village until B and L companies could secure Matanikau Village, reorganize, and fight three miles westward to join it.

B Company, 5th, was no longer the strong 180-man unit that had stormed Beach Red on August 7. A declining diet, the rigors of living in a hot climate, and the onset of exotic disease with annoying or dangerous symptoms had begun to make inroads into every unit in the division. Hawkins's company had lost its share of combat troops. Many were ill or weakened by the effects of dysentery and strange fevers and held back from the offensive.

Hawkins's company marched out of the Perimeter along the Government Track late in the afternoon of August 18 and bivouacked in the bush beside the trail. Several Asians were flushed from the underbrush during the approach and sent to the rear under escort. The troops were up for the fight when they left the Perimeter, and the discovery along the way of several decomposing, mutilated bodies of islanders raised their ire. Several individual Japanese charged from the undergrowth into the company perimeter during the night, but they were all killed.

L Company, in pretty much the same condition as B Company, left the Perimeter at about the same time, guided by MG Bill Rust, who had been leading patrols into the area for the past two weeks. The Marines were traveling light, with neither packs nor ponchos nor any other extraneous gear. It was rough going through some fairly thick growth. By nightfall, the company was safely across the Matanikau, about 2,000 yards from the beach. Just before sunset, a sniper on a hill a half-mile to the north shot a Marine sergeant through the forehead, killing him in his tracks. Three Asians were flushed at dusk, just as the company was about to establish a defensive perimeter on the west bank of the Matanikau. One was dispatched by a Marine who swung his rifle so hard that the wooden stock shattered on impact with the prisoner's skull. The second man was knifed to death, and the third simply disappeared after dark.

B Company marched to the river at dawn. As it cleared the last fringe of trees, all hands were stunned to see what appeared to be a Japanese cruiser majestically steam into view. As the warship streaked toward the beach, the Marines could actually see crewmen scurrying about on the decks and superstructure. After several anxious minutes, the vessel turned for deeper water.

L Company moved downhill through a light drizzle from its bivouac in the bush. The company .30-caliber light machine guns and 60mm mortars were set up in a base of fire and the attack commenced at 0800, right on time. A fair measure of surprise was attained at the outset as L Company struck the village almost dead center, its two lead platoons heading directly for the beach in the hope of cutting the defending force in two before it could recover.

B Company pressed its attack across the sandbar at the mouth of the river, also at 0800. Capt Bill Hawkins was caught in the open by the sudden onset of defensive fire and the stock of his submachine gun was splintered by a Japanese bullet before he could get behind some cover.

Pfc Bob Hollenbeck, a member of the medium-machine-gun platoon attached to B Company, found himself tucked up behind a huge banyan tree, looking for targets, when he felt the odd stinging sensation of hundreds of bites from residents of an ant colony he had disturbed. Though Japanese machine guns on the west bank were spitting bullets from every angle, Hollenbeck was too agonized to think of anything but getting rid of the carnivorous ants, which were crawling down his back and into his trousers. He rolled from behind the protective tree into bushes farther back and tore off his clothing to get rid of the insects.

By the time Hollenbeck recovered, the B Company 60mm mortars had been broken out. The company exec, 1stLt Walter McIlhenny, established an observation post at the water's edge and, by means of a telephone line run back to the company mortars, directed fire against the Japanese machine-gun emplacements.

On the far side of the Japanese holding B Company, an L Company platoon sergeant leading the attack to cut off the Japanese on the east side of the village was killed and several of his men were wounded. The L Company exec, 2ndLt George Mead, heir to the Mead Paper fortune, ran forward to rally the leaderless platoon, but was shot to death.

MG Bill Rust, who was with the L Company headquarters, volunteered to take charge of the still-leaderless platoon, which had to continue its attack if the company was to join up with B Company. He found only thirteen effectives on hand in a small semicircle on the beach. Incoming gunfire was very heavy, though it seemed to be letting up little by little. Rust ordered the thirteen Marines in his position to prepare the way with a barrage of rifle grenades, which was bolstered considerably when Sgt Ben Selvitelle arrived in the village with his light-machine-gun section after being ordered to abandon his base of fire to the south. B Company's 60mm mortars, which were firing from the east bank of the river, were of considerable help in getting Japanese heads down. Gunner Rust directed a scathing fire, then jumped to his feet yelling "Let's get them!" All hands rose as one and spread out in firm adherence to the tenets of their training, advancing about seventy-five yards by means of fire-and-move tactics. A spirited bayonet assault, perhaps the first of its kind by Marines in the Pacific, spontaneously developed as Rust's small group covered the last seventy-five yards to the river. Pfc Nicholas Sileo, a BAR-man, accumulated three wounds—one in the chest, one in the groin, a third through his shooting hand—but refused to relinquish his weapon. Instead, he fired with his good hand as his fellow Marines surged past. A corpsman who had become involved in the attack was shot through the heart. As soon as the small platoon had overcome resistance, Bill Rust ordered all hands to fire into all the Japanese bodies, just to be certain, then stood on the exposed bank to yell news of his attack to B Company Marines.

Capt Bill Hawkins did not hear Rust, but he was aware that the gunfire holding up B Company had abruptly ceased. He ordered a squad to probe the defenses and, when it met no opposition, ordered the rest of his Marines across the river. It was all over but the cleaning up.

Meantime, I Company, 5th, moved to take Kokumbona Village. As the boats neared the objective, Marines spotted three Japanese warships steaming up the channel. The landing craft were executing a turn to port for the run on the beach when one of the warships fired. The salvo was high, splashing harmlessly ahead of the tiny flotilla. The second salvo was much closer.

LtCol Bill Whaling was accompanying I Company as a guide and tactical commander of the three-company mission. His boat was in the lead when the warships opened fire. Whaling tried to steady his frightened coxswain by calling back from his place by the ramp, "When I think he's going to fire, I'll call you. Then you throw this thing full speed into *reverse*. Then run forward with everything you've got."

The ploy worked three times in a row, though a few near misses splashed seawater on all hands.

The boats were rapidly closing on the beach, and Japanese machine guns were getting the range. The warship was still firing, its rounds getting closer and closer to countrymen manning machine guns on the beach. Suddenly, a Japanese climbed up on a big rock at the surf line, a large Rising Sun naval battle pennant in his hand. As the Marines looked on, the man frantically waved the battle colors to attract the ship's gunners.

Bill Whaling, a veteran of fighting in France and Pearl Harbor, had been a member of the 1924 U.S. Olympic pistol team. Unable to resist any target so offered, he climbed as high up on the bow ramp as he could, holding his special scoped rifle. When the little boat rose to the crest of the next swell, Whaling sighted in on the frantic flag-waver. The boat pitched into the next trough, then slowly rose again. Thoroughly composed, Whaling gently squeezed off a single round and watched approvingly as the flag-waver pitched into the sand.

The Japanese warship came under probing fire from a captured 3-inch coast-defense gun manned by members of M Company, 5th. Twenty rounds were expended, but all fell short. Fire from another of the three ships bracketed the gun emplacement, obliging the Marines to beat a hasty retreat. The three warships countermarched, firing at Marine positions with total impunity, remaining just outside the range of Marine coast defense-guns.

Army Air Forces Maj Jim Edmundson, a professional airman since 1936, had been in the Pacific since January 1940. He had been on the ground at Hickam Field, Oahu, on December 7, 1941, and had participated as a squadron operations officer and airplane commander at Midway. Since August 13, 1942, he had been commander of 431st Bomb Squadron, a component of 11th Heavy Bombardment Group whose previous commander had been lost without a trace on a search mission over the Solomons on August 7.

Edmundson and his crew had been at the crude airstrip at Espiritu Santo—code-named "Buttons"—when word came down from Guadalcanal that Japanese cruisers were harrassing a Marine offensive operation. Theirs was the only B-17 heavy bomber that was ready to go, so they went.

The approach was made at 5,000 feet, the same height from which Edmundson had destroyed a Japanese submarine off Hawaii during a sea-search mission early in the war.

Observers near Kukum could make out the masts of the three ships, and the circling B-17, which dropped bombs as it passed back and forth over the targets. One stick of four bombs passed directly over the fantail of one of the ships, which looked like light cruisers from the air as well as from the beach. Two of the bombs exploded on the ship and the other two near-missed on either side, likely doing damage below the waterline.

While B-17 crewmen snapped photos from beside a dark pillar

of smoke, Major Edmundson continued to circle lazily over the circling victim. When Edmundson had expended all the fuel he dared, he made a low pass over excited, whooping Marines on the beach. Though Jim Edmundson was given credit for sinking a cruiser, his target was a destroyer, *Hagikaze*, and she survived.

I Company had long since landed at Kokumbona and had sent the meager opposition packing. LtCol Bill Whaling soon had the unit marching overland to join the two companies at Matanikau Village. I and L Companies joined at midday, just as B Company was crossing the river. Patrols discovered the remains of sixty-five Japanese.

MG Bill Rust, who was accompanying an I Company probe, was on the beach just to the east of Point Cruz when he and his companions found a leg encased in a Marine legging and boondocker protruding from the sand. Nearby, an oversized, handless arm was sticking out of the ground, leading Bill Rust to speculate that he had found the remains of either LtCol Frank Goettge or Capt Bill Ringer, both of whom had been very large men. Earlier, as his attack was winding down, Rust had discovered the bullet-riddled body of Cpl William Bainbridge, who had been sent for help by Captain Ringer a week earlier; Bainbridge's decomposing body was interred in the sand by the mouth of the Matanikau.

First Lieutenant Ralph Cory, the former civilian communications-intelligence expert, was not individually identified, but it is presumed that he was buried in the common grave with LtCol Frank Goettge, Dr. Malcolm Pratt, Capt Bill Ringer, and sixteen other Americans. If Cory was captured, it is certain that he did not divulge the secret of the U.S. Navy's ability to decipher Japan's most important code.

The officers were about to get the troops started on exhuming the twenty-one bodies found in the area, but an urgent recall order from division headquarters prevented the work from even beginning. The attack force boarded landing craft with its four dead and eleven wounded companions and headed for home. The precipitous recall order had been prompted by startling events to the east of the Lunga Perimeter.

14

August 20, 1942. A Thursday, about noon.

Escort carrier *Long Island*, a strange flat ship with no superstructure, turned into the southeast trade wind, black smoke pouring from her horizontal starboard funnels, and catapulted a dark blue Douglas Dauntless SBD-3 dive-bomber out over the waves.

Maj Dick Mangrum, a former flight instructor and fighter pilot with twelve years in the Marine Corps and over 3,000 hours in the air, deftly recovered control of the projectile in which he was riding and slowly raised flaps to begin his long climb. Next up was 2ndLt Larry Baldinus, a Polish expatriate and former enlisted pilot. The most experienced airman in the squadron after Dick Mangrum, Baldinus had been commissioned after Pearl Harbor. The third aircraft was piloted by a more-typical specimen, 2ndLt Hank Hise, a twenty-two-year-old Texan who had graduated from flight school with a shade over 200 flight hours in May 1942. Though Hise had amassed more flight time in carrier training in California and check flights in Hawaii, he was no veteran. The force of the catapult caused the young pilot to pull back on his joystick, so the nose of the aircraft pulled smartly up. Hise reacted by jamming the joystick in his right hand forward, then had to fight to keep the Dauntless out of the water. He regained control and pulled up to join Mangrum and Baldinus.

Three of the twelve SBD pilots were survivors of Midway. One had attacked a Japanese carrier, then had landed his crippled dive-bomber on one wheel at Midway between rows of parked aircraft. Another had been wounded in the same attack and had returned to Midway with a critically wounded radioman-gunner. Their stories, and the stories of the two or three veteran fighter pilots accompanying them aboard *Long Island*, had raised the hairs on the necks of the novice dive-bomber pilots.

The dozen Dauntlesses of Mangrum's Marine Scout-Bomber Squadron-232 (VMSB-232) formed up and orbited to await the escort of eighteen shorter-legged Grumman F4F-3 Wildcat fighters from Capt John Lucien Smith's Marine Fighting Squadron-223 (VMF-223) and a command fighter piloted by LtCol Charlie Fike, executive officer of Marine Air Group 23 (MAG-23). Major Mangrum turned his three-plane element to the northwest as the last of the fighters joined up. The Lunga Plain was 190 miles ahead.

Once the fleet had retired from Guadalcanal, the primary objective left to the abandoned Marines was getting the captured Japanese airstrip on the Lunga Plain operational as quickly as possible. Without air support, the Marines were totally at the mercy of Japanese aerial and naval attacks, and highly vulnerable to ground assault. It was fortunate that the Japanese were initially as nearly hamstrung as the Lunga and Tulagi garrisons.

The Imperial Navy's 25th Air Flotilla, at Rabaul, had been reinforced only days before the Allied incursion into the Solomons as part of a general build-up preparatory to occupying the Lunga airfield and supporting a drive into the New Hebrides. On August 9, VAdm Nishizo Tsukahara activated 11th Air Fleet at Rabaul and assumed control of air operations.

Tsukahara advocated a policy of strong reprisals against the

Americans in the Lower Solomons. However, due to severe losses inflicted upon his bomber fleet during the first two days of aerial combat, the one-armed senior air commander was restricted to mounting harassment and reconnaissance missions. Fresh units were on the way, but it would be days or weeks before the Japanese would make good the losses of August 7 and 8.

The one thing the Americans had going for them was the distance between their stronghold and the Japanese airbases around Rabaul. Though the Zero was the longest-legged operational fighter in the world, the 1,200-mile round trip between Rabaul and Lunga pushed its capabilities to the limit.

The range limitations of their aircraft obliged the Japanese to fly by the most direct route from their bases to Lunga. That meant adherence to a predictable timetable, with no margin for feints or for speeding up the throttled-back engines of the fuel-conserving fighters. The aircraft had to fly over Buka, off northwestern Bougainville, then Buin, overlooking the Shortland Islands, then straight down the Slot. A Coastwatcher station overlooking Buka was manned by Jack Read, who usually sent the first word of an impending air strike. Paul Mason, near Buin, got the next word in. It was invariably two hours between Mason's warning and the arrival of the bombers over Lunga. So, the Marines around Lunga could count upon several quiet hours after dawn and before dusk for getting work done, and upon having at least two hours in which to find cover and take aim.

Antiaircraft defense was built around the 90mm antiaircraft guns of 3rd Defense Battalion, which were bolstered by the battalion's own light-automatic-weapons batteries and numerous infantry machine guns set up on antiaircraft mounts. All levels up to 25,000 feet could be covered after a fashion, so the lone raiders of the early days usually stayed above that level, which hampered the accuracy of bombing and reconnaissance.

Almost as soon as the runway had fallen into the hands of 3rd Battalion, 5th, on August 8, 1st Marine Division's Air and Engineering officers were on the field sizing things up. They reported that they could put down 2,600 feet of usable runway by August 10, and that another 1,200-by-160-foot section could be completed in the week after that. RAdm Kelly Turner promised that aircraft would arrive by August 11.

That was the news on August 8. Some revisions had to be made on August 9, by which time Turner had retired with nearly all the equipment owned by 1st Engineer Battalion. Airfield construction commenced on August 9 when 1st Engineer and 1st Pioneer battalions and assorted helpers gathered sufficient materials to get started. A miserable fifteen percent of the engineers' equipment and supplies had been landed, so the troops had to manhandle 100,000 cubic feet of earth fill to cover a depression in the center of the field. (The Japanese had begun the strip at either extremity and built toward the middle.)

A huge steel girder served as a drag, and a Japanese road roller packed the fill. In fact, the Japanese contributed heavily to the small store of engineering equipment. In general, the captured equipment was in poor condition, but ingenious American mechanics kept it working hour after brutal hour in their lively race against time. The only earth-moving equipment was one angle-dozer the Pioneers had managed to land. Dumptrucks were nonexistent. The engineers performed incredible feats of improvisation to overcome monumental difficulties.

On August 11, MGen Millard Harmon, the administrative head of Army ground forces in the South Pacific, wrote to the Army Chief of Staff, Gen George Marshall, concerning the situation in the Lower Solomons:

> The thing that impresses me more than anything else in connection with the Solomons action is that we are not prepared to follow up. . . .
>
> We have seized a strategic position from which future op-

erations in the Bismarcks can be strongly supported. Can the Marines hold out? There is considerable room for doubt.

Navy Lt William Sampson, RAdm Slew McCain's aide, told ground controllers on August 12 that his PBY patrol bomber had developed a serious mechanical malfunction which prevented him from putting the aircraft down in the water off Kukum. He was allowed to set down amidst the dust and debris of the airfield construction effort. Mechanics who went to work on Sampson's plane found no malfunctions. What they did find was a grinning admiral's aide who had conned his way into the history books. Sampson evacuated two wounded men, the first aerial evacuation of wounded from a combat zone in the Pacific. (One was Lt Pug Southerland, who had survived his D-Day dogfight with AP1 Saburo Sakai.) Sampson pronounced the field in excellent condition, but it was really quite execrable.

Following their formation and brief training at Ewa Field, Oahu, VMF-223 and VMSB-232 had been packed aboard *Long Island* on August 2 and sent unescorted into the great unknown of the war-torn Pacific. Ground crews, key personnel from MAG-23, and all the necessary ordnance, fuel, and supplies needed to begin air operations departed from Hawaii separately aboard a transport.

When the escort carrier's captain heard about the Savo debacle, he headed for the American base at Suva, Fiji, to await clearance to launch his cargo of precious aircraft.

Upon anchoring, *Long Island*'s captain informed area headquarters that nearly all the Marine fighter pilots were too green to be committed to combat. VAdm Bob Ghormley bucked the matter to his aircraft commander, RAdm Slew McCain, a peppery, no-nonsense Alabamian with whom he had graduated from the Naval Academy in 1906. McCain suggested that better-trained pilots be transferred into VMF-223 from the Efate squadron, VMF-212.

Long Island sailed to Efate, but the better-trained pilots from VMF-212 were not forthcoming; they were merely earmarked for early shipment to Guadalcanal, perhaps within the week.

Admiral McCain learned on August 12 that transport *William Ward Burroughs*, embarking vital equipment and ground crews, had been delayed in its passage from Oahu and could not get to Lunga before August 19. Guadalcanal reported that 400 drums of aviation gasoline had been captured at Lunga, but there was absolutely nothing else of value with which to service the aircraft.

McCain had the problem whipped overnight. Maj Fog Hayes, executive officer of Marine Observation Squadron 251 (VMO-251), was ordered by Admiral McCain to mount out for Guadalcanal with elements of his squadron's ground staff.

The five officers and 118 enlisted men of the Navy's Construction Unit, Base 1 (CUB-1) were debarking at Espiritu Santo at noon on August 13 when the ensign commanding was informed that his unit would be put ashore at Guadalcanal in two days. CUB-1 had to unload, repack, and reload as much of its gear as it could, and there was a hitch. It drew transportation aboard several destroyer-transports—old World War I–vintage four-stack destroyers converted to transport amphibious troops such as Marine Raiders—and each could carry only thirty-ton cargoes. Only essential material could be embarked. The most essential materials had been stowed at the bottoms of the holds of the ship that had brought CUB-1 to Espiritu Santo, so the navymen barely had time to transship 400 drums of aviation gasoline, 32 drums of lubricants, 282 bombs of various sizes, belted machine-gun ammunition, and miscellaneous tools and spare parts. CUB-1 boarded the destroyer-transports carrying light packs and small arms, but not one tent, not even a can of food.

Lt Hugh MacKenzie, an Australian naval reservist who was to man a forward radio station at Lunga, was embarked with CUB-1 and the VMO-251 personnel. It was hoped that news of aircraft sightings directly beamed from the north to MacKenzie would end the rash of garbled transmissions and lost messages that had been plaguing the network since August 7.

The convoy disembarked its passengers and cargo at Kukum after dark on August 15. Next morning, CUB-1 moved to Henderson Field—named by MGen Archer Vandegrift for Maj Lofton

Henderson, a Marine pilot killed at Midway. The Navy and Marine groundcrewmen learned the Marine quartermaster could not make good all of the personal gear they had had to leave at Espiritu Santo. Lt Hugh MacKenzie was severely let down when he sought a suitable site for his vital radio station; he had to settle for a narrow five-foot-high dugout on exposed ground north of the runway.

Eight Japanese Betty medium bombers, the largest air strike since August 9, arrived over Henderson Field after noon on August 18. Kept above 25,000 feet by ground fire, the bombers did little harm. But it was clear to all that 11th Air Fleet was resuming work. And nothing stood in its path.

CUB-1 and 1st Engineer Battalion reported Henderson Field fit to support air operations on August 19. The facilities were crude, but the base was ready. *Long Island* had left Efate on August 18 and joined with a covering force built around *Saratoga*. The tiny, ungainly auxiliary carrier arrived off the southern tip of San Cristobal, 190 miles from Henderson Field, on August 20, and launched aircraft.

Second Lieutenant Hank Hise was surprised by the height of the hills as he flew up Lengo Channel on Maj Dick Mangrum's right wing and banked around in a 180-degree turn to begin his approach from the east. The diamond-shaped formation of four elements of three Dauntlesses each broke up with practiced ease; first Mangrum broke to the left, followed three seconds later by 2ndLt Larry Baldinus, and three seconds after that by Hise. Landing gear was lowered by the pilots at 1,000 feet as they made their downwind approaches, then flaps were lowered. Mangrum saw Maj Fog Hayes—who was a qualified carrier landing signal officer—standing on the hood of a jeep at the end of the strip, his arms held straight out in the "Roger" position, indicating that it was okay to land.

Mangrum slowly glided to a mere twenty feet, then went around again. He cut back on the throttle and his airplane smoothly dropped to the surface. Baldinus made his usual perfect landing. Intent upon his instruments, Hise nearly plowed into the high stand of trees too close to the end of the runway, pulled up reflexively, gave a last spurt of power, chopped back on the throttle, and plunked onto the ground in a cloud of dust.

While the Wildcats flew top cover, the remainder of the Dauntlesses landed. Major Mangrum followed a ground-control jeep to the dispersal area and jumped to the ground as soon as his plane's engine stopped. There, he had his hand wrung profusely by a tall, balding, elderly man—Archer Vandegrift—while thousands of thankful Marines shouted themselves hoarse and pounded one another black and blue in a thundering release of emotion.

PART VI

Baptism

15

After two weeks of learning their way around, Marines on Guadalcanal seemed to be gaining some expertise in the rugged regimen of patrolling necessary to stave off surprise assault. Small patrols, up to company strength, were the mainstay of the division's intelligence-gathering effort, and would remain so. After a time, however, the division intelligence section found reason to doubt some of the reports forwarded by subordinate headquarters.

Aged forty-four, and with twenty-five years in the Marine Corps, LtCol Bill Whaling was considered the division's foremost authority on patrolling. Long service in Central America and as canny a feel for woodsmanship as one man could possess qualified Whaling for the high esteem in which he was universally held. Where there was some doubt cast upon the validity of a particular report, Bill Whaling was asked to evaluate the data. He determined that several of the suspect patrols had never reached their objectives, that their reports were false.

Whaling reasoned that much of the problem was morale, arising from the way young Americans stranded on Guadalcanal felt about the probability of being supported if they led a patrol into real difficulty. This view, to Whaling, was invalid, for a rescue operation would inevitably be mounted by fellow Marines with a great deal at stake in an outcome that might otherwise diminish the odds in a larger fight.

Still, Whaling understood that such reactions were a logical extension of the division's experience on the island. He was confident from the outset that, as the troops and officers learned to better "read" the forest, they would begin drawing upon their own innate resources to an increasing degree, that they would eventually convince themselves that they could either stay out of trouble in the bush, or get out of it. Self-image and a sense of self-satisfaction prospered under such conditions.

The troops were slowly learning that the Japanese, though excellent fighters, were by no means invincible. On seeing the really shoddy workmanship of Japanese arms and equipment, many young Americans—who had good cause to complain about twenty-year-old ammunition and two bad meals a day—began to realize that they were far better off than their adversaries.

Though a very large percentage of Marines were of rural background, Americans of the day were fairly urbanized. Many were familiar with outdoors life, but very few were really comfortable with the rain forest, fearing it in a primal sort of way that defied mere logic. No amount of patient training could overcome the basic fears which were, in the end, at the root of the false or misleading patrol reports. Several officers were sent home in disgrace when caught playing at that dangerous game.

As one way to combat the problem, Bill Whaling was allowed to spend a large and growing portion of his time combing the ranks to find the special men necessary to lead or accompany patrols as scouts or advisors.

An important contribution to the rising level of confidence was made by one ordinary rifle platoon of 1st Marines.

The meeting at the CP of A Company, 1st Marines, was breaking up on the afternoon of August 11 when Capt Charlie Brush asked 2ndLt John Jachym, the 1st Platoon leader, to stay behind. Jachym had just volunteered to escort an engineer party slated to survey an alternative airfield site east of the Ilu River. Captain Brush revealed that the patrol, which would mount out in the morning, would be accompanied by LtCol Frank Goettge. However, word arrived the next morning that Goettge had changed his plans and would be accompanying a patrol to the vicinity of Point Cruz.

The forty-five-man rifle platoon, two Australian surveyors, and a Marine intelligence officer hiked east across Alligator Creek and set a rapid pace down the Government Track, past Beach Red, where Pioneers were still clearing supplies landed on August 7 and 8. During a rest break, a rifleman found an orange grove, and delightful greenish fruit was passed around.

A nose-count before dusk revealed that one Marine was missing. Two tracer rounds fired from the forest just after sunset spooked the Marines, so Lieutenant Jachym deployed them on the beach, backs to the sea, and sent his platoon sergeant and a rifleman into the surf to circle behind the source of the gunfire. Nothing was found. The straggler, who, it turned out, had fired the tracer rounds, found his way back to the platoon at dawn.

Next morning, August 13, the patrol trudged eastward to Tetere Village. Standing against a wind-whipped Stars-and-Stripes, surrounded by his flock, was a priest decked out in white shirt and shorts. While the survey team went to work, John Jachym introduced himself to Father Arthur Duhamel, a native of Massachusetts, who revealed that a Japanese machine-gun detachment was manning an outpost ten miles farther to the east.

Jachym and the surveyors decided to head back to Lunga. The surveying mission had been completed, and the news of a Japanese outpost in the vicinity of Tetere was important. Jachym asked Father Duhamel to accompany the patrol to Lunga, but the priest refused, explaining that neither he nor other missionaries in the area had ever been molested by the Japanese. (Father Duhamel and the remainder of his mission, including several nuns, were later butchered by Japanese soldiers.)

The patrol force-marched back to the Perimeter, arriving at nightfall on sore feet, completing its scheduled three-day job in only two. Jachym's report was the first indication that there were Japanese east of Beach Red.

C Company, 1st Pioneer Battalion, was preparing to move from Beach Red to the Lunga Perimeter on August 11 when sentries were confronted by a stocky black man with pink hair, cloth puttees wrapped above his bare splayed feet, and a large Union Jack pulled about his shoulders. Capt Halstead Ellison was called out to deal with the strange, haughty islander, whose responses to questions were in pidgin, a polyglot the Marines had not yet come to master. Ellison called division headquarters to ask that a British liaison officer be sent to help with the interrogation.

Capt Charles Widdy, who had managed the Lever Bros. plantation at Lunga, quickly learned that the islander was Jacob Vouza, a Guadalcanal native who had served for many years in the police patrol on neighboring Malaita. Vouza had retired as a sergeant major just before the war, then had volunteered his services to the British district officer at Aola Bay when the Japanese invested Tulagi. He had just completed a long hike from the hills behind Aola Bay to bring a message from his boss, Capt Martin Clemens, who wanted to bring his force of islanders to Lunga to serve as the core of a native scout force.

On instructions from division headquarters, Widdy handed Vouza a hastily scrawled message to take back to Clemens. The Pioneers were ordered to maintain their post on the Tenaru.

Martin Clemens left Vungana Village on the morning of August 14, and marched downhill through the rain forest toward the Lunga Perimeter with sixty constables, clerks, and bearers. The party was crossing a wide kunai-grass plain on the morning of August 15 when a bearer saw an airplane high overhead. Their optimism got the better of their caution, for they were nearing the safety of American lines, and everyone, including Clemens, dropped his meager bundle and frantically waved to catch the attention of the pilot. Food and ammunition packed in stout wicker baskets were parachuted by a Japanese pilot, no doubt searching for refugees from the Marine landings. Without yet realizing its source, Clemens sent scouts to retrieve the manna.

From his post on the Tenaru, Captain Ellison watched the parachutes blossom and deduced that the Japanese were dropping parachutists to go up against the Clemens party. He grabbed his rifle and helmet and jumped aboard his vehicle to lend a helping hand. Minutes later, the Pioneers were filling the scout car with the green wicker baskets and billowing parachutes.

As the Marines pulled out, a thoroughly shaken Martin Clemens emerged from his hiding place and reorganized his party for the final lap into Volonavua Village, the rendezvous designated in Capt Charles Widdy's letter.

The Marine sentry at Volonavua was shaken. Marching toward him was the strangest assortment of men he had ever seen— black men formed into two marching columns, locked in a precise parade-ground cadence. Those with weapons held them at slope arms. Leading the column was a scruffy white man followed by a scruffy black dog. The white man wore a slouch hat, ragged shirt and shorts, and a pair of shiny black oxford shoes that clearly did not fit well. The young sentry raised his rifle, but he did not fire; he had been told to expect visitors. The corporal-of-the-guard was called out to deal with the strange motley.

After eating and resting, the amiable Scots district officer revealed that he had been forced to proceed cautiously from Vungana because his scouts had reported seeing numerous Japanese in the area east of Beach Red. Someone suggested that the Japanese for whom the Clemens party had clearly been mistaken by the Japanese pilot that morning might be operating under the control of a higher authority, but no one really knew.

To cap everything, division headquarters had that very morning received word from RAdm Kelly Turner that a major Japanese attack might be launched against the Lunga Perimeter at any time.

Reports from three independent sources—Duhamel to Jachym, Clemens's scouts to Clemens, and the Naval Intelligence Division to Kelly Turner—were tied into one neat package.

But there *was* no large, organized Japanese force east of the Lunga on August 15. It arrived three days later.

Col Kiyano Ichiki commanded a force of 2,000 crack infantrymen from the 7th Infantry Division's 28th Infantry Regiment. It was as finely honed a unit of infantry as the Imperial Army boasted, its officers hand-picked by the force commander.

Ichiki Butai—Ichiki Unit—had been at Midway, ready to be hurled against the defended beaches. After the great naval air battle had been lost, *Ichiki Butai* went to Guam to train. There, Colonel Ichiki received orders to take his unit home to Japan. This news brought mingled feelings of elation and disappointment, for *Ichiki Butai* had no glorious victory tales to tell.

Ichiki Butai recovered its luck while homeward bound. When a "small" force of American Marines landed in the Eastern Solomons, *Ichiki Butai* was dropped off at Truk to await transportation to Rabaul and, ultimately, to Guadalcanal.

Responsibility for the land campaign in the Eastern Solomons passed on August 13 from the Imperial Navy, in the person of 11th Air Fleet Commander VAdm Nishizo Tsukahara, to the Imperial Army, in the person of 17th Army Commander LtGen Harukichi Hyakutake. The general was fifty-two, as was Archer Vandegrift, and had been in active service since 1909, as had Vandegrift. His 17th Army had been formed in July 1942, solely to oversee Imperial Army ground forces in New Guinea. Hyakutake did not relish the idea of pulling the Imperial Navy's chestnuts from the Solomons fire. It was his fervent wish to put the Eastern Solomons problem to rest long before at least two fresh infantry divisions earmarked for autumn operations in northern New Guinea began staging through Rabaul in late September. As might any army commander with divergent tasks to accomplish, Hyakutake could easily visualize having those fresh troops bled off to extinguish the brushfire in the Eastern Solomons at a time when he would prefer to be setting a forest fire to engulf New Guinea.

As he lacked forces for the Eastern Solomons work, Hyakutake had to rely upon higher headquarters to pass along *Ichiki Butai* as well as a veteran infantry brigade resting and refitting in the Palau Islands. The Imperial Navy offered a battalion-size *rikusentai* unit, which Hyakutake snapped up.

In Hyakutake's view, and in the view of his superiors at Imperial General Headquarters, New Guinea was by far the greater prize. An obedient soldier, Hyakutake would give the needed attention required to the sideshow in the Solomons, but the real effort, and the best troops, would be saved for New Guinea.

RAdm Raizo Tanaka, an up-and-coming amphibious specialist commanding a squadron of destroyer-transports based in Rabaul, looked at his charts of the Solomon Islands once again. His precise calculations had confirmed the obvious choice. If he was to be responsible for landing infantry anywhere along Guadalcanal's northern coast, and in secrecy, he would have to mount the operation directly through the Slot. The reasons were manifold: The Slot was the shortest route, less time would have to be spent in open waters, and friendly aircraft could provide support all the way to Guadalcanal.

There were flaws aplenty in the concept of landing troops at Guadalcanal. No matter how quickly the destroyer-transports could get there, much time would be lost ferrying soldiers and equipment to the beaches. During that time, the amphibious force would be vulnerable to naval or aerial forces operating in support of the American Lunga garrison.

Tanaka needed the dark hours to cover his approach and retirement as well as to cover the landing operation itself. If he entered the Slot just after sunset at any point southeast of Bougainville, he would have sufficient time and the cover he required, even if the Allies had aerial or naval support, which reconnaissance reports indicated they did not have.

Five hundred *rikusentai* were sent to Guadalcanal from Rabaul on the night of August 17 to test the admiral's concept. They landed near Kokumbona Village without incident. Some of them took part in defending the area against the three-company Marine sweep on August 19.

Nearly 1,000 members of *Ichiki Butai* boarded Tanaka's five destroyer-transports on the afternoon of August 18 to undertake the true inauguration of what Tanaka called "Rat" operations. Americans soon called Tanaka's service the Cactus Express, after Guadalcanal's code name. American newsmen, however, coined its enduring name: The Tokyo Express.

The Allies had nothing with which to counter the August 18 run, had no idea it had taken place. After the advance echelon of his unit had been landed at Taivu Point, well east of Alligator Creek, Colonel Ichiki began planning the attack he hoped to launch in a week against the 2,000 Americans that the 17th Army intelligence section said were defending the Lunga Perimeter. The balance of his force was expected in five days.

Before retiring to Rabaul on the morning of August 19, Admiral Tanaka gave his destroyer captains permission to bombard the Marine perimeter. One destroyer disrupted a landing operation near Kokumbona Village, but the fun was spoiled when a lone B-17 planted a stick of bombs across the fantail of destroyer *Hagikaze*. Chastened, Tanaka retired.

Capt Charlie Brush, commander of A Company, 1st Marines, summoned 2ndLt John Jachym to the company CP late on August 18 to ask how Jachym's troops were recuperating from the rigors of the forced march back from Tetere.

"The men are fine," Jachym reported.

"Good. You're going out again to get that machine-gun outfit you told us about. I'm going with you."

Jachym's reinforced platoon, about sixty Marines in all, left at 0700, August 19, and followed the same route it had taken earlier. There was great excitement when the tired Marines stopped to watch Maj Jim Edmundson bomb *Hagikaze*.

When Charlie Brush called for a lunch break, Jachym told him about the oranges his troops had found on their last hike through the area. Brush cheerfully agreed to trudge on for another half-hour to get the fresh fruit.

The Marines were only halfway to the oranges when they bumped head-on into a Japanese patrol. The astonished men of both sides who could bring their weapons to bear opened fire.

One of the Marines had the top of his head blown off as the American patrol recoiled to take stock. Charlie Brush coolly ordered John Jachym to dispatch a squad to the flank to envelop the opposition, which was milling about in a disorganized mass. Jachym put his platoon sergeant in charge of the enveloping increment and sent it packing into the trees to the right while he urged the main body of the platoon steadily forward.

The action heated up considerably as the Americans sought the upper hand in what, for all of them, was first combat. Jachym was standing in the surf with a borrowed submachine gun, trying to control its tendency to rise while being fired, when he was gently chided by a cool Charlie Brush for being a greater danger to coconuts than to Japanese. Jachym was struck by his own lack of fear, and he found himself amazed that the people he was trying to kill were also trying to kill him; he had never before considered the possibility.

Months of training paid off. The troops obeyed their leaders and went fearlessly about their work. A runner was shot and killed as he recklessly stormed across a tiny creek to get at the Japanese, and a third Marine died in the general melee.

The fight ended within thirty minutes, leaving three dead and three wounded Americans and a shocking thirty-one Japanese corpses on the beach and in the verge of the forest.

As his Marines collected souvenirs and documents, John Jachym noticed that there were too many map cases, swords, binoculars, and documents for so small a patrol. And there were far too many officers present. The corpses were too well dressed, and their helmets bore the red enamel star insignae of the Imperial

Army—not the anchor-and-chrysanthemum of the *rikusentai* who had been garrisoning the island on August 7.

Intent upon his mission, the combative Captain Brush wanted to collect the documents, proceed with the destruction of the machine-gun detachment east of Tetere, and *then* return to the Lunga Perimeter to file a report and turn in the documents. Lieutenant Jachym had three wounded Marines to think about, and he was loath to leave them behind when he was certain that at least a few Japanese had survived the fight; leaving a squad to defend them would further weaken the reinforced platoon. Brush relented. The three dead men were left in shallow graves with their boondockers sticking out to aid recovery efforts, and three stretchers were rigged from ponchos and cut saplings.

Though all hands, including the officers, took turns carrying the wounded up and down gullies, across streams, and through the loose sand of the beach, everyone was done in by the time the platoon met an ambulance that had been sent out in response to a radio report. It was well after 2100 when Brush and Jachym reported their findings and turned in their haul.

As the division intelligence linguists unravelled the history and mission of *Ichiki Butai*, those who had been following events east of the Perimeter were surprised to learn that the Japanese had been ashore for only a day when they ran into the Brush patrol. What struck them most was the graphic on a captured map; the defenses along Alligator Creek, which were quite weak at that moment, had been sketched in accurate detail.

Following deliberations with division headquarters in the morning, Col Clifton Cates ordered 2nd Battalion, 1st, to dig in at the mouth and along the west bank of Alligator Creek. A pair of 37mm antitank guns from 1st Special Weapons Battalion was sent to the sandspit, and the twelve 75mm pack howitzers of 3rd Battalion, 11th, were tightly registered upon the area. It was judged that the line would be capable of withstanding an assault by the following night, August 20.

Nothing much happened through the daylight hours of August 20. Second Battalion, 1st, put on a furious burst of entrenching activity along Alligator Creek and the beach west of the sandspit. Fifth Marines, which recalled the three-company Kokumbona assault force, went to full alert. All hands took time off to cheer the arrival of Marine fighters and dive-bombers in the late afternoon. Scuttlebutt—rumors—were rife. The blooded veterans of Jachym's platoon gave advice based upon their half-hour combat experience.

SgtMaj Jacob Vouza, Martin Clemens's chief scout, led a patrol of fellow islanders on the evening of August 20 to reconnoiter along the coast east of Alligator Creek. The small party rapidly made its way along the coastal trail until the lead scout detected movement ahead. While the main body moved ahead from a fork in the trail, Vouza dropped back to discard a tiny souvenir American flag he had foolishly carried with him. Before the scout could act, however, a Japanese patrol blundered up to him and held him stock still at rifle point.

A proud, volatile individualist, Vouza disdainfully glared at his captors and refused to answer any of their questions. He was bound to a tree and searched. The American flag was discovered, and several pointed questions were asked and ignored. Vouza was beaten, stabbed, and left to die.

The scout remained calm and immobile, awaiting the return of his strength. Then he gnawed through the straw ropes and made for the Perimeter, taking care to avoid the numerous Japanese who had by then infiltrated the area.

The Americans had no inkling as to Japanese movements, but they were fully alerted. Marines manning a listening post near the mouth of Alligator Creek detected an individual staggering toward the stream. Several men sent to investigate found the bleeding Vouza in a high pitch of agitation, incoherently babbling away. Capt Martin Clemens was called out from the division CP as Vouza was carried to the west bank.

Clemens, who furiously drove from the division CP, was shocked at the scout's condition; Vouza had been wickedly gashed across the throat and was copiously bleeding from several body wounds. He asked Clemens to take down his last will, which he proceeded to dictate at great and boring length. At once sensing that the scout would recover, while fearing that he would not, Clemens held one of Vouza's hands and furiously transcribed.

As Martin Clemens wrote, the first files of *Ichiki Butai* stealthily moved upon the listening posts guarding the sandspit at the mouth of Alligator Creek.

16

Pvt George Turzai, an eighteen-year-old serving with E
Company, 2nd Battalion, 1st, was sound asleep in his foxhole when the Japanese vanguard of scouts attacked or blundered into Marine listening posts near the mouth of Alligator
Creek, about 200 feet to the north. Turzai and his foxhole buddy, a
close-mouthed older private named Moser, were exhausted after
digging their three-foot-by-six-foot-by-three-foot-deep fighting
hole about twenty feet from the west bank of the sluggish creek.
Neither Turzai, who was asleep, nor Moser, who was on watch,
knew a thing about the Japanese advance until a piercing scream
wrenched them to full awareness.

Everything went dark and quiet for a moment. Then the sky
was lighted, clear as daylight, and rifle and machine-gun fire
erupted from within and in front of the strongpoint Marines had
built up at the sandspit at the creek's mouth. A flare landed on the
bank directly in front of Turzai's fighting hole. Private Moser, who
was older and smoother than George Turzai, urged his partner to
crawl into the open and douse the light. Turzai affixed his bayonet

to the end of his Springfield '03 rifle and crawled forward to knock the flare into the water. As Turzai lay still, recovering his night vision, he saw a sword-wielding Japanese officer leading nearly 200 soldiers from the stand of coconut palms on the east bank.

A machine gun momentarily stopped most of the Japanese, but at least six who were racing directly at Turzai kept coming. The young Marine snapped his rifle to his shoulder and put out the five rounds in its magazine as quickly as he could work the bolt and trigger. He had no idea if he was hitting anyone, and cared less, for two Japanese were upon him. Turzai stood up in time to parry a bayonet thrust; the Japanese steel clanged against the American rifle barrel, nearly severing Turzai's left pinky. The second Japanese, confused or overexcited, felled his countryman with a well-directed bayonet thrust, then his face splintered under the impact of Turzai's heavy rifle butt. George Turzai beat a hasty retreat.

Pvt Johnny Rivers was manning the .30-caliber water-cooled medium machine gun in the log-and-earth emplacement only yards from George Turzai's foxhole when the Japanese burst from the trees on the opposite bank. A promising welterweight whose reactions had been honed to perfection during a year's training as both a gunner and a boxer, Rivers snapped his weapon onto the first target he saw and squeezed the trigger. Japanese in the arc upon which the gun could bear scattered or dropped, but several who approached from the sides got to within arm's length of the burly boxer and had to be punched to submission. The very instant the gun cut loose again, a bullet from the far bank passed through the firing embrasure of Rivers's bunker and killed the young gunner. Dying fingers froze upon the trigger, and nearly 200 rounds were pumped into Japanese bodies before Rivers slowly toppled over. Cpl LeRoy Diamond resumed firing until he was wounded.

The Japanese appeared to the third man in the dugout, Pvt Al Schmid, as hysterical cattle charging into the water in massed waves. The bucking machine gun mowed down the lead rank, but Japanese to the rear pressed into view, and fell under Schmid's well-directed bursts. Within minutes, however, a hand grenade exploded at the embrasure and blinded the gunner.

Pvt Whitney Jacobs heard shouts for help from within the dugout, dashed through heavy gunfire, entered the emplacement, and hurriedly staunched the wounds of the bleeding gunners. Then he excitedly returned to his own fighting hole.

Schmid and Diamond took stock. The corporal could see, but his wounds prevented him from firing the gun. Al Schmid was blind, but otherwise able to direct the key weapon. Schmid resumed his position between the spread rear tripod legs, squeezed the release, and, with LeRoy Diamond issuing directions in his ear, lifted the trigger and resumed his job of killing and maiming Japanese soldiers.

Nine hundred Japanese in all, the half of *Ichiki Butai* that had been landed only days earlier, attacked LtCol Al Pollock's reinforced 2nd Battalion, 1st, at Alligator Creek. Most of them made for the sandspit, right into the teeth of a pair of 37mm antitank guns manned by members of B Battery, 1st Special Weapons Battalion. The gunners fired canisters into the packed Japanese, momentarily halting them as riflemen and machine gunners fought to recover from the shock of first contact.

The 2nd Battalion, 1st's ready reserve, was posted about 300 yards west of the sandspit. Second Lieutentant George Codrea's 1st Platoon, G Company, was formed into a column of squads and in motion toward the sound of the firing within minutes of the opening exchanges. The last 100 yards had to be traversed on hands-and-knees under an umbrella of Japanese machine-gun fire, which was overshooting the Marine defenses at the front.

As the platoon approached the embattled sandspit, Codrea formed his Marines into a skirmish line and ordered them forward. When the six-foot-four-inch officer was hit twice in the arm, he dropped back, prepared to sit the fight out. Then Cpl John Spillane's squad was stopped by a mortar round right beside him, and Codrea sensed the need for some drastic action. He yelled "Follow me!" and headed directly for the apex of the sandspit, a spot that would be known as Hell's Point.

Corporal Spillane was right at the lieutenant's heels when

three rounds penetrated his helmet in quick succession. Stunned but unscathed, he loosed a violent oath, grabbed the helmet from a dead man, and thrust himself back into the attack.

Pvt Harry Horsman was baptised in blood when a dying comrade, the platoon's first fatality, fell with a head wound and left brain matter all over Horsman, who dropped to the sand and opened fire on anything that even seemed like a target.

As eerie shadows played death games in the light of colored flares, bright yellow and pink tracers arched hypnotically across the silvery water and between the pitch-dark stands of stately palms. Two rifle companies, most of a weapons company, and two anti-tank guns withstood the repeated blows of nearly a battalion of superb Japanese infantry.

Jammed or balky weapons seriously affected the Marines' ability to defeat the attackers. Old ammunition and the excitement of the fight were at the root of the trouble. When Cpl John Shea's submachine gun jammed, he rolled over onto his back to fix the weapon. After a moment, he felt someone hacking at his left leg with a bayonet. Astounded, Shea pinned his assailant against the wall of his fighting hole with the injured leg and released the bolt of his weapon, pumping five rounds into the attacker. Pvt Joe Wadsworth, who was manning a foxhole right on Hell's Point, fired into the Japanese until his BAR jammed. He picked up a discarded '03 and fired it until several Japanese got within bayonet range. Wadsworth parried and jabbed for some moments, but was overwhelmed and left for dead. Pvt Ray Parker wriggled out across the sand, sheltered by a low dune, to a position from which he could place enfilade fire upon a Japanese machine gun emplaced on the east bank. His BAR jammed within minutes and he had to continue with a slow-firing '03 he happened to find. Cpl Dean Wilson's BAR jammed just as three Japanese loomed out of the darkness and charged his foxhole. He threw aside the useless automatic rifle and grabbed for the nearest weapon, a machete, with which he took a swipe at the nearest attacker. The man reached for his belly, but too late to hold back the torrent of intestines that cascaded over his feet. Wilson also hacked the other two Japanese to death.

Unable to fully assess the Japanese assault force, LtCol Al Pollock was loath to commit the remainder of his reserve company. He would hold with what he had for as long as he could, using whatever supporting arms higher headquarters could direct to his aid.

As *Ichiki Butai*'s first, major, effort subsided in the face of unexpectedly strong and determined opposition, Colonel Ichiki ordered his officers to reform the troops while his mortars and light 70mm battalion guns softened up the sandspit.

Maj Bob Luckey, commander of 1st Special Weapons Battalion, rushed to the 1st Marines CP as soon as the attack developed to coordinate 2nd Battalion, 1st's supporting arms. Messages from the line soon convinced Luckey that fire from 81mm mortars, and the 75mm pack howitzers of 3rd Battalion, 11th, were falling on friendly troops. Luckey was about to order corrections when an icy calm Col Clifton Cates told him, "That's an old trick, Bob. Keep right where you are." Cates was right; the Japanese were firing their mortars in such a way as to give the illusion that friendly fire was falling short.

The lull gave LtCol Al Pollock a few free moments to talk to observers on the line and dope out the best use for the uncommitted portions of G Company, which he had held back for forty-five of the longest minutes of his life. Following quick consultations with his company officers, sundry observers, and the regimental CP, Pollock ordered the bulk of G Company to attack the Japanese trying to force his line at the sandspit.

The G Company attack slowly forced the Japanese toward the east bank and seemed assured of success when several hundred Japanese waded into the breakers preparatory to attacking Pollock's flank. Marines met the threat with everything they could bring to bear. All twelve of 3rd Battalion, 11th's 75mm pack howitzers fired, as did a pair of halftrack-mounted 75mm antitank guns that had been rushed forward. A ghastly toll was exacted before the surviving attackers tumbled over one another in headlong flight for the coconut grove. The Japanese launched no other significant mass assaults, but hours of intense exchanges and local assaults ensued.

Pvt Andy Brodecki, of G Company, fired his BAR for so long that he had to stop to allow it to cool down. Still, Brodecki was in a good spot and felt he should do something to ward off the Japanese. He asked Marines in the rear to pass forward a weapon, and was amazed when someone handed him a Thompson submachine gun and ten clips of ammunition. That started an avalanche of weapons and ammunition from the rear to the hands of the men in the best firing positions. Brodecki and his foxhole buddies received dozens of hand grenades, which they blindly lobbed whenever they wanted to stir things up across the way.

The Marines kept the sandspit bathed in flarelight, but Japanese snipers in the coconut grove used the light to zero in on their most dangerous adversaries, the 37mm guncrews. One after another, the gunners were felled by the patient snipers.

The 37mm platoon leader, 2ndLt Jim McClanahan, took rounds in the arm, leg, and buttocks before becoming convinced that he could no longer take part in the exchange of gunfire. Nevertheless, he refused evacuation and went to work fixing numerous jammed automatic weapons. His second-in-command, GySgt Nelson Braitmeyer, launched a one-man assault against several Japanese who were setting up a machine gun which would be able to sweep the antitank-gun emplacements. He was shot to death. Pvt Elmer Fairchild, manning one of McClanahan's heavy .50-caliber air-cooled machine guns, had the three middle fingers of his right hand shot away. Nevertheless, and despite shrapnel wounds in both legs, Fairchild wrapped his bleeding right hand in his shirt and carried on.

It was getting on toward dawn when Pvt Harry Horsman, of G Company, noticed that the 37mm gun adjacent to his fighting hole had gone silent. He and another rifleman ventured over the low sandbag wall and found that no one was tending the weapon. The two riflemen decided to give it a try themselves. While the other Marine loaded, Horsman aimed and fired by trial and error. A corporal from their squad soon joined them but none of the three really knew what they were about. When Sgt James Hancock, their squad leader, came over the wall, the riflemen suddenly became a real guncrew, for Hancock had been an artilleryman before the war. The improvised guncrew fired the 37mm gun with adequate results until a tremendous explosion engulfed the gunpit and severely wounded Sergeant Hancock.

The first grey streaks of dawn were breaking over the palms on the east bank of Alligator Creek when Pvt George Turzai rose to meet several Japanese who had crossed the sluggish stream. Turzai quickly emptied a fresh five-round magazine and watched five of the Japanese falter and drop, not knowing or caring if he or other Marines had hit them. One of the attackers met Turzai's bayonet lunge with a well-timed parry. Turzai tried to jab the man head-on, but the Japanese soldier pressed his rifle's muzzle against the Marine's neck and squeezed off a round. The stunned Marine left his assailant to others and crawled and ran over mounded dead and wounded men in the hope of finding help. Marines from his platoon passed him in the opposite direction, charging a platoon of Japanese that had forced a penetration. Then Turzai passed out and fell to the ground, where he would be found and cared for hours later.

The sparring continued past sunrise. Neither side was quite able to muster a decisive blow, but while the Japanese had been spending their limited resources on futile efforts to unseat the Marine line, the Marines had been readying their reserves.

Together with LtCol Jerry Thomas, 1st Marine Division's operations officer, and LtCol L. B. Cresswell, commander of 1st Battalion, 1st, Col Clifton Cates had been planning a counterattack. Cresswell's companies had been shaken from their bivouacs in the dead of night and were ready to move at a moment's notice, as soon as the best direction for the attack had been ascertained from conflicting reports.

As the fighting around Hell's Point subsided, a company of 1st Engineer Battalion arrived to help Pollock's troops dig antitank obstacles and install a minefield across the sandspit, which was gruesomely littered with Japanese corpses. The line had been well wired-in the previous day, and that probably saved Pollock from being overrun. But for desultory sniper fire, the creekfront was fairly quiet. *Ichiki Butai* had drawn back to lick its wounds.

While 2nd Battalion, 1st, and its supports retrenched along Alligator Creek and Hell's Point, Cresswell's battalion was ordered to envelop what remained of Colonel Ichiki's command.

The battalion crossed Alligator Creek at 0700, well south of the coconut grove that sheltered *Ichiki Butai*. While posting most of the D Company weapons squads along the way to cut possible escape routes, Cresswell pushed his three rifle companies toward the enemy. After crossing Alligator Creek well south of the coast, the battalion angled slightly to the west to arrive behind the Japanese and pin them between the beach and Alligator Creek.

Second Lieutenant John Jachym spent hours listening to his platoon sergeant bitch and moan about the needless firing that had forced the battalion into the attack; the NCO was dead certain that no more than a half-dozen Japanese stragglers had set the whole shooting match off. Jachym was not so certain.

Pvt Andy Poliny, an A Company BAR-man, was in agony. His ammunition belt, loaded with 240 .30-caliber rounds, had chafed the skin from his hips; when Poliny dropped his pants during one rest break to check on the injury, he found that he was actually bleeding from the bruises.

Pvt Adam Sowa, a C Company 60mm mortar gunner who had enlisted within days of Pearl Harbor, had been spooked by the sudden onset of his battalion's movement in the night, but things seemed to be going as he had been told they would, so he found himself relaxing despite the fact that first combat was drawing closer. Sowa was happily surprised when he emerged from the rain forest and found the beach on his right; C Company, 1st, had gone completely around the Japanese in secrecy. He was particularly impressed at the way Marine artillery simply shut itself off the moment his battalion opened its attack.

The onset of the battle was sudden, startling. As 1stLt Nick

Stevenson's C Company broke out of the forest directly into the coconut grove, a Japanese infantry platoon holding tiny Block Four Village opened on the Marine point. L. B. Cresswell ordered Stevenson to back-pedal a bit to encircle the huts and isolate the Japanese rear guard from the Japanese main body, which was farther to the west. The eager C Company riflemen drew first blood when the Japanese guarding Block Four Village charged head-on. Deployed in a loose skirmish line, they blasted the attackers and turned the survivors toward the beach, where the Japanese ran into the surf. Marines standing on the beach casually squeezed off rounds at the bobbing heads.

Pvt Andy Poliny, of A Company, forgot his bruised and bleeding hips as soon as he stepped out of the rain forest and saw enemy soldiers turn to fight. Marines around Poliny cheered as they closed on the enemy, but their spirits were rapidly subdued when several of them were shot. The action turned positively grim when a dozen Japanese broke from cover to escape along the beach. They were felled, one after another, as Capt Charlie Brush coolly directed the fire of his rear guard.

The Japanese in the coconut grove were contained by 1400.

As Pvt Andy Poliny's squad was about to drag two Japanese corpses from a shallow depression in among the palms, an officer ordered them to bayonet the bodies. Two Marines moved to undertake the grisly order, but one of the Japanese rolled over and shot one of them in the face. Poliny levelled his BAR and fired on full automatic. A short time later, two Japanese emerged from the trees carrying a wounded comrade. The company gunnery sergeant bellowed, "Cut 'em down!" The two uninjured Japanese pulled hand grenades from their tunics, but died in a hail of gunfire before the missiles could be armed.

Though the Marines had clearly won the battle, the Japanese survivors were not about to concede defeat until they had had an opportunity to draw as much American blood as they could. That attitude meant a battle to the death.

The action was transformed into a hunt. Wily Japanese and

Marines used every conceivable trick to stalk one another. Bullets whisked through the coconut grove from every conceivable direction, tearing up trees and American and Japanese flesh.

Pvt Andy Poliny was caught flatfooted when a machine gun opened fire as his squad crossed a small open space. Poliny sank to his stomach in front of the nearest palm. While his heart pounded against his ribs, splinters rained down on his helmet as the Japanese gunner tried to chew the palm to pieces inches over his head. But the gunner never depressed the barrel of his weapon and Poliny was saved when other Marines destroyed the machine-gun nest.

The heat of the day took its toll. Exhausted, dehydrated Marines fell under the impact of the close air; experienced NCOs stalked among their young charges, admonishing them to conserve water by merely wetting their lips and mouths rather than gulping from their canteens. Some men obeyed, most did not.

When a large group of Japanese broke through the Marine skirmish line and headed down the east bank of Alligator Creek, a B Company platoon stood fast and obliterated the opposition. Another group ran headlong into a blocking position built around a machine-gun section and it, too, was ground to dust.

When the encirclement had been completed and tightened, several Marine F4F fighters lifted off the muddy runway that was the object of the bloodletting and mounted the first close-air-support operation of the campaign. They hit the main body of *Ichiki Butai* in the coconut grove and did a ghastly execution.

As the chaotic afternoon fight wore on, Archer Vandegrift despaired of completing the annihilation of *Ichiki Butai* by nightfall; he wanted the survivors killed or captured, every one of them. A platoon of six light tanks, which had been unable to accompany Cresswell's battalion overland in the morning, was ordered across the sandspit in the middle of the afternoon. One tank was wrecked by a Japanese soldier who died placing magnetic mines on its steel hull, and two others were damaged in accidents brought on by limited visibility and the broken ground. The last three were ordered by L. B. Cresswell to simply reconnoiter the Japanese position in the coconut grove.

When the three surviving light tanks had formed up on the sandspit, the tank-platoon leader, 1stLt Leo Case, ordered them to drive forward and direct point-blank fire at the Japanese. This was quite a bit more than L. B. Cresswell had envisioned, but the armored attack flushed numerous survivors into the guns of waiting riflemen.

The G Company commander noted that many of his young riflemen were wasting a great deal of ammunition as they fired excitedly across the sandspit at the Japanese stirred up by the tanks, so he ordered the tired troops to cease firing and called up GySgt Charlie Angus, an expert rifleman with years of competitive match shooting to his credit. Decked out in shooting jacket, glove, and campaign hat, Gunny Angus selected a suitable position with his spotter, another old salt who called out the windage while Angus coolly aimed and squeezed off the first round. It missed, as did the next, and the one after. Angus drew in a deep breath; this was the real thing, after all, and scores of impressionable young kids were looking on, not to mention several high-ranking officers. One by one, Angus's targets—heads bobbing in the surf—disappeared from sight.

The fight was pretty much over by 1700, fully sixteen hours after it began. The survivors of the advance detachment of *Ichiki Butai* fought like cornered animals, but were eradicated.

Capt Martin Clemens, who had seen SgtMaj Jacob Vouza safely to hospital, was sent to the killing ground to help collect documents from the dead. The young Scotsman was revolted by the crumpled, bleeding corpses, many half-buried by gritty volcanic sand that had been shifted by the tides. He could not fail to notice that his islanders were positively pleased with the carnage; it was something they clearly understood better than he.

LtCol L. B. Cresswell's Marines were fed a light meal late in the day. Pvt Adam Sowa wolfed down all the water he could fit in along with, of all things, a bag of captured cookies. Seventeen-year-old Pvt Joe Seifts, of C Company, drew a captured can of asparagus and some cookies, but could not get them down as his mind replayed the sudden death of another young Marine; the boy, whose lips had gone blue in a waxy white face, had been placed in a stretcher just before uttering his last words: "I'm hungry." Though Seifts knew he should eat, he handed his food to a startled neighbor and sat back to regain his composure.

Across the way from Sowa and Seifts, Marines from E and G companies, 1st, and B Battery, 1st Special Weapons Battalion, were sorting themselves out, viewing the remains of dead comrades, and working through their grief and shock.

Pvt Harry Horsman astonished himself by bagging a live Japanese. Since Horsman had taken the man, he was given the honor of escorting him to the rear aboard a truck. The prisoner clearly wanted to die, and he signed Horsman to do him in. The young Marine did no such thing mainly because he felt the Japanese might be a source of valuable information. What really amazed Private Horsman during the brief ride was that he felt absolutely no hatred toward the pathetically downcast prisoner. By the time Private Horsman returned to the sandspit, the shooting had entirely stopped and earth movers were scraping out a common grave for the putrefying Japanese bodies.

Considerable food, equipment, weapons, ammunition, and data were scavenged from the 871 dead and 15 captured members of *Ichiki Butai*. The cost was 34 dead and 75 wounded Americans.

Late that evening, Col Kiyano Ichiki buried his unit's colors in the coconut grove, drew a ceremonial dagger, and disemboweled himself in the soft sand beside Lengo Channel.

17

As LtCol Al Pollock's 2nd Battalion, 1st, battled snipers near the sandspit and as LtCol L. B. Cresswell's fresh companies waded into the coconut grove, Coastwatcher Jack Read warned that a Japanese bomber strike was on the way down the Slot. Lt Hugh MacKenzie, the Coastwatcher liaison officer at Lunga, patched into the Marine communications net, known as Texas Switch, and for the first time was able to pass the news to American aviators who could rise to the challenge.

Capt John Smith scrambled a division of four of his F4F Wildcat fighters. Smith was in the lead Wildcat with a green second lieutenant on his wing; TSgt Johnnie Lindley was right behind with another green kid on his wing. None had ever flown in combat.

The Americans were over Savo, climbing past 14,000 feet, when they spotted six Zeros 500 feet higher and on a reciprocal course. Smith opened fire head-on at the leading Zero as the two aircraft roared toward each other at a combined speed well in excess of 600 miles per hour. The Japanese pilot flinched first. He pulled up, exposing his belly to Smith's four .50-caliber machine guns, and then fell away as the Marine squadron leader was engaged by a pair of Zeros on his tail. The Wildcat's greater weight and superior diving speed saved Smith, who swooped beneath friendly anti-aircraft fire. The two lieutenants joined up, but Lindley was missing. Smith and the lieutenants climbed back over Savo, where their fighters were liberally shot up, then headed home. Meantime, Lindley, who was VMF-223's only enlisted pilot, walked away from his damaged Wildcat, which piled up on the muddy runway when he attempted a powerless landing. John Smith's presumed kill was later confirmed, the first by a Cactus fighter.

The landing of the advance echelons of *Ichiki Butai* and Yoko-suka 5th Special Naval Landing Force were preliminary moves in Operation KA, a straightforward infantry operation aimed at re-capturing the Lunga airfield. On receiving news of the disastrous demise of Colonel Ichiki's advance force, Rabaul opted to send a stronger force to take stronger measures. Leading the way would be rear echelons of *Ichiki Butai* and Yokosuka 5th Special Naval Land-ing Force, which would be carried by transports under the com-mand of RAdm Raizo Tanaka, who had already overseen the successful landing of men and material on either side of the Lunga Perimeter.

Things got quickly out of hand as Combined Fleet staffers at Truk added more and more parts to the simple plan. A powerful bombardment force would be dispatched to hold down the Amer-ican aircraft at Henderson Field, and carrier- and land-based air-craft would assist. When Adm Isoroku Yamamoto mentioned that he wanted to draw out the American fleet to expose the American carriers to attack, powerful elements of the Combined Fleet, in-cluding three carriers, were ordered out of Truk in the hope of meeting VAdm Frank Jack Fletcher's battle force. Eleventh Air Fleet would attack Henderson Field from Rabaul, and 8th Fleet would cover Tanaka's transports and bombard the American hold-ings. KA became a complex, massive blow aimed at terminating the American presence in the Eastern Solomons.

Aerial reconnaissance, sightings by Coastwatchers and radio intercepts gave early indications that a major action was in the offing. Three fleet carriers—*Enterprise*, *Saratoga*, and *Wasp*—were called to action, which was just what the Japanese wanted.

At dawn on August 23, Tanaka's transports steamed southward into open seas. All of the ships were old and cumbersome, obliging Tanaka to proceed at the speed of the slowest, a nerve-wracking eight-and-one-half knots. He was the bait.

A surge of excitement passed through the American carrier force when news got around that a shore-based patrol bomber had reported sighting a pair of Japanese cruisers and three destroyers at 0900 on August 23. For once eager to join battle, VAdm Frank Jack Fletcher ordered *Saratoga* to strike. Thirty-one SBD dive-bombers and six TBF torpedo-bombers were launched at 1445 from a position near the Stewart Islands. Henderson Field got a twenty-three-plane strike airborne at 1615.

The effort was a bust. Japanese lookouts saw the American reconnaissance bomber, so their ships had reversed course. The American warplanes flew over empty ocean until their fuel began running short, then headed to Henderson Field for the night.

As the main Japanese and American battle forces faced off near the Stewart Islands, well to the north of Guadalcanal, a diversionary force built around light carrier *Ryujo* broke away from the main battle force before dawn, August 24, and headed straight for Guadalcanal at high speed. Once in range, *Ryujo*'s fighters and bombers were to strike Henderson Field.

Second Lieutenant Mel Freeman had been landed at Lunga Point in a rubber boat launched from an American destroyer-transport on the night of August 21. No experience could have better illustrated the desperate plight of his nation to the twenty-four-year-old Wharton School graduate. The junior member of Efate-based VMF-212, Freeman had been among the first Marine fighter pilots to reach a combat area in the Pacific. His opportunity to meet the Japanese came in response to RAdm Slew McCain's vow to bolster VMF-223 with some experienced fighter pilots. However, neither Freeman nor the other four VMF-212 airmen who arrived with him were combat veterans.

Mel Freeman's chance came at about 1400 hours, August 24, when VMF-223's ready fighters were scrambled to meet an incoming raid of Betty bombers from Rabaul. Leading the American response was Capt Marion Carl, a handsome Midway survivor considered one of the most aggressive fighter pilots in the Marine Corps. Still the junior man, Mel Freeman was the last pilot to get airborne.

It was by then a given that the slow-climbing Wildcats had to be at optimum altitude and in optimum position before they could dare engage Zero-escorted bombers, so Captain Carl opted to lead his Wildcats away from the Betty strike to give them more time to gain the required altitude. By the time the American fighters spotted the Bettys, the Japanese had already released their bombs and were turning northward with their noses down to pick up speed. At the same time, however, the Americans picked up the inbound *Ryujo* strike of nine bomb-equipped Kate torpedo bombers and fifteen Zero fighters as it approached Savo from east of Malaita at a mere 9,000 feet.

Carl held his eager pilots in check for long moments in an effort to gain just that much more of a height advantage over the Bettys. The Japanese were to the left and, though Carl and the other leaders were well above them, Mel Freeman was just about at the same level and traveling in the same direction as the quarry. At 1425, Carl suddenly peeled out of formation, executed a magnificent overhead pass, and smoked at least one of the graceful twin-engine bombers.

The American formation dissolved as all hands turned into the Japanese bombers. Mel Freeman strove mightily to line up his reflector gunsight on a Betty but all he could manage was a forty-five-degree deflection shot. He saw his bullets passing right ahead of the bomber's right propeller, then felt elation as thin wisps of smoke appeared from beneath the engine cowling. He passed beneath the target and peeled off in an effort to gain speed for another attack. However, he spotted a Kate way below and decided that his dive would provide adequate momentum for catching up; the smoking Betty was forgotten.

The heavy Wildcat flew through machine-gun fire put out by the Kate's rear gunner as Freeman's thumb nudged the gun-button knob on his joystick. The four .50-caliber wing guns roared to life again and, in an instant, the Wildcat passed right over the long greenhouse canopy of the diving Kate. There, Freeman saw the dead or wounded gunner flapping in the slipstream and awed expressions upon the upturned faces of the bombardier and pilot.

Fearful that the Kate's pilot would bring his nonexistent forward-firing guns to bear, Freeman pulled around to the left and found himself looking right down the nose of a Zero fighter. The two flew straight at each other, exchanging gunfire for an eternity of seconds before the Japanese pilot pulled up and away.

No sooner had Freeman gotten clear than he saw a Wildcat spin down from above and plow into the water. That was Freeman's biggest shock of the day, for the Grumman's dead pilot was probably a longtime roommate, 2ndLt Red Taylor, a former Berkeley football player who had accompanied Freeman to Efate and Guadalcanal.

In all, the Americans claimed twenty kills, though only six Zeros and ten bombers, at most, failed to return. Marion Carl was high scorer, with a pair of Bettys and a Zero to his credit. Three Wildcats were downed and two Marine pilots were lost.

While *Ryujo's* small air group was challenging Cactus Air over Guadalcanal, *Ryujo* herself was sunk by *Saratoga's* Air Group 3. And while *Ryujo* was being hit, fleet carriers *Shokaku* and *Zuikaku*—the two surviving Pearl Harbor attackers—traded strikes with *Enterprise*. The Battle of the Eastern Solomons—the third carrier-versus-carrier battle in history—resulted in the destruction of *Ryujo*, moderate damage to *Enterprise* and a Japanese seaplane tender, and the loss of many Japanese aircrews.

The main battle forces withdrew during the night.

The only benefit gleaned by Cactus Air from the carrier exchanges was the marooning of eleven *Enterprise* dive-bombers at Henderson Field. Sent out on an evening strike, the SBDs, led by Lt Turner Caldwell and logged as Flight 300, had to land at Henderson Field when their fuel ran low.

The job of getting Tanaka's transports fell to the weak Cactus Air establishment. His own support having fled, Tanaka sent his five covering destroyers ahead to bombard Henderson Field in order to keep the American dive-bombers down. As the Japanese warships were coming on station at 0230, August 25, Maj Dick Mangrum, commander of VMSB-232, led two other SBDs aloft in an effort to get at them. However, all three Marine aircraft missed. A second three-plane strike, mounted at 0400, found the Japanese retiring past Savo, but no hit was scored. One of the precious SBDs became lost and ditched off Malaita.

Dick Mangrum responded to a PBY sighting report at 0600 by leading four Marine SBDs, three of Turner Caldwell's Flight 300 SBDs, and four Wildcats against Tanaka's force of four old destroyers, three slow transports, and light cruiser *Jintsu*.

Hours of boring flight ensued. Second Lieutenant Hank Hise, flying off Mangrum's right wing, was getting a stiff neck from constant craning to watch for trouble and keep station on the flight leader. Endless columns of puffy white clouds could be seen marching across the vast emptiness of sea and green-hued islands. The short-legged Wildcats had long since turned for home. Suddenly, at 0835, as Hise looked off to port from an altitude of 12,000 feet, he spotted three columns of ships. The strain of long hours of flying vanished.

Mangrum executed a classic dive-bombing attack, approaching from east to west, ninety-degrees to the direction in which the ships were traveling. Then he waggled his wings, broke the flight off to the left, and pitched over his right wingman, 2ndLt Larry Baldinus. When Baldinus went, Hise kicked his airplane up and over, dropped flaps, eased back on the throttle, and rolled on the left trim tab to overcome the lack of torque. As the young Texan swung on his seat harness, fighting to keep down the bile rising in his throat, he instinctively looked around for the biggest ship; he was determined to go out in a blaze of glory.

Baldinus and Hise plummeted toward *Jintsu*. It was over within seconds. Hise reached his release point, came back on the stick, and added power. All emotions were overcome by the pull of gravity on the blood supply to his brain. An instantaneous grey mind-numb vaporized. Unable to bear missing the result of his first combat dive, Hise broke a cardinal rule and, while closing his dive flaps, eased off to the right to look back at the target. The anticipated ball of fire did not emerge, but Hise did see his bomb explode in the water beside *Jintsu*'s hull. He advanced his throttle to full power, got his flaps all the way up, and joined on Baldinus, thankful to be with someone he was certain would know the way home. The two were surprised to see Mangrum execute a second dive, which did not score; the major's bomb had not released on his first dive, so he had hauled it back up to 10,000 feet and gamely tried again.

Baldinus's 500-lb bomb, which had been planted between *Jintsu*'s forward gun mounts, knocked RAdm Raizo Tanaka unconscious.

Lt Turner Caldwell led his two wingmen—Ens J. T. Barker and Ens Chris Fink—after *Kinryu Maru*. Fink, who was the last man in the Navy formation, saw Caldwell's 500-lb bomb miss the target, but he did not have time to track Barker's 500-lb bomb—which also missed—because he quickly arrived at his own release point. As Fink was pulling out, he heard his rearseatman shouting over the intercom that his bomb had hit the transport dead amidships. Fink quickly glanced back and saw smoke rising and debris settling. He also saw that *Jintsu* was afire.

All seven American dive-bombers made a running rendezvous as they headed south for home. As soon as the Navy Dauntlesses were clear of the action, Caldwell signalled his wingmen to check their fuel situation. Fink had forty gallons remaining, while Caldwell and Barker each had only twenty-five gallons aboard. All three—and all the Marine airmen—safely reached Henderson Field and went right to work refueling their airplanes, a job that consisted of straining aviation gasoline from fifty-five-gallon drums through chamois skin into twelve-quart buckets that were then emptied into fuel tanks.

As soon as the fueling was completed, all the Navy SBDs were ordered out to find Tanaka once again. All of the Navy pilots except Ens Chris Fink were able to get airborne.

Meanwhile, as soon as RAdm Raizo Tanaka came to after narrowly escaping death in the vortex of 2ndLt Larry Baldinus's 500-lb bomb, he transferred his flag to one of the destroyers and sent the damaged *Jintsu* back toward Truk under her own power. He was going on!

Kinryu Maru was definitely sinking. A destroyer came alongside to begin taking off the crew and the naval infantrymen when eight U.S. Army Air Forces B-17s from 11th Heavy Bombardment Group arrived from their base at Espiritu Santo. The destroyer captain felt safe where he was; vertical bombing was known by everyone to be highly inaccurate. The man was blown into the water when five of forty-four 500-lb bombs dropped by the heavy bombers blanketed his ship, which immediately sank at 1015. The remaining destroyers stopped at once to pick up survivors. Tough, resolute Raizo Tanaka bore on, but was soon recalled by Rabaul, well short of his goal.

The second Cactus air strike—ten Flight 300 Dauntlesses under Lt Turner Caldwell—found just one Japanese destroyer about 150 miles northwest of Henderson Field. Six of the Dauntless pilots were ordered to attack; the rest were held in reserve pending the discovery of the Japanese main force.

Ens Hal Buell, a veteran of the Coral Sea and Midway battles, was the third man in the string. He saw the first two bombs miss by a fair margin, and he saw a good deal of antiaircraft fire rising to meet him. The lithe destroyer was well into a hard starboard turn when Buell released his 500-lb bomb at what he felt was just the right instant. However, his rearseatman reported only a near miss to starboard.

The fourth and fifth pilots dropped their bombs close toward the destroyer's port side, and the last man was not even close. The destroyer appeared to have been amply damaged.

After tooling around for a while, using up precious fuel, the Navy pilots returned to Henderson Field.

PART VII

Seesaw

18

Henderson Field was a mess. It had been jury-rigged, improvised. Systems of construction that can be characterized, at best, as "novel" had been dreamed up by men who had little choice in the undertaking, men whose stake in the outcome was total. Conditions, however, were improving by fits and starts, and not a few backward steps.

In the beginning, when a bomb blast blew out so-and-so many cubic yards of runway, engineers, groundcrewmen, and CUBs ran out to the crater and filled it in with dirt, carefully premeasured, which had been loaded into trucks standing on the verges of the open area. When the fill had been dumped, all hands tediously hand-tamped it to create a hard, even surface for the aircraft, which might be circling overhead, using precious fuel. The situation vastly improved with the arrival of several pneumatic tampers. Soon, it took only thirty minutes to fill a crater left by a 500-kg bomb!

Beginning with flashlights, night landings were eventually helped along by a jury-rigged system of captured lamps.

Even without abuse from the Japanese, the ground crews had a rough time of it. The earliest method for fueling aircraft involved strapping a fifty-five-gallon fuel drum to the rafters of the uncompleted Japanese hangar, then pumping by hand. When fueler trucks were landed, the fuel still had to be hand-pumped.

The weather was a constant irritant. It rained daily, often several times daily. Each storm turned the runway and its approaches into a glutinous quagmire. Aircraft built to land on concrete runways and wooden carrier decks placed enormous stress on their wheels, which had a disturbing propensity for sticking while inertia kept the airplane's fuselage moving. Depending upon speed and the weight of the aircraft, and the viscosity of the mud, any given airplane might flip over, swerve, ground loop, drop one or both front undercarriage assemblies, lose a wheel, come to a safe stop, or become airborne.

Most of the aircraft were fairly new upon arrival at Henderson Field, but they could not be adequately maintained. The novel methods employed by ground crews at Henderson Field kept at least a minimal number of aircraft flyable.

As air raids became stronger and more frequent, early warning became a greater problem. Lacking all but the crudest radars, Cactus Air Ops was forced to rely almost exclusively upon Coastwatcher reports. When the Coastwatchers missed a strike or had radio problems, reliance fell to an almost worthless radar set whose "picture" was almost entirely obscured by intervening mountains and high stands of trees.

A second line of defense was 3rd Defense Battalion's 90mm antiaircraft batteries, one of which was outfitted with outmoded, unreliable radar, originally designed to guide searchlights. The other batteries, including automatic weapons, lacked even those crude sets, so had to be trained by sight alone. The impressive record of 3rd Defense Battalion can be attributed only to its very high standard of training.

Aggressive offensive aerial operations were, of necessity, for the future. An aggressive *defensive* effort had been waged from the moment Capt John Smith led VMF-223 to Henderson Field. The

Japanese could not be driven off, Smith knew, but they could be made to pay a very heavy toll.

John Lucien Smith, who would soon be promoted to major, was a hard-driving disciplinarian, moody and sarcastic. It was fortunate, for his inexperienced young pilots required a sure hand if they were to survive, and the taciturn Oklahoman had that, in the air and on the ground. Most important, Smith was a superb fighter tactician, a confident innovator who would painstakingly train his men to survive against the otherwise unbeatable Zero. Smith had entered the Marine Corps in 1937 as an artilleryman and had first flown dive-bombers. In fact, he did not get into fighters until just before the war started. He was an extremely intelligent man, able to adapt quickly.

The slightly obsolescent Grumman F4F-3 Wildcat Smith flew was something of a miracle fighter, not because of any inherent superiority, but because it was not worse. It had been designed as a fixed-gear biplane, but had been hastily converted *after* its acceptance by the Navy into a sturdy mid-wing monoplane with retractable landing gear. It was a characteristic of the stubby, knock-kneed fighter that it wobbled in the minute or so after take-off as the pilot cranked up the gear with one hand while holding his joystick with the other. It was said, also, that the Wildcat was a forgiving aircraft—just right for the eager but woefully inexperienced young hotshots who were to defend Guadalcanal in the weeks and months to come.

Two hours' warning from the Coastwatchers in the Northern Solomons was barely enough for the heavy, slow-climbing Wildcats to be bullied up to sufficient altitude from which to attack Japanese bomber formations. The Zero was a fast climber and highly maneuverable, and it outclassed the F4F in all but two vital categories: diving speed and ability to take punishment. These differing characteristics dictated the tactics.

It was essential for the Marine fighters to attack Zeros or Zero-escorted bombers from above and dive through the Japanese formation before the Zeros could follow. The Zero was the better

airplane, and Zero pilots were the better airmen, so the Grumman's higher diving speed was often all that kept Smith's youngsters from a dunking or death.

The other advantage enjoyed by the Marine airmen was that they usually operated over or close to home. While maintenance facilities were crude, marginal aircraft could often be nursed home and made airworthy again; Japanese cripples, and their valuable crews, were often lost. Though many American aircraft were lost, a high percentage of downed pilots were recovered after bailing out over or near Henderson Field or in areas where islanders were still loyal to the Crown. John Smith and a large number of his original pilots would have the opportunity to walk or swim home. This was an important morale factor in an effort that seemed to hold no end of frustrations for the aircrews.

If VMF-223 was a strange amalgam of inexperienced young pilots and inadequate aircraft, there is no way to accurately describe the Army Air Forces' 67th Pursuit Squadron. Formed in late 1940, 67th Pursuit had started the war providing cadres for new squadrons in the massively expanding Air Corps. By the time the squadron was shipped to the Pacific in February 1942, only three of its original complement were still flying with the unit. One, the squadron's first and only commanding officer, was Capt Dale Brannon.

Sixty-seventh Pursuit, eked out to full strength by some of the greenest pilots the Army had on its rolls, had disembarked at Noumea on March 15, 1942. Its complement of brand-new fighters was brought to the squadron's mountain airfield in crates, carried by truck over a twisting, narrow trail. When the eager mechanics uncrated the prefabricated aircraft, they were astounded to find forty-five P-400 and two P-39 fighters, and not one of the P-40 fighters with which the squadron was to have been equipped. The hybrid P-400s, a Lend-Lease version of the P-39, were to have gone to the British in North Africa, but the confusion and exigencies of the new war had seen them diverted to the Pacific. Not one of the airmen had ever flown a P-400, and only two, including Dale Bran-

non, had checked out in P-39s. And that was not all. There were no assembly instructions enclosed with the parts of fighters that arrived in New Caledonia, so the ground crews had to sort of piece the aircraft together. And they were weird planes, with a powerful engine *behind* the cockpit and a 20mm cannon in the nose. Toggle switches had been installed for British airmen in place of the levers with which American pilots were accustomed. Though Brannon's pilots craved better, familiar aircraft, they were willing to fight with anything, as long as they could fight.

The opportunity arrived on August 22, when Dale Brannon selected four other pilots for a trail-blazing flight to Henderson Field. No fighter had yet flown from Efate to Guadalcanal, mainly because of the distance. Rare belly tanks were fitted to the five long-nosed P-400s, which were shepherded by an 11th Bombardment Group B-17, which had the required navigational gear the tiny fighters lacked. The flight was uneventful. All five P-400s set down smartly and taxied to the verges of Henderson Field, where they were met by several reserve pilots and a ground team who had arrived the day before aboard a Navy transport that had confounded Japanese efforts to prevent reinforcement by sea.

Sixty-seventh Pursuit's debut came on August 24, a clear, hot sunny afternoon on which Kates from *Ryujo* and Bettys from Rabaul struck Henderson Field. Dale Brannon and his regular wingman, 2ndLt D. H. Fincher, saw the black flag (warning that an air raid was imminent) go up beside the radar van and ran for their fighters. Both airmen could already hear the drone of aircraft engines overhead as they started their engines and turned onto the taxiway behind Capt Marion Carl's flight of Marine F4Fs. Bombs began hitting the field as the two Army pilots flew through the dust kicked up by the Wildcats, then evaded Zeros sent in to strafe the field.

Both P-400s missed the main action, but not for lack of trying. Though they had both flown P-400s for months, neither Brannon nor Fincher had yet learned that they had very serious altitude limitations. Both knew that the installed British high-pressure oxygen system was unserviceable by American equipment deployed in the

Pacific, but neither realized that they would be kept from high-altitude combat. The P-400s got to 16,000 feet, but both pilots became woozy and had to drop beneath 14,000 feet to regain their senses. A lone Zero, no doubt attracted by the strange new American fighter, flew into range. Brannon and Fincher turned in and each let fly with each fighter's four wing-mounted .30-caliber machine guns and single nose-mounted 20mm cannon. The Zero disintegrated.

More P-400s were expected within the week, but it was beginning to dawn on the Cactus Air establishment that they might be of little value as defensive interceptors.

The deep inadequacies of the Cactus ground-support effort were graphically illustrated on August 25 when the CUBs, charged with caring for planes returning from morning missions, could not rearm the fighters quickly enough to intercept a strike of twenty-one Bettys as it wheeled in over Henderson Field at 1155. Forty bombs fell in a tight pattern around the Pagoda, the captured building that served as both control tower and air operations (Air Ops) center. All but three of the American aircraft managed to get airborne, and damage to the runway was minimal, but the inability to counter the strike was unsettling and infuriating.

It was at this juncture that MGen Archer Vandegrift took a good look at the hand he had been dealt. It was evident that any sort of respite brought on by the shock of the Solomons landings had ended; those twenty-one Bettys comprised the largest single strike since August 9, so it was evident that 11th Air Fleet was being reinforced. On the other hand, John Smith's original nineteen Marine fighters had been whittled down to eleven—three shot down, one crash-landed, one destroyed in a test flight, and three grounded for want of spare parts. Three of Dick Mangrum's twelve SBDs were also out of operation—one lost in a water landing and two awaiting spare parts. Lt Turner Caldwell had eleven Navy SBDs on the island, but no one knew for how long. And the five P-400s were beginning to look as though they might be useless in defensive operations. Stocks of ammunition, aviation gasoline, oxygen bottles, oils and other lubricants, bombs, and spare parts were rapidly dwindling. In a message to Vice Admiral Ghormley that afternoon, Vandegrift warned that he would be out of aircraft in a short time unless replacements and supplies were sent.

Around noon on August 26, while the SBDs and P-400s scrambled eastward out of range, John Smith got an even dozen Wildcats into position to intercept a strike of sixteen Bettys as they swept down over New Georgia. This was to be the first interception by most of VMF-223's rookies, and they nearly blew it. Smith and his exec, Capt Rivers Morrell, and Capt Marion Carl teamed with two visiting VMF-212 airmen to score three confirmed kills and a great deal of damage. Smith's lieutenants, however, merely shot off a lot of ammunition. One rookie was shot down and killed. Worse, the Bettys plastered Henderson Field and flamed 2,000 gallons of precious aviation gasoline.

Next day, August 27, fourteen new P-400s arrived, and an Efate-based B-17 ferried in three fresh Marine pilots to replace three VMF-212 pilots rotated back to the rear the day before. The Japanese August 28 air strike aborted in bad weather.

At 1700, August 28, a pair of SBDs piloted by 1stLt Danny Iverson and 2ndLt Hank Hise were tooling along on evening patrol over the Russell Islands at 130 knots when Hise spotted four destroyers silhouetted against the setting sun only seventy miles from Cape Esperance. Because they lacked radios, Hise thought Iverson might have failed to see the targets. But Iverson had seen them; he just assumed they were Americans. To Hise's chagrin, the flight leader dropped down so his gunner could flash a recognition signal with his Aldis lantern. The Japanese blinked backed with their automatic-weapons batteries. Iverson pulled up, with Hise following, to 7,000 feet, where they topped a thin layer of clouds. Without warning, Iverson pitched through a hole in the clouds. Startled, Hise armed his 500-lb bomb and followed. The Japanese were by then maneuvering every which way. Hise selected a target running straight across his flight path and continued to bore in, scared to death as he noted how many guns were firing at him. He cut his bomb loose at 2,500 feet, certain he had missed by a half-mile. Unable to find Iverson, Hise headed home, where he taxied straight up to the Pagoda to report his find. Soon, Iverson arrived safely home with his bomb to tell how he had been unable to get lined up on either of two dives.

Hise's report resulted in a late scramble by eleven Dauntlesses. Lt Turner Caldwell bored through the failing light to score a direct hit on one destroyer while Ens Chris Fink, who had hit *Kinryu Maru* three days before, planted a 1,000-lb bomb directly amidships on destroyer *Asagiri*, which exploded and sank. A third destroyer was damaged by near misses. A Marine SBD and its crew were lost strafing the last destroyer.

Transport *William Ward Burroughs* anchored off Kukum early on August 29 and disembarked the ground crews of VMF-223 and VMSB-232, the most welcome reinforcement to date. But before any of the transport's precious cargo could be ferried to the beach, she had to up anchor and run for the safety of the Tulagi anchorage. A big air strike was on the way.

John Smith led ten Wildcats and fourteen P-400s aloft, but was unable to intercept the eighteen Zero-escorted Bettys until after they had dropped their bombs from 17,000 feet. Four bombers and four Zeros were claimed by the Marines at the cost of one F4F so badly shot up that it had to be cannibalized for spare parts. The P-400s could not operate over 14,000 feet, so took no part in the fight. Two F4Fs on the ground were wrecked by bombs, and the returning fighters had to avoid the numerous bushes repair crews set out on the runway to mark bomb craters. When the smoke settled, it was noted that *Burroughs* was aground in the Tulagi anchorage, stuck fast, a sitting duck with her valuable cargo of aircraft supplies.

Five of seven Japanese destroyers making for Taivu Point, east of Lunga, were spotted during the aerial fighting of the late afternoon, but, though all available dive-bombers were launched just after midnight, the warships were not found. Fortunately, the Japanese commander was so unnerved by the sound of aircraft engines that he dropped a force of Imperial Army soldiers at Taivu Point and ran for home without bombarding the Lunga Perimeter or Henderson Field, or attacking the stranded transport off Tulagi. (He was summarily relieved when a boiling mad Admiral Tanaka found that he had disobeyed standing orders to attack American surface vessels wherever and whenever found.)

At 0930, August 30, Paul Mason, on Bougainville, reported a large formation of Japanese single-engine aircraft heading to Guadalcanal. These were eighteen Zero fighters sent to the tiny Buka reserve strip the previous day from carriers *Shokaku* and *Zuikaku*; their job was to destroy the American fighters any way they could. However, they were flying too high for positive identification from the ground, so observers assumed they were Zero-escorted Val dive-bombers or Kate torpedo bombers. When the Zeros passed over eastern New Georgia at 1100, their progress was reported by Coastwatcher Donald Kennedy.

John Smith led his last seven F4Fs and seven P-400s aloft at 1105 and parked the F4Fs at 15,000 feet, the best height for hunting Kates or Vals. The seven P-400s remained 1,000 feet below while four more P-400s circled at 14,000 feet over *Burroughs*.

The seven-plane P-400 flight had been cruising at 14,000 feet for about thirty minutes when it was jumped from out of the low clouds by Zeros roaring in from below and behind. Woozy from lack of oxygen, the pilots were a bit slow to react, but nevertheless gamely turned to meet the threat. The American aircraft were simply outclassed, so their pilots dived into the clouds, where they had to rely upon their inadequate instruments.

The weather suddenly turned from marginal to poor. The cloud cover dropped to a mere 1,000 feet and visibility was cut to a quarter-mile. The P-400s straggled out of the rain and were bounced by six Zeros, which tore them apart. Four P-400s and two pilots were lost and five of the seven surviving fighters were extensively damaged. Nonetheless, the Army pilots claimed six kills.

The Marines fared far better, though they did not at first realize that the Japanese had bounced the P-400s, the result of incompatible radio equipment. Instead, John Smith went after a second Zero element, which he saw breaking for *Burroughs*.

Ever mindful that his pilots had a tendency to switch targets too quickly in hopes of getting a piece of everything in the sky, Smith ordered his airmen to choose targets and stay with them. Then he led them out of the sun. Six of the veteran Japanese fighter pilots were shot down on the first pass, an incredibly satisfying result. Captain Smith pulled up, but turned in when he saw that his green wingman had acquired a Zero on his tail. Smith destroyed the Zero as his wingman ran for the protection of clouds over the channel. About to head for the clouds himself, Smith was obliged to make a head-on pass at a Zero boring in from below, and he blew it from the sky.

Seven Marines downed eight of Japan's best carrier pilots in three minutes, and two badly damaged Zeros were lost on the return to Buka. Unfortunately, though VMF-223 had no pilot losses, three more Wildcats were bound for the boneyard. The five remaining Wildcats were caught on the ground refueling when eighteen Bettys appeared at 1800 and sank destroyer-transport *Colhoun* as she was unloading supplies.

Burroughs, still high and dry off Tulagi, was untouched, but a good deal of valuable gear was jettisoned during attempts to lighten her while the local boat pool rushed to unload her.

The most important occurrence of that busy August 30 was the arrival of nineteen new Wildcat fighters and eighteen new Dauntless dive-bombers. Shepherded by a pair of B-17 pathfinders, Col William Wallace, commander of MAG-23, led the remainder of his group to Henderson Field. Maj Bob Galer's VMF-224 and Maj Leo Smith's VMSB-231 brought the grand totals up to eighty-six pilots for sixty-four operational aircraft.

RAdm Slew McCain, the South Pacific aircraft commander, happened to be visiting with Archer Vandegrift when the new aircraft arrived. Easily containing his true feelings in the face of the Marine general's elation, the admiral shot off a bolt on September 1, aiming it directly at the Pacific Fleet commander, Adm Chester Nimitz. It was a waste, McCain cautioned, to send good men aloft in bad aircraft—a reference to the P-400 fiasco. He asked for a significant reinforcement, and ended with this incredibly prescient pronouncement:

> Cactus can be a sinkhole for enemy air power and can be consolidated, expanded, and exploited to [the] enemy's moral hurt. The reverse is true if we lose Cactus. If the reinforcement requested is not made available, Cactus cannot be supplied and hence cannot be held.

The day before this missile was launched, on August 31, *Saratoga* was heavily damaged by a torpedo off San Cristobal. Among the injured was VAdm Frank Jack Fletcher. When the carrier was ordered Stateside for repairs, three of her four veteran air squadrons were flown off. On September 2, in response to McCain's candid message, Nimitz signaled Adm Ernest King, in Washington, and asked that the *Saratoga*'s valuable aircraft be transferred directly to McCain's command for possible deployment on Guadalcanal.

The first few days of September 1942 were momentous.

On September 1, the entire 6th Naval Construction Battalion—Seabees—was landed at Kukum and put right to work building an auxiliary fighter strip on the Lunga Plain, a task that would be completed in a week's time.

On the same day, 11th Air Fleet was reinforced by 26th Air Flotilla's twenty-four Bettys and twenty Zeros. By that time, however, the Japanese bases at Rabaul and Kavieng were coming under increasing pressure from the New Guinea–based bombers of 5th Air Force, which damaged a number of the Japanese aircraft and drew precious fighters off escort duty for protecting the bases.

An hour after sunset on September 3, a Marine R4D Skytrain transport (the military version of the Douglas DC-3) landed at Henderson Field following a nine-day flight from California by way of Hawaii and New Caledonia. The pilot was LtCol Perry Smith, commander of MAG-25, the first air service unit deployed in the

South Pacific. Stepping from the hatchway of the twin-engine transport was BGen Roy Geiger, the silver-thatched commander of 1st Marine Aircraft Wing. With Geiger were his chief of staff, Col Lou Woods, and his intelligence officer, LtCol Toby Munn. They had arrived to establish a forward air command post.

Early the next morning, following an all-night flight of some 900 miles, MAG-25's exec, LtCol Fiske Marshall, landed his fuel- and equipment-laden R4D at Henderson Field, the first honest-to-goodness American war-zone aerial resupply mission in World War II. The two R4Ds flew out later in the day filled with wounded Marines. MAG-25's dozen aircrews and R4D's would provide an important new conduit for the trickle of supplies and equipment that would keep Henderson Field viable.

Roy Geiger had arrived to take charge of Cactus Air. A 1909 Basic School classmate of Archer Vandegrift, he was also one of America's first military aviators. He was, in fact, the forty-ninth naval aviator and the fifth Marine ever to earn his wings. Geiger and a very few other men had written the doctrine by which the warplanes at Henderson Field were fighting.

Geiger's arrival had an immediate and dramatic positive effect upon the course of the air war in the Lower Solomons, for he had the experience, know-how, intelligence, rank, and perseverance to make things work. Within hours of landing, Geiger had chosen as his CP a spot near the 1st Marine Division CP, the better to facilitate the daily conferences, formal and informal, that would be held with his warm friend of thirty-three years, Archer Vandegrift. It was Roy Geiger's desire to turn the defense-oriented Cactus Air establishment into an offensive tool. As it happened, the Japanese and the weather would be helping him along.

19

On the morning of August 13, 1942, as Imperial General Headquarters was informing 17th Army's LtGen Harukichi Hyakutake that he would be responsible for retaking the Eastern Solomons, a message from Tokyo to Japanese forces in the Palau Islands was providing the means for the effort. MGen Kiyotake Kawaguchi, a burly, balding, mustachioed professional soldier, was informed that day that his independent 35th Infantry Brigade was to leave the Palaus for Rabaul on August 15.

Kawaguchi Butai had been on the move since the beginning of the year, almost as though it was viewed in Tokyo as a military fire brigade. The core of the unit was 124th Infantry Regiment, which had served as part of the crack 18th Infantry Division in Manchuria and the China coast in the late 1930s. Detached from its division before the start of the Pacific War, the regiment had been heavily augmented by artillery, support, and headquarters detachments and designated 35th Infantry Brigade. In March 1942, under Kawaguchi's command, the brigade had participated in an amphibious landing and subsequent ground fighting on Borneo, followed that same month by mopping up operations on Cebu, in the Philippines, its first experience with American infantry. April found the brigade fighting Americans on Mindanao, and June saw it shipped to the Palaus to refit.

Preparations were completed within the allotted two days, and the brigade mounted out for Rabaul aboard a large transport on August 15, sailing by way of Truk. From Rabaul, the main body of the brigade—reinforced by 2nd Battalion, 4th Infantry, a part of 17th Army's 2nd Infantry Division—was shipped to the nearby Shortland Islands, where it set up a temporary camp.

While no news of the defeat of *Ichiki Butai* reached the troops, there was news of the Imperial Navy's stunning victory over the American carrier fleet in the Eastern Solomons; it was said that Japanese naval aviators had sunk two American carriers.

General Kawaguchi remained in Rabaul to meet with RAdm Raizo Tanaka, aboard the latter's flagship. The meeting did not go well. Kawaguchi had heard about Tanaka's rebuff on August 25 at the hands of Cactus-based dive-bombers, and he gruffly asserted his preference for troop-carrying barges—so-called "Ants"—over destroyer-transports, Tanaka's "Rats."

The two strong-willed flag officers disagreed widely on how to proceed. Tanaka was convinced that night landings from his fast destroyers were perfectly feasible, but Kawaguchi noted that he had transported his entire brigade over 500 miles in barges before his eminently successful Borneo landing. Tanaka countered by pointing out that the Borneo movement had been made while Japan held local air superiority, that the same condition did not prevail in the Eastern Solomons, that Guadalcanal-based American fighters and dive-bombers held the upper hand despite anything Kawaguchi might have heard to the contrary.

Round and round they went until, at length, Kawaguchi offered a compromise: The main body of the reinforced brigade, with himself in command, would be ferried to Taivu Point, east of Lunga, aboard Tanaka's destroyers; barges would carry Col Akinosuke Oka, commander of 124th Infantry Regiment, with an augmented battalion. Why either experienced commander allowed the brigade to be split between fast destroyers, capable of completing each run in a single night, and the slow-moving barges, which might take a week or two to reach Guadalcanal, is hard to imagine. It is possible that Tanaka's superior, VAdm Gunichi Mikawa, wanted to spread oil on the troubled waters that had developed between the naval headquarters in Rabaul and the reluctant 17th Army.

Colonel Oka was overjoyed when Kawaguchi announced that he, Oka, would embark with his regimental headquarters and the reinforced 2nd Battalion—about 1,100 soldiers—while Kawaguchi would lead the remainder of the reinforced brigade to Taivu Point. As soon as the two forces were in communication again, they would deploy, along with any friendly troops they encountered on the island, and envelop the Marine perimeter in a gnashing pincer assault. It was a complex arrangement, made more complex by the uncertainty of Colonel Oka's schedule.

The advance echelon of *Kawaguchi Butai*, about 750 soldiers, was landed at Taivu Point on the night of August 31. After depositing the soldiers safely on the beach, the destroyer-transports prepared to bombard Henderson Field, but they were stalked off Lunga Point by several American dive-bombers. The American warplanes failed to locate the destroyers, but the flotilla commander became so rattled that he fled without firing a shot. When Tanaka heard that his subordinate had run without a fight, he summarily relieved the man.

On the following night, September 1, Tanaka personally led eight destroyer-transports carrying General Kawaguchi and his main body from the Shortlands to Taivu Point. The troops were landed without incident and met by the haggard *Ichiki Butai* base troops. Kawaguchi led all of his soldiers three miles down the moonlit beach to an abandoned native village at Tasimboko Point.

A routine morning patrol of P-400 fighters found some targets on the beach between Tasimboko and Taivu Point. Little of value was destroyed in subsequent bombing and strafing runs, but the Japanese were given considerable cause to wonder if the game was already up. It would be days before Colonel Oka's force could be landed and, having spoken with the grim Ichiki survivors, General Kawaguchi was loath to launch a premature assault.

Next morning, September 2, the Tasimboko encampment was awakened hours before dawn by frantic calls for the guard company to repel an assault upon the beach. Gunfire directed at incoming boats was stilled by Japanese commands from seaward. Unbeknown to the Japanese ashore, Tanaka's destroyer-transports had disembarked the half of *Ichiki Butai* that had not been landed in time for Colonel Ichiki's disastrous August 21 assault. The melee among friends resulted in two dead and eight wounded Ichiki soldiers.

General Kawaguchi was fairly rattled by the time the excitement died down. The Americans, he felt, could not have failed to hear the ruckus at Tasimboko. He vilified himself for having allowed Colonel Oka to take the slowest available means of transportation to Guadalcanal, a decision that delayed moving into the rain forest and preparing the attack.

American airmen had *Kawaguchi Butai* pinpointed. A steady stream of P-400s and SBDs bombed and strafed the village. Casualties were light, but on the rise. No one could figure out why the inscrutable Americans did not launch a ground assault.

On August 31, Archer Vandegrift ordered three battle-tested battalions to Lunga from Tulagi. Second Battalion, 5th Marines, was returned to its regiment and based near Kukum as the division reserve. On September 4, the tiny 1st Parachute Battalion and about half of 1st Raider Battalion were ferried to Guadalcanal to form a divisional strike force.

The balance of 1st Raiders, two companies under the battalion exec, LtCol Sam Griffith, were landed on Savo in response to reports from islanders that Japanese had been seen there. Griffith and his troops spent ten exhausting hours combing the island, but found nothing of value. The rugged interior yielded no clues of a recent occupation, but the beaches were littered with the debris of the disastrous naval battle that had been fought there three weeks earlier.

When Griffith arrived off Kukum aboard destroyer-transports *Little* and *Gregory* very late in the afternoon, LtCol Red Mike Edson sent a message for him to keep his troops aboard the ships to save time mounting out in the morning against the Japanese at Tasimboko. The message was not received, however, and all the Raiders disembarked. It was too late for *Little* and *Gregory*—World War I-era warships—to make for the relative safety of the Tulagi anchorage, so they cruised warily offshore to kill time until dawn, when the Raiders would re-embark.

Ens Al Gallin had graduated from the Naval Academy on December 19, 1941, with the Class of 1942, and had been serving as *Gregory*'s assistant engineering officer almost every day since. He was awakened from a deep sleep at 0056, September 5, by booming gunfire, and was struggling into his clothing when General Quarters was sounded at 0058. As Gallin ran aft to his battle station, he could hear the sound of firing, but could see no flashes. Within a minute, however, a parachute flare dropped by an over-helpful American scout plane burst about 1,000 yards off *Gregory*'s port bow, then a searchlight about 2,000 yards off the starboard quarter illuminated *Little* as she was turning to starboard off *Gregory*'s starboard bow. Three rapid salvoes plunged *Little* into flames. Al Gallin immediately ordered Number-3 Gun, a 4.5-inch naval rifle, to fire on the light, but the gun misfired. An instant later, *Gregory* turned to port, placing the light dead astern. When the ship that had been firing at *Little* began firing at *Gregory*, Ensign Gallin ordered the balky gun to return fire. The searchlight had by then found *Gregory*, but Number-3 Gun's second round got the light. The Japanese placed one salvo just short of *Gregory*'s fantail and abruptly ceased firing.

There was no time to breathe a sigh of relief. The warship that had been firing at *Little* illuminated *Gregory*, and a third Japanese vessel fired. As Number-3 Gun put out its fifth round, Al Gallin noticed that his ship was dead in the water. When Gallin turned and saw that the bridge and galley deckhouse were ablaze, he ordered the life rafts cut away, then started forward to see what had happened. He found repair and ammunition parties standing fast just forward of the after deckhouse, and ordered the sailors to set all the depth charges on "safe." Boats were being lowered to the rails by the time Gallin reached the midships section; he ordered all hands nearby to stand by the boats. Sailors were streaming up from the engine rooms, but no one was coming out of the fireroom. Gallin next found the port after side of the well deck ablaze. A lone seaman was fighting a gasoline fire on the auxilliary radio generator with a CO_2 fire extinguisher. Two men lay dead beside the radio shack.

The bridge had been abandoned, its port wing a shambles, blood all over the place. The exec and control talker were dead on the deck. There was nothing Al Gallin could do, so he climbed back down to the main deck and made his way aft, telling all hands to abandon ship. He saw that Number-3 Gun was still firing, but ordered the crew to clear out.

Gallin started forward for a last tour of the ship. He met another officer and agreed to rendezvous at the boats. Several seamen carrying a wounded officer from the bridge reported that there was no one left alive topside, so Gallin returned to the boats and found that two of three were already away. Forty enlisted sailors and one officer were embarked in the last boat. Gallin climbed aboard and was being lowered away when a yeoman reported that several injured sailors were still aboard. The other officer ordered Gallin to remain with the boat alongside the ship while he went to investigate. It was soon discovered that the boat's engine had been disabled, probably by shrapnel.

The Japanese opened fire again, spraying *Gregory*'s survivors with shrapnel. The boat's engine would not start, so Al Gallin ordered everyone to swim away from the ship. A Japanese ship illuminating *Gregory* from off the port bow and quarter placed at least six heavy-caliber salvoes near the swimmers.

At about 0120, less than thirty minutes after he had been

awakened, Al Gallin gathered all the men he could find into a tight group and continued to swim away from the burning ship. Two other fires could be seen on the water—*Little* and what had to be a Japanese ship.

The firing abruptly ceased when the swimmers were about 1,000 yards from *Gregory*. Unable to keep going without knowing what had happened to the rest of the crew, Gallin started back in the company of a Coast Guard boatswain's mate. They had gone only fifty yards when a row of five flares illuminated the port side of their ship. Certain the Japanese were circling back, the two turned away, but they could not find the group they had just left. They treaded water until about 0800, when they were rescued by a landing boat sent out from Kukum.

Gregory's captain, LCdr Henry Bauer, died in the water of his mortal wounds after giving his life jacket to a sailor who had gone over the side without one.

In the morning, when they discovered that they had no means for getting to Tasimboko, Edson's Raiders marched inland, crossed the main runway and moved up the steep slopes of a bare T-shaped ridge just to the east of the Lunga River.

Despite efforts to disperse the soldiers and their equipment around the Tasimboko base, *Kawaguchi Butai* suffered small but steady losses in men and material at the hands of American warplanes from nearby Henderson Field. General Kawaguchi was rooted to the spot by his conviction that he had to await the arrival of Colonel Oka's force to participate in the assault on the captured airfield. Kawaguchi's situation would have been far worse if the tiny Cactus Air establishment had had more bombers and fighter-bombers to spare from its daily routine of searches and combat air patrols.

Word from Colonel Oka finally arrived on September 4. The first "Ants" had reached the southern tip of Santa Ysabel, directly north of Cape Esperance, and were waiting there for the rear groups to join. It would be several days before the crossing would be made, but all was well. General Kawaguchi dispatched an officer-courier with verbal instructions detailing Oka's role in the upcoming assault. As the message had to be carried all the way around the inland flank of the Lunga Perimeter, to Kokumbona, the general took care to allow sufficient time for it to arrive.

Some time after the good news from Colonel Oka arrived at Tasimboko, American aircraft spotted Oka's barges off Santa Ysabel and around nearby San Jorge Island. As soon as BGen Roy Geiger found out about the "Ants," he took direct control of the aerial effort to exterminate them.

On one mission, Capt Dale Brannon found five armored troop-carrying barges in open water, as close to being sitting ducks as anything he had ever seen. After cautioning the two younger P-400 pilots on his wings to try for only one barge at a time, Brannon circled wide, chose a target, and throttled back to come in at a steep angle. When the squadron leader thought he was in just the right position, he nudged the firing button for the deadly 20mm cannon peeking out through his plane's propeller spinner. *Bonk! Bonk!* Two rounds left the 20mm cannon and Brannon pulled up and around to view the results of his attack. Only then did he realize that he had flown through a storm of small arms and light machine-gun fire. Brannon's wingmen reported light damage to their aircraft, but thought they had scored hits. Brannon lined up his sights on another barge as he slowly dived at a steep angle and squeezed off two more rounds from the 20mm cannon and countless rounds from his four wing-mounted .30-caliber machine guns. He hoped the cannon would hole the bottom of the barge and the machine guns would kill men shooting back at him. After several passes by all hands, it became obvious that the barges were losing way, so Brannon ordered his flight home.

Scores, perhaps hundreds, of Japanese were killed or injured during the day, and most of Oka's stores were lost.

That night a totally unnerved Colonel Oka ordered the remaining barges to ferry 700 infantrymen across the sixty-mile-wide channel separating Santa Ysabel from Guadalcanal. The last fifteen barges were only 300 yards from Cape Esperance when they were bounced by the Cactus dawn patrol—the only two serviceable P-400s, which were joined twenty-five minutes later by six Wildcats. Only one barge was confirmed sunk, but nearly 250 Japanese were killed or injured in the surf and on the beach. Of the 1,100 soldiers Colonel Oka had started with, only 450 got safely ashore.

On September 6, the day the Seabees completed the new fighter strip on the Lunga Plain, General Kawaguchi left 300 soldiers to guard reserve stores and artillery, and led 3,100 veteran jungle fighters down the beach from Tasimboko. He would attack the reportedly inferior Lunga garrison from the inland flank after cutting south at Koli Point and approaching through the rain forest. It would be a grueling march, but his troops were up for it.

Hours before dawn on September 8, Japanese sentries on the beach at Tasimboko saw the silhouettes of two large ships escorted by a small flotilla of destroyers. The air was so still that the Japanese could hear English-speaking voices aboard the ships. Convinced to a man that it was about to bear the brunt of an amphibious assault, the guard company hastily deployed.

A short time later and farther to the west, near Koli Point, many of General Kawaguchi's assault troops also heard and saw the transports and destroyers, which were passing from east to west. The brigade commander deduced that a large body of reinforcements was on the way to Lunga, and that his attack would be met by more Americans than anticipated.

The transports, which carried no ground troops, had been sent from Noumea by RAdm Kelly Turner with supplies and some support personnel. Their arrival was welcome, but it alerted the Japanese, if for the wrong reasons, to what was to befall them later in the day.

The four rifle companies of 1st Raider Battalion left Kukum at 1800, September 7, aboard two destroyer-transports and two tuna boats grandiloquently described as "yacht patrol vessels." Next morning, the predawn stillness off Tasimboko was shattered when a Raider aboard one of the ships accidentally discharged his rifle. However, there were no Japanese on the landing beach, and B and C companies were safely landed east of Tasimboko Point by 0520. While C Company secured the left flank, B Company advanced westward toward the Kema River. A and D companies landed with the battalion command group at 0615 and hurried to catch up with C Company.

When the main body had been consolidated, LtCol Red Mike Edson held B Company on the beach, placed A Company on its left flank, and sent C Company farther inland to envelop the Japanese base. The Raiders were pressing toward Tasimboko when two Marine SBDs and four P-400s arrived to drop 100-, 300-, and 500-lb bombs on the village and strafe the forest to the west. As the aircraft headed home to rearm, the two destroyer-transports laid their guns right on the village and commenced firing at a 37mm gun that had opened on the Raiders down the beach. An hour later, as the Raiders slowly pressed through the unyielding rain forest, the six warplanes returned to bomb and strafe targets in the woods.

Red Mike contacted division headquarters at 0855 to say that his Marines had overrun two light fieldpieces against negligible opposition and to ask that air cover be maintained in case the reported 3,000 Japanese in the area counterattacked.

A second progress report, at 1045, indicated that the Raiders were still on the move but that additional Marines should be landed west of the village to block what seemed to be a general retreat by the Japanese in that direction—for that was Edson's only explanation for such light opposition. Division headquarters saw no reason to take on so many Japanese in a real pitched battle and told Edson to re-embark and return to Kukum. Red Mike overlooked the order and pressed on through a heavy downpour.

Edson's third report, filed at 1130, stated that several 75mm guns had been taken and that he was meeting increasing opposition. It appeared that about 1,000 Japanese had been encountered. (Only 300 were near Tasimboko at the time.)

The Japanese fired their remaining 75mm guns point-blank

into the advancing American skirmishers. One Raider had an arm sheared off by a 75mm shell burst, and two B Company Raiders were felled by a tree burst, the only Marines to die that day. One Japanese gun was silenced when Edson's runner, Cpl Walt Burak, eased around behind it and picked off the entire crew.

Overlooking its earlier order to Red Mike to clear out, division headquarters sent A and B companies, 1st Parachute Battalion, and the Raider Battalion's weapons company (E Company) from Kukum to support the ongoing advance. The fresh 'Chutes and Raider weapons platoons were merely deployed on the beach.

Henderson Field and the new fighter strip had been closed down just after noon by unbelievably heavy rain. Nonetheless, one Marine dive-bomber and four P-400s got off through six inches of mud to undertake their third mission of the day. The aircraft pounced on Japanese soldiers barring Edson's way and, within moments, the Raiders were able to spring forward and complete the envelopment begun in the morning. They pressed through the downpour and on into the village unopposed.

Unaware that the Raiders had achieved their objective, the support aircraft returned to the muddy airfield, where they were quickly refueled and rearmed. Word arrived at 1530 that the Raiders were in retreat. (They were withdrawing but were by no means under pressure.) The last three flyable P-400s rolled out. Capt Dale Brannon lowered half flaps, stood on his brakes, and ran his straining engine to full throttle. When he reached full power, he came off the brakes and roared down the runway, spuming mud in all directions. He barely lifted off. The second P-400, piloted by 2ndLt Vern Head, cranked up to full power and began moving, but could not get off. The fighter whipped and skewed nearly to the end of the field, at which point Head pulled all the way back on his joystick and momentarily hung her on her propeller. The abused aircraft stalled, fell back into the mud, broke into three sections, and burst into flames. Second Lieutenant D. H. Fincher had a half-instant to make his decision. Though fearful that the 300-lb bomb slung to his fighter's belly might erupt, Fincher flew right through the flames. Fire fighters pulled Head from the wreckage—hurt but alive—as Fincher and Brannon joined for the run to Tasimboko. They remained aloft for two long hours, flying lazy-eights over the withdrawing Raiders and 'Chutes, and returned to the fighter strip on the last of their reserve fuel.

Intelligence estimates based on what the Raiders had seen and collected at Tasimboko pegged the Japanese garrison at about 4,000, a remarkably accurate reading. A very large cache of food and equipment was found, but it could not be hauled away before nightfall, except for what individuals carried out in their pockets and packs. The remaining supplies and artillery were destroyed.

As the Raiders ransacked his base, General Kawaguchi assembled his officers in a misty drizzle near Koli Point to explain his plan for the assault on the airfield. *Kawaguchi Butai* would march west to the Tenaru River, then turn south for two miles. The 1,000-man rear echelon of *Ichiki Butai*, along with all the artillery, would cross the river and advance to a point about 2,500 yards from Henderson Field to wait for the main body to get to an assembly area south of the runway. Minutes before 2100, September 12, the artillery east of the Lunga Perimeter would open up in the hope of drawing the Americans' attention to the eastern flank. At 2100, precisely, Kawaguchi's main body, and Colonel Oka's force, near the Matanikau, would open their assaults under the guns of warships off Lunga Point.

Kiyotake Kawaguchi, an intelligent, experienced, and forthright man of the world, had severe misgivings about the potential outcome of his mission. Everything he had seen since landing on Guadalcanal indicated that the Americans held the airfield in considerably more strength than his superiors believed. They certainly ruled the skies over Guadalcanal, and those two transports in the predawn haze had impressed the Japanese brigadier, who assumed that they were full of fresh troops. More to the point, Kawaguchi had doubts that the ordained night assault would win ground. He

was obliged to launch a night action because the required naval
support was available only at night, and because American warplanes could not then support the defenders. Kawaguchi knew that
he was outnumbered and outgunned, and that his chance of success
was remote, but he was honorbound to try.

The Ichiki soldiers and gunners were left on the banks of the
Tenaru as 2,100 infantrymen of *Kawaguchi Butai* began hacking
through the dense underbrush, measuring gains by the meter and
half-meter. Scrambling up steep, muddy hillsides and trudging
through bottomless, mucky bogs, the battle-hardened veterans
struggled forward day and night, fearful of attack from the air and
ambush on the ground. Food was scarce, and the drinking water
was contaminated. Disease was rife.

While the Japanese were struggling with the jungle, Archer
Vandegrift was struggling with Japanese aerial ordnance. Nearly
every night since the division CP had been set up near Henderson
Field, it had been the target of inaccurate but nonetheless frightening and distracting harassment by Japanese bombers. The division
staff had been losing needed sleep and thus losing effectiveness. It
was concluded, after some discussion, that the CP was merely suffering fallout from attacks directed at the runway, so the division
commander decided to move to a quieter place, a spot south of the
runway, hard by a protecting ridge, well away from the areas liable
to be hit by the relays of lone Japanese night bombers. As a precaution, he ordered the Raiders and 'Chutes to man the ridge behind
the new CP, and to mount patrols into the rain forest stretching
away to the south.

The Raiders returned on September 10 to the naked T-shaped
ridge on which they had been billeted before the Tasimboko raid,
and the 'Chutes dug in beside them along a line about 2,000 yards
south of the main runway. The twelve 105mm howitzers of 5th
Battalion, 11th, were registered as a precaution on the jungle flats

south of the ridge, but no one really expected an attack in the area, so dense were the woods.

The air war had begun to pick up on September 8, the day the Raiders struck at Tasimboko. Unable to mount a noon strike through the day's driving rain storms, the Japanese flipped in a fast evening strike by floatplane fighters based in northern Santa Ysabel. Sixteen Wildcat fighters were scrambled to meet them. One crashed on takeoff, and the others failed to make contact. The Japanese lost their way to Henderson Field and strafed Tulagi instead.

Returning Marine airmen found the base solidly misted over by a ground fog, the result of the day's rain, now drying. Two of the Grummans ran into each other on landing, and both had to be scrapped. A fourth fighter was lost when its wheels caught in the mud, and a fifth crash-landed. Together with the P-400 and Wildcat lost in takeoff in the late afternoon, Henderson Field lost six fighters that day, none to enemy action. Fortunately, no airmen were killed.

A heavy Japanese raid on shipping on September 9 resulted in claims of five Bettys and three Zeros downed. The Marines, however, lost four F4Fs, with one pilot killed, one wounded, and one missing. The missing man was Capt Marion Carl, Cactus Air's high-scoring combat ace, with twelve confirmed kills.

One of John Smith's youngsters was lost on September 10 against five Japanese downed from the noon strike. That left an even dozen flyable Wildcats on Guadalcanal.

The noon raid on September 11 was particularly heavy. While all the surviving Marine Wildcats were fighting off a strong Zero escort, twenty-six Bettys hit the main runway and facilities. A P-400 was demolished on the ground and three Army pilots, including Capt Dale Brannon, were slightly injured. In the air, Maj Bob Galer, commander of VMF-224, downed a Betty and a Zero, but he was forced to ditch and swim home. John Smith scored his twelfth and thirteenth kills, and three other fighter pilots scored one apiece, a total of seven. By 1330, September 11, Cactus Air was down to eleven Wildcats.

By 1630, it was up to thirty-five.

Alarmed by the increasing tempo of Japanese raids and the steady loss of friendly fighters, RAdm Slew McCain received approval from Adm Chester Nimitz to release the twenty-four six-gunned F4F-4s of *Saratoga*'s Fighting-5. Twenty-four veteran Navy pilots landed their Wildcats at Henderson Field at 1645 to the accompaniment of frenzied cheers from Marines and airmen throughout the Perimeter.

Twenty of the Navy fliers were baptised by fire at 1100, September 12, when they were scrambled along with the last eleven Marine F4F-4s. John Smith led the last five of his original eighteen VMF-223 fighters down from 28,000 feet to score against six Bettys at 24,000 feet, all in one pass. Smith got his fourteenth and fifteenth kills.

Lt Smokey Stover and three other grounded Navy fighter pilots had to watch the action from dugouts beside the Lunga River, but they had plenty to cheer about during the dogfight; as they watched, two Wildcats stayed on a Betty until they had smoked it, another Betty had its wings sheared off in a dive, and a 90mm antiaircraft round blew up another Betty in midair. Stover and others on the ground could hear the whine of engines far overhead, and the rattle of gunfire, and they could see white gunsmoke plume back over the wings of whipsawing Wildcats. In all, the Marines downed ten Japanese, and Fighting-5 accounted for six. The Navy squadron's exec was evacuated with severe leg wounds, and a young ensign died when his powerless Wildcat undershot the runway and hit several trees before flipping over onto a tractor. There were no Marine losses.

It was obvious that the Japanese were building up to something. In fact, one of the air raids had clearly been centered upon the ridges south of the main runway, where the new division CP had been built and Raiders and 'Chutes deployed. It could not be dismissed as a navigational error, for the Japanese made their approach at right angles to the main axis of the runway and completely overflew the airbase before dropping.

There were other indications. The force that had occupied Tasimboko Village was spotted east of the Tenaru by scouts led by SgtMaj Jacob Vouza. Capt Martin Clemens had gone to great trouble to teach the islanders, whose language concept allowed only for the numbers "one," "two," and "many," to count troops accurately. Nevertheless, the division intelligence section chose to downgrade their estimates of "several thousand" to "several hundred." Word from the scouts that the Japanese were constructing a "tunnel" through the forest south of the Lunga Plain was dismissed. In the end, no one knew when or what or by how many, but it was generally assumed that "something" was going to happen.

It happened sooner than anyone expected.

20

On September 12, in the rain forest south of the T-shaped ridge, *Kawaguchi Butai*'s main body was winding up its preparations for taking the airfield. It was only after dusk that MGen Kiyotake Kawaguchi first learned that the jumbled ridge manned by Marines lay between his assault force and the main runway. There was no time to maneuver around the ridge; the hungry, exhausted Japanese would have to advance over the defended ground.

Last-minute work parties and scouts fanned out to blaze trails and observe the enemy. The Emperor's soldiers prepared to do their duty amidst a mood of relief. Mementos were exchanged and words of encouragement passed between old friends or from officers to their men.

An afternoon patrol by LtCol Sam Griffith and two riflemen brought news to LtCol Red Mike Edson that there was a large force of Japanese to the front. Griffith had been unable to determine how many Japanese there were, or where they were heading. Edson decided to mount several strong combat patrols next morning, and he called his company commanders and staffers to his CP for an evening planning session. Most of the Raiders and 'Chutes turned in for the night while sentries settled down to what would, they hoped, remain a quiet watch.

The T-shaped ridge rose out of the rain forest about a mile south of the main runway, its stem running in a north-south direction for about 1,000 yards parallel to the Lunga River, about 600 yards to the west. The crossbar was high, clear, fairly broken ground dominated by four distinct spurs, two each on either side of the stem. Steep gullies and jungle-choked ravines isolated the bare ridge in most directions. The only feasible path from south of the ridge to the Lunga Plain was down the long axis of the spurs and stem.

Two Raider companies were on the line: B Company was on clear, high ground, its right flank tied in with C Company, Raiders, which was extended out to the right, its own right flank dangling off into the tree-choked flats beside the Lunga River. A and D companies, Raiders, were close by, in reserve. The battalion headquarters and elements of E Company, the weapons unit, were bivouacked several hundred yards to the rear, on the stem of the T. B Company, 'Chutes, about seventy troopers, was tied in with B Company, Raiders, east (left) of the center of the stem, which served as the battalion boundary; A and C companies, 'Chutes, were bivouacked in the woods just behind and below the stem. The minuscule parachute-battalion headquarters was to the rear, near Edson's CP.

An increment of 1st Pioneer Battalion was holding a hill overlooking the west bank of the Lunga, well to the right of C Company, Raiders, and elements of 1st Engineer Battalion were on another nearby hill, to the left of the 'Chutes.

It started just as Red Mike was ending his briefing. As the leading elements of *Kawaguchi Butai* briefly floundered in the jungle flats below the ridge, seeking the first line of Marine listening posts, the artillery supported by the rear echelon of *Ichiki Butai* east of Alligator Creek opened fire several minutes before 2100, dead on schedule. Immediately, a Japanese naval floatplane ranged in from over the channel and dropped a parachute flare just south of the main runway. Two Japanese cruisers and a destroyer then opened fire on the T-shaped ridge. Several "overs" killed a number of Kawaguchi's advancing infantrymen.

Shouts of "Japs!" and "Here they come!" intermingled with screams of *"Totsugeki!"*—"Charge!"

Several listening posts screening the Raiders' front were swept away in the opening rush, then the Japanese crunched up against the main line, manned at the points of impact by platoons from B and C companies, Raiders.

Spreading left and right, the Japanese screamed and yelled and hurled strings of firecrackers to rattle the defenders. The most hard-pressed of the C Company platoons slowly fell back from its position overlooking the river. Communications became unglued all along the line as attackers and defenders intermingled under the eerie glow of shellbursts and parachute flares. Before any Marines could effectively react, Japanese soldiers were cutting fire lanes through the dense underbrush and firing along them at the stunned Raiders. Within minutes, a second C Company platoon was isolated by a human wedge of oath-screaming Japanese. All the disorganized Raiders who could withdrew.

Severely disabled in the opening minutes of the fight, C Company, Raiders, was forced to give ground. This, in turn, forced adjacent B Company to undertake a fighting withdrawal to re-fuse its now-dangling right flank. When the withdrawal had been completed, B Company's right platoon was bent far back, holding a north-south line. The Japanese could not press their advantage against the main body of B Company, for they had their hands full with isolated individuals and pockets of Raiders who had not been able to withdraw with the herd. The attackers were so taken aback by the unexpectedly stiff opposition that the fighting tapered off immediately after the first successful rushes had been driven home.

Heavy skirmishing ensued through the long night, but the Japanese had all withdrawn by sunrise.

卍

Early on September 13, pilots from carriers *Hornet* and *Wasp* ferried in eighteen brand-new F4F-4 Wildcat fighters for Cactus pilots whose own Wildcats had been lost in the heavy air fighting of the previous week. The *Hornet* and *Wasp* pilots were flown out later in the day.

Lt Smokey Stover, of Fighting-5, roared aloft at 0830, one of seventeen Navy and Marine fighter pilots to greet an early air strike. Stover was at 25,000 feet peering all over the sky in search of targets when his earphones crackled with his division leader's excited voice: "Zero!"

The Americans had found two reconnaissance aircraft escorted by twenty Zeros. The Japanese were not there for a fight, did not even expect one. Their sole mission was to determine who owned the airbase following General Kawaguchi's "crushing" night assault. They gamely turned to meet the oncoming Americans. The four Fighting-5 pilots descended steeply, and were passing 18,000 feet before Smokey Stover even saw the quarry. Immediately, Stover saw his wingman bailing out of his burning Wildcat. Then he was jumped by a Zero, which doggedly chased him into clouds at 6,000 feet. Hugging the clouds, Stover got into position to bag a Zero. The Japanese pulled up right in front of him, but Stover managed to hang on and fire his six .50-caliber wing guns until the Zero burst into flames and crashed into the rain forest. Next, Stover forced a Zero into a head-on contest as it pulled away from a firing run on another Wildcat. Stover saw good hits on the Zero's fuselage. He watched as it circled, trailing smoke, but he did not see it fall, so claimed only a probable.

Fighting-5 claimed three Zeros definitely destroyed and one probable. The Marines made no claims. One Fighting-5 airman was lost with his Wildcat and another—Smokey Stover's veteran wingman, Ens Don Innis—was seriously burned before bailing out; he was picked up in the channel by a landing craft from Kukum. A third Navy pilot was wounded, but landed safely.

The reconnaissance report to 11th Air Fleet resulted in a bomber strike later in the day against "artillery" positions near Taivu Point. The Bettys destroyed most of what little remained of *Kawaguchi Butai*'s supplies. The Japanese bombers were hit first by Maj Bob Galer and two other Marine airmen as soon as they turned for home. Each of the three Marines claimed a kill. Smokey Stover, in one of seven Navy Wildcats to get in on the melee, got to 25,000 feet in time to make one pass, but with no observable results. Other Fighting-5 flyers destroyed two Bettys over Savo. However, a furious Wildcat-versus-Zero dogfight claimed the lives of three Marines and two Japanese. One Navy F4F was lost in a launching mishap.

Late in the afternoon, a pair of Zero floatplanes caught everyone flatfooted and flamed a Marine SBD coming in for a landing, killing the pilot and gunner. Ten minutes later, antiaircraft gunners opened upon a dozen "intruders," but fortunately failed to score. The "intruders" were U.S. Navy SBD Dauntless dive-bombers manned by aircrews from Scouting-3, which had been transferred to RAdm Slew McCain's Aircraft, South Pacific, following the departure of *Saratoga* after she suffered torpedo damage on August 31. Soon after, the first American torpedo bombers to be sent to Cactus—six TBF Avengers from *Saratoga*'s Torpedo-8—also landed.

The Raiders moved to recover lost ground after sunrise. Japanese snipers abounded, so the advance by elements of B and C companies was cautious and slow. B Company riflemen who succeeded in reclaiming fighting holes lost in the night found that the gear they had left behind had been rifled by the Japanese, and that much of the food they had pilfered at Tasimboko had, in the end, gotten into the stomachs for which it had been intended.

A Company, 'Chutes, had had no contact with the Japanese during the night, so was ordered down to the jungle flats to support the Raiders' attempts to regain their original positions. The company advanced only a bit before it was stopped by gunfire from concealed emplacements. Unwilling to risk a major fight while deployed on so narrow a front, Capt Bill McKennan ordered his unit to back away from the Japanese. Once clear, however, McKennan pushed in from another direction, this time with some artillery support. The second attempt brought forth a few Japanese snipers, but they did little to impede the 'Chutes, who accomplished their mission by midafternoon. A Company returned to the ridge at 1530 to find that the cooks had saved the morning meal. All hands ate their first food of the day, then lined up again to collect their afternoon meal, which was always served punctually at 1630.

C Company, Raiders, which had been badly mauled in the night fighting, was withdrawn from the front. A Company, the only Raider unit anywhere near full strength, and the remnants of D Company, which had been disbanded to fill out the ranks of the other companies, were sent to hold the Raider right.

Red Mike decided to shorten the line somewhat, and pull it back nearly 100 yards to force attackers to cross open ground through grazing automatic-weapons fire. Improved fields of fire were cut, and much of the line was wired in. Deeper fighting holes were dug, and automatic weapons were repositioned. Asked by Archer Vandegrift what he thought of the night action, the grim, unflappable Red Mike whispered that he thought it was a test. Then he smiled his peculiar, bloodless smile and added that the Japanese would be back that night. Vandegrift ordered up 2nd Battalion, 5th, which had fought beside the Raiders on Tulagi five weeks earlier.

When the reserve battalion was delayed by the day's busy air activities as it crossed the main runway on its way from Kukum, LtCol Bill Whaling, exec of 5th Marines, and the rifle-company commanders arrived at Edson's CP late in the day to look over the ground. It was a wise precaution, for the main body of the battalion would be delayed until after dark.

Late in the afternoon, all twelve 105mm howitzers of LtCol Hayden Price's 5th Battalion, 11th, were moved with the aid of prisoners from their forest revetments to more-exposed firing positions south of the main runway. The gunners quickly plotted general and direct support concentrations on their maps, and zone registrations were fired before dark.

The registration fire caused some excitement along the ridge, where Raiders and 'Chutes paused to see if they were under attack. When Capt Bill McKennan, who had been up all night and all day overseeing his A Company, 'Chutes, saw that the rounds were landing well beyond his position, he dozed off.

Once the guns were registered, everyone except gunners was moved back into the woods to man a secondary line; if the Japanese broke through the Raiders and 'Chutes, they would certainly overrun the howitzers. There was nothing between the artillerymen and the vital airfield.

First Raider Battalion mustered just over 400 effectives. They held an 1,800-yard line anchored on the southern slope of a high, projecting knob to the right of the center of the crossbar of the T. B Company was on the left, and A Company and the remnants of D Company held the right. C Company, the battalion headquarters, and elements of E Company were the reserve.

First Parachute Battalion had yet to come in contact with *Kawaguchi Butai*. B Company, mustering about seventy-five effectives, was tied in at the ridge's center with B Company, Raiders. C Company, which had landed fewer than eighty men at Gavutu and which now fielded no more than fifty, was to B Company's left rear, holding about 200 yards along a knob overlooking the jungle flats. A Company, the battalion reserve, was in the woods right behind C Company. The battalion was down to well under 200 troopers in all from the 377 who had landed at Gavutu. As with most Marine battalions in the Eastern Solomons, 1st 'Chutes had lost far more Marines to illness and disease than to enemy bullets and bombs.

General Kawaguchi reckoned that he had about 1,000 organized effectives for the coming assault, a number far exceeding the combined strength of the two battalions holding the ridge. Despite casualties suffered the previous night, and the fact that many stragglers had not rejoined their companies, Kawaguchi decided early in the day to mount a new assault.

With the onset of darkness, Raiders and 'Chutes could hear more and more talk from the woods to the front. The Raiders replied with taunts and curses. Bullets flew sporadically as each side psyched itself up.

Capt Bill McKennan, of A Company, 'Chutes, was awakened from his afternoon nap by a runner summoning him to the battalion CP. He made his way through the dense woods in pitch darkness and was advised that the situation on the front had become "threatening." A Company was to move to the ridge. McKennan returned to the company bivouac and ordered 1stSgt Marion LeNoir to call the troops out. The tension was alleviated when one young trooper said to McKennan as he passed in the dark, "I s'pose we get time-and-a-half for this, Cap'n." The men dropped down beside the road to wait for the attack to begin.

B Company, Raiders, took it on the nose at 1830, September 13. The Japanese struck most heavily on the right, just where they had hit C Company the night before. A platoon was quickly isolated from the rest of the company and surrounded. Then B Company fell apart under repeated hammer blows. Driven back, the Raiders reformed just behind the crest and surged forward to regain some of the lost ground. But the Japanese were pouring through a 200-yard gap in the line. Within minutes, B Company's front had been reduced to a series of tiny pockets and strongpoints manned by desperate men. A Company, Raiders, isolated by the Lunga on one flank and the gap torn at its juncture with B Company, was not seriously molested by *Kawaguchi Butai*'s main effort, which was aimed at the stem of the ridge, a direct path to Henderson Field.

Shortly after B Company collapsed, Red Mike moved his CP *forward* to the high knob dominating the southern end of the ridge, only several yards behind the most advanced machine-gun emplacement. As Edson sought to steady his rattled troops, Cpl Walt Burak, his runner, scuttled to the rear in search of communications wire, which was spliced in to the battalion message center and run back to the division CP, where the senior staff was anxiously await- ing news. Edson was coldly determined to stand his ground, though he, as every man around him, could barely lift his head for fear of having it blown off by the sheets of fire the Japanese were putting out. Edson presented a terse rundown to LtCol Jerry Thomas, the division operations officer, who was directing the overall effort from his operations center, just north of the ridge. (Red Mike would leave his exposed CP only once that long night, and then only to briefly spring to the rear to alleviate some of the confusion experienced by his superiors at division headquarters.)

Individual Marines drifted back through the blackness from overrun positions while others crept forward. As the life-and-death struggle raged across the killing ground, Red Mike called on C Company to defend the knob on which he had established his for- ward CP. Then beleaguered B Company was allowed to withdraw. Only sixty Raiders responded, but many other B Company Ma- rines were fighting individually and in small groups on other parts of the battleground.

Fifth Battalion, 11th, was having the most active night in its brief history. Its twelve 105mm howitzers had been brought so close to the ridge during the late afternoon that the crews had had to dig pits beneath the breech blocks in order to take up the recoil when they fired at extreme high angle. The tubes were so steeply inclined that the rounds described trajectories similar to those of mortars. Initial fire missions consisted of individual concentrations directed by trained artillery forward observers on the ridge or by infantry officers and NCOs who had open lines to the battery fire direction centers.

All that separated the howitzers from the Japanese was the line of Raiders and 'Chutes on the ridge. Pfc Larry McDonald, the nineteen-year-old O Battery recorder, was obliged to use a narrow- beamed pen-light to make certain that his records and readings were in accord. Within a short time of the onset of the action, he drew sniper fire each and every time he used the light, no matter how briefly. Despite the danger, it was imperative that McDonald and other recorders continue; all guns had been set on base azimuths, and any variation right, left, up, or down had to be noted in order to bring them back to the base.

Communication between the artillery forward observers and the firing batteries was disrupted early in the action. When Red Mike requested an urgent replacement at dusk, Maj Charles Nees, the 11th Marines' assistant operations officer, volunteered to take the job. The thirty-three-year-old reservist worked his way forward and, at about 2000, found a spot from which he could observe the front and adjacent positions. He reported to Red Mike, who had been directing the artillery, simply by shouting that he had arrived, was in position, and had established communications with the 105mm fire direction center. Nees immediately began calling the pinpoint fires the Raiders and 'Chutes needed to survive. At about the time Nees went forward, an aristocratic, silver-thatched older private first class named Tom Watson left his job as a clerk with the 105mm battalion's headquarters battery to serve as a forward observer. Watson would be a second lieutenant by morning, so flawless was his direction of the guns.

By 2100, the howitzer crews shifted from called fire to box barrages, then to rolling barrages, which entailed firing a salvo at maximum elevation and subsequent salvos outward at fifty-yard increments to 300 yards, then pulling the fire back fifty yards at a time. The gunners could not believe that Raiders and 'Chutes were calling ranges so close to their own positions, but they complied. The only time the guns stopped firing was when the battery execs, who were in charge of the fire direction centers, ordered individual tubes swabbed and cooled.

One Japanese officer was so impressed with the rapid-firing howitzers that he later referred to them as "automatic artillery." Much of the artillery's success stemmed from Japanese assault tactics: Every time the Emperor's soldiers were about to launch a new assault, they lofted a red flare from their starting position. The Japanese who managed to breast the curtain of steel often pitched calcium flares at the American lines, and those drew yet more fire. The quality and speed of the gunnery paid deadly dividends.

The tiny parachute battalion, spared the previous night, bore the brunt of a vicious head-on assault. The action on the 'Chutes' front began when two mortar rounds landed in C Company's lines, killing one trooper and wounding another. The 'Chutes responded by pitching hand grenades down the steep slopes at the sound of voices.

As the action heated up and the Japanese routes of advance were revealed, Capt Bill McKennan's A Company was ordered forward from its reserve position to man a secondary line on the reverse slope of the ridge, behind B and C companies.

Fearful that a powerful attack might breach his weak line, Capt Justin Duryea, whose B Company was holding the cleared area in the center of the ridge, directly beneath Red Mike's forward CP, ordered smoke pots ignited to screen his front. A red flare burst overhead at the moment of ignition, and its light was reflected off the smudgy black curtain. Someone yelled, "Gas attack!" Blood ran cold as the smoke oozed over the red-lighted ground; everyone had long ago discarded his gas mask.

The Japanese struck as additional flares were lofted into the red sky, surging down the spurs and wildly charging along the protruding spine and the dark edges of the low jungle flats. They punched through from dead ahead, officers waving swords aloft while yelling *"Totsugeki!"* and *"Banzai!"* at the top of their lungs. Riflemen fired their .25-caliber Arisaka rifles and 7.7mm Nambu light machine guns from their hips, hurled grenades, and fired their strange little "knee mortars." They screamed their oaths and fired their weapons and sacrificed their lives for their emperor.

Most of the B Company troopers held firm, and the Japanese rolled away to their right front, hitting Capt Dick Johnson's platoon-size C Company. Cpl Ernie DeFazio, a squad leader whose squad had been disbanded, was firing at sounds in the dark when he saw a red, glowing light coming at him. There was barely time to secure his helmet with his left hand and duck. The object, a grenade launched by a knee mortar, burst overhead and badly lacerated DeFazio's left hand. DeFazio did not dare get up, and he knew that yelling for a corpsman in all that din would be a waste of effort, so he crawled on his belly toward the rear until shock and pain caused him to faint.

Most of the C Company troopers bolted, but the Japanese were momentarily halted when a C Company machine gunner cradled his gun in his arms and charged forward firing a long burst. The attackers were held for only a moment, for the gunner was shot dead in his tracks.

The unremitting, repeated hammer blows finally forced Duryea's B Company to give ground. That in turn caused most of the remainder of Johnson's C Company to flee. While troopers from the forward companies ran headlong toward the rear, McKennan's A Company revealed itself to the Japanese by opening with powerful defensive fires centered on three well-emplaced medium machine guns. Japanese Nambus, whose muzzle-flash suppressors made them extremely hard to spot at night, reached out from the dark to duel the Marine machine guns. American gunners were going down, one after another, but volunteers from the rifle squads replaced them. A Company held its line.

Pfc Larry Moran, of B Company, ran nearly 1,000 yards down the stem of the ridge before he was stopped by 1stSgt Donald Doxey, who was reorganizing B Company stragglers in a stand of trees. Doxey ordered the 'Chutes to win back the lost ridgeline. As Larry Moran worked forward, he could hear bellowing voices from the Raider lines, exhorting the troops to keep the machine guns firing and "kill the Jap bastards!"

Elements of B Company, Pfc Larry Moran included, regained the summit, but Moran was soon blasted over the side by a concussion grenade. Uninjured, he collected his wits and scrabbled uphill to rejoin the fight. Suddenly, a challenge was hurled through the night. Moran recognized the voice as belonging to MG Bob Manning, but he could not recall the password.

"Mr. Manning," he called.

"Yeah," Manning replied.

"It's Moran; I can't remember the password."

"Okay, come on up."

Another voice suddenly called Manning's name and said that reinforcements were coming up on the right, that he should have his troopers hold fire. As Gunner Manning expected no help from any direction, he alerted the men around him to the ruse, then shouted approval. The attempted penetration was easily repulsed.

At 2200, three-and-one-half hours into the battle, Red Mike informed LtCol Jerry Thomas that his force of Raiders and 'Chutes had dwindled to about 300 organized effectives, and that the Japanese had yet to ease the pressure. Isolated groups and individuals continued to contribute to the success of the effort by stalling rushes and confusing Japanese troop leaders by firing from odd places at odd moments. Nevertheless, though many Japanese were down, the Marines were increasingly outnumbered.

Pfc Larry Moran was struck in the thigh by a red-hot sliver of shrapnel. He fought on until a lull allowed him to hobble with another injured Marine to an aid station about 100 yards back. When the two arrived at the sickbay, they were told that the corpsman was on the line, that there was no one qualified to deal with their injuries. The two continued toward the rear, permanently out of the fight.

Pfc Bill Keller, an A Company BAR-man, bowled over three Japanese who popped out of the trees directly beneath his position. One screamed for endless minutes, so painful were his wounds. A corpsman asked Keller what the trouble was. When the BAR-man said that a wounded enemy soldier was making all the noise, the corpsman sort of grinned and dropped into the trees to get at the wounded man. The screaming stopped, but Bill Keller never learned the outcome, for two Japanese concussion grenades exploded within a yard of his position. The next thing Keller knew, he was being lifted onto a jeep at the base of the ridge. Shrapnel wounds pitted the lower part of his face and upper back. His precious BAR was clutched tightly in his fists.

Capt Bill McKennan was working out of his CP, right behind

the forwardmost machine guns, when he and 1stSgt Marion Le-Noir saw a Japanese grenade sputter out of the darkness. LeNoir dived one way and McKennan went the other, right into the orbit of a second grenade he did not see. McKennan next found that he was rolling downhill, and he came to rest by the roadway running parallel to the base of the ridge, tangled up with a rifleman who had been knocked down by the same blast. The two groggily regained their feet and tried to regain their bearings, then felt their way along the trees beside the road until they reached an aid station. Both men were placed in a jeep and bounced rearward. An infiltrator hurled a grenade from out of the darkness, but the jeep rolled through the blast, and the two groggy, injured Marines were carried into a tent, where their wounds were swabbed with sulfa compounds. McKennan dropped off as morphine combined with the effects of forty-eight hours on the go.

In a conversation with LtCol Jerry Thomas at 0230, Lieutenant Colonel Edson said that he was "out of the woods." While the Japanese had not yet begun to acknowledge defeat, it was generally felt that they had spent themselves. Thomas informed Edson that 2nd Battalion, 5th, was behind 5th Battalion, 11th, and would soon be closing on the ridge to assist him.

G Company, 5th, moving up the left side of the stem of the T at 0400, was soon pinned by heavy fire from the woods to its left. It suffered numerous dead and wounded before arriving behind the 'Chutes and pressing forward against heavy opposition. In all, G Company lost thirty dead and wounded by dawn. As E Company attacked on the right of the stem, it lost five killed and nine wounded to snipers it bypassed in the dark.

The Japanese mustered one final assault at first light, but it ran directly into the guns and bombs of the last three serviceable P-400s at Henderson Field. The three Army pilots turned out of their high-powered takeoffs and dipped over the ridge, wreaking unbelievable destruction upon *Kawaguchi Butai*, which put out enough return fire to force two of the aircraft to glide back to the runway without functioning engines.

Cpl Carlo Fulgenzi, an eighteen-year-old suburban New Yorker serving with Headquarters Company, 1st Engineer Battalion, had been placed in charge of a group of engineers who, like himself, were suffering from the effects of malaria or other tropical diseases. Positioned across the jeep track at the base of the ridge, Fulgenzi's group was whittled down through the long night by Japanese infiltrators, but the survivors held.

At about 0500, Fulgenzi decided to venture up to the ridgeline to find a buddy whose machine gun had stopped firing hours earlier. He stopped dead in his tracks when he ran into about thirty Japanese—laughing, joking men who had simply sauntered through or around the American positions higher up. All Carlo Fulgenzi had to fight them off with was a Colt .32-caliber revolver he had smuggled ashore, a gift from his father. He had only the six rounds in the cylinder. As Fulgenzi ducked away from the Japanese, he found a dugout and rolled inside, silently praying for deliverance. He was shaking so badly that he had to steady the pistol between his knees.

The chattering Japanese stopped outside the dugout. Several climbed on top of the coconut logs over the engineer's head while others proceeded to rip apart tents throughout the area. They soon discovered that wounded and ill Marines were in the tents, and proceeded to flay two of them with bayonets and knives.

A grenade landed in the trench leading into Fulgenzi's dugout, and a steel sliver tore into his left leg. Immediately, four Japanese dived into the trench; they could not see Corporal Fulgenzi, but he could see them silhouetted in the entryway. The leader was only a foot away when Carlo Fulgenzi lifted the barrel of his Colt pistol and squeezed off a round into the man's forehead. The first Japanese pitched to the side, and Fulgenzi put a round into the second head. And the third. And the fourth. He started to climb out of the dugout to make his escape when he ran headlong into a fifth Japanese. The man had his rifle raised and was already squeezing the trigger when Fulgenzi shot him dead.

Fulgenzi turned toward his company area, but got only about twenty-five yards when he found twelve Japanese furtively moving through the trees. They yelled oaths as Fulgenzi dived toward a nearby machine-gun emplacement, uncertain whose it was. He found three Marines, who turned their gun to the flank and dropped all the Japanese in sight.

After one of the Marines in the gun emplacement handed Fulgenzi a submachine gun, the engineer corporal bandaged his leg wound and hobbled off to the 1st Engineer Battalion CP to issue an alert concerning the infiltration. Then he volunteered to lead a patrol to rescue the gunner he had set out to find earlier.

Four of eight engineers in the patrol were wounded as they crawled on their bellies through a rain of sniper fire toward the silent machine gun. It took what seemed like hours to traverse a mere hundred yards. Moans from the position, however, egged on the rescuers. Carlo Fulgenzi broke into the open and leaped into the fighting hole. A Japanese machine gun that opened fire as Fulgenzi was airborne put a round through his left wrist, but he ignored the wound when he saw the two Marines who had been manning the position. The dead man on top had a dozen bayonet holes through his chest. The survivor had been shot through both legs above the knees, and one leg had been slashed to the bone by a sword. Fulgenzi was helping to lift the wounded man onto a stretcher when he was shot through the right arm. Despite the excruciating pain, he helped carry the wounded Marine to safety, then turned himself in for treatment of his own wounds.

There was a moment of heart-stopping drama at the division CP when a sword-wielding Japanese officer stepped into the open with two riflemen and headed directly for Archer Vandegrift, who was in the open, alone and unarmed.

MG Sheffield Banta, an utterly unflappable old salt, stopped typing a report long enough to unholster his .45-caliber automatic pistol and plug the officer dead in his tracks. A corporal whose pistol jammed attempted to tackle one of the enlisted gate crashers, but two quick gunshots from nearby felled the quarry practically at the commanding general's feet. The third intruder was dropped where he stood and, later, a fourth infiltrator was routed out of the division commander's closet.

A and B companies, 1st Marines, were sent from reserve positions by Alligator Creek before dawn to mount a sweep below the ridge to sever the Japanese line of retreat. Though these Marines were veterans who had weathered the carnage in the coconut grove on August 21, many were utterly appalled by what they saw as they passed through the tiny remnant of the parachute battalion; mail and debris were strewn all over the place, and Marines with dark, hunted expressions nervously peered at the jungle flats below.

The two companies cautiously advanced west and south for nearly two hours without opposition. Then A Company ran into gunfire put out by a tiny blocking force. Capt Charlie Brush ordered 2ndLt John Jachym's platoon to hold the rear while the remainder of the company withdrew. Though Jachym was unable to comprehend why the powerful force was not going to launch an attack against the Japanese ahead, he fought a slow rearguard action. When A Company was reformed, Captain Brush explained that he had been ordered back to Alligator Creek to withstand an assault there. He had also received word, however, that B Company had been engaged by a far superior Japanese force. He ordered Jachym's platoon to mount a relief.

When Lieutenant Jachym reported to the B Company CP, he found four of the company officers wringing their hands over the possible fate of a rifle platoon that had been ambushed and was pinned in the dense undergrowth. As the officers talked, Japanese machine guns on the opposite bank of the nearby Lunga River opened fire on them. Then a mortar round landed at their feet. The five officers and their runners burst in all directions from the point of impact, scrambling for cover. The round proved to be a dud.

John Jachym could see that the demoralized B Company officers were not about to commit themselves to bailing out the lost platoon, and he felt he needed more than his own understrength platoon to do the job. He sent his runner after the rest of A Company, which arrived at the B Company CP in due course, winded but up for the effort. Captain Brush reported to battalion headquarters, which reported to division headquarters, which replied that it could not afford to have the two companies involved in the rescue mission. Brush was ordered to withdraw posthaste to Alligator Creek.

The abandoned B Company platoon was destroyed. In all, twenty-four Marines were killed in a fight to the last bullet. One of the few survivors, Pvt Harry Dunn, spent three days carrying a wounded comrade to safety; he hid during the day and traveled by night. It was a remarkable feat of survival and devotion.

More than 600 Japanese corpses were counted on and about Bloody Ridge, as it came to be called; many wounded were laboriously carried into the rain forest by their spent comrades; a large number of dead or missing soldiers was never found, not even by American patrols that, for days, combed the jungle flats south of the ridge. Perhaps 1,200 Japanese officers and soldiers followed their general away from the beaten zone, across the Lunga, westward to link up with Colonel Oka's battered contingent.

The march was too much for many of the injured; scores of wounded Japanese were left by the wayside with scores of dead. They had neither food nor medical supplies. By the fifth day, NCOs were beating their flagging charges with switches, cursing them onward. In the end, the survivors emerged from the forest near Point Cruz and rushed to lap up the water washing over the beach. Many died, convulsed in agony. Of the 2,100 souls Kiyotake Kawaguchi had led to the foot of Bloody Ridge on September 12, just 1,000 returned safely.

The Raiders lost 31 killed and 104 wounded, and the 'Chutes lost 18 killed and 118 wounded. B Company, 1st, lost 24 killed. Several dozen engineers and artillerymen died. Many of the wounded were flown to Espiritu Santo aboard the Marine R4D transports that landed each dawn with ammunition and supplies.

With the loss of 212 of 377 troopers at Gavutu and Bloody Ridge, 1st Parachute Battalion ceased to be an effective fighting force. The Raider battalion lost a combined total of thirty percent of its strength—not counting illness cases—at Tulagi and the Ridge.

Early on the evening of September 13, listening posts screening K Company, 1st, at the southern end of the Alligator Creek line, reported hearing strange noises all along the front. The K Company exec, 1stLt Joe Terzi, moved forward to calm the rattled observers. He got across a wide field to the bank of the creek before he and his runner spotted a large group of men. The two dropped into the water and lay doggo for some moments, until discovered by one of the 1,000 *Ichiki Butai* soldiers General Kawaguchi had left to guard his artillery. The two Marines lifted themselves over the bank and tore across the open field toward K Company's main line. Several gunshots hurried them along and alerted their fellow Marines.

The K Company commander coolly allowed the Japanese to crawl right up to the wire on the far side of the field before ordering, "Open fire!" Over 200 Japanese dead were counted on or behind the wire; only twenty-seven were found in the field.

When Japanese snipers opened on the K Company line at dawn, a platoon of B Company, 1st Tank Battalion, was sent to clear the area. The tankers made a hasty reconnaissance on foot, then six light tanks were sent forward, without infantry support. Two of the tanks were quickly disabled by antitank-gun fire, and a third fell over a thirty-foot bluff into Alligator Creek; it landed upside down, and the trapped crew of four drowned. The platoon leader was killed when an antitank round pierced the white star on his turret; his tank withdrew. The last tank threw a track about fifty yards short of a Japanese machine-gun emplacement; the crew bailed out and picked its way safely to friendly lines.

I Company, 1st, just north of K Company, mounted a strong probe, but the main Japanese force had by then withdrawn. Snipers and roving mortar teams stayed on for a week.

Sgt Ben Selvitelle's light-machine-gun section of L Company, 5th, was just finishing its breakfast on the morning of September 14 when its lone sentry yelled, "Japs!"

Selvitelle ran to the line, grabbed a pair of field glasses from the sentry, and swept the coconut grove across the way. A man wearing puttees and a sword was just running into the open. Selvitelle blinked, then focused upon several more men, all similarly dressed. Soon, a column took form. Selvitelle rattled off a string of terse commands. The last command was, "Fire!"

The .50-caliber heavy machine guns attached to the section chugged out rounds. The gunfire brought forth a Marine officer, who stood up on some sandbags and yelled, "Stop firing! That's a Marine work party." Then, "Come on in, Marines." The gunners ceased firing.

Selvitelle saw a man across the way wave his sword and urge the other men to take cover. Then the Japanese opened fire, which finally convinced the Marine lieutenant that he was in danger. Immediately, the entire 3rd Battalion, 5th, opened with everything it could bring to bear—all manner of small arms, machine guns of every variety, 37mm antitank guns, mortars, and halftrack-mounted 75mm antitank guns.

The Japanese—certainly Colonel Oka's soldiers—recoiled, then probed forward. Several nearly advanced to the American line, but were driven off when tracer rounds set the woods afire.

When all the Japanese departed at about 1500, an L Company officer asked volunteers to go out and fight the brushfire. No one responded, so he appointed Sergeant Selvitelle and several gunners to take care of the chore. The six Marines were understandably nervous as they passed through their wire. About twenty yards out they found a dead Japanese scout who had taken cover behind a coconut tree; he had laid his rifle down and taken out a pack of Lizard-brand cigarettes when a .50-caliber slug had taken off the top of his skull. The Marines were particularly impressed by the corpse's new uniform and how well fed he looked.

Nothing more was heard of Colonel Oka's command that day. The Japanese September offensive was over.

21

It was just coming up 1445, September 15, 1942. Carrier *Wasp* was off San Cristobal Island, in an area known as "Torpedo Alley." She had just launched freshly fueled fighters and scout-bombers to assume duties as combat air and anti-submarine patrols. Sixteen armed fighters were being spotted on the flight deck aft in takeoff positions, and aircraft from the noon patrol were already on the hangar deck for refueling.

A lookout suddenly yelled, "Torpedo wake on starboard bow!"

Then there was an explosion. Then a series of explosions.

The American carrier had been hit when she was most vulnerable to a torpedo attack. The fighters and scout-bombers just landed had been lowered to the hangar deck and were being refueled; the ship's gasoline-pumping system was filled with highly flammable aviation gasoline. The hits themselves were punishing, but not particularly damaging in terms of flooding. But the blasts set the hangar deck awash in burning fuel, and the fires quickly spread beyond control. Three armed SBDs were set afire, and the

500-lb depth charges slung beneath their bellies blew up. Water pressure throughout the carrier failed. Ammunition in the gun-gallery ready-ammunition areas was cooking off only five minutes after the torpedoes struck. Despite the heroic efforts of her crew, "Abandon ship!" had to be sounded only thirty-five minutes after *Wasp* was hit. The crew calmly lined up near the stern of the ship and took to the water in an orderly procession. All known survivors were picked up by escorting destroyers by nightfall; 193 men died and 366 were injured out of a complement of 2,247. Twenty-seven of *Wasp's* seventy-one precious aircraft were saved.

The new fast battleship *North Carolina* was also hit, and she had to return to the United States for repairs. A severely damaged destroyer limped to Espiritu Santo under her own power, but she later broke in two and sank en route to the West Coast. The lone Japanese submarine got clean away. *Hornet* barely evaded two torpedoes from the same six-torpedo spread that had hit the other warships. She was America's last fully operational fleet aircraft carrier.

The dispatch of America's last two operational fleet carriers to waters in which *Saratoga* had been torpedoed and damaged only two weeks earlier was made in support of the first major reinforcement of 1st Marine Division at Guadalcanal.

Adm Chester Nimitz had been ordered by Adm Ernest King as early as June 20 to facilitate the return of 7th Marines, 1st Battalion, 11th Marines, and sundry support units to 1st Marine Division at the earliest opportunity—not later than September 1. The interim would be used by the South Pacific staff to find a suitable force for replacing them in Samoa.

Then RAdm Kelly Turner got in the way. It had been Turner's intention that 2nd Marines be landed at Ndeni, in the Santa Cruz Islands, following the Guadalcanal and Tulagi landings. But all three rifle battalions of 2nd Marines had been committed in the Tulagi area and could not be re-embarked in time for Turner's forced retirement on August 9. So, on August 20, Turner issued a plan whereby the reinforced 7th Marines and 5th Marine Defense Battalion would occupy Graciosa Bay, Ndeni, to protect the airfield slated to be built there. High-level arguments briefly erupted, and they resulted in the temporary shelving of the Ndeni project.

Early in September, Admiral King proposed dispatching 7th Marines to spearhead upcoming amphibious operations in the Southwest Pacific, but Kelly Turner got *that* plan changed.

Richmond Kelly Turner was known to be extremely rigid of manner. However, he was among the most innovative of America's naval strategists, possessed of a brilliant, inquiring mind. He was far ahead of his superiors in divining how the amphibious war would ultimately be waged. By the first week of September, Turner felt that he was losing touch with the situation on Guadalcanal, so arranged to fly up with RAdm Slew McCain on September 12 to talk face-to-face with Archer Vandegrift. While McCain conferred with BGen Roy Geiger at Cactus Air Ops, Turner handed Vandergrift and LtCol Jerry Thomas a copy of a memorandum he had received from South Pacific headquarters: Without benefit of a first-hand glimpse of the holdings around Lunga by even one of VAdm Bob Ghormley's top subordinates—much less by the area commander himself—it had been decided and widely publicized that the chances of holding Guadalcanal were nil.

There had been moments Archer Vandegrift thought along the same line, but the general was by nature a positive thinker. The memorandum proffered by Turner set him back on his heels.

Turner's response to the message—and no one ever knew which way Kelly Turner was going to blow—was a proposal that the augmented 7th Marines be landed at Taivu Point to establish a second perimeter and support the building of a second airbase. Indeed, Turner hoped that elements of the fresh regiment might establish numerous small enclaves all around the coast of Guadalcanal to guard against landings by the Japanese. This was Kelly Turner, the tactician, at his egregious worst. But the amphibious force commander was within his rights to formulate such a plan, and to see it implemented. By virtue of unbreakable naval tradition—emanating from times, not several decades gone, when landing forces com-

prised small groups of bluejackets augmented by several Marines—
the naval-force commander was in all ways the superior of a landing-force commander.

Without saying that there was no point in establishing a second perimeter if the first could not be held, Vandegrift quietly suggested that 7th Marines be shipped posthaste to Lunga. The two
flag officers quibbled at length over various courses of action, but,
when they turned in under freshly erected canvas in the shadow of
the T-shaped ridge south of Henderson Field, Turner remained
unconvinced that he should support a landing by 7th Marines at
Kukum. The events of the night of September 12 changed his
mind.

First, the admiral was routed from his cot and sent scampering
for shelter, the result of the cruiser bombardment in support of
Kawaguchi Butai's first strong probe of Bloody Ridge. In the morning, a somber Archer Vandegrift took Turner on a tour of the
bloody remains of a hospital annex that had taken a direct hit in the
night. After breakfast, Turner quietly told Vandegrift that he
would recommend that 7th Marines, and all its supports, be moved
to Lunga, intact, as soon as he could assemble the necessary
shipping.

The loss of *Wasp* on September 15 was a seal on the promise.

On the afternoon of September 13, as LtCol Red Mike Edson
reshuffled his small force to withstand the expected grand assault,
Vandegrift quietly asked his operations officer, LtCol Jerry
Thomas, to draw up a plan for a guerrilla operation in the hills
behind Henderson Field—so certain had he become that the abandonment of the Lunga Perimeter and Henderson Field was imminent. Thomas bucked the job to his plans officer, LtCol Bill
Twining, who, sworn to absolute secrecy, spent the day writing a
single pencil draft of the plan, which he filed in the pocket of his
dungaree shirt.

Later in the day, Vandegrift invited his old friend, BGen Roy
Geiger, out for a walk. Geiger had spent the previous day with the
immensely positive and energetic RAdm Slew McCain, so he felt

that things were looking up. Vandegrift told Geiger about the Ghormley memorandum and about his own hitherto unexpressed doubts. He ended by telling the air boss about the plan he had asked Jerry Thomas to formulate, and that, if the time came to implement it, he wanted Geiger to get the precious aircraft to safety. Geiger's reply was a tonic: "If we can't use the planes back in the hills, we'll fly them out. But, whatever happens, I'm staying here with you."

Seventh Marines boarded ship in Samoa on September 2 and sailed to Espiritu Santo, where it awaited the outcome of the heated disagreements and constant changes in plans. Turner arrived at Noumea from Guadalcanal on September 13 and immediately met with Admiral Ghormley to urge the release of 7th Marines for duty in the Lunga Perimeter. Ghormley acceded.

Fifth Defense Battalion, which had accompanied 7th Marines from Samoa, was to remain behind, but it was replaced by 2nd Battalion, 10th Marines, a 75mm pack howitzer unit awaiting transport to rejoin 2nd Marines at Tulagi.

Kelly Turner organized a strong covering force to escort 7th Marines, 1st Battalion, 11th, and 2nd Battalion, 10th, to Guadalcanal. The force left Espiritu Santo at dawn, September 14, just as *Kawaguchi Butai* began its long march to Point Cruz. There were strong indications that large Japanese naval forces were on the move, a factor that obliged Turner to stand off lower San Cristobal on the afternoon of September 15 to await long-range air-patrol reports.

Meantime, Archer Vandegrift consolidated his position. Third Battalion, 2nd, was ordered to Guadalcanal from Tulagi to become the division reserve, and detachments from various regiments and battalions were ordered back to their parent organizations. In the end, the alert was relaxed. With his strength centered on Lunga, Vandegrift felt it was time to expand the Perimeter somewhat, so he planned for 7th Marines to man Beach Red as an eastward protrusion in his line. (The defeat of *Kawaguchi Butai* clearly had restored Vandegrift's optimism.)

Turner set out from San Cristobal early enough on September 16 to arrive off Kukum at 0550. The sea was fairly rough, so it was decided to land the reinforcements at that sheltered beach rather than at Beach Red; the plan for expanding the Perimeter eastward was quietly abandoned.

Several cargo vessels carrying drums of aviation gasoline arrived independently as the reinforcements were landing. Seventh Marines put on a spiffy performance. Spectators along the beach were surprised and gratified to see the well-trained regiment perform a precision combat landing.

Tension was running quite high among the novices of the 7th, who had no trouble seeing heavy bomb damage along the shoreline. Shortly after the landing operation began, a Marine lieutenant turned his SBD in over the channel to begin a routine approach on Henderson Field. The men in the boats, and quite a few ships' gunners, opened fire on the slow dive-bomber. It was sent skidding into the water only 100 yards from the beach. The wounded gunner was saved, but not the pilot.

By day's end, 4,180 fresh, eager Marines were ashore with 147 vehicles and a huge store of food, ammunition, and miscellaneous gear. The ammunition was the first landed at Guadalcanal since August 8.

On its return, the task force carried out the withered 1st Parachute Battalion, 162 wounded and ill Marines, and eight Japanese prisoners. The transports left the anchorage at 1800, just as that night's run of the Tokyo Express entered the channel by way of Savo. The Japanese did not give chase, but the incident unnerved Admiral Turner sufficiently for him to proclaim that no Allied transport would be allowed to remain in Sealark and Lengo channels after nightfall.

Next morning, all hands ashore were given full rations for the first time in over a month.

General Vandegrift issued orders on September 19 detailing a complete perimeter defense. Special and service units hitherto manning internal defensive cordons were moved to areas by the beach, and rifle battalions were sent inland. The Lunga Perimeter was divided into ten sectors, seven of which were to be manned by rifle battalions, of which there were by then ten on the island. With the arrival of ample troops and more supplies, the strictly defensive nature of the Perimeter was transformed; the defenses would henceforth be seen as screening a base from which limited offensive operations could be mounted.

The period of apprenticeship had drawn to a close.

At about the time 7th Marines arrived, Archer Vandegrift received a letter from the Commandant of the Marine Corps, LtGen Thomas Holcomb, authorizing the promotion *and transfer* of many officers, the better to train and lead a rapidly expanding wartime Marine Corps.

That left the Marine division commander with the task of sending several of his best senior staffers and troop commanders home. Several of the more-senior promotions and transfers were obligatory, but Vandegrift had the opportunity to choose replacements from among men who had shown great skill or drive during the opening weeks.

He replaced his outgoing chief of staff with Jerry Thomas, who was given his eagle solely on the basis of merit, for he was a relatively junior lieutenant colonel. One of the harder choices involved the relief of Col Roy Hunt from command of 5th Marines, though the relief placed Hunt in line for high command elsewhere. The jolt was buffered considerably by the promotion of Merritt Edson to full colonel and his succession to the command of 5th Marines. Bill Whaling was also promoted to full colonel and, though he should have been shipped home, was kept on to organize and train scouts. Col Pete del Valle, of 11th Marines, should have gone home, too, but Vandegrift could not bear to lose him, and proposed that he be given a star and kept on. A number of senior lieutenant colonels, some of them battalion commanders, were also sent home to make way for younger men.

By the time General Vandegrift finished his shuffling and juggling, he felt he had a tight, cohesive organization led by the best and brightest officers available to him. Of course, the opportunity to get rid of dead wood had been taken on with time-honored vigor and, though he was obliged to send home some of his very best troop leaders and staffers, Archer Vandegrift was, on balance, satisfied with the results.

22

There were big doings in Rabaul in the days following the defeat of *Kawaguchi Butai*. It was abundantly clear by then that there was a far larger force of Americans in the Eastern Solomons than anyone had dreamed the United States could field at that time. Rumblings could be heard clear back to Tokyo, and these resulted in the hurried dispatch of one of the Imperial Army's inner circle of war planners to Rabaul for command conferences with LtGen Harukichi Hyakutake, of 17th Army. It also meant making the entire crack 2nd Infantry Division available for deployment in the Eastern Solomons.

MGen Yumio Nasu, infantry-group commander of Sendai Division—as 2nd Division was known—arrived well in advance of his unit to get some idea of the type of fighting he could expect on Guadalcanal. Among others, he talked with a civilian news reporter named Gen Nishino who had accompanied General Kawaguchi, and who had been evacuated after the abortive brigade assault at Bloody Ridge. After a tentative start, General Nasu implored the correspondent, whom he had known for some time, to unburden himself, for it was clear that Nishino was holding back. The newsman did just that, relating that the soldiers had taken to calling Guadalcanal "Starvation Island," a pun derived from the first phoneme in the Japanese name for the island—*Ga*—which means, in one inflection, "hunger." Nasu next met with General Hyakutake, who was by then assuring everyone that he intended to embark shortly for Guadalcanal, to personally direct land operations.

The representative of the Imperial General Staff who arrived in Rabaul was LtCol Masanobu Tsuji, a brilliant planner known throughout the Army as the "God of Operations." Tsuji had planned the flawless occupations of French Indochina and Thailand, and the thrusts into Malaya, Burma, the East Indies, and the Philippines. His dispatch to Rabaul was the best indication that developments in the area had the full attention of Japan's highest military councils.

Tsuji's first analysis was that the naval officers in the area were erring badly in refusing to commit a major fleet component to protect a major counterinvasion of Guadalcanal. The very few ships and barges deployed by the Imperial Navy for lifting ground reinforcements to Guadalcanal necessitated a long, painstaking build-up of the larger units the Imperial Army was finally committing to the campaign. More ships and barges had to be made available so that the build-up could be made in the shortest time possible. Tsuji's solution was a personal trip to Truk for direct negotiations with Adm Isoroku Yamamoto. In a respectful but emotionally forceful presentation, Lieutenant Colonel Tsuji described how officers and soldiers on Guadalcanal were living far below subsistence level, and that General Hyakutake was determined to lose his life leading reinforcements to the island to expunge some of the Imperial Army's shame. Yamamoto accepted personal responsibility for delivering reinforcements safely to their destination.

This, of course, flew in the face of the experience and recommendations of RAdm Raizo Tanaka, who had yet to lose a man in his night landings, but who had lost hundreds in daylight attempts to get past Cactus-based dive-bombers.

But the die was cast. On returning from Truk with Admiral

Yamamoto's *written* approval, Tsuji went to work with 17th Army's senior staff officer, Col Haruo Konuma. They recommended the transfer of large Imperial Army air units to Rabaul to cover ground operations. Air support had been in the hands of naval squadrons, which were trained for guarding fleet units, and not for supporting ground forces. The idea, alas, was rejected at higher levels as there was some expectation that Russia might soon enter the war against Japan, and that required that all Japanese Army air units on the Asian mainland remain there.

Next, Colonel Konuma forestalled a move to relieve General Kawaguchi of command of 35th Infantry Brigade. Konuma knew from past association that Kawaguchi was a bright and forthright officer, so he arranged for the general to travel to Rabaul to deliver a briefing. Kawaguchi arrived as ordered, dressed in tatters, for his white dress uniform had been seized by Marine Raiders at Tasimboko. He showed severe physical symptoms of strain and hunger. There was little room to argue with Kawaguchi's testimony, so Colonel Konuma prevailed upon General Hyakutake to reconfirm Kawaguchi in his role as an infantry-force commander on Guadalcanal, where his experience would be required.

The situation on Guadalcanal continued to develop and change. While American strength rose to about 19,000 with the arrival of 7th Marines and two artillery battalions, the Japanese had also been funneling fresh troops to the island, mainly via the Tokyo Express.

Following Bloody Ridge, American patrols kept fairly close tabs on the movement and disposition of most Japanese within range. It was initially surmised that the main strength of *Kawaguchi Butai* had shifted completely around the Perimeter from east to west following the mid-September fighting. This was an accurate appraisal, though over 1,000 Japanese remained in the east. The feeling-out process also revealed that fresh units were being committed in the west. This, too, was accurate.

"Ant" operations continued through the period. Six hundred replacements were brought in to fill out the shattered 1st Battalion,

124th Infantry, which had borne the brunt of the Bloody Ridge fighting. Also, by the end of September, the rear echelon of Sendai Division's 4th Infantry (whose 2nd Battalion had been used to bolster *Kawaguchi Butai*) was landed at Kamimbo Bay by "Ants" and "Rats," as was most of the fresh 29th Infantry.

The effort to land troops and supplies did not go unnoticed, nor unpunished. On September 21, a destroyer-transport was strafed by Henderson-based fighters as it disembarked troops near Kamimbo Bay. In a rare night sortie on September 22, TBFs and SBDs caught several destroyer-transports in flare light near Visale. Two days later, two destroyers were worked over by American fighters.

Hard contacts on the ground, however, were extremely difficult to make or maintain because the Japanese kept the bulk of their infantry well out of reach. Intermittent photo-reconnaissance flights found nothing due to heavy foliage throughout the Japanese-occupied areas, which caused crucial gaps in intelligence estimates.

23

On September 22, the day Col Red Mike Edson assumed command of 5th Marines, he told MG Bill Rust that Rust would be responsible for mapping the so-called East-West Trail, a track Marines believed *Kawaguchi Butai* had hacked to Point Cruz from Bloody Ridge following the mid-September attacks.

Two days earlier, Edson told Rust, the fresh 1st Battalion, 7th, had stumbled across the trail and, in a two-day march, had discovered some abandoned booty, several Japanese corpses, several Japanese snipers, and several wounded Japanese soldiers. Rust was to report to the commander of 1st Battalion, 7th, that afternoon and guide a renewed effort by the battalion to follow the East-West Trail to its end, probably near Kokumbona.

Rust was delighted. He had not been particularly active for some time and was glad to be getting back into the bush. But his real pleasure came from having the opportunity to serve once again with the commander of 1st Battalion, 7th, a slight, sinewy forty-four-year-old lieutenant colonel named Lewis Burwell Puller, a colorful character who had been commissioned from the ranks after making a name for himself in the Banana Wars of the '20s and '30s. The two had met in the mid '30s; Puller, then an overaged captain, and Rust, a junior NCO, had found and shared a common love for the highly competitive team athletics used by the Marine Corps both to kill time and hone aggressive instincts.

The debut of Puller's battalion on September 20 had not been auspicious. On that day, the fresh unit had been sent out to patrol down the east bank of the Lunga River while 1st Raider Battalion patrolled down the west bank. All along the way, Puller's green riflemen had fired at everything that moved, including the Raiders across the way. After a time, Puller's enormous strength as a leader had won out over panic, and the troops had settled down. The Raiders did not do well that day either. Red Mike Edson, who was on his last assignment as the elite battalion's commander, became separated from the main body along with LtCol Sam Griffith, the new battalion commander, and Maj Ken Bailey, the new exec. The Raiders floundered around on the way back to the Perimeter until one of the battalion staffers took a firm grip and set things right.

Despite the confusion achieved by both units, it was certain that Puller's fresh, well-trained battalion would replace the dwindling Raider battalion as 1st Marine Division's primary patrol asset.

Puller's battalion mounted out at dawn, September 23, striking southwestward from its bivouac on Bloody Ridge and turned onto the well-worn path left by General Kawaguchi and his fleeing remnants ten days earlier. Lewie Puller and several scouts had the point, an arrangement that was and would be the combative battalion commander's hallmark.

The battalion snaked up and down grass-covered and tree-shrouded ridges, following the trail and its gruesome sprinkling of Japanese corpses across the lower slopes of Mount Austen.

At about the time Puller's battalion was tramping across Mount Austen, Capt Harry Connor's E Company, 5th, crossed the East-West Trail about four miles south of the Lunga Perimeter. Connor's Marines found a bivouac, several graves and, at length, an eight-man Japanese patrol. Signalers waved their flags at the Japanese, and one of them came to investigate while the others stayed out of range. Efforts were made to get the bold one to surrender, but he would not, and an effort to wound him in the leg failed. Grass fires were set to destroy bivouacs and equipment hidden in the bush, then E Company hiked home.

First Battalion, 7th, followed Puller, Rust, and the scouts through dense woods and across rolling savannah. On the way, the Marines picked the pockets and packs of several corpses they encountered, sweated the little water they were permitted, cursed the unrelenting heat, and bitched about the pace.

The column was buzzed shortly after noon by a Marine SBD, which went through strange aerobatics to get an unfathomable message across to the men on the ground. At length, a tiny object detached itself from the low-flying bomber—no doubt a written message attached to a tool. Though several platoons combed a field of high grass for some time, the message was not found and Lewie Puller ordered the battalion back on the trail.

Late in the afternoon, at a nameless place that did not appear on the photo montages the Marines used as maps because it had been beneath a cloud on the day the area was photographed, Bill Rust splashed across a tiny stream and moved down the trail a hundred yards before looking back. No one had followed. Rust backtracked to the stream, where he found his scouts filling their canteens and their bellies with iodine-laced water. He unleashed a few choice invectives and ordered the scouts to get across the stream before the main body closed up and made a huge target for any bushwhackers who might be preparing to spring an ambush there. The point men reluctantly reformed and followed Rust, who was by then about 150 yards down the trail.

While Rust was reforming the point, and as many Marines paused to drink, 1stLt Regan Fuller, a dark, wiry, energetic University of Virginia grad, led a corporal from his A Company platoon into the trees in hopes of finding a night bivouac suitable for the whole battalion. The two soon found themselves face-to-face with two Japanese soldiers, members of a fifty-man detachment guarding that section of the trail. Both teams recoiled in utter surprise. Regan Fuller recovered first and plugged one of the Japanese while the other fled for his life. Fuller and the corporal rushed to report.

At about the same time, Sgt Joe Goble's squad of B Company, which was behind Headquarters Company, breasted a small ridge and spotted two Japanese cooking rice over an open fire. The Japanese spotted the Marines at the same instant and slowly backed into a wall of trees. Neither group fired as B Company's 3rd Platoon slowly followed the quarry toward the trees.

Several battalion scouts were easing across the stream atop a huge mahogany log when Japanese gunners facing Rust's point, and others spread out along the banks of the stream, opened fire. The scouts plunged backward as bullets picked the bark from the fallen tree. Ahead, MG Bill Rust dived into a depression behind a tree and pulled his head into his shoulders as bullets whipped through the trees and bushes. Nearby, five riflemen from the lead A Company platoon were felled by the opening bursts.

Bill Rust's small point group quickly retrieved the dead and wounded, put out all the bullets it could, and crawled back to the stream under fire. There, Rust heard LtCol Lewie Puller's tidewater drawl, "Gunnuh, come back heah!" Rust low-crawled back across the shallow watercourse and up a slight rise to where the battalion commander was kneeling behind a huge log. He reported what he had seen, which was not much.

By the time Rust's point pulled back across the stream, A Company had been fought to a standstill. Puller bellowed an order for B Company to mount a frontal assault on two Japanese machine guns which were firing into the scattered A Company platoons, so Capt Chester Cockrell, the B Company commander, led the 1st Platoon up the right side of the trail while 1stLt Walter Olliff led his 2nd Platoon up the left. First Lieutenant James McIlwain's 3rd Platoon went right up the middle as Lewie Puller bellowed, "Bring 'em up, Cockrell!" The B Company commander, a happy-go-lucky former "Ole Miss" football player did that, leading his 1st Platoon forward into the machine-gun fire. He blasted away with a .45 automatic in each hand until felled by a round in the face.

B Company's 3rd Platoon lunged into the water, but stalled against the five-foot-high bank that was being swept by grazing fire. The platoon milled about in confusion for a few moments, then beat a hasty retreat. Sgt Joe Goble blindly ran to a huge tree and hid, then scrabbled rearward with the pack and leaped behind a huge fallen log, almost on top of a Marine who had been wounded in the buttocks. Lewie Puller was standing on his knees a few feet away, directing the fight from behind the chest-high barrier, calling for Captain Cockrell until he convinced himself that the company commander was down.

First Lieutenant Walter Olliff's 2nd Platoon, in the trees on B Company's left, managed to drive forward through heavy fire emanating from its left front. Each time the Japanese stopped firing, the two leading squads plunged ahead several yards, then hit the ground. A BAR-man was hit by several rounds in the fleshy part of his right leg, just above the knee. Already weak from a bout of dysentery, the boy turned the automatic rifle over to his assistant and crawled to the rear. The assistant was hit a minute later by a round that took off half his face. Only minutes later, Walter Olliff rose to his knees and blindly lobbed a hand grenade into the trees. He immediately caught a round through his left hip which exited his right buttock. The blond lieutenant fell over onto his face; another round passed right along his lips, filling his mouth with sand and leaves. Numb from the waist down, Olliff whiled away the time singing or humming to himself. After five minutes, he saw but could not react to a Japanese who rose from a nearby foxhole and fired at him. The bullet creased the platoon leader's left leg, just below the knee. Olliff returned the fire with his automatic pistol; the Japanese did not reappear, but Olliff could not be certain he had scored. A rifleman pulled him behind a tree moments later. Nearby, another young rifleman was shot through the shoulder; he was soon screaming "I'm dying! I've been hit!" And that thoroughly unnerved the lieutenant.

It was by then dark, and there was no point for the Marine battalion to continue fighting on strange ground at night. Puller ordered C Company, which had not been engaged, to withdraw and find a suitable, defensible night bivouac somewhere to the rear. The engaged elements of A and D companies were next withdrawn, then B Company picked up its wounded and raced to the rear through the dark, eerie forest.

Walter Olliff, one of twenty-eight wounded Marines, was treated by a corpsman who had earlier run out of morphine; he was carried, in pain and bleeding, by six Marines who hoisted him face-down and staggered under his dead weight back up the trail. He was dosed with morphine, which did not help, and placed in a poncho, which six fresh Marines carried up the ridge. Halfway up, the poncho ripped, and Olliff plunged face-first to the ground. The pain nearly killed him. He was placed on another poncho and humped up the slope until it became too steep to continue on in that manner. Two men lifted him bodily up the slope, and he finally passed out from the pain and shock. He came to later in the night to find that a poncho had been placed between him and the damp ground and another poncho was over him.

Several of the wounded died in the night, and several bodies that had been left by the stream overnight were recovered by a combat patrol after sunrise. The patrol, composed of most of B Company, swung wide around the battle site and found several graves, but no living Japanese. Emplacements for nine machine guns were also found. Thirteen Marines were buried in shallow graves and twenty-five wounded were treated by the doctors and corpsmen.

When Lewie Puller had first reported details of the skirmish and withdrawal to division headquarters at 2030 the previous evening, he had requested that air support be provided at dawn, and that seventeen litters be air-dropped for the more-seriously injured.

The situation was somewhat more serious than it seemed at first glance. General Vandegrift, who was closely monitoring the sweep, knew only too well that evacuating the wounded would cut

Puller's effective strength by at least 100 men, over ten percent of the battalion. The division intelligence section felt that Puller faced a hot fight if he advanced at dawn, so the division commander advised Puller that he would be reinforced by 2nd Battalion, 5th, and supported by fighters and dive-bombers. Next, Vandegrift allowed the aggressive battalion commander to make a decision: would he prefer to withdraw, or stand and fight a possibly superior enemy force on its own ground? Puller decided to put off answering that one until he had a better grasp of the situation.

LtCol Walker Reaves's tested 2nd Battalion, 5th, left Kukum at 0500, September 25, and force-marched to Puller's hillside bivouac by 0845. When Puller counted his force of nearly 1,300 combat Marines, he decided to press on, but he modified the plan.

C Company, 7th, its attached medium-machine-gun platoon, and the battalion headquarters would march to the coast with Reaves's battalion, but A and B companies and their medium-machine-gun platoons would return to the Perimeter with their wounded under the command of the battalion exec, Maj Buck Rogers.

The casualty column ran into no Japanese, but the wounded suffered almost beyond endurance, particularly stretcher cases like 1stLt Walter Olliff, who was borne aloft by rotating teams of six B Company riflemen. Sgt Joe Goble, who took several turns at carrying Olliff, was convinced that the platoon leader would die—and so was Olliff—but he and most of the others survived the journey. (Olliff was flown to Espiritu Santo two days later, following emergency surgery.) The half-battalion under Major Rogers returned to its former bivouac on Bloody Ridge late on September 26, a Saturday.

Puller's rump force, and Reaves's unit, moved out late on the morning of September 25, bent upon catching the Japanese who had ambushed Puller's point the previous evening. The trail led the Marine column north and west toward the lower Matanikau River, nearer the coast than expected. The going was slow and rough, the trail steep, narrow, and overgrown. The combined force, which was under Puller's command, bivouacked on a high ridge east of and overlooking the Matanikau, about 2,000 yards from the beach. Capt Harry Connor's E Company, 5th, found fires with the embers still glowing. Winking campfires on hills to the north indicated that the American force was under surveillance. When Puller reported to division headquarters that evening, he was ordered to give up his chase along the trail, cut due north to the beach, and return to the Perimeter.

Following a quiet night, the column moved northwestward, downhill toward the river. On reaching the stream, the point turned northward. MG Bill Rust assured Puller that the remainder of the route to the beach was across flat ground. As the tail of the column turned onto the river trail, several Japanese on the west bank, and quite far away, fired on it. No casualties were inflicted and the rear guard soon hustled beyond the range of the Japanese rifles. Marines at the point of the column did not hear the gunfire, nor were they made aware of it.

Puller halted the column several hundred yards short of the beach and called Reaves, Rust, and several key officers for a council of war. The officers debated the suggestion that the force sweep through Matanikau Village, west of the river mouth, before proceeding home. All opted for the sweep.

Gunner Rust, who had fought into the village from the opposite side six weeks earlier, was given the point. He deployed his scouts at ten-yard intervals, took the number-four spot himself, and ordered them out onto the sandspit. The leading element of Capt Harry Connor's E Company, 5th, was right behind the scouts.

It was about 1400, Saturday, September 26, and the lead scout was about to step from the sandspit into the stream bordering the village when a barrage of grenades flung by knee mortars burst on all sides. The sand absorbed most of the blasts, but Rust and several others were knocked down. The gunner came up running, hollering orders for the other men to pull back. All returned safely and burrowed into the root system of the nearest banyan tree on the east bank of the river mouth. Rust breathed a sigh of relief, but suddenly felt a wet patch growing on his back. He did not hurt at all, and a closer inspection revealed that a can of meat-and-beans in his pack had taken the brunt of the blast that had knocked him down. E Company recoiled and deployed where it stood in the trees bordering the stream. Light machine guns were quickly broken out and everyone who could bring his weapon to bear opened fire.

Several hundred yards downstream, the rear of the column was hit by a rain of grenades, then fired on by hidden riflemen and gunners across the stream. Everyone went to ground while Puller ordered Walker Reaves to deploy alongside the river and mount a direct assault across the sandspit. Reaves ordered Capt Tom Richmond's G Company to attack through E Company.

The lead G Company platoon, under 2ndLt Paul Moore, dropped into the water several hundred feet south of the sandspit. The bottom dropped away about midstream, forcing the Marines to swim a few yards through a growing volume of fire. One of Moore's Marines was hit just as he reached the lee of the west bank. As the rest of the platoon withdrew, Moore swam to the west bank to rescue the wounded man. G Company tried again, and Paul Moore's platoon went first once again. Despite heavy support from E Company, G Company recoiled to the protection of the trees; twenty-five Marines had been killed or wounded.

While E and G companies were battling the Japanese across the river, seaplane tender *Ballard*, an old converted destroyer, arrived off the beach and signaled that she would add her fires to the general mayhem at the river mouth if someone ashore would direct her. Pfc Johnny Smolka, a signalman with 2nd Battalion, 5th, who happened to be kneeling in the bush beside Lewie Puller, sauntered out onto the beach and responded to the Navy signalman with semaphore flags, "Wait one." Bill Rust also read the signal and, while Smolka responded, volunteered to swim out to direct the ship's fire. Smolka next signaled, "Send boat to beach to contact officer." The destroyer responded, however, "Where do you want us to fire?" Smolka had by then been forced by machine-gun fire from the tip of Point Cruz to step back into the trees. A former hobo whose nerves had been strengthened from years of riding the rails through the South, Smolka stepped forward into the fire once again and wig-wagged, "Do not fire. Officer on beach. Send boat to pick him up." The gunfire permanently forced Smolka from the open.

Bill Rust was already in the water, pulling for the ship, and was picked up after swimming 500 yards. Soon, he was sitting in *Ballard*'s battery director's chair aiming the ship's 5-inch guns. Several salvoes were fired, but their effect could not be observed. *Ballard* turned for Kukum at sunset and dropped Rust off on the beach. He immediately hitched a ride back to the river to rejoin Puller's command group.

It was too late to mount additional attacks, so the companies dug in for the night. Puller reported to division headquarters, which ordered him to renew his attack in the morning, adding that support would be sent. Division headquarters then ordered LtCol Sam Griffith's 1st Raider Battalion to cross the river south of Puller in the morning and attack the Japanese right flank.

No one thought that evening to notify Maj Buck Rogers's portion of Puller's battalion about the fight on the Matanikau. Next morning, a Sunday, Rogers carefully washed and shaved and dressed in a clean khaki shirt, riding breeches, and smooth leather puttees before heading for the open-air church service being held behind Bloody Ridge at 0900. The service lasted only a few minutes, for Major Rogers was ordered to march his group to Kukum to board boats and land in support of Puller's renewed assault at the mouth of the Matanikau. Capt Charlie Kelly, who had temporarily given up command of C Company, 7th, to nurse an ankle injured on patrol on September 20, insisted on going with Rogers; he got the battalion to Kukum while Major Rogers, too rushed to change into utilities, was briefed at Division.

The Japanese on the west bank of the river were to be hit by three Marine forces operating under the control of Col Red Mike Edson: Puller's, comprising his own Headquarters and C companies and Reaves's battalion, would mount assaults at the river mouth, pinning the Japanese or, at least, fixing their attention; the Raiders would cross the river well to the Japanese right, at a wooden bridge more than a mile from the beach; Rogers's half of Puller's battalion would land beyond Point Cruz and roll the Japanese up from the rear. It was a hastily contrived plan, the largest mounted by the Marines to date. The result of a chance encounter, it was not a carefully plotted concept.

Bill Rust joined the Raiders in the morning to guide them through the bush behind Puller's lines at the river mouth. The objective, a tiny wooden footbridge, was near the spot where Puller's force had turned downriver the previous day. The Raiders were to cross the bridge, turn north, and pitch into the right flank of the Japanese who had Puller and Reaves pinned at the river mouth. Rust did not then know that the tail of Puller's column had taken long-range fire from the vicinity of the bridge the previous afternoon, so he could not warn LtCol Sam Griffith that the crossing might be contested.

The Raiders came upon a small clearing just short of the bridge. Griffith, Maj Ken Bailey, and MG Bill Rust advanced to observe the open ground before moving to the stream. Bailey was in the middle and Griffith was on the left. Rust, who was on the right, was pointing out the trail to the west when a machine gun opened fire on the group. At the same moment, light mortars and other machine guns opened on the vanguard of the Raider column. Griffith and Rust rolled away to the right, but Bailey's instincts carried him backward, away from the guns. Seven bullets etched a crooked line up Ken Bailey's back and instantly killed him. Raiders caught in a fairly open, low-lying position about twenty feet across and between two dominating ridges, returned the fire, but they really could not see their assailants.

Severely shaken by Bailey's death, Griffith issued a string of commands aimed at establishing a base of fire and clearing his front. A reinforced company was left near the clearing while the remainder of the battalion moved into the bush in search of some maneuvering room. Progress was agonizingly slow as the larger part of the battalion moved single-file up a narrow spine. Hours were lost, but, by midafternoon, Griffith was ready to attack the

Japanese flank. As the battalion commander moved up a little side slope to get a good look around, he was painfully wounded in the shoulder and had to be dragged to cover by Bill Rust. Several other Raiders were also hit by fire from higher up.

Officers gathered around Griffith and discussed their plight. It was too late in the day to launch a meaningful assault, the Raiders were on poor ground for a night defense, and high hills all around effectively blocked communications. Nevertheless, and despite his painful wound, Griffith was prepared to hold his position or, if so ordered, deliver his assault. Gunner Rust shed some of his equipment and hiked rapidly back to the beach, where he reported to Colonel Edson, who had come forward hours earlier to direct Puller's assault at the river mouth. Revived by a shot of medicinal brandy, Rust hustled back more than a mile to the Raider CP and relayed Red Mike's instructions: Return to the beach.

The communications difficulties the Raiders had experienced throughout the day precipitated an unfortunate series of events on the coast, and on both sides of the Matanikau. An early report, detailing the initial contact with the Japanese guarding the bridge, had resulted in the misunderstanding at the division CP that the Raiders were fighting *west* of the river. This signaled the start of further attempts by Puller's force, at the river mouth, to reopen its attack. It also resulted in orders to Maj Buck Rogers, who was waiting at Kukum, to mount out and land his force on the beach west of Point Cruz.

The Japanese noon air strike hit the Perimeter just as Rogers's boats were embarking in the company of *Ballard*. The destroyer was obliged to sail into open waters to evade the strike, but the landing craft wore on westward to maintain their schedule. Many Japanese bombs hit around the division CP, disrupting communications throughout the Perimeter and, of consequence, among the elements of Colonel Edson's attack force.

Buck Rogers's boats turned at just 1300. B Company went in first to clear the beach, and landed without incident. The major was heard to exclaim, on landing, "Lord! We've landed in the wrong place! We landed too soon!"

The reinforced company quickly reorganized on the beach and pushed inland, across the Government Track and into a coconut grove. Sgt Joe Goble, whose squad was on the extreme right flank, tripped over a green communications wire in the underbrush, then entered a Japanese battalion bivouac in the trees. Two of Goble's riflemen spotted a Japanese soldier, who escaped before the Marines could fire at him. B Company advanced up a shallow slope without incident to a high, grassy ridge, the easternmost spur of Hill 84, about 500 yards south of the beach.

As riflemen deployed in a defensive arc, Major Rogers called in the B Company officers and NCOs for a briefing.

Buck Rogers had served for years in the organized Marine Corps Reserve and had been called up with his Washington, D.C., unit in November 1940. He was a mild-mannered, soft-spoken, politically active Southerner, a Post Office official who for years had been responsible for issuing America's new stamps. Though he had never before commanded Marines in combat, no one doubted his ability to do well this day.

Capt Zach Cox, B Company's new commander, called for a runner just as the officers and sergeants were gathering. A rifleman named Hoffman was turning to respond, and Sgt Joe Goble was about to join the command conference, when a Japanese knee mortar lofted a grenade into the midst of the group, right between Major Rogers and Captain Cox. Everyone for several feet around went down in a mass of arms and legs. Joe Goble and another sergeant were bowled over onto their backs, unscathed, Private Hoffman was brutally injured in the stomach and abdomen, and Captain Cox received terrible wounds in the arm. Buck Rogers, still dressed in the khakis and leather puttees he had donned for church, was blown nearly in two.

A Company landed at about that moment. As Capt Charlie Kelly, the senior man with A Company, though not its commander, was seeing to moving inland, flankers on the right spotted Japanese approaching down the Government Track in columns of threes. One machine gun held the Japanese at bay while A Company moved to join B Company on the ridge, but the guncrew was overrun before it could withdraw.

Charlie Kelly was a thoroughly unflappable troop leader who had served with Buck Rogers in the Marine Corps Reserve. He took command of the two reinforced companies and ordered everyone to dig in. The Japanese were forming in the coconut grove below the ridge.

While the Japanese force that had appeared on the Government Track west of the beach moved eastward to join units already deployed against Colonel Edson's force at the mouth of the Matanikau, the Japanese battalion whose bivouac had been uncovered by B Company, 7th, deployed on three sides of Charlie Kelly's force to hold it in place. Kelly had only one 81mm mortar along, and only fifty rounds of 81mm ammunition. This was in the hands of MGySgt Ray Fowel, a mortarman of legendary stature. Kelly gave Fowel a free hand to fire at targets of opportunity, both at the Japanese passing eastward along the Government Track and those deploying against Hill 84. Some of the rounds were placed on targets so close to the hill—within 200 yards—that the mortar had to be held steady in an absolutely vertical position by a Marine lying on his back with his feet braced against the tube. While Fowel's fire had some effect, there was little that the small, immobile force could do to stop the larger, mobile one. Kelly had no radio, so could not warn Puller or Edson of the new threat, nor even call for help.

All three elements of the Marine force were immobilized. Puller's force was trying to break the continuing deadlock at the mouth of the Matanikau; G and F companies, 5th, each sustained excessive casualties trying to force the river, but nothing was accomplished against increasing opposition. The Raiders were by then stopped short of the bridge and were snaking uphill in an effort to get around the Japanese bases of fire across the river and on

adjacent ridges. The position of Capt Charlie Kelly's two reinforced companies was only dimly perceived by the other forces.

Nerves were wearing thin among Charlie Kelly's Marines on
Hill 84. The Japanese mounted repeated efforts to sweep the ridge,
and were barely held. Most of the assaults were launched up the
narrow eastern nose of the ridge, where few Marines could be deployed. Fortunately, Sgt Roy Surles and Pvt John Giles, of D Company, were able to set up a .30-caliber medium machine gun on the
nose, and that held the attackers off. But ammunition was limited
and could not be replenished.

In the rush to get clear of Kukum in the morning, no one had
thought to bring a radio, so there was no way to get support. Late
in the afternoon, 1stLt Dale Leslie, a Marine dive-bomber pilot,
happened to pass over Hill 84. When Leslie looked down from several hundred feet, he thought he saw the letters H-E-L-P spelled
out on the ground below. A second pass confirmed his surmise;
Kelly's troops had stripped off their skivvie undershirts and "written" the message on the grass. Leslie immediately radioed a report,
which was relayed to Colonel Edson's headquarters. There, Lewie
Puller thrust out his chest and demanded a ride back to the Perimeter. He was going to secure boats and evacuate Kelly's isolated
force.

Puller boarded *Ballard* at Kukum within the hour and the de-
stroyer-turned-tender hastily beat up the coast, a line of landing
craft following at top speed. As soon as Charlie Kelly saw the
smoke-belching destroyer from his vantage point atop Hill 84, he
ordered Sgt Danny Raysbrook, the communicator who had ne-
glected to bring his radio along, to stand in the open and signal the
destroyer with semaphore flags, which he had brought. Raysbrook
got an immediate response: Kelly was to withdraw immediately to
the beach to be picked up by landing craft. Kelly replied that his
force was cut off from the beach. *Ballard* asked for fire directions,
which Kelly relayed through Sergeant Raysbrook.

Ballard opened fire, and forward observers overlooking the river directed howitzers at the western edge of Henderson Field against Japanese troop concentrations at and near the base of Point Cruz, thus preventing Japanese soldiers nearer the river from moving to engage Kelly during the ticklish withdrawal. Several friendly registration rounds landed well over their intended targets and felled several Marines.

While *Ballard* found the range and chewed up the attackers below the hill, Charlie Kelly ordered the D Company commander to lead the way to the beach with a mixed force of riflemen and gunners, and establish a base of fire. The gunners quickly dismantled several machine guns and lugged them down the steep, grassy slope toward the coconut grove. *Ballard*'s 5-inch guns fired into the coconut trees while leaving a path to the beach clear for the Marines.

Pvt Jack Ellenberger, a B Company BAR-man, helped carry a wounded Marine down the steep slope in a slippery rubber poncho. Inevitably, the carriers and the painfully injured Marine slid and skidded to a painful thump at the base of the ridge. Then it was off through the trees, bracketed on both sides by the near bursts of *Ballard*'s shells. Several misdirected rounds landed among the fleeing men, breaking up the tight unit formations that had left the ridge.

Pvt John Giles, manning the machine gun on the eastern nose of Hill 84, refused to leave his position until everyone else had dropped down off the ridge. He was last seen firing at dogged Japanese attackers. Below, already in the trees, PlSgt Anthony Malinowski, of A Company, took a BAR from the hands of a wounded gunner and told his platoon leader that he would cover the retreat. Malinowski did not make it out, but a flurry of automatic-rifle bursts could be heard by the retreating men for several precious minutes.

The reinforced companies reformed on the beach just to the west of Point Cruz within forty-five minutes of *Ballard*'s opening salvo. The landing craft that had accompanied *Ballard* turned in toward the beach and were making top speed through the light swell when they began taking enfilade fire from Japanese machine guns set at the end of the point. All of the coxswains hesitated and slowed their craft, then took evasive action beyond the range of the guns, *away from the beach!*

Though Capt Tom Cross, the A Company commander, had earlier been wounded in the wrist, he ran into the waves and kicked through the surf, determined to swim out to direct the boats to land. 1stLt Dale Leslie, who was orbiting overhead in his dive-bomber when the boats turned back, immediately overflew the milling craft, wagged his wings to get their attention, and fired his .50-caliber fixed nose machine guns over the heads of the Marines on the beach to show the boat crews that he would support them.

The Japanese had long since recovered their aplomb following Kelly's unexpected fighting withdrawal through their bivouac, and they were leaning heavily upon the tiny Marine enclave. It took the boat crews thirty minutes to get up the nerve to breast the Japanese fire from Point Cruz and land on the twenty-five-by-one-hundred-yard strip of sand.

The first boat grounded on a sand bar thirty yards from the beach. Captain Kelly ordered the casualties out first. Six-man teams carrying the litter cases in ponchos stumbled through the surf in relays, depositing their charges on the deck of the landing boat until it was too crowded for more. Other boats had by then pulled up onto the sand bar and wounded were carried out to them. Kelly was gratified to see that all the carriers returned, as ordered, to the beach for new burdens or to fight.

When the last of the wounded had been loaded, Charlie Kelly told his officers and noncoms to get the rest of the troops off the beach. The tiny perimeter slowly contracted as the Marines withdrew and the Japanese pressed in, too close to be fired on by *Ballard*'s ready guns.

One boat remained longer than the others. Its coxswain, Coast Guard Signalman 1st Class Douglas Munro, was also the landing-boat group commander. When one of his boat's gunners was felled, Munro leaped to the gun mount and fired the exposed .30-caliber machine gun at Japanese positions in the trees. Following an exchange of many nerve-wracking minutes, Munro was killed when a Japanese mortar round burst beside his boat. He thus became the only U.S. Coastguardsman ever to be awarded a Medal of Honor.

Pvt Jack Ellenberger, of B Company, was aboard Munro's boat when it left the beach. He had helped carry aboard the same Private Hoffman who had been seriously wounded beside Maj Buck Rogers hours earlier. The tiny plywood craft was barely off the sand when its steering went out, and it circled three times through heavy fire from the beach and Point Cruz as the crew frantically worked to correct the problem. Suddenly a lone Marine burst out of the trees by the beach and ran through the surf, screaming for the boat to wait for him. Breathless and fearful, the man lurched through the waves, his hands extended in front of him. As he grabbed at the plywood gunwale, he was lifted aboard, and the boat picked up speed to join the pack headed for Kukum. Private Ellenberger and the others got down to see how Private Hoffman was doing. The boy asked for a cigarette, and one was immediately placed between his lips. He took a deep drag and expelled the smoke with his last breath. Ellenberger and the others watched in stunned silence as tendrils of smoke drifted out through the dead man's perforated abdomen.

Buck Rogers's force lost twenty-four killed and twenty-three wounded in its abortive operation.

All of the Marines had withdrawn into the Lunga Perimeter by nightfall. Intelligence estimated that 1,800 Japanese had performed in the widespread fighting, and that about 60 of them had been killed and about 100 had been wounded. The cobbled-together operation had come close to being a first-rate fiasco. The Marines had been aggressively led, but they had been outfought.

It was a strong lesson.

24

Adm Chester Nimitz, the U.S. Pacific Theater commander
in chief, landed at Henderson Field on September 30 as
part of a lengthy and ambitious effort to take stock of the
forces deployed under his command.

The Nimitz trip had begun some weeks earlier with a journey
to San Francisco for ultra-high-level consultations with Adm Ernest King and the Navy officers directing the Pacific War. The con-
ferees detailed a series of sweeping command changes, almost
worldwide, aimed at bringing the effort in the Pacific, and particularly in the South Pacific, to some sort of order.

Of immediate interest in the South Pacific was the replacement of RAdm Slew McCain, the area aircraft commander, who
would be assuming delicate and important duties in Washington.
He was to be replaced by RAdm Aubery Fitch, an aggressive and
successful Coral Sea veteran. VAdm William Halsey was to command the carriers.

While stopping over at his Pearl Harbor headquarters on September 20, Nimitz hosted Gen Henry "Hap" Arnold, commander

in chief of the U.S. Army Air Forces. Arnold told Nimitz that he had been greeted in Hawaii by MGen Delos Emmons, commander of Army aircraft in the Pacific, who was just back from a tour of the South and Southwest Pacific areas, which included a stopover at Noumea to speak with VAdm Bob Ghormley. Emmons had reported that his meeting with Ghormley was charged with a sense of defeat—a feeling many senior officers had experienced at meetings with Ghormley.

On September 25, Nimitz departed Pearl Harbor with members of his senior staff. A fortuitous meeting at Canton Island with Slew McCain, who was on his way home, gave the theater commander a fair understanding of what he might find in Noumea. A day was gained in crossing the International Dateline, so the admiral's party arrived in Noumea on September 28, east longitude time. And there Nimitz met a tired, depressed Bob Ghormley. Part of the area commander's attitude was formed, Nimitz guessed, by remaining cooped up for weeks at a time aboard his command ship, *Argonne,* a condition brought on by the refusal of his French "hosts" to offer more cheerful accommodations ashore. But the physical surroundings were only part of the story. Ghormley seemed mentally burned out from having had to face insurmountable tasks for nearly half a year.

A top-level conference was convened aboard *Argonne* in the afternoon, and it ran well into the evening. In attendance, besides Nimitz and Ghormley and members of their staffs, were General Arnold and MGen Richard Sutherland, Douglas MacArthur's Southwest Pacific chief of staff. The discussion revolved largely around Guadalcanal. Nimitz was surprised to learn that numerous combat aircraft had been amassed in the South Pacific, but that most were being held in reserve. Arnold was so dismayed that he stated that no additional Army aircraft would be deployed in the area until those in reserve had been put to use against the Japanese.

Nimitz wanted to know what Ghormley planned to do with several Army regiments stationed in the rear, and why none had yet been transported to Guadalcanal. And he asked several pointed questions about the singular lack of aggressive surface patrolling by naval units in the waters adjacent to Guadalcanal, and why the Tokyo Express was allowed to operate there with impunity. Nimitz was deeply affected by Ghormley's reaction to two urgent messages from Guadalcanal that arrived during the session. In both cases, Ghormley muttered, "My God! What are we going to do about *this?*"

Nimitz spent September 29 touring Noumea, New Caledonia, and Espiritu Santo, and speaking at length with RAdm Aubery Fitch, and MGen Al Patch, whose newly formed Americal Division would eventually replace Marine units on Guadalcanal. Then Nimitz flew to Guadalcanal aboard a B-17. Following some excitement when the bomber was nearly lost in a storm, the admiral's party arrived at Henderson Field in the midst of a fearsome downpour.

Despite the rain, Nimitz insisted upon touring Bloody Ridge, where he exchanged pleasantries with his old shipmate, LtCol Lewie Puller, and made a trip to the hospital, where he spoke to the ill and wounded Marines who filled the tents. Nimitz saw how confident the Marines were; nothing he heard warranted the depression he had seen in Noumea, though he saw much that disturbed him.

After a pleasant dinner, Nimitz and Archer Vandegrift at last found an opportunity to hold a frank private discussion on a wide range of issues. Vandegrift made a point of telling Nimitz how he felt about the meddling of Kelly Turner in the conduct of the land battle. Vandegrift had an ambivalent attitude toward Turner, whom he certainly respected and with whom he felt a kinship born of adversity. But there was a negative side to the relationship, neither wholly personal nor wholly professional.

Turner was an austere, brilliant traditionalist with a decided bent for technical innovation, though he tended to mix in matters not entirely within his ken. A surface officer, he had seen enough potential in naval aviation to have put himself through the rigors of flight training at age forty-two. Marked early in his career as a "comer," he had the opportunity to function in a wide range of disciplines, and he excelled in all of them.

However, from the moment Archer Vandegrift's command had been flung into the Lower Solomons, Turner had been a constant source of well-meaning irritation. He had shown a particular bent for meddling with ground operations on a tactical level, something for which he was neither trained nor possessed of any extraordinary insight or talent. He had irked many senior Marine officers on quite a few memorable occasions, and his meddling was having a negative influence upon operations and, ultimately, upon the security of the Lunga Perimeter. It is not surprising, however, that Turner felt he was uniquely suited to assist in making decisions on the ground, for he had built his reputation on the opinion of others that he was good at whatever he took on.

The amphibious-force commander's latest contribution was the suggestion that 2nd Marine Raider Battalion, which in mid August had won laurels for the famed Makin Raid, be landed at various points around the coast of Guadalcanal to destroy Japanese observation stations. With 1st Raiders weakened by repeated combat and illness, General Vandegrift felt that he needed the tough 2nd Raiders as a strike force based at Lunga. He had written several blunt letters to Turner, each expressing this simple imperative, but the matter was far from settled.

In fact, there was a larger issue at stake, and Vandegrift took the opportunity to lay it before Admiral Nimitz. Tradition viewed the Marine Corps as subordinate to the Navy, and Marine officers were viewed as being subordinate to naval officers of equal rank. This rule applied particularly where a landing force was involved; the fleet commander ruled supreme. However, tradition had never contemplated a landing force as large as the augmented division holding Lunga, nor had it contemplated the catch-as-catch-can method of doing business then prevailing in the South Pacific. Vandegrift was a superb ground commander. In truth, he was the commander of a ground force operating quite independent of a naval force. Turner, however, had long chosen to overlook that last point.

Little real or lasting harm had yet been done by Turner. As the senior representative of his junior branch of service—a service which proudly espoused a unique doctrine for the conduct of amphibious warfare—Archer Vandegrift felt constrained to look to the future. And he saw in that future situations that would be direly affected by Turner's strongly held views.

Vandegrift told Nimitz unequivocally that he viewed the protection of Henderson Field as his division's primary mission, that Turner's proposed landings elsewhere were beyond the capability of his command, and that committing the fresh troops needed at Lunga to such ventures would jeopardize the security of the Lunga Perimeter and the vital airbase it guarded.

Asked to comment upon what he considered the most important lesson learned thus far on Guadalcanal, Vandegrift referred to the tendency of senior naval officers to place the safety of individual vessels above the outcome of the mission, of the tendency of many commanders to hold back rather than fight through. Vandegrift referred to the need for a new set of naval regulations he knew Nimitz wanted to write: "Leave out all reference that he who runs his ship aground will suffer a fate worse than death. Out here, too many commanders have been too leery about risking their ships."

By the time the talk broke up, Archer Vandegrift was certain he had found a new and willing ally. The days ahead were to show the accuracy of that surmise.

Despite Admiral Nimitz's very best intentions, it would take time to weed out the faint-of-heart before truly aggressive actions could take place. The shocking losses at Savo, the sinking of *Wasp*, and the damage sustained by *Enterprise* and *Saratoga* militated against truly bold use of what remained of the U.S. Fleet.

The Japanese had taken a relatively conservative course, though their strategy was based on a view somewhat different from that taken in the United States. While American admirals were fighting a waiting game and would eventually marshal the fruits of an unprecedented fleet expansion, the Japanese never expected to fully replace their shipping losses, and they certainly had no expectation of exceeding them, as would in time their American adversary. The result was that both navies were loath to engage in surface actions near Guadalcanal. Rather, each was looking for a larger stroke involving a decisive, massive naval battle in open waters. Small fights in Lengo Channel would gain no strategic advantage for either side, though Nimitz was coming to realize that important tactical considerations had to be fulfilled by picking fights with Japanese surface vessels.

In time, a bizarre accommodation was established: Japanese destroyer-transports unloaded at night, when American aircraft were ineffectual, and American transports worked by day, when friendly aircraft could cover them.

Daily, Admiral Tanaka's fast destroyer-transports hovered in the Shortland Islands until the late afternoon, then steamed the final 200 miles to Cape Esperance, where most of the unloading took place. American aircrews had just enough time before sunset to launch a single strike upon the Japanese ships, which maneuvered erratically as the aircraft approached. Few hits were scored, and few ships were sunk, and all but a few airmen refused to strafe the troop-laden vessels.

While the Japanese destroyer-transports were landing troops and cargo, those that had already unloaded, and their escorts, often ran to Lunga Point and fired salvoes at the runway and defenses. Nightly, four-engine flying boats from Rekata Bay dropped parachute flares, as much to disturb the sleep of men on the ground as to provide illumination for ships' gunners. The amphibian bombers nearly always dropped a sprinkling of 100-kg anti-personnel bombs, again as much to keep men awake as to hurt them. The night harassment was not often effective, but it took its toll. First Lieutenant Danny Iverson, of VMSB-232, was severely wounded and 2ndLt Larry Baldinus was killed one night when a naval shell burst in their tent. Second Lieutenant Hank Hise was hit by a truck and suffered a shattered pelvis when he was caught in the chaos of a night bombing in early September.

Each Japanese destroyer-transport was able to lift 150 combat-equipped infantrymen to Guadalcanal, so runs of five or six ships each night were gradually shifting the odds even more in favor of 17th Army. So successful was the effort that, by early October, the cocky Japanese were landing within ten miles of the Lunga Perim-

eter. There was little short of night patrols by strong American
surface naval forces that could stem the flow.

Still, while numerous fresh infantry units were being committed to the fight at Guadalcanal, the Imperial Army had yet to view
the campaign as being of decisive importance. High-ranking Army
officers still saw the stalled New Guinea offensive as being the
more crucial, a view which precluded for a time their total commitment to a crushing offensive. They allowed Guadalcanal to become
the sinkhole Slew McCain had earlier predicted it would become;
Japanese war might was disappearing on and about Guadalcanal a
little at a time.

The burgeoning Japanese strength would mount to 20,000 effectives by mid October. The Marines could field a force of roughly
equal size. The arrival of 7th Marines and the transfer of several
battalions from Tulagi had bolstered Lunga's strength considerably,
but by the end of September there seemed to be little hope that the
U.S. Army would assist and ultimately relieve 1st Marine Division
before the Japanese could mount a major land offensive.

American garrisons far from Guadalcanal had gained little
strength since arguments over the deployment of 7th Marines had
been waged a month earlier. To make matters worse, the scrubbed
Ndeni operation was being actively supported by the U.S. Joint
Chiefs of Staff. No one seemed inclined to support Archer Vandegrift's view. As the haggling over the availability of troops continued, and despite assurances from Admiral Nimitz, Vandegrift
continued to witness an erosion in the effectiveness of even those
forces already on the island.

More than 800 air and ground personnel who had suffered
wounds had been evacuated by early October, perhaps three percent of the men committed. Another 2,000 had come down with
malaria, dengue fever, beriberi, and other exotic illnesses.

MGen Millard Harmon, the U.S. Army South Pacific
ground-force commander, had long been unhappy with the way
things were going and, while he controlled too few troops to provide relief and reinforcement of the Marines, his contacts at the War

Department included some of the highest policy-makers. In a letter to Admiral Ghormley, dated October 6, Harmon vented some of the rage he felt about what he saw as a declining situation on Guadalcanal. He pointedly asked Ghormley to permanently scrub the Ndeni operation, which had by then been resurrected to employ 2nd Marine Division's 8th Marine Regiment, then in Samoa, and 5th Marine Defense Battalion. He questioned the logic of readying troops for the operation when they and many others were urgently needed at Lunga. He questioned the value of Ndeni as a base since the Japanese would undoubtedly bypass it in a move upon Espiritu Santo once Guadalcanal had been won back. And then he hit upon the very essence of the matter. If Guadalcanal could not be held, there was absolutely no need to take Ndeni:

> In the final analysis [plans for taking Ndeni] are not . . . vital to the success of the main offensive operation . . . of maintaining security of South Pacific bases and lines of communication. . . .
>
> It is my personal conviction that the [enemy is] capable of retaking [Guadalcanal and Tulagi] and that [they] will do so in the near future unless [our garrison is] materially strengthened. I further believe that appropriate increase in strength of garrison, rapid improvement of conditions for air operations and increased surface action, if accomplished in time, will make the operation so costly that [the Japanese] will not attempt it. . . .

Archer Vandegrift could not have said it better, and Slew McCain already had. Ghormley endorsed Harmon's views, though he retained a fascination for the Ndeni occupation. More to the point, however, Ghormley ordered Harmon to prepare a regiment of fresh infantry—*Army* infantry—for deployment on Guadalcanal, and Kelly Turner was ordered to transport it as soon as possible. Chosen was the 164th Infantry Regiment of the American Division, a full battle force of National Guardsmen, tough prairie men from North and South Dakota and western Minnesota. There was even a faint promise that more Army units would follow.

25

Late in the morning of September 15, a dugout canoe paddled by one of Capt Martin Clemens's constables put in at Lunga Point and deposited a haggard, beaming Marine aviator, Capt Marion Carl. A veteran of Midway and an aggressive high-scoring fighter ace, Carl was back from the dead five days after being shot down east of Lunga.

The aviator was taken to the Pagoda, the advance command post of 1st Marine Aircraft Wing, where BGen Roy Geiger made a special point of welcoming him back and needling him with the news that Carl's friendly rival, Capt John Smith, had pulled ahead of Carl's score of kills, sixteen to twelve (Carl had been ahead by one when he was downed). "What," Geiger asked, "are we going to do about that?" After a moment's deep thought, Carl replied, "Goddammit, General, ground *him* for five days!"

There is much of the boyish spirit of the Cactus fliers in that response, for they were very young men bearing up, some better and some worse, to pressures that should have staggered them and would certainly have staggered most older men.

One older man who was bearing up well was Roy Geiger. On the morning of September 22, the fifty-seven-year-old aviation pioneer strapped on a parachute, climbed into the cockpit of a Marine SBD, and flew down to Visale to deposit a 1,000-lb bomb on goods left during the night by the Tokyo Express. Geiger flew—just once—to make a point, and to set an example. While new pilots and aircraft continued to dribble in, the air war was still very much in the hands of the few who had begun it. But they were slowly folding. Some cracked up on landing or got shot down. Some lost all fear and became too reckless in combat. Some avoided fights because they had been too brutally stressed for too long to carry out a fighter pilot's primary mission—to kill, or to be killed trying. Bomber pilots had similar difficulties, and the results were about the same. Geiger demonstrated that if a fifty-seven-year-old could fight, there was really no reason why men in their early twenties could not better stand the strain. The act also erased the barriers that separate the order-giver from the order-taker; Geiger was a combat Marine.

The last two weeks of September were cloudy and stormy over the Slot, so 11th Air Fleet all but shut down, giving the Cactus fliers an opportunity to regain some of their moral strength and composure while ground crews overhauled the beat-up, over-worked aircraft. Now and then, pilots from rear squadrons or units that were slated to move up to Guadalcanal ferried up new aircraft. Morale, for a time, was high. But only for as long as the pressure was abated.

Its aircraft used up, the last of Lt Turner Caldwell's *Enterprise* Flight 300 crews were airlifted out on September 27, the day 11th Air Fleet resumed operations over Guadalcanal in a big way. Twenty-seven Bettys escorted by forty-two Zeros were perfectly intercepted by thirty-four Navy and Marine Wildcats. Four of the Japanese medium bombers were downed outright, and three others never reached home. Five American aircraft were damaged, but none were lost, and there were no pilot injuries.

Then 11th Air Fleet changed its tactics. Nine Bettys set out from Rabaul and Kavieng on the morning of September 29, as did twenty-seven Zeros. The bombers flew only as far as New Georgia before turning back, their job having been merely to guide the fighters to the Guadalcanal area. Rabaul simply wanted to draw the effective Cactus fighters into the air, and destroy them. While the new grass fighter strip, Fighter-1, launched thirty-three Wildcats, only fifteen Fighting-5 pilots led by LCdr Roy Simpler found the raiders, and each side gave up a pilot and an airplane before the Japanese all broke for home.

There were no air operations on rainy September 30, the day Admiral Nimitz arrived, or again on rainy October 1. Before Nimitz left, he awarded Navy Crosses to John Smith, Bob Galer, and Marion Carl. Nearly a dozen other Army, Navy, and Marine pilots received Distinguished Flying Crosses from the admiral.

VAdm Nishizo Tsukahara was relieved of command of 11th Air Fleet on October 2 by VAdm Jinichi Kusaka, who had been serving as commander of 26th Air Flotilla since August. Kusaka immediately embarked upon an aggressive program to destroy Cactus Air.

Coastwatchers on Bougainville missed the October 2 fighter strike, and Cactus radar picked it up in only enough time for thirty-three Wildcats to get off the ground, but not by much. Thirty-six Zeros with the advantage of altitude struck the Wildcats from out of the sun. Two of John Smith's aces, who had received Distinguished Flying Crosses from Admiral Nimitz, were shot down and killed in the first pass; Maj Bob Galer, skipper of VMF-224, had to ditch for the second time in a month, and a pilot visiting from a rear squadron was shot down and killed, as was one of Fighting-5's veterans. John Smith flamed one of three Zeros he caught flatfooted, but the other two got him; he pancaked into a clearing six miles southeast of Fighter-1 and walked home until met by a jeep sent out by Col Clifton Cates, who had seen the Wildcat disappear into the distant trees. In all, four Zeros were claimed, all by fighter-squadron leaders: two by Maj Bob Galer, one by Capt John Smith, and one by LCdr Roy Simpler. Counting the losses and other fighters damaged on October 2, the Americans found they had only twenty-six serviceable Wildcats by day's end. Kusaka had nearly eighty Zeros.

October 3 was in no way a repeat. Alerted in plenty of time by the Coastwatchers, all of the Marine fighters ambushed the incoming Zeros. The last four VMF-223 Wildcats, led by Capt Marion Carl, went all the way through the Japanese formation; Carl got one, and two of his companions got one apiece. The fourth man got two, but had to bail out.

The hero of the day was LtCol Joe Bauer, the visiting skipper of VMF-212, who had scored his first kill on September 27. He went the rest of the way to "ace" on October 3 by scoring four times in quick succession.

During the vicious melee, three Zeros broke away to strafe the main runway, but two were downed by ground fire, for a total of eleven kills. Two F4Fs were lost, but no pilots were hurt.

The bomber war had been going downhill from mid September. Japanese bombers and warships tended to overlook Fighter-1 in favor of the larger runway and the bombers parked on the ground. The result was the steady loss of Cactus bombing aircraft.

Morale among the bomber crews in late September and early October was extremely low. Constant, boring searches, conducted mainly by Scouting-3 Dauntlesses, resulted in uniformly unsuccessful late-afternoon strikes against small Japanese destroyer groups by tired airmen in worn aircraft. The crews that had to ditch or bail out as a result of battle damage or mechanical failure usually did so a long way from home, with little certainty they would be rescued. Many crews disappeared without a trace.

Far worse than missing the boat far up the Slot was missing it as it disgorged men and supplies at any of a dozen beaches along the northern coast of Guadalcanal. Experience taught the bomber crews the likeliest places for such landings, and Coastwatcher reports coupled with air-search findings usually gave a pretty good idea as to the number of ships involved and when they might be found. But accurate bombing in near darkness or in the harsh, quavering light of flares dropped by aircraft forced to keep well apart to avoid midair collisions was nearly futile.

On October 3, for example, Rabaul dispatched a fat seaplane tender, *Nisshin*, loaded with troops and munitions. Afternoon searches were grounded until 1430, following the big fighter-versus-fighter battle of the day, but *Nisshin* was sighted 190 miles out at about 1530 by two SBDs, which barely survived a melee with ten Zeros escorts. A report from another search element at 1600 revealed that three destroyers were accompanying the tender. A bomber strike left Henderson Field at 1615. Six SBDs attacked *Nisshin* at 1725, but her antiaircraft batteries and those of six escorting destroyers put the aircrews off the mark. All the dive-bombers missed, as did three accompanying torpedo bombers.

When word of the failure reached Henderson Field, five SBDs thrown together from four squadrons were sent off at 2200 under LCdr John Eldridge, of *Wasp*'s newly committed Scouting-71. Of the five, only Eldridge and a Scouting-3 pilot found the Japanese in the dark, and they both missed.

Several SBDs launched around midnight spent hours dropping flares and monitoring the unloading of what turned out to be the first shipment of Japanese heavy artillery consigned to Guadalcanal. Her unloading completed before dawn, *Nisshin* beat it back toward Rabaul, her wake dogged by Dauntlesses and Avengers, which claimed hits but really missed altogether. Well over twenty bomber sorties were launched against that one target, and not one hit was scored in the twelve hours the Americans could reach her. Failure was chalked up to bad luck, pilot error, weariness, overexcitement, bad visibility, and poorly functioning aircraft.

The jinx was broken on October 5 when nine SBDs caught six Japanese destroyers in the Slot. Two of the warships were severely crippled by near misses and forced to turn back.

Then the pendulum swung all the way back. Two bomb-armed Torpedo-8 TBFs were lost as they attacked the four surviving destroyers by flare light; one Avenger flew into the sea and sank before the three-man crew could get out, and the other ditched, lost and out of gas, near San Cristobal, its veteran pilot and radioman both lost.

Nisshin was spotted again on October 8, but the two-plane search element that found her and other Japanese warships at 1530 was bounced by the large Zero escort. Both pilots and rear-seats were wounded, but they got off messages to alert Cactus Air Ops. Unfortunately, the big attack group sent up the Slot goose-egged.

Col Lou Woods, 1st Marine Aircraft Wing chief of staff, was sent to Espiritu Santo from Guadalcanal on October 1 to organize the flow of men, aircraft, armaments, and aviation supplies to the front. Woods, who was promoted to brigadier general on October 7, launched a potent campaign to back Cactus with adequate support. As a result of his efforts, a fresh fighter squadron, VMF-121, went aboard escort carrier *Copahee* at Espiritu Santo and sailed toward Guadalcanal. Also, a fresh scout-bomber squadron, VMSB-141, was readied to fly forward in increments.

Copahee arrived well off Guadalcanal's southern coast on the afternoon of October 9 and catapulted twenty brand-new VMF-121 Wildcats flown by twenty fresh Marine fighter pilots. The new squadron, commanded by Maj Duke Davis, would be replacing VMF-223, which had flown to Guadalcanal less than eight weeks earlier. Of eighteen original VMF-223 pilots, six were dead and six had been evacuated with injuries. The squadron had scored eighty-three kills, a number that was to be eclipsed by newer units, but not so dramatically and certainly not against such incredibly long odds, or under such adverse conditions.

John Smith, who was promoted to major before being flown out on October 11, was the squadron's high scorer with nineteen kills. His record—the highest then attained by an American airman in World War II—was soon surpassed, but John Lucien Smith was the first of America's air heroes, and was destined to meet briefly with President Franklin Roosevelt the following February to receive a Medal of Honor. Capt Marion Carl, the Marine Corps' first

World War II ace, never did make good the five-day early September hiatus, but he ended his stay with 16½ confirmed kills. Seven of the original eighteen VMF-223 aviators became aces, with at least five kills apiece.

On the same day VMF-223 was officially relieved (there were but four pilots left on October 12), the last of newly promoted LtCol Dick Mangrum's scout-bomber crews were flown out, thus ending one of America's closest-run holding actions of all time. An era drew to a close on October 12, just as a newer, more dangerous phase of air, sea, and ground operations was about to begin. The Guadalcanal Campaign was about to boil over.

26

Heartened by Adm Chester Nimitz's promise to help, and alarmed by the build-up by the Japanese on his western flank across the Matanikau River, MGen Archer Vandegrift decided in the first week of October 1942 to mount a limited but powerful attack aimed at upsetting whatever plans all those Japanese had in mind. In the first phase of the operation, two battalions of Col Red Mike Edson's 5th Marines were to advance upon the mouth of the Matanikau to engage and hold in place the Japanese encountered there. Next, three rifle battalions would cross farther upstream and march in echelon toward the coast to pocket the engaged Japanese between themselves, Edson, and the channel.

For the inland action, the fresh 3rd Battalion, 2nd, was placed directly under Col Bill Whaling, who had devoted the last weeks to training and leading a picked group of scouts and snipers. Known as Whaling Group, the scouts and the rifle battalion were to cross at the forks of the Matanikau, 2,000 yards from the coast, and immediately wheel to the north to attack the right flank of the Japanese engaged near Matanikau Village by Edson's two-battalion force.

Next, LtCol Herman Hanneken's fresh 2nd Battalion, 7th, was to follow Whaling across the river, advance to the first line of ridges, and likewise wheel northward and emerge near the east side of Point Cruz to attack the Japanese right rear. Finally, LtCol Lewie Puller's tested 1st Battalion, 7th, was to follow Hanneken, advance to the second line of ridges and wheel northward to cut off the Japanese line of retreat just to the west of Point Cruz.

The operation was to be supported by three artillery battalions and a mixed bag of aircraft. Third Battalion, 1st, was placed in bivouac at Kukum in the event an amphibious envelopment was required as the action developed. Division headquarters was so confident in its ability to control the multi-pronged operation that no overall commander on the scene was appointed; Edson was in charge of his part of the fight, Whaling was in charge of his column, and Col Amor Sims was to direct the two battalions of his 7th Marines. Movement was to begin October 7.

As it happened, 17th Army had instructed Sendai (2nd Infantry) Division to launch an offensive against the western Lunga Perimeter with a regiment of fresh infantry then in the vicinity of Point Cruz. Elements of a newly arrived independent heavy-artillery regiment was to go into position near the Matanikau and 17th Army wanted it screened in depth.

The Japanese force was built around 4th Infantry Regiment, one battalion of which had been shipped to Guadalcanal with *Kawaguchi Butai* in early September. The regiment was directed to strongly probe the 5th Marines' sector and effect a penetration if possible. The Japanese offensive was to commence October 8.

The American and Japanese battalions were thus to fight a "meeting engagement," where neither would enjoy the advantage of striking an unprepared enemy nor the advantages of a defensive deployment to ward off the attacks of the other. To prevent the spread of demoralizing rumors through his command, the Sendai Division commander, LtGen Masao Maruyama, expressly forbade his troops from mixing with the malnourished survivors of 35th Infantry Brigade. When one of his field officers handed him a soldier's letter home which read in part, "The news I hear worries me," Maruyama issued a general order to the division:

> From now on, the occupying of Guadalcanal Island is under the observation of the whole world. Do not expect to return, not even one man, if the occupation is not successful. Everyone must remember the honor of the Emperor, show the strong points as of steel or of rocks and advance valiantly and ferociously. Hit the enemy opponents so hard they will not be able to get up again.

On the evening of October 6, elements of 3rd Battalion, 4th, crossed the Matanikau at the ford about 2,000 yards from the beach, and 1st Battalion, 4th, began slipping across the sand bar at the river's mouth to secure a bridgehead from which the October 8 attack would be launched.

Whaling Group's vanguard ran into outposts held by elements of 3rd Battalion, 4th, at about 1000, October 7, as it was moving on the ford. The two forces scrapped a bit, but the Japanese appeared unsure of themselves and refused to be drawn into a major fight.

After engaging in sniping and counter-sniping for a time, the American vanguard was ordered to bypass the Japanese and get back on schedule. The small Japanese force had by then determined that it was vastly outnumbered, so it withdrew, allowing Whaling to establish a night bivouac on high ground.

While Whaling Group was moving to the south, 5th Marines set out from the Perimeter at 0700, October 7, in the hope of establishing a secure base from which an assault at the river's mouth would be launched the next morning.

Things were going fine at the point for L Company, 5th, until about 1300, when it became fragmented in the woods about 200 yards short of the river. Weapons Platoon, which should have been well to the rear, found itself out in front, so the machine gunners and mortarmen immediately halted and took cover. As the L Company first sergeant stood beside Sgt Ben Selvitelle's tree explaining that he could see five Marine scouts directly ahead—they were bound hand-and-foot and clearly dead—he was felled by a single bullet. Selvitelle crawled from cover and found a tiny hole in front of the man's shoulder and a huge exit wound through the collarbone. He sprinkled sulfa on the holes and bound them, then sent the fully conscious man to the rear.

Selvitelle low-crawled back behind his tree through a hail of gunfire and went to work digging in with his mess spoon. The Japanese fire was so close over Selvitelle's head that splinters clipped from the tree fell down his open collar.

L Company's Weapons Platoon sustained its first casualty of the war when a 60mm ammunition carrier took a slug through the thigh. When Ben Selvitelle realized that he was senior man in the area, he gathered up his courage and dashed across ten open yards to the wounded man—just enough time for one "Hail Mary" before he tumbled back to earth. After patching the injured thigh, Selvitelle ran back to his tree.

As the firing from the front became more intense, pinned Marines fired back, though they had no firm targets.

The leading element of 3rd Battalion, 5th, had been engaged as it moved along the narrow coastal plain by about a company of the Japanese 1st Battalion, 4th Infantry. Without adequate room to maneuver, L Company, 5th, was obliged to advance on an extremely narrow front. The 150 Japanese barring the way had the support of other, stronger units on the far side of the river.

A rifle platoon deploying to the right of the L Company Weapons Platoon sustained several casualties before the platoon leader yelled at Sgt Ben Selvitelle to move one of his light machine guns forward. Selvitelle tried to ignore the order, but the lieutenant said, "Move it!" Selvitelle picked a spot and ordered one gun team into action. The gunner took off to emplace the tripod, then the assistant gunner, a strapping veteran, casually stood up, shouldered the gun, and caught a burst in the right side. He fell on top of Ben Selvitelle screaming, "I'm hit! I'm hit! I'm bleeding." When the gunner dropped the tripod and ran back to help, a bullet creased the side of his foot. Selvitelle and another Marine stripped the pants off the assistant gunner, but could find no wound. They did find that both his .45-caliber automatic pistol and canteen had been shattered and that he was drenched with water; he was scared but uninjured. The tripod the gunner had left in the open was retrieved, but the machine-gun section was not called back into action.

While L Company remained pinned, the bulk of 3rd Battalion, 5th, eased around the inland flank of the holding force and slowly advanced. An attempt by the Japanese to recross the river was stopped in the late afternoon.

It was evident by midafternoon that 3rd Battalion, 5th, could neither advance around nor quite destroy the Japanese it had pinned near the sandbar at the river mouth. The center and left companies, L and K respectively, had been stopped and had gone into defensive holding positions while only I Company, which had worked into the line on the beach, could maneuver. But I Company was getting nowhere.

Inland, Maj David McDougal's entire 2nd Battalion, 5th, was working its way toward a small creek in the vicinity of the East-West Trail, but the rifle companies could not quite penetrate to the creek nor firmly engage the Japanese. At 1530, in response to Colonel Edson's request, Archer Vandegrift ordered A Company, 1st Raider Battalion, to assist 5th Marines. Until the sixty Raiders could get into position, Red Mike ordered his two operating battalions to disengage for the night along nearly a mile of riverfront.

After dark, Edson had motor-transport units and elements of 1st Amphibious Tractor Battalion simulate the noisy preparations of a large-scale river crossing. The ploy came to nothing because an extremely heavy downpour in the middle of the night turned all possible approaches to the river into bottomless streams utterly incapable of supporting even the phantom assault Red Mike had in mind. The rains shattered hopes that the real assault on Matanikau Village could be launched.

On October 8, as the 3rd Battalion stirred to clear the Japanese pocket on its front, 2nd Battalion, 5th, moved toward the bank of a small tributary cutting across the front. E Company pushed forward to engage a small Japanese force digging in just to the south. As G Company maneuvered to launch a flank assault, it was stopped by some of the heavy fire that was by then smashing into E Company. Maj Dave McDougal, the new battalion commander, was up with E Company when he was seriously wounded in the leg and hand. McDougal and other wounded Marines were evacuated, and the battalion was ordered to pull back and establish a fortified position.

By that time, Archer Vandegrift was forced to call off the 5th Marines' attack. Red Mike's two battalions were to reduce the pocket east of the river and hold in place while Whaling, Hanneken, and Puller mounted their sweeps.

At 0500, October 8, 1stLt Bob Neuffer, commanding A Company, Raiders, was visited by his old company commander, Maj Lew Walt, now the 5th Marines operations officer, who had been sent by Edson to oversee the reduction by the Raiders of the Japanese pocket by the sandbar at the mouth of the Matanikau. It was still raining, but Walt ordered the Raider company, hardly more than a reinforced platoon, to cross the river by day's end. Asked about support, Walt told Neuffer that there might be a few fighter-bombers if the weather cleared.

Information from the front was beginning to make sense to the division intelligence section, which finally saw that Edson was fighting a meeting engagement and that a Japanese attack of significant proportions would probably be mounted by day's end. Coast-watchers and Allied patrol aircraft reported large concentrations of transports and warships in the Bismarcks and Shortlands, an indication that a major effort was under way.

As A Company, Raiders, marched to the beach and through I

Company, 5th, which it was to relieve, Sgt Frank Guidone's squad was struck by machine-gun fire as it started through the trees in column. The Raiders hit the deck and scanned the front for targets. Guidone spotted three Japanese clustered around a Nambu light machine gun, hidden in the jumbled roots of a banyan tree only twenty yards away. The squad BAR-man moved up under covering fire and carefully squeezed off a short burst. He felled the three Japanese. When Sergeant Guidone reported to Lieutenant Neuffer, the company commander told him to advance if possible or at least hold where he was.

Meantime, tiny B Company, Raiders, moved up to support A Company as did a pair of 37mm antitank guns, which were concealed on the sandspit over which the anticipated Japanese assault would have to be mounted. Lieutenant Neuffer established his CP near the guns and tied into the communications net of the adjacent 3rd Battalion, 5th.

Soon, 2ndLt Cliff MacGlocklin's 1st Platoon was withdrawn just enough to skirt the Japanese defenses at the river mouth. The Raiders dug in and strung barbed wire as soon as they reached the beach. On MacGlocklin's left, tied in with I Company, 5th, was PlSgt Joe Buntin's 3rd Platoon. On the right, nearest the river, 2ndLt Richard Sullivan's 2nd Platoon was manning a 200-yard defensive line.

Nothing much beyond some mutually ineffectual exchanges occurred through the late morning and early afternoon of October 8. At about dusk, Maj Lew Walt ordered Sgt Frank Guidone to lead a group of Raiders into no-man's-land to stir things up with a few hand grenades. Guidone personally led one other Marine in toward murmuring Japanese voices, and the two hurled several grenades. The two Raiders scuttled back to their own line amidst a hail of bullets and cries of pain from the enemy line.

Lieutenant Sullivan and his platoon sergeant were caught in the open just before sunset by a mortar barrage as they crawled to the company CP to confer with Lieutenant Neuffer. Sullivan dragged the seriously wounded NCO to safety, but returned to his

platoon after his own wounds were treated. On reaching his platoon's sector, Sullivan learned that several of his Raiders had been
hurt and that, as a result, his platoon's left flank was riddled with
gaps. He was just leaving to return to the company CP to scrounge
replacements when he was injured again, in the open, by another
mortar barrage. When he thought he heard a voice during a brief
lull, he hurled a challenge, though he had forgotten the evening's
password. No matter, for he drew as a response a furious burst of
small-arms fire from Japanese moving through the gloom.

Then the Japanese mounted their assault.

It was nearing 1830, and nearly dark, when ranks of Japanese
infantry, standing shoulder-to-shoulder, surged in the direction of
the sandspit, stepping into the carefully concealed zone of fire
claimed by a medium-machine-gun section loaned to the Raiders
by M Company, 5th. Lieutenant Sullivan bellowed a warning that
Japanese were also in the rear, got off a quick burst with his submachine gun, then slowly back-pedaled with his men toward their
own barbed wire. Headquarters troops and mortar gunners were
soon being hit as the Japanese pressed closer. Sullivan fired two
magazines before he was drilled through the shoulder and forced to
drop his submachine gun. Pvt Bill Dodamead spotted a sword-
wielding Japanese coming at him, and lifted an arm just in time to
ward off the blow, though it cut deeply into his back. The Raider
dropped his rifle, but he ripped out the Japanese officer's windpipe
with his bare hands.

Lieutenant MacGlocklin faced a major dilemma. If his 1st Platoon opened fire, Marines might get caught in the crossfire; if not,
his platoon might be overrun. There was no moving back; the river,
the channel, and MacGlocklin's own wire had him boxed in. The
young officer brayed to the Raiders on his front to drop to the
ground, then ordered his own men and the two 37mm antitank
guns to fire. The Japanese were sent reeling.

Sullivan's 2nd Platoon was in grave danger. Hit from the rear,
it had turned to fight, but had been steadily pressed back into its
own wire. Machine guns were manhandled to new firing positions,

from which one gunner felled fifteen Japanese with slow, measured bursts while another fired full tilt at the oncoming Japanese with a machine gun in the crook of his arm.

Lieutenant Sullivan and Sgt Donald Wolf were cut off and went to ground in a foxhole as the Japanese surged by in the dark. Wolf and another Raider, also bypassed, dropped several attackers with rifle fire.

It was by then pitch dark. Second Platoon had been all but routed, but the Japanese had broken in confusion when they plowed into the wire at the "rear" of the Marine position. As the Japanese drew back to find a way around the wire, Raiders quietly crawled from their fighting holes and sniffed the air to find the telltale odor of their adversaries. (Many Raiders said the Japanese smelled like cooked rice.) Wherever the Raiders found Japanese soldiers, they silently went to work with knives and bayonets, killing many Japanese and demoralizing the rest.

Lieutenant Sullivan and his two companions elected to exploit the confusion to effect their escapes. One man went his own way and was not seen again. Sergeant Wolf led Sullivan in another direction, but they stumbled upon several Japanese. Sullivan heard a scuffle while diving for a tangle of vines to escape detection; he was nearly caught, but made good his escape. Sergeant Wolf was injured in the melee.

Raiders straggled home all night, and 1stLt Bob Neuffer directed those who could still bear arms into a new line on the sandspit, which was already seriously threatened. The company commander phoned Red Mike to say that A Company was coming apart, but that he thought it might hold until help arrived.

Edson, who well knew that night actions could be terribly confusing and that the situation was nearly always better than the men on the spot realized, sent Maj Lew Walt to take charge. When Walt and his runner found Neuffer, the lieutenant was too busy rebuilding his line to talk, so 2ndLt Cliff MacGlocklin conferred with the major, who immediately ordered him to pull his 1st Platoon back. The opposing lines were seriously intermingled, so the withdrawal was extremely difficult. (At one point, Walt shared his foxhole with another warm body, thinking nothing of it. Walt's returning runner discovered that the major's companion was Japanese and shot the intruder.)

As it turned out, Walt and his runner were the only reinforcement A Company, Raiders, received. Fortunately, the fight began tailing off shortly after the major's arrival.

Lieutenant Sullivan appeared during a lull, bleeding from numerous wounds and scratches, his left arm dangling uselessly, and Walt ordered him to the rear for treatment. When Sullivan finally reached Red Mike's CP, he stopped to tell the colonel all he could about the fight and the condition of A Company. Edson ordered the weak, ashen-faced lieutenant to report to the sickbay; he had done more than enough for one night.

First light found the Raiders and Japanese staring at each other. A flurry of gunfire erupted, and several Raiders engaged in hand-to-hand combat, but the fight was over. The Japanese bridgehead had been eradicated.

The approach by Whaling Group and the headquarters and two battalions of 7th Marines (accompanied by a large force of local bearers recruited by Capt Martin Clemens) on the Matanikau ford was nerve-wracking, and very slow.

Pfc Guy Creamer, a machine gunner with H Company, 7th, developed a terrible thirst during one of the many long breaks that hot afternoon, so he gathered the canteens of other members of his squad and strode off to find a stream. Following a rugged climb over a steep ridge, Creamer had just lowered the first of his canteens into the brackish water when a Marine nearby queried, "Hey, Mac, you sure you need that water?"

"Sure do," Creamer replied.

"Well, there's about a thousand dead Japs upstream." Undaunted, Creamer filled all the canteens and reclimbed the steep ridge, which about did him in. When he reached a clearing he had passed earlier, he allowed his instincts to carry him leftward, but a Marine with whom he had exchanged a greeting earlier warned him that he was heading into enemy country. "No," Creamer averred,

"I'm sure I'm right." He was back in the clearing soon enough, prodded by several Japanese snipers in the high kunai grass. When the weary gunner reached his platoon, he asked the corpsman to lace the water with iodine. Capt Bob Farrell, the weapons company reconnaissance officer, asked if the water was okay to drink, and Creamer replied that it had come from a stagnant part of the stream; to mention that it was contaminated by dead bodies was to deny his buddies the thirst quencher altogether. The iodine did the trick, for no one fell ill to that batch of water.

LtCol Lewie Puller's 1st Battalion, 7th, at the tail of the column, finally arrived at a tributary stream, bridged by a huge submerged banyan log, in the middle of the afternoon of October 7. Puller, who had charge of the point, was highly suspicious of the crossing—despite the fact that over 1,000 Marines had preceded him—and ordered his Marines to cross one at a time.

By the time Capt Charlie Kelly, now the battalion exec, arrived at the crossing, it was evident that the battalion would either have to proceed with less caution or operate well into the night. Kelly dispatched small fighting groups upstream and down, then sent the remaining troops across three at a time. Still, it was quite dark before the tail of the battalion clambered up a steep, slippery, water-logged trail on the west bank. Several Marines were so done in by the climb that they literally tumbled back down and had to be helped up the incline once again. It was pitch dark before Charlie Kelly was certain that all hands had made it safely to the bivouac on high ground.

A torrential downpour developed before dawn and continued unabated through the day, slowing progress, covering the approach of groups of Japanese bent upon inflicting casualties upon the thoroughly miserable Marines. It was too overcast for air activity, and the artillery fire the troops heard seemed to be far away. There was little to do for most of the day except struggle forward when the line moved, or hunker down in the rain and shoot the breeze.

The second night in the bush, still short of the Matanikau, was punctuated by flares and bombs from lone Japanese raiders. When 2nd Battalion, 7th, was hit by harassing fires after dark, a platoon leader took a small patrol out to try to silence the Japanese. The group thrashed about in the trees and vines for an extended period, found nothing and returned to the battalion bivouac. A jumpy sentry fired several rounds and brought down the lieutenant, whose serious but treatable wounds would prove fatal because the only way out was with the battalion, which was at least a full day from the coast.

October 9 dawned sunny and bright. Whaling Group waded across the Matanikau near Hill 65 at dawn and turned north along the first line of ridges, Hills 73 and 75. Next, Hanneken's 2nd Battalion, 7th, passed the tail of Whaling's column and turned north after hiking about 1,000 yards to the west to follow Hill 72 toward the coast. Puller's battalion passed behind Hanneken's and turned north toward Hill 81. The 7th Marines command group remained on the east bank of the Matanikau.

Whaling Group moved rapidly toward the coast and crossed Hill 78, overlooking the beach, without encountering serious opposition. Hanneken's 2nd Battalion, 7th, made good progress before running into at-first scattered opposition and then stiffer resistance as it drew nearer to Hill 78. While Hanneken was organizing his battalion to fight through the opposition, he was called by regimental headquarters. Col Amor Sims, who had elected to keep his command group east of the Matanikau, told Hanneken that the operation had been cancelled and that 2nd Battalion, 7th, was to break contact with the Japanese on its front and join Whaling Group on the coast as soon as possible. Hanneken, a forty-nine-year-old regular who had been commissioned from the ranks following his assassination of a Haitian guerrilla chief named Charlemagne (for which he was awarded a Medal of Honor), reluctantly ordered his Marines, few of whom were actually in contact with the Japanese, to disengage.

Meantime, B Company, 7th, was crossing a narrow valley filled with waist-high kunai grass when a pair of concealed machine guns opened from a hummock to the right and killed two Marines. A large portion of the company wheeled toward the source of the fire. The machine guns kept firing and mortar fire impacted among the B Company troops, wounding several.

Sgt Joe Goble, of B Company's 3rd Platoon, directed his squad to fire rifle grenades at the spot where he thought the machine guns were hidden. The guns were destroyed, but there was too much going on for Goble to be certain, so he sent a rifleman back to the column to get more rifle grenades. The second batch was used up almost as soon as the puffing Marine returned.

Unable to locate his platoon leader, Sergeant Goble ordered the troops to dig in along the military crest at fifteen-yard intervals; he was prepared to hold through the night, though he could not understand why no help was being sent. Before Goble could re-solve that question, however, he was called up to the line, where he found Cpl W. O. Rust, rocking back and forth beside a tree, his stomach opened by a gunshot wound. Goble treated the wound, then grabbed Rust under both arms to carry him down from the ridge.

The next thing Goble knew, he was on his back and Corporal Rust was on top of him. He felt an indescribable pain in the back of his skull and sensed that someone's foot was under his head. He yelled for help before it dawned on him that the foot was his own; he had been shot by a sniper as he bent over to take Rust's weight, and the single round had shattered about eight inches of bone in his left femur. A corpsman gave Goble a shot of morphine and splinted the wreck of his leg, then members of his platoon jury-rigged a poncho stretcher. As Goble was waiting to be carried, one of his Marines killed the sniper.

Goble's platoon received no support because Capt Marsh Moore's C Company had flushed bigger game. As C Company worked across a high, grass-covered ridge to close in on the Jap-anese with whom Hanneken's battalion had become embroiled be-fore Hanneken was called off by Colonel Sims, scouts found a very large concentration of Japanese infantry in a deep, circular ravine between Hills 80 and 81 and between the two battalions—or what would have been between the battalions had not Hanneken acceded to Sims's peremptory order to withdraw. The Japanese were initially deployed to take on Hanneken, so C Company was able to approach almost unhampered.

Even as C Company was putting its full weight into the fight, the regimental CP contacted Lewie Puller and ordered him to make for the coast to "reconnoiter" the beach west of Point Cruz. Puller was not precisely a team player, nor was he capable of disengaging from a fight in progress to look for what might or might not be trouble elsewhere. And his low appreciation of staff and command above the battalion level had left him with an all-too-obvious loathing for Colonel Sims, who had been a fine combat troop commander in France a quarter-century earlier. Puller's response to the remote-control order: "How the hell can I disengage? We're in a heavy fire fight. You can't give orders from back there. Why the hell don't you come up here and see what the hell's going on!" He ordered the phone line to the regimental CP cut and turned his full attention to destroying the Japanese he had within his grasp. (The line was not cut, but neither was Puller annoyed again with messages from regimental headquarters.)

First Lieutenant Jess Mehrlust, an artillery forward observer from C Battery, 11th, was called to the C Company lines to bring in artillery concentrations. Though Mehrlust had been on active duty since 1940, he had never before called a live fire mission. He did not know precisely where his firing battery was located, nor was he particularly certain of his own whereabouts. All he could do was order up two rounds on the same azimuth but at different ranges. If he could see where the rounds landed, he would be able to determine a direct line back to the battery and gauge his relative position to it. The trouble was that he did not know where friendly troops might be lurking. He ordered the rounds fired with great trepidation. The first was heard when it impacted, but no one could spot it. The second landed so close that Mehrlust was certain he had hewed down fellow Marines. He crawled out of his safe spot to help with the wounded, but there were none. Mehrlust returned to his post and called in precise salvoes; at least he knew precisely where *not* to fire.

C Company Marines quickly developed a winning solution to

the problem of flushing the Japanese from the jungle-choked ravine. First the company 60mm mortars would fire. When the Japanese bolted up the far side of the ravine—the side that had been held by Hanneken—the company machine gunners and riflemen mowed them down or forced the survivors back into the trees. The ploy worked again and again.

Most of the serious opposition came from a machine gun the Japanese hoisted into the branches of a huge banyan tree on the near side of the ravine; each time this gun fired, one of the three 60mm mortars lofted rounds into the tree until the gun was silenced, but the Japanese continually remanned the position. Both of Captain Moore's young runners and several other Marines were killed by this gun or snipers manning positions near it.

Lewie Puller decided at length to commit Capt Regan Fuller's A Company to extend Moore's right flank around a greater portion of the ravine. In time, elements of Capt Bob Haggerty's B Company were likewise committed on Fuller's right, but the fight remained essentially C Company's. A timely run by several P-400s all but wiped out the Japanese in the ravine just as the mortar crews were reporting that ammunition was about exhausted.

Regimental headquarters eventually managed to coax Puller into agreeing to withdraw to the beach; the fight had come pretty much to a close after two-and-one-half hours, and Colonel Sims had cancelled the reconnaissance mission that had riled Puller earlier.

As the battalion slowly disengaged, with C Company fighting a slow rearguard action, Capt Charlie Kelly was sent ahead with the casualties. Kelly's was a bizarre mission. He went ahead of the column with a few scouts to reconnoiter and kept finding 2nd Battalion corpsmen treating wounded Marines who had been left by the wayside. These wounded were dutifully added to the ragtag safari, but Kelly had no idea how Hanneken's people could presume that 1st Battalion would be coming that way, and he shuddered at the possible alternatives. When Kelly paused atop a bare knob well short of Matanikau Village to see if it was safe to go on, he spotted the regimental command group plodding northward on the far side of the river. Semaphore signals revealed that Point Cruz and the river mouth were clear of Japanese. It was still a long way to the coast, and there were abundant signs that Japanese soldiers were roving through the area, but the column of wounded made it to the beach without incident, though several of the more seriously wounded succumbed to shock or dehydration.

When Sgt Joe Goble regained his senses he was on the beach next to a litter with a blanket pulled up over a dead man's face; he lifted the blanket and stared into the face of Cpl W. O. Rust, the Marine he had been trying to rescue when he was shot.

Boats carrying the regimental surgeon and jerrycans of water and medical supplies landed just as Kelly's column cleared the trees. The wounded were quickly evacuated, but Charlie Kelly remained on the beach to greet the rest of 1st Battalion, 7th, which emerged from the forest at about 1530. C Company was the rear guard while the battalion crossed the Matanikau by way of the sandspit. Someone had thoughtfully provided trucks to take the weary Marines back to their bivouac on Bloody Ridge.

The three-day operation—the largest ever run entirely by Marines under Marine commanders—cost 1st Marine Division 65 killed and 125 wounded. Japanese losses at Puller's hands alone, according to Japanese sources, amounted to nearly 700 members of 3rd Battalion, 4th Infantry, killed. Another 70-odd Japanese soldiers died at the mouth of the Matanikau. (More Japanese were killed in 150 minutes by C Company, 7th, than had been killed by two battalions in the nightlong battle at the mouth of Alligator Creek *or* in two nights at Bloody Ridge!)

Control of the battle had been less than adequate. Archer Vandegrift and his staff had been too far from the fight to exert any meaningful control, though they certainly tried. Col Bill Whaling, senior to Col Amor Sims, and far better prepared for the jungle operation than Sims, had been given no command function beyond the control of his own battalion-sized column. Sims had isolated himself from the only significant fight west of the Matanikau, and had not contributed a thing to its success. Col Merritt Edson, still getting into form as a regimental commander, had been uncharacteristically passive throughout his portion of the fight.

The destruction of Sendai Division's 3rd Battalion, 4th, and the reduction of the two bridgeheads east of the Matanikau had given the Marines a significant victory, but it was by no means a brilliant triumph.

27

tGen Harukichi Hyakutake landed at Cape Esperance with key members of his staff and the bulk of Sendai Division's artillery group on the night of October 9. Many of the Ichiki and Kawaguchi soldiers who unloaded the large store of rice the general brought made off with the food in as complete a breakdown of discipline as Japanese soldiers could exhibit. It is interesting and revealing that Hyakutake did nothing about the massive theft.

The incident points up the basic tenuousness of the Japanese situation on Guadalcanal, about which the 17th Army staff had been amply and forcefully forewarned by MGen Kiyotake Kawaguchi. However, 17th Army took the view that, as long as it had access to seemingly unlimited human resources, no effort would be made to rehabilitate units that were shattered in combat or through privations brought about by inadequate logistical administration.

Far from coming to grips with the reasons for the Ichiki and Kawaguchi defeats—superior American strength and mobility on the ground, and local American air superiority—many senior Jap-

301

anese officers chose to view "lack of offensive spirit" among their own troops as being at the root of all their problems.

The 17th Army commander said before arriving at Guadalcanal, "The operation to surround and recapture Guadalcanal will truly decide the fate of the Pacific War." In echoing the precise sentiments of many of his adversaries, Hyakutake drew from all the information and impressions reaching him the essence of what both sides had at stake in the Eastern Solomons. Though Hyakutake had seen with his own eyes the emaciated Ichiki and Kawaguchi survivors, and he saw the extent to which they had been driven in order to merely subsist, he remained so confident his side would prevail that he ordered his staff to draw up plans for the recapture of Tulagi and the seizure of Rennell and San Cristobal islands. And he looked to the day when he could breathe life back into his stalled New Guinea offensive.

By the middle of the second week of October, nearly all of Sendai Division, along with the remnants of 35th Infantry Brigade and advance detachments of 38th ("Nagoya") Infantry Division, were on hand for the coming land offensive.

LtGen Masao Maruyama's crack, veteran Sendai Division, which had been assigned to 17th Army in early September, had fought on Java at the start of the war and 4th Infantry had seen duty in the Philippines in July 1942, while 16th and 29th Infantry regiments remained in Java. Twenty-ninth Infantry was considered one of the best regiments in the Imperial Army.

LtGen Tadiyoshi Sano's Nagoya Division had been commissioned in September 1939 and had participated without distinction in the siege of Hong Kong. Its 228th Infantry Regiment and part of 229th Infantry had fought on Timor and Amboina, and the balance of 229th Infantry and the entire 230th Infantry had seen action on Java.

In addition to its two infantry divisions and 35th Infantry Brigade, 17th Army mustered several antiaircraft and antiaircraft artillery batteries, a mountain infantry battalion, an engineer regiment, an independent medium tank company, a mortar battalion, and numerous supply, medical, service, and communications units and detachments. Sendai Division's 4th Field Artillery Regiment was in the process of building up a formidable establishment of 15cm howitzers, the largest artillery pieces on Guadalcanal at the time.

Americal Division's 2,850-man 164th Infantry Regiment was scheduled to leave New Caledonia in time to arrive in Lunga Roads on October 13 with 210 groundcrewmen and 85 Marine riflemen. The American GIs were embarked in a pair of fleet transports escorted by three destroyers and three minelayers. Farther out, in the vicinity of Rennell Island, was a force of four cruisers and five destroyers under RAdm Norman Scott. A force built around the new fast battleship *Washington* and America's last operational fleet carrier, *Hornet*, was on station 180 miles south of Guadalcanal and about fifty miles east of Malaita.

Admiral Scott learned on October 11 that an 11th Bombardment Group B-17 had spotted two Japanese seaplane tenders and six destroyers in the Slot. This was the same group that had, on previous missions, slipped through the fingers of Cactus air strikes. Attuned to the criticism leveled at the Navy following the Savo debacle, Scott had painstakingly trained his force over many weeks to undertake night engagements in restricted waters. The October 11 sighting gave Scott the opportunity he had been seeking; he ordered his battle force to proceed to Guadalcanal at a speed of twenty-nine knots.

Unbeknown to Scott, RAdm Aritomo Goto was leading a special bombardment force of three cruisers and two destroyers to Guadalcanal to inflict damage upon Henderson Field. He had escaped detection simply by shaping a course outside the Slot. While Scott would have the advantage in numbers and firepower, he was bound to be surprised by the size and composition of the force he would be facing.

During the afternoon of October 11, thirty long-range Zeros and thirty-five Bettys left Rabaul for Guadalcanal to draw off the American Wildcats and prevent the regular afternoon search missions from being launched, so that Goto's force and the rein-forcement group could run into the area after dark. The Japanese formations were broken up by bad weather and, though the Coast-watchers missed them, seven Bettys and two Zeros were downed by American fighters. Cactus lost a Wildcat and a new P-39 fighter. Although the reinforcement group was detected by American search aircraft late in the afternoon, no strikes were launched be-cause Roy Geiger felt there was little or no chance of success.

⊕

Admiral Goto's bombardment group picked its way toward Savo and, by 2200, was within sight of Guadalcanal. Speed was increased to twenty-six knots, guncrews were put on alert, and lookouts were busily calling out landmarks. No one had any reason to suspect that an American battle force might be in the area.

At 2330, a spotter plane off heavy cruiser *San Francisco*—the only one aloft—found the reinforcement group sixteen miles from Savo, just off Cape Esperance.

The bombardment group was closing on the American war-ships, virtually on a collision course, but neither Scott nor Goto had an inkling as to the other's presence. Scott merely happened to be making for a point between Goto and the station from which the Japanese expected to bombard Henderson Field.

The Americans had a distinct advantage in that they possessed surface-search and gunnery radars, while the Japanese had none. But it was a mixed blessing, for both types of radar were new, and neither had yet been employed in combat, day or night. Several of the American captains were impressed with the results in practice, but Admiral Scott, a 1911 Annapolis graduate, was not particularly knowledgeable of radar and inclined to disregard it. Moreover, the radar operators had not yet gained the edge of experience that would prevent them from wrongly interpreting often confusing data. Several of the sets were not in operation, some by choice of individual captains and others because of malfunctions or lack of spare parts.

There was also the human element. The weeks and months of

304

almost incessant sea duty and the subduing influences of defeats of
the Savo variety had caused morale in many ships to plunge or, at
least, edge downward. Typical of many men in the ships under
Admiral Scott that night was Boatswain's Mate 2nd Class Vance
Carter, of *San Francisco*, a twenty-three-year-old gun trainer with
nearly six years' naval service. Carter never went anywhere without his lifejacket and belt knife, nor would he take off his clothes
except to change or take an infrequent salt-water shower aboard his
ship. His only shore leave in months had been a week earlier, when
San Francisco stopped off at Noumea at the express request of her
senior medical officer, who told her captain that the men needed
some time off from the mental and emotional strain of months on
end at sea. Carter and most of his shipmates slept, when they
could, at or near their battle stations, ever ready to defend themselves in the event of surprise attack. Indeed, Vance Carter had
slept in his own bunk only once in many weeks. On that occasion,
he had awakened in the middle of the night, fearful of being caught
below decks by a Japanese torpedo. Despite the strains, *San Francisco* remained an efficient, clean ship; discipline was maintained
above all else.

In anticipation of engaging the Japanese reinforcement group,
Admiral Scott had placed his two light cruisers, two heavy cruisers, and five destroyers in a column formation: three destroyers,
four cruisers, two destroyers. While such a formation obviated a
number of desirable options in action, it allowed Scott to know
where all his ships were at all times. A lifelong destroyer and
cruiser sailor, Scott knew what he was about. His force was a
mixed bag and would require firm control.

The Americans entered the contested area from the southeast
of Cape Esperance. Their quarry was inshore. Scott planned to hit
the transports after first checking the far side of Savo for possible
undetected screen warships.

The American column was on a northeasterly heading at 2332.
Scott ordered a reversal in course by column, a maneuver akin to a
freight train taking a sharp curve. The three van destroyers, with

Farenholt in the lead, made the move without incident. However, *San Francisco*, the flagship, turned prematurely in the mistaken notion that the admiral had ordered the column to execute a *simultaneous* turn. The error was discovered in short order, but not before the van destroyers had been thrown out of the battle line. *San Francisco* became the lead ship.

As the Japanese reinforcement group was expected to be engaged to port, the destroyer-division commander elected to lead the van destroyers up the starboard side of the cruiser column to resume their places ahead of the flagship.

The three destroyers were rushing up beside the cruisers when several ships contacted hitherto undetected targets on their gunnery radars. *Duncan*, the last of the van destroyers, made an excellent contact to starboard and issued an immediate verbal warning by voice radio. Light cruiser *Helena* made a firm contact, reporting several vessels bearing 315 degrees at 2,700 yards. Light cruiser *Boise* reported several "bogies" to starboard, giving rise to fear of an air attack; "bogey" usually meant "airplane."

Norman Scott remained unconvinced. There was no previous word of a second Japanese surface force and no direct information from the radars aboard his own flagship; he was fairly certain that the contacts were his own van destroyers, which did not explain *Duncan*'s report. Scott decided to wait and see.

All of the American captains trained out guns on the approaching Japanese, though Scott still refused to allow them to commence firing. After two attempts to gain permission to fire on the basis of his firm radar contact, *Helena*'s Capt Gilbert Hoover acted on his own. As soon as *Helena* opened, heavy cruiser *Salt Lake City* and *Boise* also began throwing out 5-, 6-, and 8-inch rounds, though the task-force commander had issued no such command.

As soon as the firing began, the middle American van destroyer, *Laffey*, abruptly swung around and joined up at the tail of the cruiser column, leaving *Farenholt* and *Duncan* between the opposing cruiser columns.

Fubuki, the lone right-hand Japanese destroyer, attempted to turn to starboard to parallel the American column. She was lighted by several American warships and became the focus of a merciless pounding. Within moments, her grey-painted sides were peeled back by numerous hits. She broke in two and sank.

The three Japanese heavy cruisers were in the center and the second Japanese destroyer was on the left. *Aoba*, with Admiral Goto aboard, had the van, and she was immediately hit. Admiral Goto was grievously injured and several members of his staff were killed. *Aoba*'s captain, who was in nominal command of his battle force, concentrated on saving his own ship. He ordered a turn to starboard, which caused *Aoba* yet more damage as she momentarily paralleled the American track before laying a smoke screen and running for safety.

Furutaka was immediately astern the flagship. Boatswain's Mate 2nd Class Vance Carter, manning a telescope in *San Francisco*'s Turret-2 watched with surprising sorrow as the graceful cruiser was mortally pounded by shells from his ship and the other American cruisers and destroyers.

Kinugasa's captain coolly turned his ship to port and, followed by destroyer *Hatsuyuki*, escaped both detection and harm.

Admiral Scott was still trying to sort things out. Radars were registering targets, but the confusion of battle had rendered most of the operators uncertain as to the relative positions of friendly vessels. *Boise* had had no radar for several minutes, the result of a blown fuse. Scott was yet uncertain of the position of his van destroyers. Even after several minutes of intense firing and adequate visual evidence that the fight was real, the skeptical American task-force commander heatedly enforced a general cease fire. Then *Boise* took sudden evasive action to comb the wakes of a pair of torpedoes, and another fish barely missed *Helena*.

Kinugasa had returned.

The American captains ordered their batteries to resume firing. They gave as good as they got. *Farenholt* took two quick hits from guns that could only have been friendly. *Duncan*, off on her own after firing torpedoes at receding targets, was set ablaze by friendly and unfriendly guns and soon abandoned by her crew. *Boise* took numerous hits and lost both forward turrets to induced ready-powder explosions. *Salt Lake City* was hit, and she temporarily lost portions of her electrical grid.

Admiral Scott directed destroyer *McCalla* to pick up swimmers, then reformed his remaining warships and led them away to Espiritu Santo. *McCalla* picked up nearly all of *Duncan's* crew. She also placed a salvage team aboard the stricken destroyer at first light, but *Duncan* had to be scuttled late in the afternoon.

Fubuki was sunk outright, and *Furutaka* went down twenty-two miles north of Savo. *Aoba* had been severely damaged, and RAdm Aritomo Goto died from his wounds. Two Japanese destroyers were detached from the unmolested reinforcement group to see to survivors, but these were recalled at first light because of the proximity of American warplanes.

Led off Henderson Field at 0515 by LCdr John Eldridge, commander of Scouting-71, sixteen SBDs escorted by many F4Fs and P-39s found destroyer *Murakumo* and near-missed her as she was running northward, her decks packed with *Fubuki* and *Furutaka* survivors. A second strike found *Murakumo* and destroyer *Shirayuki* at 0800. American fighters strafed both destroyers, then dive-bombers again near-missed *Murakumo*. Finally, six TBFs from Torpedo-8 weaved through the friendly fighters and split into two groups of three to launch torpedoes on either bow. *Murakumo* went up in a great cloud of steam and debris, and hundreds of Japanese sailors took to the water, most for the second time in a day. The destroyer was scuttled in the evening.

Shirayuki, which remained on station to collect survivors, was joined in the afternoon by destroyer *Natsugumo*. They were attacked by a mixed bag of SBDs led by Eldridge, whose bomb struck *Natsugumo*. Two other Americans near-missed *Natsugumo* before she blew up.

For the loss of one destroyer sunk, one light cruiser severely damaged, and one heavy cruiser moderately damaged, the American battle force managed to sink a Japanese heavy cruiser and a fleet destroyer by gunfire, while Cactus Air sank two additional destroyers. The victory clearly went to the Americans, despite the fact that the object of Admiral Scott's sally, the unmolested rein-forcement group, had been able to add appreciably to 17th Army's burgeoning strength. More by accident than design, the U.S. Navy had gone a long way toward avenging and balancing the humilia-tion of Savo.

PART VIII

Crisis

28

Tuesday, October 13, 1942, was a day long-awaited. Two nights earlier, the jungle-weary Marines of Guadalcanal had heard the thundering boom of big guns in the channel beside their beleaguered Lunga Perimeter. Sailors and Marines on the beaches had seen the brilliant flashes of naval guns.

In the morning, on October 12, word had gone out that the Tokyo Express had been turned back by American surface warships.

All that day, the Marines had waited to see what the Japanese would do about their defeat, and all the following night had been spent awaiting some fearsome retribution. But nothing had happened.

Tuesday, October 13, dawned bright and clear. Men on the beaches watched excitedly as a pair of fat fleet transports hove into view and dropped anchors in Lunga Roads. They watched incredulously as men streamed down the cargo nets slung over the transports' sides and boarded landing craft. They stood stupified as the boats disgorged those men on the beach. Reinforcements—the first U.S. Army soldiers to be sent to Guadalcanal—had arrived.

The long-promised relief of beleaguered 1st Marine Division was under way.

The Dakota and Minnesota National Guardsmen of 164th Infantry Regiment took the inevitable intramural ribbing good-naturedly and marched off to their bivouacs between the beach and Henderson Field. An odd assortment of jeeps, British Bren carriers, trucks, and engineering equipment and, most important, food followed the fresh, green dogfaces off the beach. Outward-bound, the tough, aged young men of 1st Raider Battalion turned their backs on Guadalcanal.

At just two minutes past noon, twenty-seven Bettys, with a heavy Zero escort, dropped in unannounced over Henderson Field. Cactus Air launched all of its forty-two operational Wildcats, which clawed for altitude, but arrived at combat level too late. The Bettys dropped their payloads of 250-kg bombs from 30,000 feet. The bombs cratered both Henderson Field and Fighter-1 and destroyed 5,000 gallons of precious aviation gasoline. The Americans claimed a Zero and a Betty destroyed, but one of the scorers, a green VMF-121 airman on his first sortie, had to be picked up just off the beach following a harrowing water landing.

Black Tuesday had begun.

A second strike of eighteen Bettys and eighteen Zeros arrived over the airfield between 1330 and 1400. Unbelievably, the American fighters were again caught on the ground, still refueling after the earlier raid. Capt Joe Foss, a green VMF-121 division leader, led a dozen Wildcats after the Zeros, but the Bettys plastered both runways, causing severe damage.

Only one American scored, and that was green, twenty-seven-year-old Joe Foss. Jumped from behind, Foss was nearly killed, but his attacker came by too fast and gave the Marine a chance at an easy kill. Foss recovered and fired a light burst, and the Zero blew up. But Foss allowed himself to be jumped by three other Zeros, who shot his plane to pieces. With Zeros still on his tail, Foss rocketed into Fighter-1, making a deadstick approach at full speed. He slowed only a bit before his Wildcat went out of control and piled up at the end of the dirt-and-grass runway. An ambulance arrived in time to give the thoroughly chastened Foss, who climbed from the wreckage unaided, a ride to his tent. This was the breathtaking start of a brilliant combat career in which Foss would become the first American to match Capt Eddie Rickenbacker's World War I record of twenty-six kills.

The bombing raid had been a complete success. The runways, which Seabees had just gotten back into shape, were holed from end to end. Six B-17s arriving back from a raid to the north were ordered to stay clear, for the twisted steel Marston Matting that covered a patch of Henderson Field large enough to land a heavy bomber had to be replaced.

The fresh Guardsmen managed to get ashore without loss. There was no reason for them, or anyone, to consider October 13 an exceptional day—yet.

Seventeenth Army artillerymen had for days been painstak- ingly hauling a regiment of 15cm howitzers to fresh emplacements west of the Perimeter. Safe beyond the range of Marine counterbat- tery fire, the howitzers were ready to fire as the second air raid flew out of sight to the west.

The Japanese gunners registered their pieces with slow, me- thodical precision. This was a new, more serious threat than any- thing the Lunga garrison had experienced in over two months of merciless poundings. "Pistol Pete," as the heavy artillery was soon dubbed, was by far a more potent weapon than any bomber or warship could ever be.

Pvt Fred Harris, of M Company, 5th, happened to glance toward Henderson Field in time to see several Seabees stepping from the shadow of a small hill into the open of the Lunga Plain. A 15cm shell burst right in front of them. The Seabees turned back toward the protection of the hill, but their path was again barred by a huge geyser of dirt and stone. Private Harris would have bet on the Japanese forward observer at that point, but the scared Seabees foxed them all by continuing on toward the hill as the third 15cm round landed on the spot where the first round had impacted.

The new hazard, not yet fully perceived, killed more than one conscientious Seabee or Marine engineer working in the open around the runways.

Pistol Pete pumped shells into the Perimeter until nightfall; not too many, or too fast, for the China War veterans directing the fire were just limbering up. But the quantum leap in danger was perceived by day's end.

A Japanese task force built around battleships *Haruna* and *Kongo* slowly lurked toward Lunga Roads, undetected by American search aircraft grounded as the result of runway damage. Each carried 500 36cm high-capacity bombardment shells, a type never before used against land targets.

It began with the *put-putting* of an underpowered fabric spotter floatplane arriving over Lunga Point to drop flares for the battleship gunners. Cpl Frank Blakely, at the 1st Marines message center, near the beach, thought he heard a sound from the channel like a cork being pulled from a champagne bottle—a gentle *pop*!

MGen Archer Vandegrift, Col Jerry Thomas, and several division staffers crowded into a bombproof bunker, prepared to sit out another boring bombardment. As the first incendiary shells burst on the runway, Thomas blurted out, "My God, those aren't 5-inchers they're throwing at us." He was right. Once the target area had been sufficiently lighted, *Kongo*'s captain ordered his gunnery officer to begin registering the new 36cm shells.

The first salvoes walked right up the beach toward the 1st Marines CP. Cpl Frank Blakely and two other communicators leaped into Blakely's radio dugout and buried their heads in their hands just as the top of a coconut palm crashed down across the entrance. Blakely reflexively reached down to finger an object that had fallen on his leg, but all he felt was a searing pain from a white-hot shell splinter. The youngest of the three communicators, a boy who had earlier boasted about how many Japanese ears he expected to collect, screamed uncontrollably and tried to pull himself through the twisted branches until Frank Blakely decked him with a solid punch in the mouth; the boy continued to blubber and whine.

Three green Guardsmen were passing through the 1st Marines galley area when the first shells hit; they dived into the nearest dugout with three Marines, and all six sat down, three men facing the channel and three facing inland. Immediately, a 36cm round hit at such an angle as to shatter the bodies of the two Marines and GI facing inland; the Marine and two GIs facing the sea were buried, but emerged without injury.

When the fire on the 1st Marines sector abruptly ceased, Col Clifton Cates ordered Cpl Frank Blakely to relay news of the bombardment to the 1st Marine Division CP. Blakely, whose knees were actually knocking together, was certain that the proximity of the shelling had temporarily unhinged the normally unflappable regimental commander, for Archer Vandegrift's bunker was less than a mile away, and there was no question but that the folks at the division CP knew more than enough about the shelling.

Satisfied that his guns were on target and could be manipulated with ease, the Japanese task-force commander ordered his flotilla gunnery officer to resume firing as soon as the moving warships could turn at the end of their firing leg and beat back up the channel off Lunga Point. The subsequent holocaust was horrible, chaotic, as stunned, waking men burst from their sleeping places and bolted for secure underground shelters. Buildings, huts, and tents were ripped open, spilling their contents onto the trembling earth. Steel splinters, wreckage, purple-dyed 36cm baseplates cut through the air to slice holes in trees, tents, trucks, aircraft, and men. Gasoline—more precious fuel—went up in smokey circles of unbearable heat, casting enormous shadows before the exulting Japanese gunners. In the target area, throughout the Perimeter, terrified men were beset by tens of thousands of terrified rats, which were shaken from their shelters by the awful shelling and sent scurrying in their multitudes into the holes and across the backs of cowering Marines, sailors, and soldiers.

A near-miss lifted Archer Vandegrift from his perch at the end of a bench and unceremoniously dropped him on the damp earth. Another blast injured men around the 11th Marines CP. Field telephones whose wires survived the pounding brought steady news of irreparable damage and mounting despair throughout the Perimeter.

The Marine battalions occupying Bloody Ridge took the brunt of the "overs" aimed at the main runway, but were spared the worst possible fate by the soft, rain-soaked earth, which absorbed most of the killing effects of the huge rounds and smaller shells from accompanying cruisers and destroyers.

Dr. Victor Falk, VMSB-141's flight surgeon, had just dozed off at dusk when he was awakened with news that it was his turn to fly to the rear base at Espiritu Santo next morning with the daily air-evacuation run. Falk protested to no avail, so had to leave the company of the dive-bomber squadron's senior officers for a tent nearer Air Ops. The squadron tent received a direct hit that night which killed Maj Gordon Bell, the squadron commander, and a ground officer and three senior pilots.

Meantime, Dr. Falk was sent scrambling for a dugout, from which he watched towering geysers of burning aviation gasoline and felt the deep vibrations of exploding shells rippling through the ground. He soon joined Dr. Henry Ringness, another flight surgeon, in rounding up wounded men and treating them wherever there was space and a modicum of shelter. Ringness was eventually felled, but continued to treat other men for as long as he could drag himself about. When Victor Falk found him, Ringness gave a detached, clinical explanation of his injuries, calmly noting that his spinal cord had been severed; he had no knowledge that his buttocks had been shredded by a Japanese shell. Falk dragged Ringness to the division hospital, but the grievously injured physician later succumbed to his wounds.

In the midst of the destruction, as huge shells burst and great pyres of burning gasoline leaped skyward on every side, 2ndLt Denny Doyle, a newly arrived Marine dive-bomber pilot, paused before lighting a calming cigarette with trembling hands in order to ask his three cowering companions if they thought the match might give their position away to the Japanese gunners.

Kongo and *Haruna* and their cruiser and destroyer escorts used the last of their ammunition at 0230, and left the channel, their wakes ineffectually dogged by four newly arrived American motor torpedo (PT) boats.

Before anyone in the Perimeter could organize damage-control parties, a chain of Japanese night bombers arrived to make matters worse. A direct hit on Texas Switch, the garrison's main radio station, prevented word of the disaster from going out until nearly dawn. By that time, forty-one American officers and men were dead, and dozens of others were wounded, some mortally.

The material damage was staggering. Thirty-two of thirty-seven SBDs were damaged or destroyed, and all of Torpedo-8's remaining TBFs were gone for the time being. Only two new P-39s and four old P-400s survived the night. Cactus Air's offensive capability was ruined, though Fighter-1 had only been lightly shelled and bombed, and most of the American fighters had escaped serious damage.

Henderson Field was incapable of supporting any sort of flight operations. Nearly every gallon of aviation gasoline had gone up during the night or was burning off in the light of the new day. Air operations had to be switched to Fighter-1.

Among the hostages of the bombardment were the crews of six B-17s under Col Blondie Saunders, the 11th Heavy Bombardment Group commander. The B-17s had struck Japanese transports on October 13 in an unprecedentedly long mission to both Buka Passage, in the Solomons, and Buna, in New Guinea, then had been obliged to stop off at Guadalcanal to refuel. Saunders and his crews had been kept aloft by the noon bombing, then grounded by BGen Roy Geiger, who could not spare the required fuel from his burning stocks. As soon as it was light enough to work, Saunders sent his airmen out onto the main runway to clear a path through the sharp shell splinters that littered the area in thick profusion. (As one of the B-17 crew chiefs prepared his airplane for the journey to Espiritu Santo, he boosted a seventeen-pound hunk of shrapnel out of the pilot's seat.) Only four of the six B-17s were airworthy, and those barely managed to fly off the abbreviated 2,000-foot patch of Marston-Mat-covered runway optimistically referred to as "operational." Blondie Saunders reluctantly ordered the destruction of the two grounded B-17s, which were crammed with super-secret devices.

Archer Vandegrift arrived at Air Ops to find a dejected Roy Geiger viewing the wreckage of his headquarters building. Geiger ordered the structure demolished, believing that it had served as a registration point for the Japanese gunners.

With no fuel, there would be no defense. Someone remembered that BGen Lou Woods had hidden small caches of fuel here and there around the Perimeter weeks earlier. Roy Geiger had been given a map with the locations of the caches clearly marked, but he had misplaced it. A search was given top priority and, as the day lengthened, the small horde was painstakingly assembled. Even the nearly empty tanks of the two scuttled B-17s were sucked dry. But it was not nearly enough.

The fighters were scrambled at 0930 on the strength of a Coastwatcher report, but no Japanese aircraft materialized. Twenty-six Bettys, which had flown far off course to kill time while the American fighters used up their limited fuel, struck Henderson Field while the fighters were refueling on Fighter-1.

Thirteen F4Fs and eight Army fighters met an 1130 strike of eighteen Bettys, and creamed it. Navy fighter pilots destroyed five of the bombers, and the Marines got four Bettys and three Zeros for one loss of their own. It was a meager salve.

An afternoon search to the north by several SBDs uncovered two separate convoys. The first consisted of six troop-laden transports and eight destroyer-transports heading for Cape Esperance. Two cruisers and two destroyers were also coming on fast, undoubtedly to bombard the runways.

Roy Geiger told his airmen that they would fly to the last, then join ground units to repel land or amphibious assaults.

As 15cm shells burst in and around their repair shops, Marine groundcrewmen wrestled with the damaged aircraft, cutting parts from the wrecks to build flyable bombers and fighters. The first offensive strike of four SBDs and seven P-400s went after the transport convoy at 1445, but scored no hits. A second attack mounted at 1745 by seven Navy SBDs and six P-400s was met by heavy antiaircraft fire over the transports and came up empty; an accompanying P-400 was shot down, and a second was lost in a landing after dark.

Eighth Fleet struck the Lunga Perimeter that night while the six transports disembarked the infantry and their gear. In all, the cruisers dumped 750 8-inch shells on the Perimeter. GIs of the virgin 164th Infantry were certain after only two nights ashore that bombardments of such magnitude were common fare.

Thursday's dawn was a relief. But the sunlit waters to the west disclosed an act of damning gall. In easy view of Lunga Point, the six Japanese transports were methodically and unhurriedly disembarking troops and supplies at Tassafaronga.

The first American aircraft aloft were a pair of P-400s, armed with 100-lb bombs for their routine dawn patrol. No sooner had the pilots gotten their wheels up than Air Ops announced the arrival of numerous Zeros in the area. Both Army airmen turned inland and followed a line of clouds around toward Cape Esperance, where, Air Ops said, there were ample targets.

First Lieutenant Frank Holmes's war had begun at Pearl Harbor, where, dressed in the brown pinstripe suit he had worn to Mass that Sunday morning, he had managed to get an aged P-36 fighter aloft to chase, but not to fight, the Japanese attackers. This morning, less than a year later, Holmes had less than thirty gallons of fuel aboard as he lined up on one of the Japanese transports. Three Zeros were on his tail and every one of ten destroyers was putting out rounds at him and his wingman. Certain this was his last flight, Frank Holmes bored through the fire and placed his tiny bomb on the forward hatch cover of the vessel that had become his target. The hold, filled with artillery shells, blew. Holmes hauled back on his stick to come out of his dive, but he had time to see that his gunsight was aligned on the stern of the next transport. He pressed the trigger and saw rounds strike the ship. He also saw hundreds of kneeling and standing riflemen firing at him from the transport's deck. Instinctively, Holmes moved to bank around for another strafing run, but the power of his diving turn froze his controls and took him down low over the palm trees lining the shore. Every ship in range was firing at him, so he highballed for home on the last of his fuel. There were thirty-seven holes in his P-400 from bullets and shell fragments.

Another early riser was Lt Smokey Stover, who took off at 0800 in the company of another of Fighting-5's three remaining Wildcats. The two F4Fs climbed westward to 7,000 feet and executed a forty-five-degree dive on three of the six transports they found lined up west of Point Cruz. The two Wildcats flew through thick antiaircraft bursts to mast-top height, but neither was damaged, and both pilots saw their .50-caliber bullets strike home before ducking into a nearby valley running to the interior of the island. Well out of range to the southwest, they climbed and executed a second attack. Neither Wildcat was damaged, but neither did Smokey Stover see any results from his gunfire.

Stover was pulling out of his second dive when he spotted a fabric float-biplane coming down on his tail from 7,000 feet. He turned ninety degrees to the biplane's course and climbed, as did the Japanese pilot. Unable to gain altitude on the fabric airplane while topping 8,000 feet, Stover turned his sluggish Wildcat toward the quarry and approached to within a half-mile. The Japanese pilot fired a pair of 20mm cannon through his aircraft's propeller disc, but the rounds dribbled off to Stover's left. Meantime, Stover closed to within 500 yards of the floatplane and pressed the gun-button knob on his joystick. Only four of six wing guns fired.

The two warplanes were roaring right at each other, but neither pilot would break off. Stover's right wing neatly knifed through the biplane's top fabric left wing.

As soon as Stover recovered from the unintentional midair collision, he looked around for the biplane. It was still flying, but was clearly in trouble. Stover made a quick pass with guns ablaze, and the biplane rolled into a spin. Stover's wingman, who had not been able to get in on the sudden action, saw the Japanese crash. Disgusted with his poor marksmanship, Smokey Stover landed and recovered two huge fabric swatches from the leading edge of his Wildcat's right wing; one of the swatches was emblazoned with an entire Rising Sun emblem.

This gut-wrenching action proved to be Smokey Stover's last on Guadalcanal, an incredible finale to a tour that began with a strafing run against Japanese-held Henderson Field in the predawn hour of August 7.

Obsessed with an unquenchable rage, Roy Geiger's crews drained the last of the fuel from the tanks of wrecked aircraft and gasoline drums for the last three undamaged, flyable SBDs.

Maj Joe Renner took charge of getting the three SBDs airborne, marking many of the obstructions and holes in the runway. The path, alas, could not be seen from the high aircraft cockpits, so Renner trotted ahead of the first taxiing bomber, which nevertheless nosed over into a shell crater before even reaching the main runway.

The second dive-bomber, piloted by VMSB-141's senior surviving officer, 1stLt Robert Patterson, had to be scrapped when its undercarriage was left in a small crater. Undaunted, Patterson drove over the field in a jeep with Major Renner, then climbed into the last airworthy bomber on Guadalcanal and managed to get airborne, only to discover that the hydraulic system had failed and that he could not raise his landing gear. After all the trouble to which he had already gone, Patterson was not about to abort. He delivered a wheels-down attack against one of the stationary transports—and missed.

Ground crews pieced together more SBDs from the profusion of spare parts that littered the field and its environs. As the morning wore on, aircraft composed largely of other aircraft rolled off the reassembly lines one-by-one and took off to deliver solo attacks on the transports down the beach, which were protected at all times by shipboard antiaircraft guns and no less than thirty-two long-range Zero fighters. Hits were scored and two of the ships had to be beached, afire, amidst the cheers of the shell-shocked gawkers lining the beaches around Lunga Point. But the toll in airmen and aircraft became prohibitive, so Roy Geiger ordered the bombers grounded until a reasonable number could be collected for a coordinated strike.

Gasoline continued to be found throughout the Perimeter in forty- and fifty-drum lots, each drum representing an hour's flying time for a Cactus Wildcat. And word from rear-area headquarters indicated that several large gasoline barges were being towed up, and that ships were on the way with deck-loads of aviation-gasoline drums.

Roy Geiger ordered literally everyone to work. He was out for blood. Those who could fly would fly, those who could not would do what they could; Lt Swede Larsen, whose Torpedo-8 had no TBFs left, took his pilots and groundcrewmen out to Bloody Ridge to fight as infantry.

One who could fly was Maj Jack Cram, the pilot of Roy Geiger's personal PBY-5A Catalina flying boat, "Blue Goose." Cram, a fighter pilot, had been shanghaied into his chauffering job months before by Geiger himself. He was itching to get into the fray and volunteered his services as a pilot. The situation was desperate enough to warrant the risk of the lumbering flying boat in battle, though Cram's mission was bound to be suicidal.

Arming Blue Goose was a simple matter. In addition to the toilet paper and tin cans he had been hauling regularly from Espiritu Santo, Jack Cram had brought up two aerial torpedoes on his last run, and these remained slung beneath the parasol wing of his patrol bomber. Nimble hands jury-rigged hand-release toggles, which gave Cram an opportunity to become a combat pilot once again. He had no torpedo experience, and with the Torpedo-8 pilots back in the hills, he was reduced to getting directions from Fighting-5's skipper, LCdr Roy Simpler, whose brother was a TBF pilot.

Maj Joe Renner asked Cram to join the next strike, a mixed bag of Navy and Marine SBDs and Army fighter-bombers. But Cram pointed out that his PBY-5A had an operational speed of 90 knots,

324

too slow for keeping up with the SBDs. Renner ordered Cram to leave early, never expecting to see him or his crew again.

Blue Goose headed south over the forest before turning west toward Cape Esperance, then came about to an easterly heading and began a shallow dive from 6,000 feet. As Cram plummeted earthward, he glanced at his airspeed indicator, which registered an unprecedented 270 knots; Blue Goose had been built to do 140, maximum. A slight movement to the left caught the pilot's eye; the wing was flapping. So was the right wing.

Jack Cram forced himself to stare straight ahead at a sea full of ships. No one was firing at him, and his run was dead perfect. He pulled the release toggles at 100 feet. The Catalina leaped and lurched as the heavy torpedoes fell clear. Thoroughly engrossed, Cram hauled back on the control yoke to keep the cumbersome bird aloft, to claw for needed altitude. One of the torpedoes porpoised in the waves and harmlessly exploded. The other stove in the side of a transport, forcing her to beach.

The SBDs were already bearing down from the east. To avoid being hit by their falling bombs, Major Cram pulled around in as tight a 180-degree turn as he would ever manage and hauled back on the control yoke once again to find some flying space. The destroyers' antiaircraft got him there, amply ventilating Roy Geiger's personal airplane. Cram manhandled the awkward bomber back toward Fighter-1, certain that every second he lived from that point on was a bonus.

Upon clearing the ships' fire, Cram ran into the Zero umbrella, which went after him with a vengeance. Ever a fighter pilot, Cram cautioned his green nose-gunner, whom he could see from the flight deck, to lead his targets, of which there were six buzzing in and out from all directions. As Cram bullied his way into the traffic circle over Fighter-1, 1stLt Roger Haberman passed overhead in his F4F. Quick to note Blue Goose's predicament, and without taking time to raise his landing gear, Haberman flitted in behind the Zero and squeezed off a short, easy burst. The Zero—

Haberman's first kill—rolled over and fell away into the rain forest. Haberman followed Cram down for a neat landing.

Later, a much-relieved Jack Cram nursed Blue Goose off Fighter-1 and headed back for Espiritu Santo—to pick up a load of toilet paper and tin cans.

B-17s from Espiritu Santo scored three hits against the Japanese transports for dozens of bombs dropped from high altitude, and SBDs, P-39s, and P-400s caused additional damage at the cost of three Marine aircraft and crews.

With the Cactus Air establishment growing stronger by the hour, the Japanese decided to leave before the remaining three transports were sunk or severely damaged. Despite the very best efforts of the American aircrews, a company of medium tanks and nearly 4,000 crack infantrymen and technicians from 16th and 230th Infantry regiments were landed with many tons of supplies.

Only one major air strike was launched by 11th Air Fleet, though harassment continued unabated through the day. At 1245, twenty-seven Bettys and nine Zeros were over Henderson Field without a Cactus fighter anywhere in the vicinity. Several fighters did get aloft, but only one Zero was downed by Fighting-5's last F4F.

Air strength ebbed and flowed through the afternoon of October 15. Without aircraft to fly, fifteen exhausted Army and Navy fighter pilots and Marine dive-bomber pilots were evacuated by air from Guadalcanal that afternoon. On the plus side, six pilots from LtCol Joe Bauer's VMF-212 ferried up the last six spare SBDs available in the South Pacific; these pilots were returned to Espiritu Santo by air to rejoin their fighter squadron, which was to move to Cactus the next day. In all on October 15, one float-biplane and six Zeros were downed at a cost of three Dauntlesses, two P-39s, and an F4F. Four American pilots and three aerial gunners were killed.

Farther afield that day, October 15, an emergency resupply convoy that had been scraped together at Noumea two days earlier was spotted at dawn by Japanese search planes off San Cristobal, a day away from Lunga.

Composed of two attack cargo ships, a PT-boat tender, and a fleet tug escorted by two destroyers, the convoy was not only brimming full of needed supplies and ammunition, each cargo ship towed a barge loaded with 1,000 barrels of aviation gasoline and five hundred 500-lb bombs.

The dawn sighting by the Japanese snooper was followed at 0608 by orders from South Pacific Area Headquarters to transfer one of the barges to fleet tug *Vireo*. While both cargomen and the tender sailed to safety at top speed in the company of one destroyer, *Vireo* was to haul the vitally needed barge in the company of the second destroyer, *Meredith*.

At 1050, two Japanese patrol bombers attacked the tug, but they were twice beaten off by *Meredith*'s antiaircraft guns. However, at the conclusion of the air attack, the destroyer received word that Japanese warships were in the area. *Meredith*'s captain ordered *Vireo* to reverse course and bend on all the speed she had.

The tug could barely sail at 14 knots, far too slow to race the oncoming Japanese warships. The destroyer's captain was thus obliged to order *Vireo*'s crew to abandon ship and come aboard his faster vessel. When the tug's crewmen had all been safely transferred to *Meredith*, the destroyer drew off to scuttle the abandoned vessel with a torpedo.

At that precise moment, 1215, twenty-seven Japanese carrier bombers and fighters struck.

Three Japanese warplanes were shot down by *Meredith*'s antiaircraft gunners, but the destroyer was torn to scrap by bombs and bullets, and she quickly sank.

Vireo, which was not struck by a single bomb or bullet, provided a tantalizing haven for the bilged crews of both vessels, but she was pushed farther and farther from the survivors by a steady wind. Only one raftful of survivors eventually reached her.

Attracted by the scent of blood, sharks struck at swimmers

with appalling swiftness to tear hunks of flesh from men already brutalized by their fellow men.

Those who lived beyond the pain of the wounds, the deadly sun, and the unremitting scavenging by sharks, drifted for three ghastly days before they were sighted and rescued by two destroyers and a fleet tug. Of a combined total of 309 officers and men manning *Meredith* and *Vireo*, 73 survived.

The larger part of the original convoy was attacked by five Vals, and one of the cargomen was damaged, but all four ships and the one barge safely returned to Espiritu Santo.

When the South Pacific Area command learned on October 15 that there was at least one Japanese carrier on the prowl, all American ships in the region were ordered to head for bases far in the rear lest they get caught in another air strike.

Henderson Field was struck for the third night in a row on the night of October 15, this time by a cruiser force sent down from the main Japanese fleet anchorage at Truk. Nearly 1,500 8-inch shells were fired beginning at 0030, but Fighter-1 and the repair shops were spared serious harm. It was by then obvious that the Japanese did not know the importance of the little grass strip, for they invariably fired at the main runway.

At dawn, Friday, October 16, Roy Geiger counted ten SBDs on line with four P-39s and three P-400s, plus a reasonable number of Wildcats. While talking to LCdr Roy Simpler early that morning, Geiger blurted out in frustration, "Roy, I don't believe we have a fucking Navy." Simpler had been through the worst of times with Geiger, but he retained his loyalty to his service. "General, if we have a Navy, I know where to find it." Geiger told Simpler to do that little thing, and Simpler climbed into the cockpit of one of his squadron's two remaining Wildcats. As soon as he was aloft, he flew southward, across Guadalcanal, and straight out to sea. He had about reached his point-of-no-return when he spotted an American carrier task force, a sight to take the breath away on the best of days. Aircraft had been launched, so Simpler approached with caution, fighting the impulse to declare an emergency so he could land aboard the carrier and partake of a decent meal. But he could not; he flew to his home away from home and landed at Fighter-1 as air strikes from *Hornet* hit the Japanese west of Lunga.

Hornet's fresh Air Group 8 assumed responsibility for protecting the sky over Henderson Field and for launching a strike against the Japanese seaplane base at Rekata Bay. This sufficiently relieved Cactus Air to allow it to mount a steady succession of strikes at known Japanese dumps along the northern coast and troop concentrations wherever they could be found. One Marine SBD was lost to ground fire during the day, and several P-400s all but fell apart from wear.

Late that afternoon, the last pilots and aircrewmen of Fighting-5, VMF-224, and VMSB-231 left Henderson Field aboard Marine transport aircraft, and the staff of MAG-23 was replaced by the staff of MAG-14.

One of the day's most important arrivals was seaplane tender *MacFarland*, a converted four-stack destroyer that brought up over 40,000 gallons of aviation gasoline in 750 deck-loaded drums. The first 400 drums had been unloaded and dispersed when nine Val dive-bombers that had been out all day vainly searching for *Hornet* passed overhead on the way home to Buin.

There were many aircraft aloft as the Vals came up from the usually friendly south, so no alert was issued. LCdr Roy Simpler, who had decided to sail south aboard *MacFarland* when there proved to be one seat less than needed aboard the transport aircraft that had taken out the last of his Fighting-5 pilots, noted the heightened activity over the field and told the ship's captain that he had better get some sea room fast, for Cactus airmen never went aloft for training. Next thing Simpler knew, several Vals were heading right for him. A single bomb hit the barge carrying the last 350 fuel drums, spreading flaming gasoline all over the place. A second bomb hit *MacFarland*'s fantail, killing or maiming nearly a dozen departing Fighting-5 groundcrewmen.

LtCol Joe Bauer, who had knocked down four Zeros in one sortie about a week earlier, was in the traffic circle over Fighter-1, the last aloft of twenty VMF-212 pilots who had just flown up from

Efate by way of Espiritu Santo. He went after the Vals alone as soon as he spotted the pillar of smoke from the burning barge, and caught them as they were pulling up. Down they went: one, two, three, four. Bauer landed at Fighter-1 on the last of his fuel. He had earned a Medal of Honor for his two back-to-back four-plane kills.

Half of 40,000 gallons of aviation gasoline had been lost.

MacFarland, which had shot down one of the Vals herself, limped to a hidden estuary in Florida's shoreline for repairs.

The night of October 16–17 passed more quietly than previous nights; most of the Japanese warships in the area were out looking for *Hornet*, which was retiring. That evening, Cactus Air learned that Pacific Fleet Intelligence had tumbled to Japanese plans to launch two massive air strikes the next day.

While on a routine dawn patrol around Cape Esperance, 1stLt Frank Holmes, of 67th Pursuit, lucked upon a find of incredible importance. Flying nearly at wavetop height, paralleling the beach, Holmes saw odd reddish shapes, the same color as the ground, humped up beneath the trees along the beach. Mindful that untoward curiosity might warn the Japanese, Holmes highballed it for Fighter-1 and commandeered a ride to Air Ops to tell of his find—hundreds of square yards of tarp-covered supplies carried ashore from Japanese transports on October 15. Air Ops at first thought to call in a heavy-bomber strike, but two American destroyers anchored off Tulagi were ordered across the channel to walk 5-inch shells from the inland side of the dump toward the beach. They took an enormous toll of the goods the Japanese had landed at so much cost.

The first Japanese air strike arrived early. Eighteen Vals and eighteen Zeros, all from carrier squadrons temporarily based on fields in the north, were intercepted at 0720 by eight VMF-121 Wildcats led by the squadron commander, Maj Duke Davis. The Vals went after the destroyers that were shelling 17th Army's main forward supply dumps. The destroyers were not hit, but six Vals and four Zeros were downed. One of Davis's Wildcats was lost, but its pilot was saved.

Following the morning strike, three SBDs spotted targets for the destroyers which, with a succession of Army fighter-bombers and a flight of six B-17s, blasted the dumps to oblivion.

Numerous Japanese destroyers and cruisers managed to reach Guadalcanal unnoticed that night, but, while most unloaded troops and supplies at Cape Esperance and Tassafaronga, only five destroyers fired an ineffectual ten-minute barrage at Fighter-1.

On October 18, a morning air strike was spotted over New Georgia by a Coastwatcher. Sixteen Wildcats downed three of fifteen Bettys and four of nine carrier Zeros. The Marines lost one F4F in a take-off mishap and two in combat—without pilot loss.

Also on October 18, rescue vessels which saved the surviving crewmen of *Vireo* and *Meredith*, which had been lost on October 15, recovered the bargeload of aviation gasoline abandoned by *Vireo*, and this was sent straight through to Lunga.

Eleventh Air Fleet's offensive against Henderson Field had shot its bolt; the Japanese air groups were gutted. Now, with plenty of gasoline in stock and on the way, and a growing crop of fresh aircrews in operation or coming up, Cactus Air was clearly resurgent.

29

When Adm Chester Nimitz returned from his tour of the South Pacific, he put the lessons he had learned to good use. It was evident from Nimitz's own findings, and more so from the naval action off Cape Esperance and the massive bombardments of the following days, that the battle for Guadalcanal was approaching the critical stage. Fleet Intelligence estimated that 17th Army had achieved frontline strength nearly equal to that of the reinforced 1st Marine Division. A command summary put it succinctly: "It now appears that we are unable to control the sea in the Guadalcanal area. Thus our supply of the positions will only be done at great expense to us. The situation is not hopeless, but it is certainly critical."

It was a bad time for the Allies worldwide. Not only were the Japanese still free to do as they chose, the Axis in Europe and North Africa remained victorious. The Wehrmacht had been demoralized in the Russian winter of 1941–42, but had regained lost ground and was digging in for another siege of winter warfare. Afrika Korps had been stymied at various times over the preceding months, but it stood before the gates of Cairo, readying itself for the final showdown. The Germans held Western Europe in a firm grip. It was this grip that the Allies decided to break, and nearly everything they had in the way of men and material would be directed against Hitler. Thus, Admiral Nimitz had to make do until America's war-making potential could be realized. It would take time. All of the very limited resources in the Pacific would have to be used.

Nimitz ordered bomb-damaged *Enterprise* out of drydock and on her way to the South Pacific. The new battleship *South Dakota*, which had been damaged when she hit a reef, was also ordered out of Pearl with *Enterprise*, though neither had had repairs completed. The U.S. Army's 25th Infantry Division, on garrison duty on Oahu, was alerted for shipment to the South Pacific, and VAdm William Halsey, an aggressive and knowledgeable carrier commander, was ordered south to replace the injured VAdm Frank Jack Fletcher as commander of the fleet carriers.

But the rushing of ships, troops, and senior officers to the South Pacific was, in many ways, cosmetic. There was something at the root of the conditions in that area that needed fixing. So Nimitz called a special meeting on the evening of October 15. It was attended by the small group of staffers that had accompanied him on his South Pacific tour. Most of the officers present—all Nimitz intimates—noted that the ordinarily jovial commander in chief had an icy cast in his usually merry blue eyes. He was getting down to business.

It was clear, Nimitz noted, that the Japanese were about to open a major offensive against the Lunga garrison, so he wanted to hear impressions regarding the situation in the South Pacific. He asked if anyone thought VAdm Bob Ghormley was capable of handling the pressure in a way that would inspire his subordinates.

After some discussion, the staff registered its overwhelming opinion: Ghormley was not cutting it; he had become bogged down in minutiae, and was overwhelmed by pessimism.

Nimitz asked each officer in turn: "Is it time for me to relieve Ghormley?"

The answer from each man: "Yes."

The talk turned to possible replacements. Though Kelly Turner was a junior rear admiral, he seemed an obvious choice. But his cantankerous and overbearing manner had him at direct odds with the ground commander at Guadalcanal. No, Turner probably needed a more-senior officer to arbitrate his inevitable disputes. Halsey's name came up. There was an initial positive reaction. He was a fighter, and well respected throughout the U.S. Fleet. It was said that the carrier sailors had cheered aloud when his return following a lengthy illness had been announced. Nimitz, however, wondered whether the combative Halsey had the administrative savvy to handle the post. Unwilling to commit himself either on the question of relieving Ghormley, or on whom he might choose as a replacement, Nimitz adjourned the meeting.

Late that evening, while resting in his private quarters, Nimitz was called to the phone. A staff officer who had not been in on the meeting, and who did not know what had transpired, was calling to ask if the admiral would grant a brief interview; he represented a small group of staff officers that had an opinion to express. Nimitz invited the man over for a chat.

The entire group of staffers arrived to find Nimitz dressed in pajamas and dressing gown, ready for bed, so they came to the point: While Nimitz undoubtedly had feelings for Ghormley as a brother officer and friend, the situation clearly warranted a change. The group recommended that Halsey replace Ghormley. Without committing himself, Nimitz expressed his appreciation for the group's concern and said that he would give its views every consideration.

In the morning, October 16, Nimitz cabled Adm Ernest King to ask permission to replace Ghormley with Bill Halsey. A very prompt affirmative was received.

The impact of the decision was instantaneous. As soon as Halsey assumed command in Noumea, he asked for a briefing by staffers who had been to Guadalcanal. When he learned that not one of Ghormley's men had yet been to the front, his first impulse was to make the trip himself. But he realized that he would need the coming days and weeks to hammer the supporting services into shape, and that the task would require every waking minute until it could be completed. So, he did the next best thing to going by inviting Archer Vandegrift to Noumea.

❧

For his part, Vandegrift was totally immersed in the reorganization of his defenses and in clearing up the debris of the bombings and shellings of the past week. It would be nearly a week, he thought, before he could get away, and only if the situation warranted his departure.

There arrived at Henderson Field on October 21, Vandegrift's most-welcome guest to date, the venerable Commandant of the Marine Corps, LtGen Thomas Holcomb. While Vandegrift feared for Holcomb's safety, he was thrilled to mark the arrival of the one man to whom he felt he could completely unburden himself. Beginning with a tour of the lines and talks with troop commanders, Vandegrift happily noted that Holcomb, whom he considered the Marine Corps' best tactician, seemed enthusiastic about the troops and their deployment.

At a private meeting before dinner, Holcomb complimented Vandegrift on the job he was doing, then probed him on a matter of some importance to the Marine Corps. Holcomb was then sixty-three, and would be facing mandatory retirement in less than a year. While he expressed a willingness to continue his tour beyond retirement if asked to do so by President Roosevelt, the commandant felt that the mantle should be turned over to a younger man. He was, he said, going to recommend Archer Vandegrift when the time came. Vandegrift politely and humbly demurred, but Holcomb persisted.

Talk eventually turned to the pressing matters of the moment, particularly to the continuing misunderstandings with Kelly Turner. Then, inasmuch as Holcomb was leaving the next morning via Noumea, Vandegrift decided to avail himself of Bill Halsey's

request for a meeting; he would fly to Noumea with the commandant, who would thus participate in the talks.

Following a cordial dinner with Kelly Turner aboard the admi-
ral's flagship, Vandegrift went over to *Argonne* to meet Bill Halsey.
Besides Vandegrift and Halsey, the meeting included General
Holcomb, Admiral Turner, MGen Millard Harmon (the Army
South Pacific troop commander), MGen Alexander Patch (the
American Division commander), Halsey's chief of staff, and several
key members of the respective staffs.

Halsey began by asking Vandegrift to outline the situation on
Guadalcanal. The commanding general did this, stressing the poor
physical condition of his Marines due to a restricted diet over a
period of more than two months. He further stressed the need for
material support and added the obvious request for reinforcement
and eventual relief. He specifically recommended that General
Patch's division be committed in its entirety, and added that the
balance of 2nd Marine Division might be sent in.

Generals Harmon and Patch fully concurred with the troop
requests, adding that American Division would be ready to move
just as soon as it could be relieved of garrison duties. With Harmon's vigorous concurrence, General Holcomb wholeheartedly endorsed every one of his protégé's requests.

Halsey patiently listened. When the tall, patrician-looking
Marine division commander had completed his presentation, the
new area commander lifted his bushy grey eyebrows and asked
Vandegrift, "Can you hold?"

"Yes," the reply came, "I can hold. But I have to have more
active support than I've been getting."

Halsey nodded. "You go on back there, Vandegrift. I promise
to get you everything I have."

A direct result of the conference that evening was the final
cancellation of the Ndeni operation, which for months had been the
bad dream affecting all of Vandegrift's best intentions. In addition,
Halsey endorsed a dispatch from General Holcomb to Admiral
King outlining the command relationships that should be hence-

forth maintained between naval and landing-force commanders. This direct attempt to circumvent for all time the headaches brought about by Kelly Turner's strong views was subsequently endorsed by Admiral Nimitz, at Holcomb's personal request, and was soon adopted at the specific order of Admiral King.

While the higher order of command decisions was being debated aboard *Argonne*, the business of winning and holding Guadalcanal was in grave conflict. With BGen Roy Geiger temporarily minding the store at Lunga, American forces on Guadalcanal were facing the most serious threat of the campaign.

30

Over 5,500 Sendai and Nagoya division veterans were marching around the western flank of the Lunga Perimeter.

In view of 4th Infantry's defeat on the coast a week earlier, LtGen Harukichi Hyakutake had opted for an all-out attack against the interior Perimeter line. Unlike MGen Kiyotake Kawaguchi, whose tactics he otherwise sought to emulate, Hyakutake sent engineers to cut a trail for the assault forces.

It was hoped that LtGen Masao Maruyama, the Sendai Division commander, would be in position to launch his inland thrust on the night of October 21. To support Maruyama, General Hyakutake decided that 4th Infantry would mount a tank-supported assault across the bar of the Matanikau, both as a diversion and a serious effort in its own right. While the main force would haul some light 70mm artillery with it, the coastal force would be supported by 10cm and 15cm artillery.

General Hyakutake was so confident of success that he withheld the order that would have brought the balance of Nagoya Division to Guadalcanal. There seemed no need for the reinforcements, which he hoped to divert to New Guinea.

The plan for the assault was complete in every detail. In fact, Adm Isoroku Yamamoto's staff had included instructions for the surrender ceremony, detailing the precise time and place at which Archer Vandegrift would relinquish his sword to Hyakutake.

The vanguard of General Maruyama's inland assault force moved out on October 16, some days behind the trail-blazing engineers. Accompanying the division commander was MGen Yumio Nasu, Sendai Division's infantry-group commander, and the weak, pale MGen Kiyotake Kawaguchi, elements of whose reorganized brigade would participate in the assault. Also along was LtCol Masanobu Tsuji, acting both as a representative of 17th Army's senior staff officer, Col Haruo Konuma, and of Imperial General Headquarters. The assault force was built around the fresh 16th and 29th Infantry regiments. Elements of 230th Infantry were in reserve.

Despite the best efforts of the engineers, the going was extremely tedious for everyone. Transport was left entirely to the bent backs of soldiers trudging single-file for up to sixteen hours a day along the narrow, winding, undulating jungle path. General Maruyama pulled himself up the steep, muddy hills with the aid of a white cane. Nasu, whose body was wracked by malaria, leaned heavily upon his sword, refusing help or relief. No cooking fires were permitted, so everyone subsisted on a half-ration of cold rice. When sheer cliffs barred the way, nimble soldiers climbed them to secure ropes for those who followed. Dismantled field guns, mortars, and machine guns were hauled up the steep, slippery hills, then hand-carried to the next obstacle, endlessly it seemed. The gooey muck left by each downpour pulled at the feet of the brutalized infantry, taking their shoes from them, leaving them exhausted and in need of rest every few hundred yards. The nights were chilly, forcing men in rotting clothing to huddle together for warmth. Only the hardiest could keep pace by the third day in the rain forest. Gun after gun had to be abandoned, and so did many of the sick.

The vanguard lost its way, so did not reach the upper Lunga

until October 19, some days behind schedule. General Maruyama decided to postpone the offensive until the night of October 22.

General Kawaguchi, whose thin brigade was to launch an attack on the right flank of the Perimeter, grumbled over the lengthening chances of success, for it soon became evident that Maruyama was stubbornly clinging to a plan that the elements and the terrain had already modified. After thinking the matter through, the wan Kawaguchi left his brigade and trudged off alone to find Maruyama, whom he hoped to convince of another, more realistic plan. Instead, the brigadier found the politically powerful LtCol Masanobu Tsuji, to whom he outlined his plan, which called for an attack across the more open, rolling ground southeast of Henderson Field rather than through the dense jungle below Bloody Ridge. Kawaguchi said that his assault, combined with General Nasu's attack in the south, would crush the defending Marine battalions in a gnashing pincers.

Tsuji privately loathed the decent, urbane Kawaguchi, but he attentively listened and said that he would not only relay details of the suggested plan to Maruyama, he would strongly urge the commanding general to adopt it. Satisfied, Kawaguchi began the arduous walk back to his waiting troops.

Far from urging Maruyama to change his plan, Tsuji urged him to replace Kawaguchi with a more reliable officer. In due course, Kawaguchi was relieved by Col Toshinari Shoji and sent back to Rabaul, where he spent many weeks in the hospital recuperating from his efforts to claim Lunga.

When it became clear that the assault could not be launched before the night of October 23, LtGen Masao Maruyama sent a message to MGen Tadamasu Sumiyoshi, the Sendai Division artillery commander, who had been left in tactical command of the coastal assault. No response was given, so it was hoped rather than known that Sumiyoshi had received the vital signal.

The first probe was made on October 20, from the west, near the coast. A Japanese combat patrol accompanied by two medium tanks ventured into view of 3rd Battalion, 1st Marines, which was holding a new outpost line on the east bank of the Matanikau. As soon as the small force came within range, a 37mm antitank gun facing the sandspit disabled one tank with a single round. The other tank fled from sight along with the accompanying infantry. Division headquarters did not quite know what to make of the tanks, but it had been preparing itself for the worst for some time.

Artillery salvoes struck throughout the Perimeter during October 21, and became hotter as the day wore on, then rose in crescendo as nine tanks supported by a very large infantry force made a dash for the sandspit at the mouth of the Matanikau. When the 37mm guns covering the sandspit disabled one of the tanks, the Japanese again turned tail.

Twice rebuffed, the Japanese on the coast refrained from mounting probes during October 22, preferring instead to augment the heavy artillery fire with that of their 90mm mortars. During the day, General Maruyama attempted to contact General Sumiyoshi about a further twenty-four-hour delay.

It was quiet through most of October 23, except for the by-then-usual artillery fire from the west. Then, at about 1800, mortars struck the lines of 3rd Battalion, 1st. The bombardment soon considerably intensified, with most of the shells directed at an 800-yard line along the river and back along the Government Track for several hundred yards. General Sumiyoshi was clearly trying to pin the Marines on the line while preventing reinforcements from using the road.

Pfc Jim McClinchy, of B Battery, 1st Special Weapons Battalion, had drawn first blood almost precisely two months earlier, when he remanned one of the 37mm antitank guns at the mouth of Alligator Creek. Battle casualties and attrition through illness had resulted in the six-foot-three-inch New Yorker's elevation to the command of one of the B Battery gun sections that very day. The promotion came after the section was ordered up to man the sandbagged 37mm gun emplacement at the mouth of the Matanikau, an isolated and exposed position only five yards from the Government

Track used by the Japanese tanks two and three nights earlier. A second relief guncrew was sent to the 37mm gun emplacement fifty yards downstream. McClinchy's only protection was the twenty-two-man rifle platoon commanded by 2ndLt Bill Wright, of I Company, 1st. Additional support was in the hands of a pair of forward observers manning a bunkered forward observation post linked by a telephone line to M Company, 1st's 81mm fire-direction center. Artillery, mortars, and halftrack-mounted 75mm antitank guns were on call, but the nearest radio was fifty yards behind McClinchy's bunker.

The Japanese artillery fire, which began at 1800, scored several direct hits upon the roof of Jim McClinchy's gun bunker, but none penetrated the position thanks to an extra layer of sandbags.

Pfc Bob Marks, half of the 81mm forward-observer team, was running a new communications wire inland to the line companies to replace the old shrapnel-severed link when the Japanese artillery fire abruptly ceased; it was as though someone had thrown a switch. As soon as their ears cleared, troops on the line, and particularly those on the sandspit, heard the rumble of tank engines. Nine medium tanks clanked out of the woods on the west bank of the Matanikau and headed directly for the sandspit. Just back of the tanks, huddled along the edge of the trees, was most of what was left of 4th Infantry, ready to divert attention away from General Maruyama's main assault. (General Sumiyoshi had *not* received word of the last delay and, at the insistence of General Hyakutake, was sending his diversionary force into battle.)

The Japanese were outnumbered two to one. Third Battalion, 1st, and 2nd and 3rd battalions, 7th, were in the immediate vicinity, and the entire 5th Marines was only a short distance to the rear, holding the main Perimeter line. There was ample support on hand, thanks particularly to BGen Pete del Valle, the 11th Marines commander.

As soon as it became obvious that the Japanese artillery fire of the early evening was softening the way for a major assault, del Valle committed ten of his twelve 75mm and 105mm batteries to the endangered zone. Division headquarters was gambling its main supports on the premise that the assault on the Matanikau front would be the only Japanese activity of the night.

The batteries around the airfield were displaced across the Lunga, over the only bridge available, and placed in battery sites south of Kukum. As there was no opportunity to register any of the arriving guns, General del Valle assigned each battery a strip zone parallel to its line of fire; thus, each four-gun unit had merely to increase or decrease ("ladder") its range as firing orders were relayed from the front.

As the howitzer batteries were being brought into place, Pfc Jim McClinchy kneeled to the left of his 37mm gun's breech block. To his right was the loader, Pvt Fred Augustynowicz, who would respond to McClinchy's requests for specific types of rounds. Pvt Milo Kosanovich and Pvt Sam Bennett were at work in the rear of the bunker, pulling the tops off crates of ammunition. The black-headed armor-piercing shells were stacked nearest the gun, for it was obvious from the noise of tank engines that they would be needed first and most. Yellow-headed high-explosive rounds were also broken out, for finishing off the tanks and heading off the infantry.

McClinchy and Augustynowicz strained their eyes to pierce the evening darkness; there was plenty of noise, but no targets could yet be perceived. The crew of a 75mm halftrack which had roared into a prepared emplacement on the beach behind McClinchy's gun at the close of the Japanese artillery preparation was similarly blinded by the darkness.

Atop a low rise to the rear, overlooking the 37mm bunker, Sgt Silvio Sangueldolce, of M Company, 1st, directed the four 81mm mortars of his platoon upon a blind depression the Japanese had earlier used as an avenue of approach upon the sandspit.

At long last, Pfc Jim McClinchy made out a dark shape emerging from across the sandspit. He attempted to locate the murky target in his gunsight, but the battery-operated lamp in the sight was inoperative, rendering the device useless. McClinchy spun a pair of wheels, one in each hand, to bring the gun barrel to bear upon the target, then pressed a plunger in the center of the left wheel with the heel of his left hand. *Crack!* The first round left the gun. McClinchy tracked its red trajectory out across the sandspit until it disappeared. The tank opened with its hull machine gun and the 37mm gun in its turret. Pvt Fred Augustynowicz rammed three more rounds into the smoking breech, but each failed to find the target. The tank was virtually on top of the bunker, so close that McClinchy could no longer track far enough to the right to hit it. Fearful that the tank driver would make a sharp right turn and flatten the emplacement, McClinchy screamed, "Get out!" and scrambled with his crew into the trench alongside the river that led to the 37mm gun downstream. The tank passed the bunker and continued down the beach until Pfc Joseph Champagne, of M Company, 1st, reached out from his foxhole to stuff a hand grenade between its wheels. The tank wildly skewed about on one track, then stopped. The three crewmen were shot to death as they bailed out.

The 37mm crew ducked back into its bunker. McClinchy lined up on a second dark shadow and fired. There was a tremendous flash only fifty yards away. A hit! Each of three new dark forms creeping from the woods was hit in quick succession.

Jim McClinchy switched to high explosives to completely destroy the three burning tanks, then he switched to canister to discourage any infantry who intended to advance behind the tanks. It was absolutely deafening inside the cramped emplacement. Red-hot shell casings piled up between gunner and loader, searing their thighs, but both were too wrapped up to notice. The breech block became so hot that Fred Augustynowicz had to use a screwdriver to pry out the spent casings. McClinchy just stared ahead, keeping the barrel lined up on targets until the loader hit him on the shoulder to signal that a fresh round was in the breech.

Jim McClinchy accounted for four tanks, Private First Class Champagne got one, and the halftrack-mounted 75mm gun got four. The 37mm gun fifty yards downriver was disabled by gunfire at the outset of the tank attack; one gunner was killed and two were wounded and evacuated. Three additional tanks spotted on the far side of the river were destroyed by del Valle's gunners.

Third Battalion, 1st's 81mm mortars put out so many rounds that all four tubes had to be replaced. Japanese counterbattery probing the Marine rear in search of mortars knocked out the line from the observation post to the fire-direction center four times that night, necessitating four trips to the rear by Pfc Bob Marks, whose job it was to keep the link open.

The Japanese infantry was blown apart by 11th Marines and the mortars. Second Lieutenant Bill Wright, whose rifle platoon was right out on the sandspit, never saw a Japanese infantryman, but he called fire so close to the sandspit that the gunners asked if he had been overrun. Several hundred Japanese were caught at the edge of the trees by the Marine batteries south of Kukum, and hundreds were killed in the devastating fire by 2200, when the gunners were ordered to stand down.

Just before daybreak, as Pfc Bob Marks lay slouched against a tree that formed one support for his observation bunker, he heard a nearby blast and a strange, throaty sound. He called out to see if his fellow forward observer, Sgt Silvio Sangueldolce, was okay, but there was no answer. Sangueldolce had been peering out through the embrasure in search of targets, and a shell splinter had sliced open his abdomen; he expired before Marks could move to his side.

In all, 1st Marine Division lost twenty-five Marines killed and fourteen injured that night. Only one of them died on the sandspit.

Sumiyoshi had attacked; Maruyama had not. Hundreds of Japanese officers and soldiers had died.

31

There was something in the wind, but Allied intelligence organizations throughout the Pacific were unable to divine Japanese intentions. It seemed to 1st Marine Division that the Japanese were building toward an all-out assault across the mouth of the Matanikau. Three fresh rifle battalions had been dispatched to the area in a week's time, including LtCol Herman Hanneken's 2nd Battalion, 7th, which was transferred from Bloody Ridge to Hill 67, overlooking the river, on October 23.

The Japanese had planned well, for the so-called Maruyama Trail took the main body of General Maruyama's reinforced regiments far beyond the range of Marine patrols. Indeed, there were no patrol contacts through the third week of October.

The transfer of Hanneken's battalion to the Matanikau front on October 23 left LtCol Lewie Puller's 1st Battalion, 7th, with the rather awesome task of covering a 2,500-yard line on and near Bloody Ridge without supports. The line stretched from the Lunga River to a point about two-thirds the distance to Alligator Creek, about twice the frontage occupied by the Raiders and 'Chutes in mid September.

Puller's battalion mustered fewer than 700 effectives, less than the number that had defended Bloody Ridge under Red Mike Edson. Earlier in the week, following the massive bombardments, Puller approved a scavenging foray to the aircraft boneyard at the end of Henderson Field in order to remove machine guns from the wings and fuselages of damaged fighters and bombers. Thus, the battalion was better armed than the Japanese had reason to suspect. (On the first Sunday after 164th Infantry landed, Puller's supply officer ordered the Catholic members of his section to attend Mass on the beach, and not to return to the battalion area without first stopping by the Guard regiment's supply dumps to steal certain specified items.)

When Hanneken's battalion moved on October 23, it was Puller's first impulse to spread his three rifle companies rightward, to cover both the original battalion line and Hanneken's former positions. He discussed the matter at some length with Capt Charlie Kelly, his exec, and they decided that the best solution was for Kelly to take a platoon from each of the three rifle companies, plus attached machine guns, and occupy the forward slope of the T-shaped ridge, which Hanneken's battalion had vastly improved during its stay. The terrain was quite favorable for even so small a force. Kelly went to work bringing up ammunition and supplies, and familiarizing himself and his Marines with the defensive area.

To Kelly's immediate left, occupying a low, jungle-choked flat, was Capt Bob Haggerty's B Company, now down to two rifle and one weapons platoons, though it was heavily augmented by its share of the salvaged aircraft machine guns. Capt Marsh Moore's C Company and Capt Regan Fuller's A Company, in about the same condition as B Company, were strung out leftward. Anchored on A Company's left, at the corner of the Perimeter line, was LtCol Art Timboe's 2nd Battalion, 164th, 1,000 fresh, green Guardsmen. The vulnerable battalion juncture was guarded by a 37mm antitank gun and several .50-caliber machine guns Puller had begged from higher headquarters. Timboe placed similar heavy weapons near the curving corner of his line, another naturally vulnerable area. Unlike Puller's Marines, Timboe's Guardsmen had the advantage of clear fields of fire across a broad meadow fronting their positions. Both battalions had rigged numerous noisemakers and booby traps to the double-apron barbed wire protecting their lines. If Japanese infiltrators could not be seen, they would certainly be heard and hurt.

Reports concerning General Maruyama's main force began mounting up late on October 24 when an observer on Bloody Ridge spotted a Japanese field officer carefully studying the ridge through a pair of binoculars. A short time later, one of Col Bill Whaling's scouts reported many "rice fires" in the Lunga Valley, about two miles south of Puller's line. By that time, Puller's troops were making feverish last-minute adjustments and refinements to their defenses.

C Company, for example, had a *cheval-de-frise*—a barbed-wire gate—in the middle of its line to facilitate the comings and goings of patrols. Capt Marsh Moore did not like the looks of the contraption and suggested that the gap be sealed with double-apron barbed wire. It was late in the afternoon, and a decision could not be delayed. A detail was called out and heavy gloves were issued for the dangerous work. The new wire was strung and tripwires were snaked through the brush. The job was completed at dusk.

Puller placed a direct call to BGen Pete del Valle, who assured him, "I'll give you what you want. I know you won't be unreasonable. Just call for all you need." The batteries that could reach Puller's lines were registered at dusk upon the jungle flats in front of the line.

Field telephones were placed in every company and platoon CP, and Puller ordered the entire circuit to remain open. A final line check was made just after dark. By then, there was nothing for Puller's Marines to do but wait in the rain, which began at nightfall. Half turned in while half remained in their holes, ready to withstand a surprise assault.

One of the sleepers was Capt Charlie Beasley, Puller's operations officer. A slight, spare twenty-two-year-old Notre Dame graduate, Beasley had put in a rough day preparing the battalion to defend enough ground for two battalions against a massive onslaught. Truly the brains of the battalion, the young tactician had had to fight mainly losing battles with superiors all day; the regimental commander insisted upon this, the battalion commander upon that. To cap it, Beasley was not even given the meager luxury of nodding off in his own cot. Since Capt Charlie Kelly was up with the platoons on Bloody Ridge, Lewie Puller insisted that Beasley sleep on Kelly's cot. Beasley had removed himself from his operations center to sleep beneath a dripping tent fly; he kept his helmet on and had a live telephone receiver tucked up beside his ear.

The main body of Maruyama's infantry had negotiated the final lap of its torturous advance from Kokumbona. Most of the light artillery and mortars littered the trail to the rear. But most of the hearty infantrymen had completed the struggle and were being formed up after wading the Lunga and advancing to staging areas south and just to the east of Bloody Ridge.

General Maruyama readied his exhausted soldiers for the job of killing that lay ahead. His plan had been appropriately scaled down for want of General Sumiyoshi's diversion and lack of artillery. As Kawaguchi's before it, Maruyama's infantry was hungry, tired, and somewhat dispirited, really in no condition to take on such a task. But the plan had been set, as if in stone.

In the hope that the night would be clear and moonlit, MGen Yumio Nasu ordered a narrow-front assault just east of Bloody Ridge. Col Masajiro Furumiya's superb 29th Infantry was the spearhead, and Col Yoshio Hiroyasu's 16th Infantry was to exploit penetrations. To the west, the skeletal 124th Infantry, supported by mortars and machine guns, was to assault Marine positions on its front. Unfortunately for the Japanese, the problems General Kawaguchi had forecasted in positioning the brigade had not gone away with Colonel Shoji's assumption of command; *Shoji Butai* was not in position, and would not participate.

Directly in the path of 29th Infantry, on a knoll about 300 yards south of the main line, was a platoon outpost manned by forty-six A Company Marines under PlSgt Ralph Briggs.

Capt Charlie Beasley had argued long and hard with regimental headquarters over the placement of the Briggs outpost. As far as Beasley was concerned, Briggs's platoon was being sacrificed to no advantage. He knew there were Japanese on his front long before the phone receiver by his ear came alive at 2130, waking him. Briggs was on the circuit, whispering, "There're Japs by the thousands coming around both sides of this knoll."

"For God's sake," Beasley cautioned, "keep down! Shut up! Don't open your trap! If they get past you, cut out to the east, through the high grass, and get the hell into the jungle to your right. I'll hold fire." Word went through the battalion like an electric shock. Sleeping men tumbled from their tents, instantly awake.

The Japanese knew that the outpost had them spotted, but they did not know that Briggs had spoken with the battalion CP. Fearful of losing the element of surprise, Colonel Furumiya decided to bypass Briggs and press on toward the main line.

There would come a point, Beasley knew, when Briggs's platoon might have to be sacrificed in the interest of larger realities, but he wanted the platoon to have as much time to get clear as he could afford to give it.

The heavy rain was Briggs's key to saving himself and his Marines. Under cover of the incredible torrent, the platoon stealthily moved eastward between the opposing lines of infantry. Crawling through muddy tangles of vines and bushes, small groups of the stranded men got away, and Colonel Furumiya lost track of them in the press of more important business.

The rain was a mixed blessing for both sides. With their visibility cut and mud barring the way in many places, the Japanese had to advance slowly, cautiously, to maintain cohesion. This gave

Puller's Marines more time to prepare. On the other hand, Japanese skirmishers reached the wire without being seen.

Charlie Beasley's phone rang again at about 2145. Capt Regan Fuller whispered a curt warning: Japanese sappers were cutting through the barbed wire on A Company's front. Beasley went on the battalion net and told his officers to steady the troops; no one was to fire until he issued a direct command.

Shouting along the front broke through the drumming of the rain at nearly 2200: Marines and Japanese soldiers were exchanging obscenities. A minute later, a hoarse scream dominated all other voices: *"Totsugeki!"*

The nerve-taut columns of Japanese infantry sprang forward, catching Puller's line from far left to just left of center with a deep, narrow penetration in C Company's sector.

Puller's Tidewater drawl resounded over the battalion net: "Commence fahring!"

Immediately, upon the first discernible movement on the front, the battalion's mortars and supporting artillery roared. The troops on the line opened with steady, heavy fire. Machine guns dominated the Marine response as the fast-moving lead ranks were followed by massed units seeking to exploit the initial penetrations through the protective wire barrier.

The high proportion of old salts to which 7th Marines had fallen heir when it shipped out to Samoa the previous spring was crucial. Puller had a large number of the Marine Corps' best machine gunners and mortarmen knitting his line together, and they took a fearsome toll from 29th Infantry. A machine-gun section in the center of C Company's line put out so much fire that, during the first lull, its chief, PlSgt John Basilone, had to send a detail to flatten out the mounds of corpses that were obscuring his field of fire.

The hardest fight was along A Company's front, where great gaps were blasted in the Japanese files by the canister-firing 37mm gun, eighteen massed BARs, and four .30- and .50-caliber machine guns. A Company's single operating 60mm mortar fired most of the

600 rounds it was to fire during the entire night. Hundreds of Japanese were felled in the open field in front of the company.

The first heavy assault lasted all of fifteen minutes. Then the Japanese fell back, unable to advance and unable to hold their meager initial gains. The retreating soldiers were caught in enfilade by guns from the adjoining 2nd Battalion, 164th.

The first lull in the attack was just taking hold when a strong Japanese force bounded back and made directly for the *cheval-de-frise* in the center of C Company's line. Stymied by the extra wire that had been strung in the late afternoon, the brave Japanese were piled up in front of the gate.

As both sides took a breather and settled down for the next phase, Lewie Puller called BGen Pete del Valle: "Give us all you've got. We're hanging on by our toenails."

"I'll give you all you call for, Puller, but God knows what'll happen when the ammo we have is gone."

"If we don't need it now, we'll never need it," Puller's soft drawl advised. "If they get through here tonight, there won't be a tomorrow."

The lean, patrician brigadier, Puller's opposite in every way but for a shared combativeness, firmly replied, "She's yours as long as she lasts."

"Totsugeki!"

Twenty-ninth Infantry had reformed for its second assault. Slipping and sliding on the rain-soaked, blood-soaked jungle flats and upon the southeastern slope of the ridge, the lead ranks swept forward and crushed themselves upon the wire, pressed from behind by fellow Japanese and ripped from ahead by Marine machine guns and rifles.

The mindless determination of the Japanese hammer blows made a doubter of Capt Charlie Beasley. "Colonel," he muttered to Puller at about 2300, "we're gonna lose Henderson Field tonight. I want to call General Vandegrift." That made quite a few simultaneous impressions upon the combative battalion commander, but he assented to his subordinate's request. The call was bucked

Top (left to right): MGen Archer Vandegrift, BGen Bill Rupertus, Col Red Mike Edson, Col Bill Whaling, and Col Herman Hanneken in Australia in 1943.

(Official USMC Photo)

Above (left to right): RAdm Slew McCain, commander of South Pacific Aircraft; Col Blondie Saunders, commander of 11th Heavy Bombardment Group; and MGen Millard Harmon, commander of U.S. Army forces in the South Pacific.

(Courtesy of J.V. Edmundson)

Top: A Marine 75mm pack Howitzer crew prepares to fire.

(Official USMC Photo)

Above: A Marine patrol probes the rain forest west of the Matanikau River.

(Official USMC Photo)

Top: Sgt Joe Goble, of B Company, 7th Marines.

(Courtesy of Joseph Goble)

Above: Smoke from fires partially obscures the damage inflicted to an aircraft hangar near Henderson Field during the night bombardment of October 13.

(Official USN Photo)

A direct hit by a Japanese bomb turned this
radio station beside Henderson Field into a
mass of debris.

(*Official USMC Photo*)

Top: Wrecked Dauntless dive-bombers line Henderson Field's main runway in the wake of Black Tuesday. In background behind wrecked airplanes are 11th Heavy Bombardment Group B-17s awaiting clearance for takeoff.

(*A.C. Timboe*)

Above: One of the Japanese medium tanks destroyed on the Matanikau sandspit by Pfc Jim McClinchy's 37mm guncrew on the night of October 23. Point Cruz is in the background.

(*Official USMC Photo*)

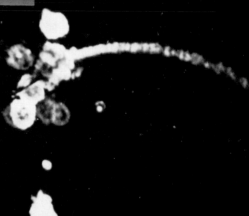

Above: One of four Imperial Army transports ordered beached at Doma Cove by RAdm Raizo Tanaka on November 15.

(*Official USN Photo*)

Left: 500-lb bombs from 11th Heavy Bombardment Group B-17 flown by Maj Jim Edmundson hit light cruiser *Yura* from 13,500 feet on October 25.

(*Courtesy of J.V. Edmundson*)

Inset above left: Maj Jim Edmundson (*right*), of 11th Heavy Bombardment Group.

(*Courtesy of J.V. Edmundson*)

Inset below left: A Japanese bomb scored a directy hit on this Marine Dauntless dive-bomber during a raid on November 2, 1942.

(*Official USMC Photo*)

RAdm Raizo Tanaka

(*Official USN Photo*)

One of more than 35,000 Japanese soldiers who died on Guadalcanal

(*Unknown*)

through regimental headquarters to division headquarters, which informed Beasley that the commanding general was off the island. At last, Col Jerry Thomas, the division chief of staff, took the call. "Colonel," Beasley opened, "we're gonna lose Henderson Field tonight. We need some reserves." Thomas said that there was another fight going on near the Matanikau. "Well, Sir," Beasley countered, "that's a two-pronged attack. They're trying to swing around the field tonight." Thomas promised he would call back.

One group of Japanese infantry penetrated the main line and moved to capture a mortar emplacement. The penetration was sealed off in time, but the Japanese desperately tried to hold their gains. Farther on, another sudden rush brought a Japanese platoon against one of Puller's water-cooled .30-caliber medium machine guns. The guncrew was shot down, but two Marines evaded injury and manned the weapon against repeated assaults until help arrived.

Marines knocked back from the line by the hammer blows from at least eight assault waves coalesced into small, grimly determined groups, then slashed their way back to their former positions. The captured mortar site was retaken after a bloody fight, and the tube was back in action within minutes.

A call from the regimental CP which had displaced west of the Lunga to oversee its two battalions near the Matanikau, earned a blistering Puller rebuke: "What do you mean 'What's going on?' We're neck deep in a fire fight, and I've got no time to stand here bullflinging. If you want to find out what's going on, come up and see."

The regimental exec, LtCol Bull Frisbie, called back to ask if Puller still needed reinforcements. It was 0300, five hours into the vicious fight, and Puller was on a taut rein. "Sure we could use help, but if it's coming, for God's sake, don't hold back. Send it on in."

Col Jerry Thomas rang up Puller's CP to speak with Capt Charlie Beasley. "I'm going to commit the only battalion left in reserve on the whole island. I think the Matanikau battle is a feint and the main effort is coming through where your men are." Thomas cleared the way for moving LtCol Bob Hall's fresh, green 3rd Battalion, 164th, to Puller's aid. The hitch was that Puller, who was down to under 500 effectives, would have to further weaken his position in order to provide Hall with guides. Staffers combed the rear for men they could press into service. As soon as Capt Charlie Kelly heard about the call for guides, he got on the battalion net to offer as many men as he could reasonably spare; Kelly's positions on Bloody Ridge had barely been touched and, because his Marines had been drawn from each of the three rifle companies, he had men available who knew all the trails from the rear to the threatened line.

Hall's battalion was bivouacked a dark, rainswept mile from Puller's. While their comrades on the line held the Japanese, the guides met the first groups of Guardsmen and led them toward the rear of the Marine line. It was so dark that many Guardsmen had to hold hands to keep from going astray.

The Japanese reformed time and again.

Capt Regan Fuller told Puller that A Company was holding, but was getting low on ammunition; the platoon-sized company had already fired enough to weigh down a battalion. Puller asked if Fuller's Marines still had their bayonets. When an affirmative answer was heard over the line, the battalion commander drawled, "Awraht then, Old Man, you'll hold."

Senior NCOs had always been minor gods in the Marine Corps, and those who commanded weapons sections were the gods' gods. Tough, strange men, they were acknowledged as the finest technicians in the service, and every major clash on Guadalcanal had gone far to reinforcing that sense of superiority.

MGySgt Ray Fowel, the genius ramrodding Puller's 81mm mortar platoon, got so much mileage out of his gunners that he nearly brought the riflemen he was supporting to grief. The gunners put rounds out so quickly that the overheated tubes caused the powder increments of many rounds to flare before hitting the bottoms of the tubes. This caused the rounds to fall short, some well within friendly lines. Fortunately, none of these short rounds became fully armed before they dropped into the mud, where they would be discovered after sunrise, too close for comfort, but harmless.

The man of the hour was PlSgt John Basilone, a regular from Rahway, New Jersey, known as "Manila John," because of his several tours with the U.S. Army in the Philippines.

Basilone's guns, double the authorized number, were set up in support of C Company, dead in the center of the battalion line, around the *cheval-de-frise*, and they made all the difference between C Company's holding and being overrun. Basilone had seen that the guns were well protected behind sandbag emplacements, and he personally oversaw the firing that scattered Japanese platoons at each rush; guns firing 500 steel-jacketed rounds per minute ripped the Japanese ranks apart.

Manila John discarded his disintegrating boondockers and raced barefoot along dark, muddy, rainswept trails to the battalion CP to collect spare barrels and ammunition, then back along narrow, muddy paths to distribute them. Lewie Puller saw the half-crazed gunner passing through several times, but stopped him only once, to get a report on the fighting.

When two of his guns were captured, Basilone spread eagled a 100-pound, water-cooled .30-caliber machine gun on his back and sprinted ahead of the rifle squad he had drawn for retaking the lost guns. As the riflemen pushed the Japanese back and held off a new attack, Manila John worked feverishly to clear jams.

Clearing jams, running ammunition and spare parts, repositioning guns and their supports, finding solutions to every sort of problem—PlSgt John Basilone was the first enlisted Marine in the war to receive a Medal of Honor.

The first of LtCol Bob Hall's Guardsmen arrived, and the exhausted, wet Marines who had been fighting in water up to their thighs for over six hours were glad for the help. Hall was met by Lewie Puller on the muddy jeep track that ran behind the main line. As pink tracers from Japanese machine guns passed overhead, the two agreed that Puller would run things until they could determine who was senior. As the two talked, Puller could only hope that the dark shadows passing on either side would turn the tide in his favor.

Capt Fox Parry, a member of the Naval Academy class of 1941 and commander of C Battery, 11th Marines, was directly behind Puller's embattled infantry line when the first of Hall's Guardsmen began appearing out of the gloom. Parry's four 75mm pack howitzers were so close to the infantry line that Parry had to order them to cease firing to avoid hitting the Guardsmen as the rounds left the tubes. The sight of the Guardsmen passing silently through his battery's gun line, perfectly aligned in squads and platoons, rifles held at high port with bayonets fixed, took the battery commander's breath away.

The Japanese attacks, which were noticeably losing strength, eventually might have pushed through Puller's thin battalion. But they were about to be stopped cold by the combination of Puller's Marines and nearly 1,000 fresh Guardsmen armed with new eight-shot, semi-automatic M1 Garand rifles.

With six rifle and two weapons companies facing them on the immediate front, and elements of 2nd Battalion, 164th, able to lend a hand on the left, the thinning ranks of 29th Infantry were doomed.

To Puller's far left, a pair of Army 37mm guns ceaselessly firing canister from well-chosen emplacements at the curve of 2nd Battalion, 164th's line hewed down Japanese attackers in platoon-sized clumps before the Japanese could even clear the trees on the far side of the broad meadow fronting Timboe's lines. Light, medium, and heavy machine guns, and hundreds of new Garand rifles lashed back and forth along the shattered lines of men emerging from the carnage of the antitank-gun fire. The Japanese never really got close to Timboe's Guardsmen, so telling were the American defensive fires.

Despite initial reports of success—including a message reporting the fall of Henderson Field that was actually relayed to Admiral

Yamamoto—General Maruyama could see no point in wasting more lives. The Japanese infantry commander, MGen Yumio Nasu, wracked by a critical malaria attack, called the assault off and ordered the infantry to pull back to safety.

The main body of 29th Infantry had moved beyond range of American fire by daylight. Some mopping up was necessary, but most of the exhausted Americans opted for gargling down some coffee and cold, greasy C-rations or Spam. Ammunition and water details were sent to the rear, and lightly wounded Marines and Guardsmen who had fought through the night despite their injuries swamped the sickbays and aid stations. Strongly guarded details cautiously moved into the corpse-strewn jungle flats to try to piece wire barriers back together, and intelligence teams began the gruesome task of rifling the pockets of dead and injured foes.

Machine gunners went to work on their weapons. One Marine gun section had used up its entire supply of barrels in the night, and one gun had been disabled when its steam condenser exploded under exceptionally heavy use. A detail from the section, sent forward to reclear the fire lanes, was itself fired on by jumpy Marines and lost three of its number before control could be regained.

PlSgt Ralph Briggs turned up on the line of Timboe's 2nd Battalion, 164th, and stragglers from his platoon arrived through the day. In all, thirty-three of the forty-six tramped home that first day. Of the remaining thirteen, nine would eventually return, the last a full two weeks later. Four were never found.

Henderson Field came under steady, heavy artillery fire through the day and, combined with the damage caused over more than a week, the big runway was often closed down. Fighter-1, less well bombarded, had been transformed into a fairly muddy quagmire by the steady rains of the preceding two days. For all intents, Cactus Air could do little about defending the Perimeter against raids by 11th Air Fleet or the warships of 8th Fleet.

To help stave off naval bombardments from the channel, the Navy had decided to base a squadron of PT-boats at Tulagi. Six of the new boats were towed from Espiritu Santo by *Trever* and *Zane*, a pair of World War I–vintage destroyer-minesweepers.

The two old minesweepers put into the wharf at Tulagi early on October 25. After untying the PT-boats and off-loading two full deck cargos of aviation-gasoline drums, Cdr Dwight Agnew, the task-unit commander as well as *Trever*'s skipper, was prevailed upon to carry a Marine surveying team to a potential new airstrip site on Guadalcanal's northern coast, well east of Lunga Point.

Trever was about to sail at 1000 when Commander Agnew was informed by the signal station ashore that three Japanese cruisers were standing in toward Lunga Point. Agnew saw that his only route out of the area through the restricted channel would bring *Trever* and *Zane* close to the Japanese track, but there was no alternative.

Closer inspection revealed that the three "cruisers" were three modern destroyers. This was a small consolation, for two of the Japanese vessels mounted guns that far outranged the Americans' 3-inch batteries.

As the two groups approached to within three miles of each other at 1030, Commander Agnew ordered his helmsman to "chase salvoes" when the Japanese opened fire. This maneuver sent *Trever* toward the Japanese when they fired short and away from them when they fired over. Though only one of Agnew's guns could bear—and even it could not reach the enemy—he ordered his gunners to commence firing, more for morale than in the hope of drawing blood.

The sparring continued for about ten minutes. *Zane* lost three killed when she was hit amidships, but *Trever*'s starboard waist gun set off ready ammunition aboard one of the Japanese warships. Several Wildcat fighters bounced the Japanese at 1040, allowing *Trever* and *Zane* to get clear and head out for Espirutu Santo at full speed.

The Japanese destroyers continued to sail along a curving southerly and southwesterly track. At about 1050, they flamed an American yacht-patrol boat as it towed a barge loaded with aviation gasoline toward Kukum.

Seminole, a seagoing tug, had been ordered out of Tulagi Harbor earlier in the day to deliver a deckload of aviation gasoline drums and several 75mm pack howitzers to a 10th Marines unit at Kukum. It was a routine mission similar to two others *Seminole* had undertaken in the past two days.

Most of the tug's crew was below decks eating when General Quarters was sounded. Gunners immediately climbed topside to man *Seminole*'s main armament, an ancient 3.5-inch naval rifle and several .50-caliber machine guns. As the gunners watched three smoke plumes on the horizon growing larger by the minute, the tug's captain ordered his helmsman to steer for the nearest land. He had no hope of putting up a serious fight, and did not even order his gunners to commence firing. Rounds from one of the Japanese destroyers set the aviation gasoline on *Seminole*'s deck ablaze and killed one American sailor. The exploding fuel drums forced the tug's entire crew to abandon ship.

Emboldened by their string of victories over the U.S. Navy, the Japanese warships swung in toward Lunga Point to have a go at some U.S. Marines. Several 5-inch coast-defense guns manned by 3rd Defense Battalion crews scored several hits. This pleased the American gunners immensely, for they were usually on the receiving end in contests with Japanese warships. The chastened Japanese retired behind a smoke screen.

October 25, 1942, was called "Dugout Sunday." Unable to defend themselves against the long-range artillery salvoes that hit the Perimeter every ten minutes, many Marines, Guardsmen, and sailors simply sat the day out in their bunkers, waiting for the sun to sufficiently dry Fighter-1 for the safe launching of combat aircraft.

The first Japanese over the field were two Zero-escorted twin-engine reconnaissance aircraft, no doubt sent to see if the airfields were in the hands of 29th Infantry. Antiaircraft fire kept the Japanese too high to see much, so one of the Zero pilots flew the length of Fighter-1 right on the deck. Every Marine in range cut loose in a mass emotional catharsis, and the Zero lazily rolled into the trees beyond the field and exploded in flames.

That was at 0800. At 0930, Capt Joe Foss, by now one of America's premier fighter aces, led four Wildcats off the still-muddy fighter strip and climbed to 6,000 feet despite intermittent attacks by Zeros stationed over the Lunga Plain. Five Zeros were downed by the aggressive American aviators.

In a series of running fights through the day, Marine Wildcats brought down twenty-two Japanese bombers and fighters. Joe Foss, who claimed four kills, was the day's high scorer. The Americans lost three aircraft, but suffered no pilot losses.

While the F4Fs fought over the island, LCdr John Eldridge's Scouting-71 caught light cruiser *Yura* and five destroyers in the Slot near Santa Ysabel; they left *Yura* dead in the water. Bombing-6 and three Army fighter-bombers hit *Yura* at about 1500, causing additional serious damage.

Refueled and rearmed, Scouting-71 hit *Yura* again at 1700. As Lieutenant Commander Eldridge's SBDs were pulling up through a heavy antiaircraft screen, six 11th Bombardment Group B-17s under Maj Jim Edmundson arrived over the milling warships. Edmundson wobbled his wings to signal the other pilots to close formation, then ordered his bombardier to open bomb-bay doors and line up on the largest vessel, *Yura*. It was 1700 and light was failing, even at the 13,500-foot altitude at which the B-17s were approaching. Two of the heavy bombers sustained minor damage from the ships' fire. Edmundson's bombardier made a perfect run on the target; when he called "Bombs away!" his payload of eight 500-lb bombs left the aircraft at sixty-foot intervals. Two bombs in one aircraft hung, so a total of forty-six were dropped. The bombers remained on course over the target so photographs could be taken. The antiaircraft seemed impenetrable, but the photographer finally said "Photos taken" and Edmundson pulled away. His crewmen, who could see the bombs explode, cheered and yelled over the interphone, congratulating the pilot and bombardier for scoring at least two hits, and possibly as many as six.

It was by then too late for another strike at *Yura*, but the Japanese ended the matter by taking off her crew and torpedoing the hulk. The Cactus airmen also sank a destroyer. When the records were tallied, it was found that, despite the slow start, Dugout Sunday was Cactus Air's busiest day yet.

On the southern perimeter, Puller's battalion tightened up to the right, occupying Bloody Ridge, leaving its former left flank to LtCol Bob Hall's 3rd Battalion, 164th. Four 37mm guns were dug in at the junction of the battalions, behind the *cheval-de-frise*. Both battalion lines were bristling with weapons, but the entire sector reserve comprised 175 members of 164th Infantry's Service and Antitank companies.

MGen Yumio Nasu, who had a temperature of 104 degrees, hoped to live long enough to lead 29th Infantry back to battle. The new attack was to be delivered in echelon, with 16th Infantry following the remnants of Colonel Furumiya's 29th. Col Toshinari Shoji, whose 35th Infantry Brigade had gone completely astray in the woods on the previous night, was led into position by a Sendai Division staffer. As preparations were being completed, General Maruyama received word that the Americans might counterassault his eastern flank. *Shoji Butai* was ordered to screen the flank, even if it meant missing the assault.

The entire assault force was to penetrate to the wire, then mount a straightforward massed frontal assault and breach the American line by sheer weight of numbers. It was a simple, oft-used tactic that had yet to succeed on Guadalcanal.

Nasu personally led the vanguard of 29th Infantry toward the wire. He was hobbling painfully forward, leaning on his sword, gasping heavily at each step—a gallant soldier determined to breathe his last in battle.

The soldiers directly behind Sendai Division's infantry-group commander had survived one night of futile combat. Fragmented by the undergrowth into groups ranging in size from under a dozen to 200, the thin 29th Infantry and the far stronger 16th approached the wire. Col Masajiro Furumiya was behind the first assault files, accompanying his regiment's color company. There would be no support this night but for the light machine guns the infantrymen could carry forward themselves. The assault was to be delivered with rifles, pistols, and swords.

General Nasu was just crossing the barrier when a volley of rifle shots rang out. The general took a slug in his chest and folded to the rain-soaked ground. Others fell by his side.

An officer majestically waved his sword over his head and screamed over the din of American gunfire: "*Totsugeki!*"

Upon clearing the wire, the lead files charged directly into the muzzles of Hall's and Timboe's guns without reforming. The attack hit the *cheval-de-frise*, now at the juncture of Puller's and Hall's battalions. The first men to breach the wire were members of two heavy-weapons companies, converted to riflemen for the venture. They charged directly into the face of 37mm canister fire, augmented by machine guns from both American battalions and the small arms of hundreds of riflemen.

Americans emptied whole cases of hand grenades into the faces of the closing Japanese. Screams of pain and pity mingled with shouts, taunts, and dying oaths, but these were all but lost against the thunder of massed weapons fire and explosions of hand grenades, rifle grenades, and mortar and artillery bursts.

The 29th Infantry's color company—the best in the regiment—smashed itself against the American line, forcing an entry. Colonel Furumiya, two officers, and six infantrymen carried the regimental colors to the rear of 3rd Battalion, 164th. When Furumiya turned to deliver orders, he saw that the breach had been sealed. He and his fellow soldiers hid.

The first wave had been beaten back, leaving nearly 250 fresh corpses littering the ground centered on the *cheval-de-frise*. Riflemen all along the American line blazed away at the piles of bodies in hopes of hitting snipers.

A company from the division reserve moved up to bolster the left of Hall's line, covering the open field where Capt Regan Fuller's A Company, 7th, had fought the night before. A short time later, LtCol Art Timboe dispatched a rifle platoon from his unmolested right company to reinforce the juncture with Hall's battalion. The

164th Infantry's regimental reserve was alerted for a move to the line.

Then the Japanese returned. The second assault, far feebler than the first, was easily turned. And so were continuing efforts to breach the line, each weaker than the one before, each more futile. The Japanese could make no headway, and gave up at midnight to haul away the wounded. Among the grievously injured was MGen Yumio Nasu, who was carried on a litter to General Maruyama's command post. The gallant Nasu breathed his last as the division commander gripped his hand.

32

LtCol Herman Hanneken's 2nd Battalion, 7th, was fighting for its life.

The battalion arrived near the Matanikau on October 23 to relieve 3rd Battalion, 1st, at the mouth of the river, but was prevented from doing so by daylong heavy shellings. Next day, because of increased Japanese activity, Hanneken was assigned a position facing south and running east and west across the forward slope of Hill 67, about 900 yards from the beach and parallel to it. The battalion was isolated on both flanks and so was expected to mount security patrols to help fill the gaps. Far to the left, well beyond support range, was the main Perimeter line manned by 5th Marines. On the immediate right, 3rd Battalion, 1st, was holding a north-south line near the mouth of the Matanikau and, on its left, 3rd Battalion, 7th, was also dug in along the river. The result was a vulnerable miles-wide salient—only 900 yards deep—appended to the main Perimeter.

Hanneken's battalion had not the numbers to cover the entire distance between the river and the Perimeter. So, with neither flank joined to any friendly unit, the battalion spent all of a brutally hot October 24 digging into the sun-dried soil. Mortars were emplaced near the beach, and the battalion and 7th Marines CPs were set up in the woods to the left rear. As the ridgeline just north of the main line was actually higher than the defended knobs, artillery and mortar observation posts were dug in there.

Most of the work took place in full view of the Japanese, under intermittent sniper fire. This harassment, and shellings through the day, prevented Hanneken's Marines from completing their work, so no one felt particularly secure at nightfall. As it turned out, a mortar observation post to E Company's right rear was overrun by Japanese infiltrators in the middle of the night.

卐

Hanneken's battalion was improving its positions on October 25 when 2ndLt Peyton Harris, an E Company platoon leader, spotted a large Japanese formation moving through the rain forest east of Mount Austen. This was the main body of Col Akinosuke Oka's 124th Infantry. Artillery and air were called to impede Oka's progress, but the entire column disappeared into a jungle-choked ravine about 1,000 yards south of Hill 67 before the effort could be mounted. However, Hanneken's 81mm mortars tracked the column into the ravine and opened fire. Immediately, Japanese mortars which had already been emplaced near Hill 67 lashed out at the defended military crest of the ridge, catching many Marines in the open. A senior NCO died from concussion, without a mark on him, and the E Company commander was mortally injured. A third Marine had a leg blown off, another fatal wound.

At dusk, October 25, F Company, 7th, was holding a high bare knob on the left (eastern) end of Hanneken's line; G Company was holding a slightly lower saddle; and E Company was holding another open knob on the far right. An F Company rifle platoon was detached just after sunset and sent to the right to screen E

Company's open right flank against infiltrators, who had probed the area in force the previous night.

The Japanese launched a strong probe against F Company at 2130, and the left elements of G Company were drawn into the sharp, brief fire fight.

A major probe by at least a battalion, and supported by snipers in trees overlooking the Marine positions and by observed artillery fires, was next launched against F Company and the left elements of G Company. It was beaten back with some difficulty.

A massed assault at 0300 struck F Company, whose commander clutched. The thin rifle platoons held for a time, but many Marines were sent tumbling down the reverse slope toward the battalion CP. The company was saved, however, by the timely arrival of reinforcements led by Capt Joe Buckley, the regimental-weapons-company commander, a legendary former enlisted Marine known for his bellicose personality and driving spirit. Buckley assumed control of the F Company sector, and the effects of that control were almost immediately felt by the Japanese, who became unable to exploit their lodgment.

Fearful of being overrun in the event Hanneken's main line collapsed, Col Amor Sims, the 7th Marines commander, next ordered his CP security force to the F Company line, to help hold the Japanese at the point of contact. Capt Claude Cross, the commander of the reinforcement group, grabbed a sack he thought was filled with hand grenades. It was, however, filled with C-ration cans, which Cross nevertheless hurled at attackers.

A Japanese force which managed to get through or around the main line thrashed about in the forest near the regimental CP for a time, but the handful of officers and technicians left to run things wisely lay doggo until the Japanese left.

PlSgt Mitchell Paige, a .30-caliber medium-machine-gun section chief, had carefully dug his guns in on the far left flank of F Company's sector, along the nose of the ridge just above the forest. Farther to the left was open, hilly ground, unsecured during the night. Directly ahead was a nearly sheer drop into a densely wooded valley. Overlooking the nose was a thick stand of extremely tall trees which Japanese riflemen had climbed after dark; the tree-tops and, thus, the snipers, dominated Paige's position. The ridge nose had been lightly probed the preceding night, but the Japanese had drawn back when gunners dropped hand grenades on them from the heights.

After nightfall, October 25, Paige and his gunners heard low voices from just below the ridge. Then it became dead quiet but for the sound of bodies brushing bushes below the knob. The night was suddenly rent by the bursts of hand grenades among the gun-pits. Japanese infantry screamed obscenely and hurled more hand grenades. The gunners responded to the shower of grenades with grenades of their own.

Then, as the pressure mounted, Paige ordered his guns into action. The entire nose came alive as the pivoting machine guns roared fury at the charging files of Japanese. The H Company machine guns were able to put out many more rounds than standard American .30-caliber mediums, for they had been modified months earlier at the insistence of a former company commander. That extra rate of fire no doubt saved Paige's section and, by extension, Hanneken's entire battalion from being sideswiped and overrun.

Mitchell Paige saw one of his ammunition carriers, a likable seventeen-year-old private, go to one knee. The section chief grabbed a rifle and scared off two of the young boy's assailants, but a third Japanese drove his bayonet into the young Marine's body, killing him. Paige shot that Japanese dead.

The Japanese swept in among the guns, forcing the Marines into a hand-to-hand free-for-all. A gunner whose leg was hacked by an officer's sword kicked out and connected his heavy boondocker under the officer's chin, breaking the man's neck.

The firing died down after some moments as the Japanese pulled back to regroup. When one of the guns was disabled by a jam, Paige crawled over to get it back in operation. Just as the section chief was feeding in a belt of bullets, he felt a hot chill run through his hand, and a sharp vibration. A Nambu light machine gun had put a full burst into the feeding mechanism.

Then the second wave hit, and hit hard. The Japanese carried the machine-gun section's left and seemed to have penetrated to the rear. Three riflemen held them at bay. In the center, three gunners were injured and evacuated. Then, within moments, every one of Paige's gunners was disabled, and he lost track of one of the guns. Fortunately, the Japanese pulled back again, giving the section chief time to find some help.

PlSgt Mitch Paige moved to the right, toward G Company, and found two gunners willing to help him manhandle a new gun into position. The three zig-zagged across the exposed ground under heavy fire, followed by several riflemen Paige had begged from the nearest rifle platoon. The new gun was hurriedly set up and Paige opened fire, sweeping the opposition.

It was light by then, barely, and Paige could see the gun he had lost several hours earlier. He crawled to the abandoned weapon, which was nearer the center of the nose, and used it to disperse a small enemy group that seemed about to rush him.

Three riflemen volunteered to hump in ammunition for the machine guns. The first Marine made it with several belts, but took a round in the stomach. The second was hit in the groin just as he reached Paige. A shoulder wound disabled the third Marine.

A Japanese machine gun tried to get Paige, but fired too far to the left. When Paige realized that he was too exposed, he fired a suppressive burst, grabbed the 100-pound gun, and moved. He followed this routine every few minutes, each time drawing a shower of grenades just as he got clear.

At one point, a Japanese platoon popped up without warning in clear view. The Japanese officer raised his field glasses to peer at Paige, who cut loose with a long burst, bowling the Japanese over where they stood.

Paige was by then thoroughly wound up. He organized several riflemen for support, and cradled his gun in his arms. Then he charged straight off the ridge nose. Including two belts of ammunition he had hastily thrown across one shoulder, Paige was humping nearly 150 pounds of palm-searing metal down the slope. He dropped a Japanese major in his tracks and led the riflemen into the trees. But there was nothing left to shoot at.

Dawn found the Japanese in possession of most of the F Company line, and repeated efforts to clear it came to nothing. An hour before, Maj Tex Conoley, Hanneken's exec, had scoured the battalion CP for cooks, communicators, and clerks. He managed to corral only seventeen Marines before he had to move out. The tiny band started up the slope.

The sun was just peeking over the hills to the east when Conoley spotted condensation rising off the barrels of two Japanese machine guns. He urged his small force forward, leading it up the slope, dropping two hand grenades into a gun pit. Then the major stepped aside as his troopers spread out to pry the Japanese from their holes.

As Conoley's Marines were mopping up, a group of Japanese formed up at the foot of the ridge. Mortars *thungged*, and the Japanese disappeared amidst bursting shells.

Second Lieutenant Bill Wright, whose twenty-man platoon of I Company, 1st, was in reserve just to the east of the sandspit at the mouth of the Matanikau, was ordered to report to Hanneken's CP. It took Wright some time to find Hanneken in the dark, but he eventually deployed his riflemen at the rear of the CP and patiently waited while the calm, thoroughly collected battalion commander followed the action on his command phone. Wright was directed to move to the sound of the gunfire at first light.

The fresh platoon passed seven or eight wounded Marines on the trail. All of them were still clutching personal weapons, and none seemed to be panicked. One of the first commented that a twenty-man platoon would be of little use in the fight, which seemed to upset the fresh riflemen. Lieutenant Wright merely asked directions of the other men he passed, cutting them off before they could express any negative feelings to his men.

The sound of gunfire was most intense on the left, so Wright moved that way, and topped the ridge in broad daylight. He and his Marines could see ample targets, and all immediately opened fire or lobbed hand grenades at the Japanese below the bare knob. The fight just sort of petered out. Second Battalion, 7th, had held. The October land offensive had ended.

Absolutely nothing had gone right for the Japanese. The Americans had fought well, perhaps superbly, against heavy odds. But the Japanese had in large part defeated themselves.

MGen Yumio Nasu was dead. Col Yoshio Hiroyasu, 16th Infantry's commander, was dead. Over 1,050 officers and soldiers of 29th Infantry were dead, missing, or wounded. Col Masajiro Furumiya, of 29th Infantry, was missing with the regimental colors. (The men of Furumiya's color guard all wandered off or died of exposure and starvation, and the colonel burned the 29th's colors and killed himself.) In all, both west and south, Sendai Division and *Shoji Butai* had lost 3,500 dead, wounded, and missing in a week of combat. Indeed, Sendai Division, the toast of the Imperial Army, had ceased to be an effective fighting organization.

Japanese soldiers were found wandering about the Perimeter for days, confused and docile because they could not find their units. Three were found sitting at the end of the bomber strip, precisely on the spot at which they had been told to rejoin their battalion to witness the meticulously planned surrender ceremony.

Short, bitter skirmishes continued for several days. As had Kawaguchi's before it, Maruyama's retreat left a wake of dead and pathetically dying men on the trail to Kokumbona. The Imperial Army's assault had accomplished nothing. In all, ninety Americans died in the action, and another 200 were injured, mainly among Puller's and Hanneken's battalions.

The Imperial Navy was having mixed results in the seas to the north of Guadalcanal, near the Santa Cruz Islands. A minutely detailed Combined Fleet plan for the support of 17th Army's land offensive and Adm Isoroku Yamamoto's thrice-attempted defeat of the American main battle fleet was intercepted by the Pacific Fleet intelligence section nearly two weeks before the offensive was to take place.

At that time, only *Hornet* was guarding the approaches to Guadalcanal. *Saratoga* had barely reached the West Coast after suffering torpedo damage on August 31, and *Enterprise* was still in drydock following her encounter with Japanese bombs on August 24. Though repair work had not been completed, *Enterprise* and her fresh, new air group were precipitously ordered south from Pearl Harbor on October 16 by a worried Adm Chester Nimitz.

The first brush came on October 25, when Cactus aircraft caught *Yura* and other bombardment vessels in the Slot in broad daylight. When *Yura* was lost, the bombardment force turned back for Rabaul.

Also on October 25, South Pacific patrol bombers found elements of the several surface and carrier forces the Japanese had deployed in the vicinity of the Santa Cruz Islands. A late-afternoon strike by *Enterprise's* new Air Group 10 failed to locate any targets, and six new American TBFs and one fighter were lost during night landings.

The four Japanese carriers and two American carriers traded punches throughout October 26, when two Japanese carriers were damaged. Dozens of Japanese aircrews—the last of the best the Imperial Navy had—were downed over the American task force, many by American pilots, but mainly by American antiaircraft gunners fighting for their lives. *Enterprise* received several serious bomb hits, several American surface vessels were damaged, and, finally, *Hornet* was sunk.

By the end of October 26, 1942, America had not one fleet carrier that was fully operational. Japan failed, however, to achieve any of her strategic aims on land or at sea; her tactical victory at Santa Cruz was, in the long run, her last serious effort and her last best chance to win the Pacific War. Never again did Japan risk her fleet carriers in any meaningful confrontation with the U.S. Pacific Fleet.

PART IX

Resurgence

33

The greatest threat facing the Lunga garrison and Cactus Air following the defeat of 17th Army on the southern and western flanks remained the proximity and near invulnerability of Japanese 15cm howitzers.

The defeat of Sendai Division had left 17th Army at a tactical as well as numerical disadvantage. For the first time following a defensive victory, the Americans had an opportunity to strike before the Japanese could reconsolidate. If they could push 17th Army beyond the Poha River, Henderson Field, Fighter-1 and Fighter-2, a new coral-topped all-weather strip near Kukum, would be well beyond the range of the Japanese artillery.

A considerable force was earmarked for the new offensive: the depleted 5th Marines, the untested 3rd Battalion, 7th, and the fresh 1st and 2nd Battalions, 2nd. A battalion of 164th Infantry would be in reserve, and support would be provided by units of 10th and 11th Marines and Cactus Air. If available, naval gunfire would be employed near the coast.

The new offensive was to be Archer Vandegrift's first opportunity to oversee maneuvers by a force approaching a division in strength and power, and the first time he planned to seize *and* hold Kokumbona.

On October 31, 5th Marines replaced LtCol Herman Hanneken's 2nd Battalion, 7th, on Hill 67, and the newly arrived battalions of 2nd Marines were brought forward. Engineer stores and reserve equipment were moved to dumps on the east bank of the Matanikau, and patrols brought in increasing volumes of vital, current data. South of the main troop concentrations, Col Bill Whaling prepared to lead 3rd Battalion, 7th, across the river in secret to screen the inland flank of the main force.

Hours before the scheduled 0630 advance, three engineer companies prefabricated three footbridges and set them beside the river preparatory to crossing. The bridges were meant to free the assault forces from having to cross by way of well-known fords, at which previous efforts had invariably been slowed or stymied.

Shortly before H-Hour, one E Company, 5th, rifle platoon boarded rubber boats, quickly paddled to the unsecured east bank, and deployed in a defensive cordon. The moment the head of the first engineer bridge was in place, Maj Lew Walt ordered 2nd Battalion, 5th, which he had been commanding for several weeks, to the west bank. Next, Maj Bill Enright's 1st Battalion, 5th, moved onto the west bank by 0700 and attacked eastward up the beach while Walt drove toward the high ground inland. Maj Bob Bowen's 3rd Battalion, 5th, the regimental reserve, followed in Enright's traces and, farther behind, 1st and 2nd Battalions, 2nd, crossed and deployed to act as a force reserve. Colonel Whaling's force crossed on schedule and without incident and began a cautious advance through the forested ridges south of Walt.

For a change, artillery and air support was ample, and functioned smoothly. Cruisers *San Francisco* and *Helena*, and a destroyer, struck the Point Cruz area while SBDs, P-39s, and B-17s bombed and strafed Japanese positions near Kokumbona.

Walt's battalion jumped off in the face of meager opposition and achieved rapid gains along the inland ridges. It reached its second phase line and dug in at 1440. Nearer the coast, Enright's Marines contacted strong emplacements centered on a deep ravine near Point Cruz, a natural defensive area made stronger by the cunning use of camouflage and superb deployment.

Progress dropped to a virtual crawl as Enright's vanguard probed the Japanese positions. In a short time, the left elements of 1st Battalion, 5th, had lost contact with the unimpeded, faster-moving 2nd Battalion. Farther south, Whaling was meeting no opposition of consequence, leading 5th Regiment and higher headquarters to conclude that the Japanese were concentrated around Point Cruz.

Enright's battalion drew the hard chore, and it was paying the price. The last remnant of the shattered 4th Infantry was making what amounted to a last stand in the natural defensive terrain just south of Point Cruz. There were less than 300 defenders concentrated in a small area honeycombed with natural and man-made defensive emplacements. Unable to maneuver, these Japanese were determined to die where they stood.

A Company, 5th, advanced down the beach against moderate opposition, but to its left Japanese machine guns and mortars had been preregistered within the first strip of coconut palms and the first steep rise. Second Lieutenant David Crosby led C Company's vanguard into the beaten zone.

Crosby's platoon maintained a steady, aggressive advance for some time. When the platoon was finally stalled, the young lieutenant personally led the point into the bush to probe the defenses. He was shot dead and the point was sent tumbling back on the main body of the platoon.

Japanese surged from the trees and made directly for two machine guns that had been deployed to anchor C Company's front. Crosby's leaderless platoon back-pedaled through the gun emplacements, temporarily routed. The Japanese recoiled under heavy fire, reformed, hurled hand grenades at the guns, and set up their own machine guns. In minutes, only three Marines were left to man their machine guns; the rest were dead or in retreat.

377

Almost as soon as Cpl Louis Casamento settled down behind the one machine gun that could still be fired, one of his two companions was injured and lapsed into unconsciousness. Then the second was injured. Despite his protests, he was ordered to the rear by Casamento, who furiously swiveled the single gun, loading it himself despite severe grenade wounds in his right hand. His right ankle was shattered, he had a hole through his right leg, and his right hip, torso, and shoulder had all been hit. He stripped off his shirt during a brief lull to staunch the blood that ran from a hole in his throat. Blood from a wound in his temple ran into his eyes as he aimed. In all, Louis Casamento had suffered fourteen separate wounds. But he held until elements of C Company drove back up the ridge and eventually forced the Japanese back.

B Company was committed to plug a widening rift between its sister units and, while A and C companies applied pressure on the flanks, struck at the main Japanese strongpoint.

Capt Jake Holland, B Company's new commander, led ten Marines forward in an attempt to skirt the main defenses and go for what he hoped was the softer flank. But the small force was spotted and driven back.

While Captain Holland was trying to work around the flank, Capt Walter McIlhenny, his executive officer, waved his riot gun at the men near him and mounted the ridge upon which the Japanese base of fire was deployed. A thin B Company squad broke from cover and followed McIlhenny up the slope. The Japanese on the ridge immediately rolled hand grenades down the slope, and there was heavy mortar and small-arms fire. But the defenders facing grimly determined Walter McIlhenny and less than a dozen Marine riflemen spilled down the forested reverse slope and took refuge in the dense undergrowth there. The Marines humped forward and reached the top of the steep slope, where they went to work clearing Japanese fighting holes of the men who held them. Before long, however, many of the Japanese who had been thrown from the ridge reformed and counterattacked. The Marines expended all the hand grenades they had carried up the hill and sent for more. The squad BAR-man was firing full tilt when a huge explosion engulfed him and the squad leader. A corpsman who had just clambered up the slope helped the remaining riflemen hurl a fresh supply of hand grenades at the climbing Japanese until the immediate danger passed. But the Japanese eventually prevailed, sending the B Company riflemen to cover in the jungle flat facing the hotly contested ridge.

After continued unsuccessful efforts by his 1st Battalion to breach the main Japanese defenses, Col Red Mike Edson called up Maj Bob Bowen's 3rd Battalion, 5th, and placed I and K companies in line nearest the beach, which allowed 1st Battalion, 5th, to concentrate leftward.

The commitment of most of Bowen's battalion, along with the development of more advantageous positions by Maj Bill Enright's 1st Battalion, nearly pocketed the Japanese along their eastern and southern flanks; their backs were pinned against the west side of Point Cruz and the beach. But the envelopment also obliged the defenders to hold their ground with yet more spirit.

The assault battalions could not advance far in the few remaining hours of daylight, so Colonel Edson ordered all of his troops to dig in for the night.

As the only Japanese encountered thus far were on the coast, Red Mike decided on the morning of November 2 that he could risk moving Maj Lew Walt's 2nd Battalion, 5th, to cover the rear of the Point Cruz pocket. Walt detached two companies under Capt Harry Connor, who had been elevated from command of E Company to battalion operations officer, and these wheeled to the right, in line abreast. They cautiously advanced without opposition or difficulty upon the coast along the yet-to-be-found periphery of the most-heavily defended ground.

G Company stopped when it closed on the Japanese pocket, but F Company, on the far left, missed the extremities of the Japanese defenses, and drove to the beach. Japanese phone wires linking the pocket with Kokumbona were cut. Just as F Company was settling in, and before the remainder of the battalion could join, many Japanese soldiers arrived from the direction of Kokumbona to trace the break in the communications wires.

Heavy firing suddenly engulfed F Company's front and rear, forcing the thin platoons to deploy back-to-back to save themselves from being overwhelmed. No assistance was immediately available as the remainder of Walt's battalion was fully engaged in the effort to spring Enright's embattled 1st Battalion loose for a frontal assault on the Japanese pocket.

Of particular danger was a hidden 37mm gun that fired into F Company from point-blank range. Lew Walt arranged to get Capt Harry Connor directly in touch with the fire-direction center of E Battery, 11th. Connor, who had never before directed live fire, had to cut it really fine because of the proximity of the Japanese 37mm gun to his positions and the sketchiness of the Marine maps. Fortunately, the first registration round impacted just off the beach, in plain view. Connor ordered, "Up 100 yards and left fifty yards." The next round landed right on the beach road and quite close to F Company. "Up fifty," Connor ordered. Then, "Battery, three rounds for effect." Twelve 75mm howitzer rounds blanketed the area around the 37mm gun, and destroyed it. The Japanese from Kokumbona pulled back.

L Company, the only 5th Marines unit not committed to the fight, was moved to the line to link C Company with Walt's battalion. The encirclement was thus complete, and the Japanese were trapped between heavily manned Marine battle lines and the channel. When the exact outline of the pocket had been determined, Colonel Edson felt it was reasonable to call his riflemen off while mortars and artillery pounded the area.

Before the fire mission could commence, however, the forwardmost Marines had to pull back to avoid shorts and overs. The withdrawal was immediately sensed by the closely engaged Japanese, who violently harassed the back-pedaling Marines. The infantry fighting stopped while 60mm and 81mm mortars and supporting 75mm and 105mm howitzers pummeled the Japanese.

Late in the afternoon, after the entire area had been heavily pounded, Red Mike ordered a frontal assault. I and K companies, nearest the beach on the right, were stopped cold by outlying emplacements not directly in touch with the main Japanese force. To break the stalemate, Capt Erskine Wells, a hard-driving, twenty-four-year-old Mississippian who had recently assumed command of I Company, ordered a bayonet assault. The spirited attack through fitful resistance carried Wells's company down the narrow beach all the way to F Company's position on the regimental left. The last remnant of 4th Infantry was totally surrounded.

The remainder of 5th Marines had considerably more difficulty. To bolster the riflemen in the dense growth, Edson called up halftracks mounting 75mm guns, but they encountered impenetrable terrain well short of the objective.

Maj Bob Bowen's 3rd Battalion, 5th, bulled its way forward and took several successive lines of coral-and-log pillboxes and rifle pits, but at considerable cost.

The second day of battle near Point Cruz saw substantial gains against fewer but more-determined Japanese. Fourth Infantry was clearly doomed, but its officers and men were prepared to acquit themselves with honor to the last.

The November 3 fight began at 0630 with a Japanese bayonet attack aimed at breaking through in the sectors of I and K companies, but the effort was beaten to a standstill.

E and G companies opened the American drive at 0800 by attempting to roll back the defenses near the southwest corner of the pocket. F Company followed shortly thereafter from the extreme left, and I and K companies moved off in column on a narrow front. Behind the two 3rd Battalion companies, elements of D Company, 164th, a weapons unit, were committed along the Government Track to mop up outlying and bypassed pockets.

The underbrush was extremely dense, forcing individual and small groups of Marines into isolated hand-to-hand fighting. Too close to fire effectively, many Marines had to pry the Japanese from their holes with bayonets. It was a costly, bloody way to fight. H Company machine gunners had to be sent forward to fight as riflemen; there was no way to fire machine guns in such close undergrowth and every man who could hold a rifle was needed on the line. When the 2nd Battalion advance faltered, 37mm antitank guns were manhandled forward and canister was fired, more to tear away concealing undergrowth than to kill defenders.

The Japanese were slowly forced back by Maj Lew Walt's 2nd Battalion under intense pressure from direct weapons support and the determined efforts of the fragmented Marine formations. So intense and determined was the American effort that the last of the Japanese defenses collapsed by midafternoon. One minute, the battle was being pressed to the limit, but it was over the next, surprising everyone. A number of Japanese filtered through the Marine ranks, but at least 239 Japanese—among them the 4th Infantry's colonel and twenty-seven other officers—were buried on the killing ground; no one knows how many other bodies might have been overlooked in the broken, densely overgrown terrain. Considerable stores were taken, and a dozen 37mm guns and one 75mm howitzer were captured, as were thirty-four machine guns. Most important, 4th Infantry Regiment had been destroyed. Beginning with the massacre of its 3rd Battalion by Puller's 1st Battalion, 7th, on October 9, the regiment had been relentlesly pared down and, finally, annihilated.

The way to Kokumbona lay open. Fifth Marines should have had no major difficulty taking the village and all the ground as far as the Poha River. The long-sought goal was momentarily within reach.

Then an urgent warning arrived from out of the blue. It seemed that a substantial force of Japanese had landed east of the Perimeter, near Koli Point. It looked as though General Hyakutake was preparing to mount another major assault on Lunga.

Though substantial American ground reinforcements were then en route to Guadalcanal, General Vandegrift did not feel that he could risk all in the face of the renewed threat. The battle-weary 5th Marines was ordered back to the Perimeter, as was Col Bill

Whaling's force. But in a radical and significant departure from the pattern of past withdrawals from the Point Cruz area, 1st and 2nd Battalions, 2nd, were left on the conquered ground, and 1st Battalion, 164th, was deployed on Hill 87. The Japanese harassed the holding forces as soon as 5th Marines withdrew, but the ground was easily held.

34

Only after the defeat of Sendai Division in late October did the Japanese military lords even begin facing up to some important realities. While Adm Isoroku Yamamoto and members of his senior staff felt that the campaign to win back Guadalcanal was a lost cause, it was decided to assemble all the facts before embarking upon a possibly rash course of action. To that end, one of Combined Fleet's top staff officers, Capt Toshikazu Ohmae, who was already on his way to Guadalcanal to look into the many delays encountered by 17th Army in launching the land offensive, was asked to look into the defeat. Ohmae arrived at Cape Esperance from Rabaul on October 26 and went immediately to General Hyakutake's headquarters in Kokumbona to confer with the army commander and his senior staff officers.

Captain Ohmae's first impression was negative; the resolve that had filled these men in early October had withered away. Still, the beleaguered Imperial Army officers seemed to desire a positive outcome to the campaign. Ohmae immediately saw that the defeat had come as a result of the inability of the Japanese field commanders to coordinate their efforts, a circumstance which left their field forces vulnerable to defeat in detail by a mobile force of Americans exploiting internal lines of communication. Captain Ohmae further noted that the Army officers had no insight into the vast problems encountered by naval forces in coordinating their own movements with those of the land forces, or that many fleet surface and air units had suffered losses because of the delays on land.

A naval career professional, Ohmae had no inkling as to the brutal truths involved in moving several regiments unobserved through a dense rain forest. The 17th Army staff had set the timetable, and Combined Fleet had complied. What Ohmae and most of his peers entirely missed was General Hyakutake's desire not so much to reconquer Guadalcanal as his need to *secure* Guadalcanal for the sake of covering his northern flank and remounting his stalled New Guinea offensive. Port Moresby was Hyakutake's strategic goal, and, in this, the 17th Army commander had the complete support of Imperial General Headquarters, which had not forgotten that 17th Army had been drawn into the Solomons fracas as a means of pulling the Imperial Navy's chestnuts from the fire. Hyakutake remained loath to commit the main strength of Nagoya Division to the Solomons so long as there remained a glimmer of a chance to shunt it to New Guinea. In the end, the destruction of Sendai Division forced the 17th Army commander's hand; if he needed a secure Guadalcanal to screen the flank of the New Guinea advance, he would need the whole of Nagoya Division to do the job.

Given the Imperial Navy's line of approach, and 17th Army's need for naval supports, it is not surprising that Captain Ohmae prevailed upon Hyakutake to drop his plan for renewing the New Guinea offensive in favor of putting all his eggs in the Solomons basket; in any event, the conclusion was inevitable. Without further ado, General Hyakutake ordered LtGen Tadiyoshi Sano to mount out with all that remained of Nagoya Division from bases in the Northern Solomons.

In taking advantage of 17th Army's critical need for his support, Admiral Yamamoto overstepped his command prerogatives somewhat by prevailing upon Hyakutake to build up a significant infantry force near Koli Point, well east of Lunga. In fact, Yamamoto demanded that the strong tail of Nagoya Division be landed there, a demand to which Hyakutake reluctantly acceded. As his own contribution to the operation, the 17th Army commander ordered *Shoji Butai* to march overland to Koli Point to secure the beaches and inland areas. (Thus, Hyakutake allowed precisely the sort of meddling against which Archer Vandegrift had barely prevailed in September: succumbing to a seemingly universal penchant on the part of admirals to impose poor land-fighting policies upon trained but disadvantaged and troop-starved ground commanders. In this case, Admiral Yamamoto succeeded in forcing General Hyakutake to split his land force when every rule demanded a concentration of that force.)

Southeastern Fleet, of which Captain Ohmae was senior staff officer, got to work creating a detailed, ambitious plan. The movement of troops would be undertaken by high-speed Imperial Army transports under the protection of 8th Fleet. As soon as the fresh units had been landed and deployed, strong naval bombardment units would begin yet another protracted and systematic pounding of the Lunga Perimeter and Cactus Air. As in all previous plans, a heavy commitment was to be made by naval air units, though 11th Air Fleet had been defeated in October and was nowhere near full—or even fighting—strength.

As soon as the prolonged bombardment had done sufficient damage, the reorganized Sendai Division would strike from the west while Nagoya Division attacked the eastern defenses.

It was a bold, intricate, and ultimately unrealistic plan, mixing past approaches with some fresh ideas. And it came under the immediate attack of RAdm Raizo Tanaka, who favored dropping Guadalcanal altogether. He hoped that in so doing Japan might save the remaining ground forces, which could be used to better advantage in defending as-yet-uncontested ground to the north and west. Tanaka's opinion was shared by many—but by no means all—high-level Navy staffers. In any case, the die had been cast and the dissenting voices went unheeded.

In a rather grandiose effort to bolster the morale of *Shoji Butai*, General Hyakutake announced plans for the construction of a new airstrip at Koli Point once the area had been secured and engineering troops and materials could be landed. It is likely, however, that the 17th Army commander recognized the futility of such an effort, for he undertook no real steps toward the avowed end.

35

Dawn, November 1, 1942.

In a hobo camp on the Lunga Plain, beside Henderson Field, 350 skinny, begrimed men, all dressed in the ripped and filthy remnants of green utility clothing, bestirred themselves and boarded trucks for a ride to the Tenaru River. Once there, the men were evicted from the wheeled transport and formed into a column to begin a deliberate hike down the Government Track east of the Lunga Perimeter. The leader of this hobo column was LtCol Herman Hanneken, and he had, the day before, volunteered the remnant of his 2nd Battalion, 7th, to investigate intelligence reports about increased Japanese activity on the long-dormant eastern flank. It was a painful march, for the men had no socks, and their boondockers were in execrable condition.

During a midday break, as the weak and tired Marines picked through cold and unpalatable lumps of greasy food, a great rumbling and tearing noise erupted in their midst. A great old banyan tree, its enormous roots undermined by incessant rains, crashed into the midst of the eating men. An officer and four enlisted Marines were crushed to death in an instant.

The battalion continued to trudge eastward toward Tetere, where it was to intercept and ambush an advance party of the regiments 17th Army wished to employ in its next great assault upon the Lunga Perimeter. Intelligence reported that the Japanese would be landed before midnight, November 2.

No hostile contacts were made during November 1, or on the final leg to Tetere on November 2, though it was correctly assumed that a Japanese infantry force *(Shoji Butai)* was operating in the area. The battalion passed Koli Point, crossed the Metapona River, and went into defensive positions just inside the trees near the beach that regional intelligence organizations had designated as the objective of the Japanese troops landing at 2330.

A light rain was falling on Koli Point at 2325, November 2, when observers on the beach saw what they took to be a transport, a cruiser, and three destroyers dropping anchor off the point.

Whoop! Whoop! Whoop! Ships' sirens cut through the still night air. Capt Reed Taylor, the battalion intelligence officer, heard Japanese NCOs and officers barking orders at their troops, followed by the *put-put* of small motors. Marines in the treeline could see the slitted running lights of small, troop-carrying landing barges.

The *only* thing high intelligence had gotten wrong was the precise spot at which the Japanese would come ashore. Hanneken's companies were strung out along the western curve of a small inlet, and the Japanese landed on the eastern arm, beyond reach. Hanneken passed the word: No one was to open fire.

Just before dawn, November 3, eight Japanese soldiers blundered into Hanneken's outpost line. Four were cut down, the others escaped. Hanneken ordered his battalion's four 81mm mortars to fire on the Japanese units camped on the far side of the cove.

As mortars and machine guns fired at the Japanese, the three small rifle companies moved forward along the beach under the command of the battalion exec, Maj Tex Conoley. The initial move brought no immediate response from the Japanese so, after a prudent wait, Hanneken ordered his vanguard to press on.

As soon as the van stepped out, a large Japanese force moved against the battalion's open right flank. Before the Marines could react, Japanese mortars and 37mm guns placed rounds in treetops over the heads of the advancing Marine platoons. F Company, the most exposed of the Marine units, took heavy casualties and quickly sought cover.

Hanneken turned to Capt Reed Taylor, his intelligence officer, and confided, "I don't know whether to retreat or attack. If we attack, we might get annihilated." The battalion commander pondered his words and the scene before him for a moment longer, then said, "I don't see any reason to get annihilated, do you?" Taylor expressed his total agreement with the battalion commander's view. "Well, then, tell Conoley to bring them back, company by company."

Hanneken was immediately faced with the problem of recrossing the Metapona River, which had been forded the previous afternoon. The wide sandbar at the river's mouth was under direct Japanese observation, so Hanneken decided that he would have to use a less-exposed spot. Patrols found a ford some distance inland and F Company, which had sustained twenty-four casualties, crossed first and established a defensive screen through which the remainder of the battalion could safely pass. Next, G Company recrossed the river and set up on the far side of a tidal lagoon while E and F companies held the Japanese off. Then E Company pulled back and set up. F Company passed through E Company and joined G Company at the lagoon, following which E Company passed through the rest of the battalion to yet another stream. The rest of the battalion then passed through E Company again.

While both sides settled down to plugging away at one another, Herman Hanneken vainly sought to gain radio contact with the division CP, with which he had been out of contact for over twenty-four hours and from which he hoped to procure some air support. Contact with the division CP was finally resumed and, after requesting immediate air support, the battalion commander asked General Vandegrift to send landing craft to pick up the injured.

The first SBD arrived overhead at about 1445 and dropped its bomb—on Marines. One Marine ran out onto the beach and waved an American flag in the hope of getting the dive-bomber pilot's attention. He did, for the pilot returned and strafed the beach with his plane's two fixed .50-caliber nose guns. The Marine with the flag ran into the trees, just in time.

A little while later, cruisers *San Francisco* and *Helena* and a pair of destroyers moved in to shell the Japanese.

Though Archer Vandegrift did not know quite what Hanneken had stirred up, but largely in view of the Point Cruz victory and the seeming ability of Hanneken's battalion to hold its ground, he made a snap decision to strike the Japanese near Koli Point.

BGen Bill Rupertus, 1st Marine Division's assistant commander, had relinquished command of the Tulagi base that morning and happened to be on his way to Kukum by small boat when Vandegrift made his decision. As soon as Rupertus landed, he was whisked to the division CP and briefed to move to Koli Point with LtCol Lewie Puller's 1st Battalion, 7th. Sometime later, 2nd and 3rd Battalions, 164th, and their supports were added to Rupertus's force. Col Amor Sims and Col Bryant Moore, commanding 7th Marines and 164th Infantry respectively, assembled with the battalion commanders at the division CP to help draw up a plan.

Meantime, Hanneken was having as much trouble with friendly aircraft as he was with the Japanese. His position west of the Metapona was heavily bombed and strafed twice despite his profane protests, which were relayed directly to the pilots themselves.

When Hanneken was told of the plan to mount a three-battalion reinforcement and sweep, he finally decided that it would be best if he pulled back to better ground nearer Koli Point. He began doing so late in the afternoon. The battalion carried its by-then-sizeable burden of wounded and fought through the small force in its rear to arrive on the ground within the fan of the Nalimbiu River in time to establish a strong night defensive position.

The two battalions of 164th Infantry were alerted for an overland march to Koli Point; they would be supported by a Marine 75mm pack howitzer battalion. Puller's battalion was to embark in landing craft along with regimental supports to land within Hanneken's lines at Koli Point; the boats would carry out Hanneken's casualties on the return trip.

Very late in the afternoon, LtCol Lewie Puller marched his veterans to the beach and loaded them aboard sixteen boats. The boats set out in two groups after dark, Puller in charge of the first group and Capt Charlie Kelly in charge of the second.

By the time Kelly's boats rounded Koli Point, they had lost contact with Puller's group. Two white lights, widely separated, could be seen on the beach, but no one had any idea whose lights they were. Kelly decided against landing blind and gathered his boats into a tight knot. His first impulse was to hover offshore until sunrise, but he soon decided that was too risky. Puller had made an identical decision.

No so Capt Ralph Wismer, the 7th Marines communications officer and nominal commander of the regiment's advance headquarters detachment. After becoming separated from Puller's boats, Wismer found the same lights on the beach as had Charlie Kelly. He tried to query by signal light, a method he had long since found deficient in the extreme, and received no answer. Finally, Wismer ordered his coxswain to close on the nearest light. The coxswain agreed, but added, "If anybody starts to fire, why, I'll back out." He brought the boat right into the middle of Hanneken's beach defense line. In asking his way to the battalion CP, Wismer was most struck by how very tired the young Marines seemed; most of them just stared vacantly wide-eyed at him when he asked directions to Hanneken's or Maj Tex Conoley's tents.

Puller's Marines, with General Rupertus and Colonel Sims, were dumped on the beach at first light. The three senior officers made immediately for LtCol Herman Hanneken's CP.

It was to be another play-it-by-ear action. Hanneken's little companies held the beach and a short line inland; Puller's Marines were fed in on the right. C Company penetrated the farthest inland and swung around along the west bank of the Nalimbiu. While his company was digging in, Capt Marsh Moore, the C Company commander, could see that the Japanese were doing the same. He was startled to note that a Japanese major and a handful of soldiers were intently staring at his preparations. Neither side fired on the other. Then several Japanese tried to fill their canteens in plain sight of the Marines, and the Americans opened fire. The Japanese were driven off, but others returned the fire. They injured several Marines and sustained casualties of their own. Later in the morning, A Company was ordered across the river to probe the Japanese line. The defenders immediately drove the Marines to ground with substantial casualties.

Very early on November 4, just as Puller's battalion was landing at Koli Point, BGen Edmund Seebree, assistant commander of Americal Division, landed at Kukum to prepare the way for the arrival of the main body of his division. As soon as Sebree reported to the 1st Marine Division CP and had been briefed on the doings at Koli Point, he left to catch up with the two National Guard battalions rushing to join the Marines.

Meanwhile, following the rebuff of A Company, 7th, BGen Bill Rupertus decided to hold in place pending the arrival of the two Army battalions. The force across the river did not seem particularly strong or threatening, but it was manifestly capable of putting up some pretty heavy resistance. The Guardsmen were coming, but slowly because the inexperienced soldiers were badly weighted down with heavy packs and a profusion of equipment too heavy to be efficiently dragged through the rain forest.

The bulk of the Guard regiment reached assembly areas east of the Nalimbiu and some miles south of Koli Point at about noon, November 4. The regimental headquarters stopped on the west bank for the night, as did LtCol Bob Hall's 3rd Battalion. LtCol Art Timboe's 2nd Battalion, 164th, pushed toward the river, swung southward in a long arc, and headed northward again; it finally came to rest in the bush in the late afternoon. The Guardsmen made no contacts through the day.

On the morning of November 5, Hall's battalion crossed the

Nalimbiu about 3,500 yards south of Koli Point and advanced near the east bank in the hope of driving into the flank of the Japanese near the coast. Timboe's battalion crossed well north of Hall's, but pushed southward across Hall's line of march before looping back northward to the east of and parallel to the 3rd Battalion; a lot of walking for no gain. The Army battalions drew some fire as they neared the coast and, in time, two 2nd Battalion platoons were stopped cold by intense automatic-weapons fire. American mortar and artillery fire probed the Japanese position and soon scattered the opposition. The 164th Infantry had yet to make more than tenuous contact with the Japanese. Both battalions and the regimental headquarters company settled into jungle bivouacs for the night.

On November 6, 1st Battalion, 11th, moved its twelve 75mm pack howitzers into position about two miles west of Koli Point to support the sweep division headquarters planned to mount as soon as the area west of the Nalimbiu had been scoured and secured.

Action through the day was inconclusive. When it appeared that the Japanese had withdrawn in the face of the Army battalions' flanking movement, General Rupertus ordered his Marine battalions across the Nalimbiu, where they were joined rather late in the day by the Guardsmen.

The heavily augmented American force moved out on the morning of November 7. The Marine battalions proceeded eastward about 500 yards apart in a column of companies. There was zero opposition. Contact between the battalions was impossible to maintain in the thick bush; only when elements of both units emerged into a common clearing could either determine the position and rate of the other. Late in the day, while the vanguard was still a mile from the Metapona, General Rupertus was notified that there might be a very large Japanese force landing somewhere east of Koli Point. He immediately deployed both Marine battalions on the beach near the river and cordoned off the interior with the two Army battalions.

While Allied intelligence sources had correctly determined the original intentions of the Japanese, who planned to land the bulk of

Nagoya Division between Koli Point and the Metapona, the initial contact between the advance party and Hanneken's battalion had dissuaded 17th Army from proceeding with the plan. On the night of November 5, the Japanese advance-detachment commander and Colonel Shoji, who had by then joined him, were ordered to disengage and march to Kokumbona.

Marine patrols were shaken out at dawn, November 8. Reversing the positions they had held the previous day, Hanneken's battalion moved off in a column of companies on the inland flank while Puller's moved out nearer the beach. Timboe's battalion was right behind Puller's as force reserve.

Capt Charlie Kelly had just crossed the sandbar at the mouth of the Metapona with the battalion vanguard when he met Hanneken's operations officer, who had news that Japanese artillery had been observed on the beach the evening before, swapping fire with American destroyers in the channel. He cautioned Kelly to keep his people off the beach. Kelly sent A and C companies on while he waited by the river for LtCol Lewie Puller to join up with the battalion rear guard. When Puller arrived, the exec pointed out the suspected gun position, then he ran ahead to catch up with the vanguard.

The American force advanced on Gavaga Creek, a stream 2,000 yards east of the Metapona. It made extremely good progress under the urging of the two Marine battalion commanders, the two regimental commanders, and the two assistant division commanders, who all hoped to surround the retreating Japanese.

General Rupertus was felled in the afternoon by the sudden onset of a bad case of dengue fever. He was evacuated at once and, under the long-range direction of General Vandegrift, BGen Ed Sebree, a chipper forty-four-year-old 1919 West Point graduate with no combat experience, became the first U.S. Army officer to command an offensive operation on the island.

As Capt Marsh Moore's C Company, 7th, neared Gavaga Creek, it became evident that the only crossing was by way of a sandspit at the mouth. Moore had not been made privy to the warning concerning Japanese artillery, but his practiced eye immediately discerned that the sandspit was ideal for an ambush. He called a halt to push several scouts across the creek.

It was by then late afternoon. LtCol Lewie Puller had been at the tail of the column through the long day, and he had frankly lost patience with the slow going. He shook out several of the intelligence scouts and communicators he favored and stepped out of the trees to the beach, the better to catch up with the point. Pfc Dan Le Fevre, the pointman of Puller's group, was forty yards ahead of the battalion commander when he came abreast the C Company vanguard platoon.

For reasons Dan Le Fevre could not fathom, for he had no reason to do so, he focused his attention just inside the next point, a spot just across Gavaga Creek from where Capt Marsh Moore had halted C Company. He saw a tiny grey, donut-shaped puff emerge from the trees and expand and grow as it hurtled right at him. The scout instinctively threw himself face-first into the soft sand as a great blast engulfed the men right behind him. As Le Fevre rolled over to see what had happened, he heard Lewie Puller bellow an order to keep down.

Four C Company Marines had been instantly killed in the blast. No other rounds impacted, so Dan Le Fevre got up and looked to the battalion commander for instructions.

Puller was up and running through heavy gunfire, his short-stemmed pipe grasped firmly in his teeth, his jaw thrust forward. But he was limping; a steel splinter was in his leg. Puller ordered a communicator to call the regimental CP, but the man reported that the line was cut. The battalion commander painfully hobbled to the phone to help splice the break. He was shot through the arm twice by a sniper, and that finally subdued his ardor. (Puller claimed five wounds; in his mind, five holes was five holes, no matter how many bullets or shrapnel slivers it took to make them.)

Despite the four dead, two missing, and thirty injured it sustained in the fight, 1st Battalion, 7th, had lucked out. Capt Marsh Moore's momentary hesitation had caused the Japanese gunners to think that they had been spotted, and they had fired prematurely to avoid missing their best opportunity altogether.

Air support was ordered up within minutes, and many Japanese guns switched over to tracer to have a go at the aircraft. That was a blunder of the first magnitude, for the Marines fired into the bush wherever they saw the pink tracer rounds emerge; many of the machine guns were thus quieted.

Puller's 1st Battalion, 7th, held the Japanese in place while, by prior arrangement, Hanneken's 2nd Battalion, 7th, peeled off and headed northeast in the hope of coming up behind the Japanese. Hanneken's weary Marines met no opposition and crossed the main channel of Gavaga Creek about 1,000 yards from the mouth. They then trudged through another 700 yards of dense undergrowth and turned north along the east bank of a smaller stream, following it out to the beach. This placed Hanneken's battalion on a line nearly parallel to Puller's and about 700 yards away. Hanneken estimated that a Japanese force of battalion strength lay in the middle.

Dawn, November 9, found an injured, sleepless LtCol Lewie Puller in no condition to resume command of his battalion. LtCol Bull Frisbie, the 7th's exec, came up to have a talk with the combative battalion commander, who had spent the night in a foxhole. Though Puller vigorously protested, Frisbie ordered him to turn the battalion over to Maj Jack Weber, formerly commander of M Company, 7th. Defiant to the end, Puller attempted to walk back to Koli Point under his own power, but he got only a half-mile before sinking to his knees. He was furious because he had failed within sight of some of his own Marines, but he allowed himself to be carried the rest of the way.

While the 3rd Battalion, 164th, marched back to Lunga, BGen Ed Sebree ordered LtCol Art Timboe's 2nd Battalion, 164th, to close off the southern flank of the Gavaga Creek defenses. Timboe established his CP near Major Weber's and committed his two operating companies, with weapons platoons, to Weber's command. (E

Company, 164th, was guarding the regimental CP.) The two augmented companies were led by Marine guides to the right flank and started across the creek.

On the far side of the pocket, Hanneken's Marines came upon an abandoned bivouac; undoubtedly it had been occupied by the force Hanneken's battalion had been sent to ambush on the beach a week earlier. Large quantities of stores and ammunition were discovered and destroyed.

Hanneken next prepared to mount an assault in concert with a noon move by Weber. G Company was on the right, its flank on the beach; E Company was inland; F Company was wrapping around the Japanese southern flank; and patrols were out in anticipation of meeting up with elements of Timboe's battalion.

Hanneken moved out at 1151 and advanced without opposition until 1330, when a small Japanese force was sent running. The main Japanese force was found at 1448, dug in along the top of the high, steep far bank of the small creek.

It took a full hour for one platoon of G Company to bully its way far enough through the nearly impassable rain forest to contact the Japanese, and it was another twenty minutes before the platoon reached the west bank of the stream. The rest of G Company remained on the beach, unengaged.

Although G Company had penetrated the Japanese line at its extremity, E Company could not advance. The E Company commander, 2ndLt Peyton Harris, started into the woods with the rear elements of his unit, but soon motioned his runner to join him in an effort to get to the point to see what was holding up the advance. The two passed the engaged G Company platoon, which was in chest-deep water, using the high east bank for cover. They pushed forward to find the lead E Company platoon engaged in a newly erupted fire fight. Harris's runner was immediately shot in the buttocks, and the only officer Harris still had serving under him was shot in the chest; the company commander helped pull him up onto the west bank of the creek and had him carried to the beach for treatment. It was another full hour before Marines were able to wade the armpit-deep water to the Japanese side. The Japanese fire was too intense for E Company to deploy on the west bank, and the Marines were unable to scrabble up to relatively dry ground. The weary riflemen had to stand in the water and blindly fire through the dense undergrowth at the presumed positions of Japanese dug in right over their heads. All Lieutenant Harris could do to help his tiny company was pass hand grenades down from the bank to the men in the water. They, in turn, blindly lobbed them into the trees overhead, hoping the shrapnel bursts would shower the defenders.

Hanneken realized early on that his Marines could not spend the night armpit-deep in the creek, so he reluctantly ordered them to break contact and withdraw 200 yards to dominating ground. The battalion had suffered eighteen killed and thirty wounded, which was a very high proportion for so small a unit—now barely 300 effectives, if that.

Meantime, two companies of 2nd Battalion, 164th, had spent the afternoon trying to close the gap between Weber and Hanneken on the inland flank. By nightfall, these Guard companies still were not in physical contact with either Marine battalion.

Late in the day, E Company, 164th, was boated from Koli Point to a beach behind Hanneken's lines and given a place to the left of F Company, 7th, thereby extending Hanneken's line another 300 yards around the southern flank. Hanneken's 6omm mortars maintained harassing fires through the night.

On November 10, Maj Jack Weber's battalion was to hold in place while LtCol Art Timboe's parceled-out Guard companies on the southern flank sealed contact with Hanneken's battalion to the east. Unfortunately, neither Timboe nor any other senior officer knew where the two companies were nor how they had fared the day before. Weber sent a patrol to find them and was stunned to learn that they had both withdrawn to overnight bivouacs near the inland end of his own line; they were nowhere near their supposed positions.

While senior Army officers urged the derelict companies to stretch themselves over the gap and contact Hanneken's force, a planned 81mm mortar barrage by the Marine battalions went off at

1030 in the mistaken notion that the struggling Guard companies had had sufficient time to accomplish their mission.

About all the mortar concentrations accomplished was a series of near misses scored by each battalion on the CP of the other. Hanneken and Weber agreed to cease firing and to cancel a planned artillery barrage in view of everyone's obviously imperfect knowledge of the terrain.

The floundering Guard companies reported at 1105 that they had contacted small groups of Japanese and that both companies were moving *away* from the area under fire.

In the middle of the afternoon, Hanneken learned that E Company, 164th, had wandered away from its link with F Company, 7th. A radio check revealed that the lost company was not in touch with its sister companies, which were still bogged down. Unable to bear much more, Hanneken withdrew G Company, 7th, from positions near the beach and dispatched it to the left flank of F Company, 7th, to extend itself into the unknown until it contacted some friendly Guardsmen.

While G Company, 7th, probed westward in search of the lost Army battalion, Col Bryant Moore, the patrician 1917 West Point graduate in command of 164th Infantry, reached the end of his patience. He and BGen Ed Sebree arrived by boat late in the afternoon and informed LtCol Art Timboe that he was being posted to head the intelligence section of XIV Corps, the newly formed command that would, within weeks, assume operational control of the American effort on Guadalcanal. Sebree and Moore also sent all of Timboe's company commanders back to Kukum.

The day was too far gone for anything else of note to be accomplished, so all units dug in for the night, the front riddled by vast gaps.

The hitherto defiant Japanese, who had been less an object of attention than the pokey Guard battalion, could see that nothing could be gained at Gavaga Creek. Senior officers ordered the troops to leave the area. During the night, nearly 1,000 defenders made it to staging areas well to the south.

On the morning of November 11, 2nd Battalion, 164th, faced

northward and slowly advanced to the beach. Opposition was negligible, composed of the last gasps of soldiers too ill to have withdrawn during the night. The Guard companies stood on the beach by noon, and a thoroughly disgusted Ed Sebree ordered the entire force back to the Metapona River. The American force had lost approximately forty killed, two missing, and 120 wounded.

The ten-day operation claimed an estimated 350 Japanese lives. *Shoji Butai* and the Nagoya Division advance force began a forced march across the foothills of Mount Austen, bound for Kokumbona.

No further efforts were made by the Japanese to build a force east of Lunga. In time, an aerodrome rivaling Henderson Field and its satellites was built by Americans at Koli Point.

PART X

Decision

36

Things were looking up at Lunga. On October 26, the day after Dugout Sunday, BGen Roy Geiger had barely been able to muster a dozen Marine F4Fs, eleven Navy and Marine SBDs, three P-400s, three P-39s, and one F4F-7 photo-reconnaissance plane. Nothing else could be flown, and the airstrips were barely salvageable.

But Cactus Air was not molested for the next four days.

Suddenly, all four squadrons of fresh MAG-11 were made available to Geiger. VMSB-132 flew its first mission on November 1. On November 2, ten VMF-112 pilots arrived at Cactus to begin operations in borrowed Wildcats the next day. The remaining two squadrons, a dive-bomber squadron and the Marine Corps' first torpedo squadron, were expected by mid November.

As important as the arrival of fresh combat crews and aircraft was the beefing up of MAG-25's lone R4D squadron by another Marine air-transport squadron, and a similar Army Air Forces unit. These units, totalling thirty-six Skytrain transports, constituted the only reliable means for bringing supplies to the island from rear areas, though their carrying capacity was severely limited. Equally important was what amounted to the first organized air-evacuation flights of wounded from any combat zone in the world.

Also in early November, 11th Heavy Bombardment Group was beefed up to a strength of fifty brand-new B-17s, and another group of twenty-three B-17s was on the way from Hawaii. A squadron of Army Air Forces B-26 medium bombers had also been brought up to Espiritu Santo, and these would soon be shuttling through Henderson Field against targets in the north. Even a new Marine B-24 heavy-bomber squadron was made available, though it was first used to help map the still-largely-unknown scene of the campaign.

November 7 was BGen Roy Geiger's last day as Cactus Air commander. Although it was never officially acknowledged, the hard-driving fifty-seven-year-old was on the verge of a breakdown from overwork and stress, and everyone around him seemed to sense it. The matter was handled with great tact and, in the end, he traded places with BGen Lou Woods, who had been running the 1st Marine Aircraft Wing CP at Espiritu Santo.

It was at this precise point that the tempo and direction of the air war in the Lower Solomons changed. Eleventh Air Fleet had been defeated in the air. Within weeks, the thrust of Cactus Air operations would become almost wholly offensive in nature.

Archer Vandegrift broke away from his operations center on November 8, 1942, long enough to spruce up his best uniform and drive to Henderson Field to greet an incoming Skytrain transport. When the airplane had taxied to the strip's apron, a Marine stepped forward to open the door and place a small aluminum ladder in the hatchway. Then a burly man with thick salt-and-pepper eyebrows appeared as the men gathered around the ladder came to attention. VAdm Bill Halsey had arrived for his promised tour of the Lunga Perimeter.

Halsey was shown all the sights because Vandegrift knew it was imperative that he see the condition of the men who had been on the island the longest, and time was set aside for the admiral to speak with the troops and troop leaders. The experience made a deep impression upon Halsey, who could not help but note that many Marines looked hungry and seemed ill. While the Noumea conferences had resulted in a promise by Halsey to relieve the Marine division, the first-hand experience in November convinced the area commander that he had better do so quickly.

Upon returning to Noumea the next day, Halsey put pressure on his subordinates to speed the flow of fresh troops to Guadalcanal. The first unit to go would be American Division's 182nd Infantry Regiment, a Massachusetts National Guard outfit.

The Japanese were also taking forthright action, not so much to relieve their forces on Guadalcanal as to bolster them with physically alert cannon fodder. Following the Santa Cruz carrier battle, Tokyo asserted that Guadalcanal would have fallen in October had there been more in the way of planning, patience, and effort on the part of the senior officers on the scene. Nagoya Division was to be deployed in its entirety for a final push, and the effort would be fully supported by the enormous resources of the Imperial Navy.

To support the movement of 182nd Infantry to Kukum, Bill Halsey decided to deploy most of the naval force then available in the South Pacific. Even damaged *Enterprise* was sent to guard the four transports bearing the fresh regiment.

With the Japanese girding for their own build-up—an operation that was to coincide with the arrival of 182nd Infantry—a showdown neither side desired seemed inevitable.

37

RAdm Kelly Turner sailed with 182nd Infantry on November 9, 1942, and RAdm Norman Scott followed later in the day with a supply convoy. On November 10, RAdm Dan Callaghan, formerly VAdm Bob Ghormley's chief of staff, left Espiritu Santo with five cruisers and ten destroyers.

Scott passed Turner at sea and was off Kukum on November 11 unloading supplies and replacements when Japanese aircraft appeared over the channel. The unloading was halted, and the three cargo ships took evasive action, but all were damaged.

Turner's four troop transports arrived at dawn, November 12, and began disembarking two infantry battalions and headquarters of 182nd Infantry, a Marine replacement battalion, and a naval base-defense force. Two vessels were fired on by heavy artillery emplaced near Kokumbona late in the morning, but land and naval counterbattery fire dissuaded the Japanese from pressing the issue.

Word of a bomber strike was received from Coastwatcher Paul Mason late in the morning, and Cactus Air Ops pinpointed the strike on radar at 109 miles out at 1335. The unloading off Kukum stopped at 1445 and all the ships ran at high speed.

Nineteen torpedo-laden Bettys popped out of the clouds over Florida in a ragged formation doing well in excess of 300 knots. Capt Joe Foss and seven other VMF-121 fighter pilots dived from 29,000 feet and caught up with the Bettys as they began their torpedo runs. At the same time eight VMF-112 Wildcats and eight 67th Pursuit P-39s trapped the Bettys between themselves and the fire of the twenty-seven American warships in the channel.

The Bettys streamed along in line-abreast formation only fifty feet above the water, low enough and fast enough to rattle *San Francisco*'s gunnery officer into ordering his main batteries to train out and fire in the hope water geysers from the bursting 8-inch rounds would distract the onrushing bombardiers. Nothing of the sort happened, but the show was spectacular.

Boatswain's Mate 1st Class Leighton Spadone, a 1.1-inch gun captain aboard *Atlanta*, the Navy's first modern light antiaircraft cruiser, saw to it that his well-trained gunners put out rounds at a steady clip, but he had to keep ordering them to cease firing to avoid hitting nearby ships; the Japanese bombers were so low that tracking them for any distance invariably brought friendly vessels into antiaircraft-gun sights.

Few of the Bettys dropped their torpedoes, so intent were the pilots upon outrunning the hammer-and-anvil tactics of the darting American fighters. Bomber after bomber cartwheeled into the water. One Betty sideswiped *San Francisco*, taking down her after control tower in a sheet of flaming fuel, killing or injuring fifty. Destroyer *Buchanan* was hit by an antiaircraft round from another ship. Three Wildcats and one P-39 were shot down, though all the pilots were saved. Seventeen of the nineteen bombers and several Zero escorts were downed.

American warships raced toward the wreckage of the downed Japanese aircraft, their crews intent upon saving the surviving Japanese airmen. As *Atlanta* neared one floating Betty, the Japanese airman on its wing opened fire with his pistol. The cruiser passed him by, bilging him or leaving him to be picked up by a smaller vessel after his ire had cooled.

Radioman 3rd Class Bill Potwin returned to the flag bridge from *San Francisco*'s emergency radio cabin in time to take a call to RAdm Dan Callaghan from a destroyer skipper whose ship was drawing fire from downed Japanese airmen. The admiral took the mike from Potwin's hand and ordered the younger officer to return fire. Potwin saw tracer immediately erupt from a nearby vessel.

Unloading resumed as soon as the transports could get back to the anchorage.

At 1800, November 12, RAdm Raizo Tanaka, aboard destroyer *Hayashio*, led a large flotilla of troop transports out of the Shortlands anchorage. Tanaka was unenthusiastic about leading a dozen slow Imperial Army transports into Cactus Air–dominated waters. He was loath even to risk his fast destroyers, for they had come under increasing and increasingly accurate American air attacks. Less than a week before, on November 7, eleven destroyer-transports carrying 1,200 soldiers had been hit 125 miles north of Guadalcanal by a mixed Dauntless-Avenger strike led by Maj Joe Sailer, commander of newly arrived VMSB-132. Two first-line destroyers had been severely damaged. A run the next night was challenged by a Tulagi-based PT-boat squadron and, though the speedy plywood boats did not score, the destroyermen had been given something new to consider.

Intelligence data had been streaming in for a full week, beginning with a sighting by Coastwatcher Jack Read, in Northern Bougainville. Read had been chased out of an excellent lookout some days earlier, then ordered off the air until things cooled down. On November 8, however, he broke radio silence to report that twelve Japanese transports were steaming southeastward.

Farther south, on a high hill overlooking the Shortlands anchorage, Paul Mason counted thirty-three vessels in the anchorage on November 6. The count mounted until, on November 10, there were sixty-one vessels at anchor, including six cruisers and thirty-three destroyers.

Allied intelligence networks were literally overwhelmed by sightings, warnings, alerts, and surmises. It was extremely difficult to piece together a cogent picture, but it was evident that something was up. For example, large Combined Fleet components had left Truk anchorage some days earlier and had been tracked southward. Radio intelligence indicated that a major bombardment group was on the way to cover what seemed to be another major reinforcement attempt; at least two battleships were involved. But the numerous reports were confusing, and any number of previous scares had come to nothing.

Inasmuch as the unloading at Kukum had not been completed, RAdm Dan Callaghan was ordered to remain in the channel, and the destroyer force under RAdm Norman Scott was added to Callaghan's flotilla. Many of the ships involved had spent time in the area, particularly over the past several weeks; it was no longer unusual for American warships to operate out of Tulagi for days at a time. The channel was by no means secure, but the growing American naval presence and the relative stability of local air cover had removed some of the risk.

Dan Callaghan did not like his assignment. Radioman Bill Potwin, who remained on the flag bridge until relieved at 1730, was struck by the handsome, white-haired admiral's demeanor. A highly respected officer who had been Franklin Roosevelt's naval aide prior to the war, Callaghan endlessly paced the bridge, muttering that he was reluctant to carry out his orders, expressing his desire to talk things over with Halsey, admitting that there was not time to do so, revealing to rattled officers and seamen that they were in for a rough night.

Boatswain's Mate 2nd Class Vance Carter was taking an evening breather beside his battle station, Turret-2, when he happened to glance up at the flag bridge. There he saw Admiral Callaghan, who had been *San Francisco*'s captain prior to winning his flag and a place as Bob Ghormley's chief of staff the previous spring. Carter was struck by the look of absolute, somber concentration on the admiral's face.

VAdm Hiroaki Abe, a blooded destroyer specialist, was in charge of the bombardment force, and RAdm Raizo Tanaka was leading the transports. At stake were the lives of 12,000 Japanese soldiers, many tons of supplies, and, in the minds of many, the future of Guadalcanal. This knowledge weighed heavily upon Abe, who felt that the repetitive, monthly pattern of build-up, attack, and defeat was draining Japan of her best ships and men. The fact was that Abe, known throughout the Imperial Navy as an extremely cautious man, left his briefing at Combined Fleet headquarters, at Truk, with a firm conviction that his bombardment force would be challenged by a strong American surface force in the restricted waters off Guadalcanal. He was not at all happy with the prospect, and he frankly transmitted his feelings to several of his ship captains.

Eight destroyers and one light cruiser left Truk on November 9 and joined with two battleships and three destroyers in the Shortlands early on November 12. A lone B-17 began shadowing the battle force at 0830. While the new fleet carrier *Junyo*, also in the area, launched several Zeros to chase the B-17, which got away, the contact deepened Admiral Abe's conviction that he would meet the enemy off Guadalcanal that very night.

With reports of hostile movements mounting almost by the hour, headquarters throughout the South Pacific were alerted to assist Guadalcanal. RAdm Willis Lee, who had for weeks been guarding the carriers, rushed toward Guadalcanal with two modern fast battleships in hopes of intercepting the Japanese dreadnoughts, but it was doubtful that he would arrive before November 14, two days hence.

BGen Lou Woods needed aircraft, and men to fly them. RAdm Aubery Fitch scoured his command for flyable warplanes and came up with more and better aircraft than even he had thought possible: a squadron of new B-26 twin-engine bombers was flown to Espiritu Santo from the Fijis and placed on stand-by for deployment to Henderson Field; 67th Pursuit was bolstered with a dozen new P-39s; six new TBFs from VMSB-131 arrived with a three-plane F4F escort; portions of a new Dauntless squadron arrived; Maj Dale Brannon, who commanded 67th Pursuit until injured in early October, had just finished forming 339th Fighter Squadron in New Caledonia, and he sent all eight of his brand-new twin-engine P-38 Lightnings, the hottest Army fighter available; and Gen Douglas MacArthur sent all of his eight P-38s from Milne Bay.

When RAdm Dan Callaghan had escorted RAdm Kelly Turner's transports clear of the channel, he returned with his large force of cruisers and destroyers. The intelligence reports were confusing, but it seemed that the Japanese flotilla on the way down the Slot comprised, perhaps, two battleships and a large number of cruisers and destroyers.

Abe's bombardment force included two old battlecruisers, *Hiei* and *Kirishima*, neither of which had ever fired in anger, though both were thirty years old. Abe also had a light cruiser and eleven destroyers. Callaghan was badly outgunned and outnumbered, but at least he knew positively that there was to be a surface action. Abe felt it, but he did not know. In truth, he had been specifically enjoined from engaging American warships; all Japanese naval commanders had. The heavy air raids of the day had been designed to sweep such forces from the area. The no-combat decree worked for Callaghan in at least one other very important respect: The new-type bombardment shell that had been fired by the battleships against Henderson Field in October, on Black Tuesday, had been so highly rated by senior Japanese officers that the battlecruisers' magazines were choked with them; neither ship was capable of engaging in a protracted hot surface action because neither had many armor-piercing shells.

Abe acted upon his fears by placing his destroyers and light cruiser in an unwieldy battle formation comprising two protective arcs around the two battlecruisers. Further hampering—and protecting—the Japanese was a fortuitous squall, which happened to be heading in the same direction and at the same twenty-knot speed as Abe's bombardment force. The squall rendered absolute protection against feared submarine attacks or aerial sightings, but the complex deployment of the two screens would be impossible to maintain, and the risk of misadventure was high in the restricted waters leading to Lunga Point.

Dan Callaghan had no set plan for the battle, nor did he undertake any advance scouting. As with RAdm Norman Scott before the Cape Esperance Battle, the cruiser commander placed his ships in a single column, destroyers in the van and rear, cruisers in the middle. The cruisers were a mixed lot, few of the most-modern design or with the most-advanced equipment. More out of nostalgia than anything, Callaghan kept his flag aboard *San Francisco*, though her gunnery radar had been disabled in the afternoon air attack; Callaghan was a native of the city for which the cruiser was named, and she had been his last command. Admiral Scott remained aboard *Atlanta* as second-in-command; she also lacked modern surface-search radar. The destroyers were also a mixed lot, ranging from the very old to the very new.

It was an exceptionally dark and cloudy night. The new moon disappeared long before any contacts were made.

After midnight, it was Friday the thirteenth.

38

Adm Hiroaki Abe's bombardment force had lost the complex deployment in which it had begun its final 300-mile leg to Savo. The moving squall that screened the Japanese warships from American eyes also screened potential targets from Japanese eyes. Warned by a scout floatplane launched by battleship *Hiei* hours earlier that a dozen American warships were off Lunga, Abe decided to get out of the rain and into the open so that he could see the enemy ships or, at the least, see targets on land. It was simply a matter of letting the squall get ahead of his ships.

At midnight, Abe ordered all ships to prepare to execute a simultaneous 180-degree turn, then left them standing by for many minutes while his staff communicators attempted to reach two of the five ships in the leading arc of screening destroyers. The turn, when it came, made a shambles of the outer screen, sending two groups on diverging courses.

The Japanese sailed north, away from Cape Esperance, for over thirty minutes before escaping the rain at 0400. Abe ordered another turnabout and directed his warships toward Guadalcanal at twelve knots. Savo was spotted sixty degrees to port, then lookouts reported seeing the shape of mountains dead ahead.

Hundreds of sailors aboard *Hiei* and *Kirishima* were hard at work stacking one-ton 36cm incendiary shells in and around the main turrets of both battleships, all ready to be fired. The Japanese were about twelve miles offshore at 0140, clearly prepared to bombard the Lunga Perimeter—strangely unprepared to engage in a surface action.

Destroyer *Yudachi* reported at 0142: "Enemy sighted."

Abe roared at his flag signal officer, "What is the range and bearing? And where is *Yudachi?*"

Cdr Kiyoshi Kiikawa, *Yudachi*'s veteran skipper, did not know precisely where he was, for *Yudachi* had gone astray from the leading screen during the first 180-degree turn in the rain.

Suddenly, *Hiei*'s masthead lookout shouted, "Four black objects ahead. Looks like warships. Five degrees to starboard; 8,000 meters. Unsure yet; visibility bad."

Abe was totally frustrated with *Yudachi*'s performance, and thoroughly preoccupied with it. He took no part in the shouting of questions and answers between his staff officers and the lookout in the masthead. At long last, however, he ordered the battlecruiser gunners to unload the bombardment projectiles and bring up armor-piercing rounds from deep within the bowels of the main-battery magazines. Hundreds of sailors jumped to comply, for a single hit among the unsheltered stacks of incendiary rounds would doom the great battlecruiser and all who were aboard.

By sheer luck, the confusion of the two 180-degree turns had left *Hiei* and *Kirishima* screened by a seven-ship arc centered on light cruiser *Nagara*, dead ahead of *Hiei*. The first screen of five destroyers had been broken up into two groups, which were now ahead and to starboard, screening the flank at some distance. It would be impossible for the single American column to engage—or even pinpoint—all of the dispersed Japanese warships.

As at Cape Esperance, a month to the day earlier, the Japanese entered the channel south of Savo. As before, light cruiser *Helena*'s modern radar picked them up first, at 0124, November 13. Her skipper, Capt Gilbert Hoover, immediately informed the flagship that there was movement off his port bow at 27,000 and 32,000 yards. Two minutes later, RAdm Dan Callaghan ordered a slight shift to starboard, bringing his eight destroyers and five cruisers head-on to the Japanese.

Helena maintained the contacts. At 0130, she reported that the opposing forces had closed to 14,500 yards, that the strongest contact was off the port bow, coming on at twenty-three knots. The two forces were closing on each other at a combined rate of over forty knots. Callaghan ordered course shifted to due north; it is likely that he hoped to "cross the T," though the fact that the Japanese were not in column would have obviated most of the advantage from his having done so.

Boatswain's Mate 1st Class Leighton Spadone, captain of *Atlanta*'s sternmost starboard 1.1-inch antiaircraft gun, was fairly relaxed. The tinny voice in Spadone's headset told him that the Japanese were to port, on the opposite side of the ship. Routine reports followed, then the voice said, "I can see them now, just off the port beam, range three-oh-double-oh." Then, "Stand by action to port!" Then, "Range two-three-double-oh." Spadone had worked in 5-inch guns before the war; he knew how very hard it was to miss a target at that range.

As the two forces closed, the extreme Japanese flankers, destroyers *Yudachi* and *Harusame*, surged ahead of the main body, swung over to port and assumed station directly in front of the main body at 0140. All Commander Kiikawa, in *Yudachi*, wanted to do was find the other three destroyers of the dispersed first screen. But the maneuver aimed the two Japanese destroyers right at the lead American destroyer, *Cushing*, whose skipper instinctively ordered the helm shifted hard aport, then hard to starboard. That broke up the American vanguard.

All four American van destroyers were thrown into violent

evasive maneuvers as each captain in turn instinctively sought to avoid collision with the ship dead ahead.

Strangely, though the Japanese had been pinpointed on radar for twenty minutes, Admiral Callaghan refused to allow his vessels to open fire. Neither did Abe, though his gunners used the time to bear on targets. The wait drove the tense Japanese captains to utter distraction, but they obediently withheld fire to give the battleship crews more time to replace incendiary shells with armor-piercing rounds.

LCdr Bruce McCandless, *San Francisco's* communications officer, standing this watch as officer-of-the-deck, saw *Atlanta* suddenly swing out of line dead ahead to avoid the milling destroyers. McCandless shouted down the voice tube to the flag deck for permission to follow. Admiral Callaghan at first denied the request, but permission was granted a moment later, allowing just enough time to destroy the integrity of the cruiser column.

Finally, at 0200 Callaghan passed: "Commence firing!" It was too late. At 0201, *Hiei's* searchlight shutters snapped open, catching *Atlanta*, the first cruiser in line, in stark twin beams of sight-destroying light.

Boatswain's Mate 1st Class Leighton Spadone instinctively pivoted his head toward the bridge. The cruiser's boats, after stack, foremast, and rigging were sharply distinct against a stark black background.

The cruiser's gunnery officer screamed, "Commence firing!" and ordered his searchlights to counter-illuminate. Too late! As *Atlanta's* sixteen 5-inch gun mounts sought the distant lights, *Hiei's* main batteries, only 5,000 yards distant, opened up, grievously harming her. Though *Atlanta's* rapid-fire 5-inch guns opened, their roars diminished while the roars of the Japanese guns dramatically increased moment by moment. RAdm Norman Scott was cut down, dead on *Atlanta's* flag bridge with most of his staff.

A member of *Atlanta's* commissioning crew, Leighton Spadone could hardly believe his ship was being hit as he was thrown across the gun mount and slammed hard into the splinter shield. *Atlanta* was rocked by the detonation of a torpedo, possibly two. Then she went dead in the water.

Both forces became utterly intermingled, thanks to the early, panicked dispersion of the American van destroyers and their subsequent vain attempts to regain formation. *Cushing* was hit amidships and slowed as a result of power-line breaks. As she was pointed north, her captain spied the giant *Hiei* and ordered six torpedoes fired. None hit. The destroyer's gunners also missed the mark, over-reaching the battlecruiser and nearly hitting flanking destroyer *Amatsukaze*, whose captain, Cdr Tameichi Hara, temporarily lost his night vision to the flashing tracer and bursting 5-inch shells.

The second American destroyer, *Laffey*, moved to within 500 feet of the darkened battleship and loosed a salvo of torpedoes. The range, however, was too short, so none of the fish could arm; all bounced off the battlecruiser's great steel sides. *Laffey* continued toward the Japanese flagship; she came so close that she had to abruptly fishtail to avoid colliding with the behemoth. Her automatic-weapons batteries raked *Hiei*'s bridge, killing her captain and wounding Admiral Abe. Then two large-caliber salvoes from *Hiei*'s guns and a torpedo in the fantail from flanking destroyer *Terutsuki* fatally damaged the aggressively handled American destroyer. *Laffey*'s crew hit the water, and many died from the concussion of her own depth charges.

As *Sterett* lashed out at *Hiei*, the obvious target, she took a hit that damaged her steering control. Then a second hit in the foremast put out her radar. Still, her skipper refused to back down, steering after *Hiei* on his propellers, firing four torpedoes from 4,000 yards.

The last of the van destroyers, *O'Bannon*, was briefly illuminated at the start of the action, but sharp, abrupt turns during the disintegration of the destroyer vanguard carried her to relative safety. She was close enough to *Hiei* to fire with telling effect, but too close to be fired upon. Within minutes, however, she had to swerve to avoid the burning *Laffey*. She stopped long enough for crewmen to throw flotation gear to their countrymen in the water. By then, the fight had passed her by.

San Francisco, the sixth American ship in line, directly astern *Atlanta*, was illuminated by ships of both sides. She got off seven full salvoes at an unidentified ship, probably the leading Japanese destroyer, then shifted to the second Japanese vessel, which reversed course and fell back upon the center group of Japanese warships. As *San Francisco*'s gunners attempted to follow the receding target, however, they pumped several salvoes into a darkened ship that drifted into their line of fire. A huge fireball well beyond the drifting target spouted flame hundreds of feet high, backlighting *Atlanta*, which had been hit by at least eighteen of the American flagship's 8-inch rounds.

Admiral Callaghan and *San Francisco*'s skipper, Capt Cassin Young, both yelled "Cease firing!" an order intended only for *San Francisco*'s guns, but shouted in haste over the open voice circuit to all ships. No sooner had the command been given than *San Francisco*'s main-battery spotter saw *Hiei* looming out of the darkness.

Boatswain's Mate 2nd Class Vance Carter, peering through a training scope in Turret-2, watched *Hiei*'s huge shape loom out of the darkness; it was the biggest moving object he had ever seen. Carter felt the turret's right gun lurch, and lurch again, as it put out round after round at *Hiei*.

Hiei returned fire, but two four-gun salvoes fell short, filling the air with eerie greenish pyrotechnics; she had only the incendiary rounds intended for Henderson Field to use against the armored warship in her sights.

Ahead of *Hiei*, light cruiser *Nagara* fired from 3,000 yards and scored direct hits with her second 5-inch salvo. A larger vessel, possibly *Kirishima*, also opened fire. *Hiei*'s third salvo was brought on target just as destroyer *Akatsuki* charged *San Francisco*'s port side and raked her superstructure. But *Akatsuki* was caught in a devastating crossfire between the guns of the American flagship and an American destroyer. She was sunk in moments with almost her entire crew.

Below decks, in the blind compartment known as Radio-3, the flagship's emergency radio cabin, Radioman 3rd Class Bill Potwin's earphones were alive with chatter from the flag bridge. Suddenly, RAdm Dan Callaghan's authoritative voice boomed over the open circuit, "Tell the navigator to get us out of here!"

In Turret-2, Boastswain's Mate Vance Carter was lifted from his seat, then flung back into it, when a huge projectile burst about six feet beneath the gun chamber to his immediate right.

Incoming fire from at least three Japanese warships felled the men on the flag and command bridges. RAdm Dan Callaghan and three of his senior staffers were killed. Capt Cassin Young, who had won a Medal of Honor at Pearl Harbor, was mortally wounded, and most of the rest of the men on the flag and command bridges were also dead or dying. Indeed, only two men on the command bridge remained on their feet: LCdr Bruce McCandless and the steersman, Quartermaster 3rd Class Harry Higdon, who reported that he had no steering control. At that moment, *San Francisco* was making eighteen knots and uncontrollably swinging to port.

Heavy cruiser *Portland* began the action dead astern *San Francisco*. She attempted to defend the stricken flagship by firing at assailants to starboard, but was herself struck by shellfire. Her captain had pointedly ignored Admiral Callaghan's general cease-fire order. Instead, he radioed the flagship to see if the order had been somehow garbled in transmission. The affirmation had momentarily checked *Portland*'s fire, but a target three miles to starboard was too good to pass up, so the main batteries were ordered to resume firing. Then the cruiser received a crippling torpedo blast in the stern; a chunk of the fantail was blown out, and torn underplating forced her to run in a circle. However, when *Portland*'s lookouts visually spotted *Hiei*, her forward turret lashed out at the battlecruiser until it passed from range. The unsteerable cruiser circled away from the battle, in the direction of Guadalcanal's coast.

Light cruiser *Helena* opened fire to port at the searchlights that had caught *Atlanta*—at *Hiei*—and was taken under immediate counterbattery fire. One round impacted between Turret-1 and Turret-2, another blew the bloomers off the guns in Turret-4, a third hit the deck near the stern, and two holed two of the stacks. Damage was nil. Capt Gilbert Hoover skillfully conned his ship clear of the carnage ahead, and *Helena*'s gunners rapidly moved from target to target. Automatic weapons fired at a large ship, possibly *Nagara*, at a range of 3,000 yards, and forced her to retire at high speed.

Before *Nagara* was hit, she served briefly as a screen for destroyer *Amatsukaze*, which surged past to starboard, toward the American battle line. *Amatsukaze*'s captain, Cdr Tameichi Hara, saw numerous American warships in the murky glare; the darker coastline of Guadalcanal was clearly visible behind them, to Hara's right. Hara ordered his ship to turn toward them at flank speed. He was about to order his guns into action when the familiar silhouettes of three friendly destroyers masked the quarry. Hara was frustrated almost to tears, certain he would be denied an opportunity to strike a meaningful blow. The three destroyers swerved to port to cover *Hiei*, whose main mast was fully ablaze. Hara was about to join up at the rear of the friendly column when flares from departing *Nagara* fixed at least five American ships in his sight. The nearest was only 5,000 yards off *Amatsukaze*'s starboard bow, a perfect torpedo shot.

Commander Hara was considered the Imperial Navy's best torpedo tactician. He had made his mark in prewar years, and had won early promotion to his first command by developing Japan's radical torpedo doctrine. This was Hara's first live-action opportunity to positively prove his tactical theorem.

Hara's torpedo officer, Lt Masatoshi Miyoshi, also felt the time was ripe, for he impatiently yelled from his station, "Commander, let's fire the fish!"

"Get the fishermen ready," Hara responded, and his crew sprang to action as he rattled off orders in an excited voice. The distance to the targets steadily closed. When only 3,000 yards separated the hunter from the hunted, Commander Hara brayed, "Ready torpedoes, fire!"

Eight fish *whoosed* into the water at 0154 as *Amatsukaze* came hard aport beneath the glimmer of newly fired star shells. Only two minutes after the perfect launch, Hara and his elated crew watched two great pillars of flame and smoke erupt from the side of one of the targets, which immediately broke in two and sank. The Japanese, Hara especially, were astounded.

By that time, *Amatsukaze* had looped back to the west. *Hiei* was seen in the distance, silhouetted by her own fires as she retired toward Savo. Hara turned his ship to help, but dim, intermittent flashes to port drew his attention to a new target, an American cruiser. Four torpedoes were readied.

"Torpedoes ready," Lieutenant Miyoshi called to the bridge.

"All right. Hold it," Hara cautioned. "Hold it." He was looking for the perfect set-up. "Steady. Steady. Fire!"

It was 0159. The launch was perfect.

Light antiaircraft cruiser *Juneau* engaged *Yudachi* before one of Hara's torpedoes struck her forward engine room at 0205. Her crew concentrated on keeping her afloat despite a broken keel, and she stopped dead in the water. Commander Hara passed up an opportunity to blast the cripple with his guns only because he wished to remain hidden in the darkness, able to launch more killing fish.

The four rear American destroyers had to wait some time before they could engage the distant Japanese. At length, *Aaron Ward* got ten full salvoes away, with many hits observed. Her gunnery, however, was upset when she was thrown into reverse to avoid *Yudachi*, which Commander Kiikawa boldly sailed through the American battle line, succeeding in his hope of drawing attention from burning *Hiei*. After only a moment's pause to recover from the hard turn, however, *Aaron Ward* resumed firing at a distant searchlight. When her gun director was hit, she came back on local control, pitching in wherever she could find an opening.

Barton had been commissioned May 29 and had taken part in the Santa Cruz battle. Now, in her first surface action, she fired her 5-inch guns, loosed four torpedoes, and momentarily stopped to avoid colliding with a friendly vessel.

Veteran destroyer *Monssen* was next-to-last in line, and had plenty of time to choose targets and prepare for action. Before she could fire, several torpedoes passed beneath her, all failing to detonate. Her acting skipper, LCdr Charles McCombs, spotted a huge target off the starboard bow and ordered his torpedo battery to fire. Two of the five fish possibly detonated on target. Another detonation was seen on a smaller vessel following a second launch.

As their ship passed to starboard of the slowing *Barton*, *Monssen*'s lookouts spotted a pair of torpedo wakes on the starboard bow. Lieutenant Commander McCombs swung his ship to starboard at flank speed. He also put full power on the port engine to pivot faster. Both fish missed by no more than fifteen yards. They crossed *Monssen*'s bows and hit *Barton* in her forward engine room within four seconds of each other. As *Monssen*'s startled topside crew (and *Amatsukaze*'s jubilant topside crew) looked on, *Barton* was blown out of the water and, within forty seconds, was completely submerged. Eleven members of her fantail crew survived.

Monssen fired her 20mm guns at several destroyers passing on a reciprocal heading 500 yards to starboard, then opened with her main battery to assist *San Francisco*, still very much the center of Japanese attention. *Monssen*'s spirited firing, however, soon drew a good deal of attention her way, from vessels of both navies. The first hit caught her in the handling room of Turret-1, starting a fire. Then hits began penetrating from all sides, too many to count. A blast in the wardroom killed the surgeon and a corpsman; one in the radio room knocked out all communications; another burst in the superstructure. Eleven rounds struck the engineering spaces: three in the forward fireroom, three in the forward engine room, two in the after uptake, and three in the after engine room. One of the latter hit the throttle manifold; superheated steam escaping under 650 pounds of pressure caused many gruesome casualties.

Cdr William Cole's *Fletcher* (designated DD445; the numbers added up to thirteen) was the last warship—the thirteenth—in the American line this Friday the thirteenth. Her modern radar had forewarned her captain of the coming battle and, once it was joined, of the relative size and disposition of every ship involved.

The main battery was laid on a likely target, but this was taken under fire before *Fletcher* could open, so Commander Cole ordered a shift to a more-distant target. Excellent long-range gunnery, aided by excellent radar control, started fires on the enemy ship. *Fletcher* obediently ceased fire when RAdm Dan Callaghan's order was passed, but soon resumed firing on a new target, then shifted to yet another. As the superbly handled destroyer passed *Barton*'s grave and burning *Monssen*, she slowed for a better look. Then Commander Cole reared his ship back and burst forward at thirty-five knots, running completely through the center of the Japanese formation. *Fletcher* was fired on by every ship in sight, American and Japanese, and combed numerous torpedo wakes. But she came through without so much as a scratch.

Fletcher's topside crew saw a multitude of shells arcing back and forth over the holocaust midst the sickening green glare of star shells and the yellow-red glow of burning ships. The scene was so horrid, and confusion so complete that individual captains of both nations began retiring on their own authority.

෫

Cdr Kiyoshi Kiikawa, whose unpredictability had made his *Yudachi* an extremely potent weapon this night, cut through the American rear destroyer line and closed on *Portland*'s port quarter to launch eight torpedoes, of which one hit the American heavy's fantail and sent her out of the fight. But minutes later, *Aaron Ward* dropped a salvo of 5-inch shells upon *Yudachi* and, at 0213, she burst into great gouts of reddish flame and pulled away from the fight to limp along the coast toward Cape Esperance.

Cdr Tameichi Hara watched *Yudachi* flare up to the west and, in so doing, nearly missed a huge silhouette as it loomed out of the darkness. Hara's *Amatsukaze* barely responded to the helm, almost collided with the dark form, then pulled away. It took a few moments for Hara to realize that he could fire his last four torpedoes at the receding target. This he did, following with orders to his gunnery officer to illuminate the target with searchlights and open with *Amatsukaze*'s six 4-inch guns. The target was *San Francisco*, and she was in for a beating. Round after round after round roared from *Amatsukaze*'s guns. As they did, however, Japan's premier torpedo expert mentally kicked himself for committing the most elementary of errors; he had fired his last four fish while only 500 yards from his target, too close for the torpedoes to arm.

As Hara silently raged at his blunder, he added to it by forgetting to order his ship's searchlight doused. An unseen American cruiser—*Helena*—opened from port. This shook Hara from his lethargy. The light blinkers were snapped shut and the first tendrils of smoke from *Amatsukaze*'s smoke generators were just beginning to spread when two of *Helena*'s 6-inch shells splashed water over Hara and the bridge watch. Then solid hits were scored. Commander Hara was thrown to the deck and all thoughts were blasted from his mind. He slowly rose, feeling for wounds that were not there. A quick look around the bridge catapulted the captain's heart into his throat. The gun-director station over the bridge had taken a direct hit; its complement and several men on the bridge were dead. A second round had penetrated the radio room, directly beneath Hara's feet; everyone there was dead. The helm was unresponsive and communications throughout the ship were out. Fires burned here and there, but the danger lay in Hara's inability to control his ship. A trusted runner was sent below with orders, then Hara ordered his guns back to action. That came to nothing, for the hydraulic system was out and the mounts were inoperable. The gunnery officer had been shredded where he stood; all that remained aboard the ship was one of the officer's legs.

The engineer sent a runner to Hara to report that the engines were not damaged and that there were no fuel fires. As *Helena* continued to pour fire at the cripple, Hara stolidly regained control and steadfastly refused to crumble as shrapnel from near misses caused more damage and started more fires.

Amatsukaze seemed doomed, but three thus far unengaged Japanese destroyers made a pass at *Helena* from out of the darkness and forced her off the scent. Commander Hara's crew managed to regain steering control by shifting the rudder to manual power—ten sturdy, sweating sailors. *Amatsukaze* turned her bows to the north and slowly sailed from the scene.

Atlanta was dead in the water, slightly down by the head, listing slightly to port, drifting toward Guadalcanal. She had sustained at least fifty hits. Fires were burning forward, and it was very quiet.

Boatswain's Mate 1st Class Leighton Spadone was crouched behind the splinter shield of the aft starboard 1.1-inch gun with the rest of his crew. The earphones he had on were dead. It was pitch dark when he asked if anyone was hurt. There were several affirmative responses; half the crew was wounded. When Spadone moved to get the first-aid bag, his right arm refused to respond as he would have liked. Shrapnel had gone through his right leg above the knee, and splinters were embedded near his groin and in his right ankle. As Spadone could not reach or be reached by central authority, he ordered his gunners to clear the mount. It was dark, but he could see that the foremast was down and that all boats save one were splintered. When Spadone climbed down to the main deck, he saw other dark forms moving among the wreckage. An officer he knew was leaning against a bulkhead, in shock. No one with whom Spadone spoke had heard anything official regarding the state of the ship, which was clearly in bad shape. Someone had to do something, so Spadone ordered the undamaged whaleboat filled with wounded and lowered into the water. The lines got away from the handlers and the stern dropped too quickly, jostling the injured men, who were at least clear of the ship and relatively safe.

Leighton Spadone began worrying about his younger brother, Phil, a gun pointer in a 1.1-inch gun mount on *Atlanta*'s starboard—engaged—side. It took some doing, and a good deal of pain from his stiffening wounded leg, but Leighton found Phil among the wounded, resting in their own berthing compartment, which was filled with the injured and dying. The younger Spadone had been given morphine, and his slurred speech and pallid complexion spoke volumes of his overall condition. His lower left leg was badly lacerated and the outer portion next to the calf was gone. Large splinters had entered his pelvis and back, but there was no spinal damage. Barring complications, Phil Spadone would make it. Whether the ship would survive was still a question only time could answer.

When LCdr Bruce McCandless discovered that *San Francisco*'s helm would not respond, he passed control of the runaway warship to Battle-2, the secondary command center that had been restored after being hit by the Betty bomber that afternoon. No sooner was that done, however, than Battle-2 was obliterated by a direct hit, its crew wiped out. The heavy cruiser was making good speed through the battle area, and an eventual collision was all but inevitable. Mc-Candless despaired of regaining control of the runaway vessel when a tinny voice wafted from the voice tube leading up from the compartment beneath his feet; Quartermaster 3rd Class Floyd Rogers, the secondary steersman, shouted that he had steering and engine control. McCandless gleefully gave Rogers a new heading between Savo and Cape Esperance. Unaware that the trailing column had disintegrated long before, McCandless hoped the American battle group would be able to regain the initiative in the relatively open waters beyond Savo.

Below decks, in the blind emergency radio compartment, Radioman 3rd Class Bill Potwin feverishly worked to restore communications throughout the ship. Without it, *San Francisco* had only a glimmer of a chance to recover from her multiple wounds. For the moment, there was no way to restore the voice lines, but Potwin and the other communicators in the airless compartment were soon tapping out Morse messages on old key sets.

Fortunately, *San Francisco* had sustained no hits below the waterline because she had been so close to the enemy warships, none of which had been able to depress their guns far enough to hole her watertight spaces. But *Hiei*'s 36cm bombardment shells and many lighter rounds had devastated her upper works.

Command of the cruiser temporarily passed to LCdr Herbert Schonland, the first lieutenant. (Her exec, injured in Battle-2 during the afternoon air attack, was killed in his bunk.) Schonland, however, was the cruiser's senior damage-control officer, so he returned the command to LCdr Bruce McCandless while he personally directed the battle against the spreading flames, often at grave personal risk. Both he and McCandless were awarded Medals of Honor for their night's work.

Portland's torn and warped underplating kept her moving in loops and turns for the remainder of the night. Though hers was the senior captain, he could not assume command of the battle force, even had he known of the deaths of both American admirals.

Capt Gilbert Hoover, of *Helena*, could raise neither RAdm Dan Callaghan nor RAdm Norman Scott by radio, so he elected to lead the survivors to safety. He ordered a general retirement to the east, though few enough ships were capable of responding. *Juneau* managed to get under way against all odds by the end of the midwatch, and her captain set course through Indispensable Strait behind Hoover's small group of survivors.

At about 0240, with fires burning from forward of the chief petty officers' hatch to the machine shop, with no power and no water to fight fires (even the little gasoline handy-billy had been holed by a shell fragment) and only a few fifty-lb CO_2 extinguishers left, with all torpedoes expended, with three of four guns out of commission and the fourth only manually operable, it appeared that the only additional big bang *Monssen* could make would be when the fires reached her magazines. There were numerous casualties, and the superstructure was fast becoming a huge pyre. LCdr Charles McCombs gave the command, "Abandon ship!"

The only way down for many was to jump. *Monssen's* helmsman climbed down the after vertical ladder from the bridge without realizing the bottom half had been shot away. He stepped off and fell to the torpedo deck. The navigator did the same and fell on top of the helmsman. A shell impacted nearby and killed the navigator, but the helmsman was uninjured.

When all the living had left *Monssen's* bridge, Lieutenant Commander McCombs carefully removed his binoculars (so they would not be broken!), kicked off his shoes, climbed the bridge rail, and jumped.

Aaron Ward lay dead in the water, her engine spaces flooded.

Fletcher successfully pressed her luck by making a second full-speed run against a Japanese warship that seemed intent upon mauling the American cripples. Commander Cole ordered the firing of his last ten torpedoes, then retired eastward through Indispensible Strait. *Fletcher*'s torpedo tubes were empty and her magazines were depleted.

Destroyer *Akatsuki* was the only Japanese vessel sunk outright. Destroyers *Yudachi* and *Yukikaze* were both severely damaged. And *Hiei*, which this night had first fired her giant guns in anger, was a cripple. Raked from stem to stern by the full might of the outgunned American force, she slowly shaped an unsure course around the southeast coast of Savo in the hope of using the island to mask the seriousness of her condition.

Daylight brought mixed feelings of relief and horror to the thousands of sailors in the battle area. *Yudachi* was dispatched by six salvoes fired by, of all ships, the circling *Portland*. The destroyer's crew, however, had already transferred to a sister destroyer in the dark, and had escaped.

Atlanta's crew put up a courageous but losing struggle to save its ship.

Boatswain's Mate 1st Class Leighton Spadone worked at jury-rigging a communications system among the after guns, which were remanned. Many of the wounded were being moved topside aft of Turret-6 as a safety precaution when the turret suddenly swung to starboard, clearly tracking a target. From out of the gloom there appeared a Japanese destroyer, which passed *Atlanta*'s stern from starboard to port. She was moving at eight knots or less, barely kicking up a wake, obviously searching for Japanese swimmers. Her main guns were trained on *Atlanta*, but she made no hostile move. Neither ship fired, which was a real blessing for the wounded American sailors near Turret-6. In time—an eternity—the Japanese warship passed from sight.

Daybreak found Boatswain's Mate Spadone standing beside his 1.1-inch gun. He peeked over the edge of the mount at the main deck, where he saw the cruiser's executive officer standing just outside his cabin. The commander had been hit in the elbow, which was bandaged. He held a photograph in his hands; perhaps it was his wife and children. He looked at the photo for a very long time, then held it over the side of the ship and dropped it into the water. Spadone could see the photo drift back and forth for a few moments before it sank from sight.

The water was filled with flotsam and men for as far as Spadone could see. Sailors aboard *Atlanta* were armed with rifles and other personal weapons to repel Japanese boarders, though no such danger was evident.

All of her wounded and nonessential crewmen were transferred to fleet tug *Bobolink*, out from Tulagi, and to landing boats from Kukum. The tug moved *Atlanta* to a safe spot off Kukum, but the damaged vessel's list dramatically increased. As there was no salvage gear available, the last of her crew was ordered off after scuttling charges were set. *Atlanta* blew up and sank three miles off Lunga Point at sunset.

Destroyer *Cushing* burned fiercely until late in the afternoon, then turned turtle. Rescue craft picked up her survivors. The small boats passed up many Japanese adrift throughout the area, less for lack of space or compassion than for the refusal of the Japanese to be rescued.

Portland continued to run in circles despite the efforts of straining landing boats to pull her about. *Bobolink* finally gave her a mighty shove, which set her in the right direction. She anchored safely off Tulagi an hour after midnight.

LCdr Charles McCombs, of *Monssen*, was rescued by a landing boat from Kukum at about 0900. A final muster on the beach re-

vealed that, of 236 members of his crew, 100 had gotten off and
seven had died in the water or on the beach. Of *Monssen's* eighteen
officers, eight left the ship and one died in the attempt. *Monssen*
drifted and burned through the day, then disappeared the following
night. It was estimated that she had sustained forty-two direct shell
hits.

San Francisco, Helena, Juneau, O'Bannon, Sterett, and *Fletcher*, all
under *Helena's* Capt Gilbert Hoover, retired in the direction of the
New Hebrides at eighteen knots. At 1101, well clear of land, a
Japanese submarine fired a spread of torpedoes at the column.
Juneau was hit once, portside beneath the bridge. The light antiaircraft cruiser simply disintegrated and instantaneously sank.
Fearing further loss, Captain Hoover ordered that his survivors sail
on. A B-17 which happened to be overhead shot off a message to
Noumea, but it was not received, and rescue operations did not get
under way. Of the estimated 100 men who survived the blow, only
ten lived. Three drifted ashore on a remote island and were rescued
at length by a PBY, and another PBY found six in the water. The
last man was eventually found by a destroyer, alone and adrift in
the endless sea. Well over 700 of of *Juneau's* officers and men died.

39

A Marine Dauntless crew on a routine dawn search in the direction of Santa Ysabel found *Hiei* just north of Savo at sunrise. The battlecruiser was doing just five knots, smoke was billowing from her forward main turrets, and her secondary turrets aft were dangling over the water. A destroyer which was burning amidships opened fire on the American warplane, but the pilot attacked, missed, and continued on his way after filing a report with Cactus Air Ops.

Lacking credible details, Air Ops sent Capt Joe Foss, now Guadalcanal's high-scoring ace, to look over the battle area and report back. Foss indeed found *Hiei*, and Air Ops ordered an immediate strike against her and the three destroyers left to guard her.

Five SBDs from VMSB-142, on their first combat strike, got away at 0615. One got a direct hit and another got a near miss. An hour later, four Marine TBFs delivered their first combat strike of the war, scoring once. After yet another hour, Maj Joe Sailer, VMSB-132's commander, led six SBDs against *Hiei*, but none scored. The Marine TBFs returned at 1010, followed by Capt Joe

Foss and five other Wildcats. The torpedo flight leader hit *Hiei*
amidships, then Foss veered off from strafing a destroyer to make a
tight turn virtually on top of the battleship's superstructure. He
was seen thumbing his nose at the white-clad enemy officers gathered on *Hiei*'s bridge! Sometime later, eight F4Fs returning from a
search for a nonexistent Japanese carrier tangled with the battleship's newly arrived air cover. The Marines claimed seven of the
hovering Zeros.

The same erroneous carrier sighting caused a whirlwind of activity for *Enterprise*'s Air Group 10, which scrambled from the damaged carrier at dawn. Unable to find a target, a large strike was
vectored to Cactus to help there as well as to mask the presence in
the area of America's last operational flattop.

While coming into Henderson Field's landing pattern at 1000,
a flight of nine Torpedo-10 TBFs spotted *Hiei* and launched an impromptu attack. The bombers split into two divisions and, watched
by Zeros that refused to join battle, attacked both bows. *Hiei* actually fired a salvo from her forward 36cm main turrets, though the
chance of hitting the aircraft was remarkably remote. The Navy
TBFs got three hits; one in either flank and the last in the stern,
which wrecked the battlecruiser's rudder.

Fourteen B-17s from Espiritu Santo dropped a total of fifty-six
500-lb bombs from 14,000 feet with one hit and one near miss. As
the heavy bombers left, Maj Joe Sailer returned with six of his
SBDs. These scored three hits with 1,000-pounders. Then a flight
of four Torpedo-8 and two Marine TBFs got a hit amidships and
one on the port bow. Two hours later, at 1435, Torpedo-10 got
three hits for six tries.

The last strike, Maj Joe Sailer's third of the day, was broken up
by deteriorating weather. Of eight pilots, only Sailer found the target. He managed only to near-miss one of the picket destroyers.
Two of Sailer's aircraft and their crews were lost from the mission,
the only Cactus losses of the day.

Shortly after dark, at about 1800, *Hiei*'s destroyer escorts came
alongside to take off survivors; 450 of her complement had been

killed during the night surface engagement and by American aerial ordnance. As the destroyers pulled away, the battlecruiser's scuttling charges ignited, and the great ship went down stern first five miles north-northwest of Savo. She was the first battleship ever destroyed by Americans in war.

A large surface force under VAdm Nobutake Kondo, composed of a pair of heavy cruisers and the seaworthy remnants of Admiral Abe's battle force, was spotted by 11th Bombardment Group B-17s north of Ontong Java. Another B-17 found RAdm Raizo Tanaka's transport-and-destroyer flotilla in the Slot north of Vella Lavella; on hearing of the action of Friday the thirteenth, Tanaka had reversed course in mid Slot and spent the day at Faisi.

Four heavy cruisers, two light cruisers, and six destroyers all under VAdm Gunichi Mikawa were missed by American planes. The warships had left the Shortlands to bombard Henderson Field in the time-tested hope of covering Tanaka's approach and unloading operation. Forging ahead despite Tanaka's daylong retirement, Mikawa was not challenged because he cannily took the long way around north of Choiseul and Santa Ysabel. While part of the battle force took up patrol stations near Savo around midnight, November 14, two heavy cruisers, one light cruiser, and four destroyers blasted all three runways for thirty-seven minutes. Later, Mikawa's cruisers and destroyers were attacked by Tulagi-based PT-boats, but they retired without damage.

Only one Dauntless dive-bomber was destroyed on the main runway during the bombardment, but seventeen fighters were demolished and thirty-two were damaged on Fighter-1. Cactus Air's vast permanent reinforcement and the loan of Air Group 10 had provided the Japanese warships with more targets than usual.

Search missions over the Slot on November 14 found Mikawa 140 miles from Cape Esperance as he retired toward the Shortlands. Five SBDs and three Marine and three Navy TBFs left Henderson Field under Maj Joe Sailer at 0715 and began launching attacks at 0800. A heavy cruiser was near-missed and damaged by the SBDs while three Torpedo-10 pilots and one Marine hit heavy cruiser *Kinugasa*, a Savo veteran, with their torpedoes. Though *Kinugasa* was left burning and trailing fuel, her crew quickly extinguished the flames and got speed up to an impressive thirty knots.

A sizeable contingent of Air Group 10 was launched from *Enterprise*, then about 200 miles south-southwest of Guadalcanal, and sent after a supposed Japanese carrier following a report at 0708 that a pair of *Enterprise* scouts had seen ten Japanese warplanes far out over the sea. At 0915, after the carrier strike was airborne, the same searchers pinpointed "two battleships, two heavy cruisers, one possible converted carrier, [and] four destroyers" in the Slot. This was Mikawa.

As they were low on fuel, the searchers attacked *Kinugasa* and set her afire again with two good hits. Another pair of *Enterprise* searchers found Mikawa's main body, but one was lost to gunfire after scoring an unconfirmed hit.

The *Enterprise*-launched dive-bombers had some difficulty finding the Japanese because the contact reports were misunderstood. The strike group eventually lost its fighter escorts, which had to duck into Henderson Field when they ran low on fuel. But luck and perseverance helped LCdr Bucky Lee's Scouting-10 Dauntlesses find Mikawa's main body at 0950. Ten of the sixteen dive-bombers were sent in after the cruisers while Lee led five others onward to look for a reported but nonexistent carrier. Five of the Dauntlesses dived through heavy flak to near-miss and damage heavy cruiser *Chokai*, Mikawa's flagship. The second group of five SBDs ruptured *Kinugasa*'s fuel tanks, which reignited enormous fires. Having failed to find the nonexistent carrier, Bucky Lee's six SBDs returned to score four near-misses against a light cruiser.

A short time after Lee's dive-bombers reformed and flew from sight, *Kinugasa*, which had stubbornly resisted numerous attacks, slipped beneath the waves.

By the time any additional strikes could be mounted, Admiral Mikawa's battered, shattered force had run from range.

Eleven Japanese transports carrying 12,000 fresh soldiers and hundreds of tons of supplies, weapons, and ammunition were coming on. RAdm Raizo Tanaka was repeatedly spotted, beginning at dawn, but the heavy attacks on the Mikawa force kept the Americans off his trail. In fact, Tanaka had actually seen Bucky Lee's Scouting-10 Dauntlesses on their way to pick up Mikawa, but he had gotten away by making smoke and zig-zagging his slow formation.

The first American aircraft to hit Tanaka were two *Enterprise* scouts, which found him at 0949 only 120 miles from Guadalcanal. The two veteran search pilots made their report and launched their attack just after 1000. The element leader missed his target by ten feet, but his wingman scored a perfect hit well aft on his. The two rearseatmen fired their twin .30-caliber free guns at everything that moved as the two dive-bombers streaked along the surface and pulled up and away.

The first strike against the transports, launched as soon as the *Enterprise* searchers reported, was composed of nineteen Marine SBDs, seven *Enterprise* TBFs, and six Marine Wildcats. The dive-bombers opened the attack at 1100, when the tireless Maj Joe Sailer led his pilots in; they got two 1,000-lb hits on one transport and one hit on another. Another half-squadron of SBDs got six hits on a third troopship. Three Torpedo-10 TBFs scored on another pair of ships, both of which sank. The water was filled with flailing, drowning soldiers and sailors. One badly damaged transport turned for home in the company of two destroyers.

Next up, at 1335, was a mixed strike of *Enterprise* and Marine Dauntlesses. In a series of piecemeal attacks lasting over an hour, the dive-bombers sank another transport and severely damaged two others. Later, another pack of *Enterprise* SBDs went four hits for eight tries. And a late-arriving Scouting-10 Dauntless launched a

437

solo attack through heavy antiaircraft fire to score a breathtaking direct hit.

The Cactus Air commanders worried through the afternoon that darkness would prevent their shuttling torpedo- and dive-bombers from completing the destruction of the transports. The aircrews were drained of energy.

Two flights totaling fifteen B-17s launched high-level attacks beginning at 1430. The results were negligible; fifteen tons of bombs were dropped and several pilots claimed hits, but none was confirmed. In passing through, however, the many-gunned Flying Fortresses downed six Zeros without loss.

The last eight SBDs launched by *Enterprise*, which retired to Noumea with only ten Wildcats aboard, found Tanaka at 1530. Each of the first three hit different ships, and the next four managed two near misses. The last man set his target ablaze with a 1,000-lb bomb dead amidships. Then eight of twelve Wildcat escorts strafed everything they could reach.

Seven unescorted Bombing-10 Dauntlesses left Henderson Field at 1530 and ran into trouble over the Japanese transports when Zeros, which hitherto had run from American fighters all day, stood their ground. Three of the SBDs were shot down and two others were seriously damaged and forced to retire without attacking.

The incredibly aggressive Maj Joe Sailer led the last strike of the day: twelve SBDs, four TBFs, and seven Marine F4Fs. As there were no aerial torpedoes left on Guadalcanal, the TBFs were armed with four 500-lb bombs apiece. The SBDs sank the sixth transport of the day and damaged two others, and the TBFs scored two hits on yet another transport.

One American loss, and an important one, was LtCol Joe Bauer, high-scoring skipper of VMF-212 and, more recently, the Cactus fighter commander. An extremely aggressive pilot known for his utter disdain for hostile fire, Bauer was downed—not for the first time—in a wild melee over the transports as the last dive-bombers were going in. Capt Joe Foss saw Bauer get clear of his sinking Wildcat and wave at friendly fighters stacked overhead.

Several Wildcats hovered over Bauer while Foss ran for home to get an amphibian scout plane with which to rescue the pilot everyone called "the Coach." By the time Foss returned, however, all the friendly fighters had left, one by one, as their fuel reserves dwindled. Though Foss searched until well after sunset, he was unable to find any sign of the Coach.

With one transport retiring and six lost, RAdm Raizo Tanaka had but four of the original eleven left when he passed the Russell Islands. Darkness was Tanaka's only ally. He had lost most of his ships. There were no more than 5,000 living Nagoya Division soldiers aboard the last of his damaged transports. Escort destroyers had been left behind, one at a time, to rescue swimmers; only four of ten remained.

The last gamble to land significant reinforcements on Starvation Island had failed. In the hope of salvaging what was left, the harried transport chief asked VAdm Gunichi Mikawa for permission to beach the ships at Doma Cove, near Cape Esperance. Mikawa said no, but his superior, VAdm Nobutake Kondo, said yes, then sent *Kirishima* and several cruisers to defend the unloading operation.

40

As the last of RAdm Raizo Tanaka's beleaguered troop transports steamed past the Russell Islands, VAdm Nobutake Kondo's improvised force of one battleship, two heavy cruisers, two light cruisers, and nine destroyers was making for Guadalcanal by way of the Slot. And RAdm Willis Lee's two battleships and four destroyers were closing on Sealark Channel from the southwest.

To Japanese minds, the night surface action off Guadalcanal on November 13 had been a victory of very mixed proportions. Japanese preliminary estimates, by no means sorted out since the battle, indicated a clear victory for their side; the Japanese accounted for the sinking of virtually all the American warships engaged in the action. But Admiral Abe's handling of the action resulted in his peremptory relief and forcible retirement within four months. Then the debacle at the hands of Guadalcanal-based American warplanes had further confused the sense of victory among Japanese naval commanders.

The job of retaking Guadalcanal was placed in the hands of

VAdm Nobutake Kondo, who had been named deputy commander in chief of the Combined Fleet only two weeks earlier. Kondo rushed south from Truk on November 13 with heavy cruisers *Atago* and *Takao* to join *Kirishima* and the smaller battleworthy survivors of Friday the thirteenth.

Kondo's appointment troubled many younger officers, who felt that his showing at Santa Cruz, where he held his surface units back when they might have engaged American surface warships, rendered him unworthy for so important a task as securing the waters adjacent to Guadalcanal.

Submarine *Trout* spotted the Japanese battle force, fired three torpedoes which all missed, and sent a plain-language sighting message which was also monitored by the Japanese. Thus, Kondo knew that an American battle force was approaching. Confirmatory aircraft sightings indicated that the enemy force was composed in part of heavy cruisers or battleships. Kondo thus divided his battle force into three groups, two for attacking the Americans, and one for covering Tanaka.

RAdm Willis Lee had no plan. Moreover, *South Dakota*'s forward turret had been hit by a bomb at Santa Cruz, and she was not yet up to full fighting trim. Furthermore, neither the two battleships nor any of the four destroyers had ever operated together, and no single officer was in charge of the four destroyers.

That two battleships were being risked in a possible surface action in restricted waters reflected the all-or-nothing attitude VAdm Bill Halsey had adopted, for they had been committed at his express command.

Lee's task force first sniffed the western approaches to Ironbottom Sound from west of Savo as it swept northward before shifting to an easterly heading. Lookouts were able to see the dim glare of fires on the western horizon. Shortly after 2100, November 14, Lee ordered course shifted to ninety degrees—due east—in order to enter Ironbottom Sound. Lee hoped to hit the main Japanese force first, then the covering force, then the transports, then whatever the transports had already landed on the beaches.

Lee's hurried departure for Guadalcanal had left him without knowledge of recent events at the scene, without even a radio call sign. Eager to get the latest word, the admiral simply broke into the radio frequency in use that night and asked for information. The radio watch officer had no knowledge of Lee or his force, so rejoined with a terse, "We do not recognize you!" Before that could be straightened out, Lee's radiomen picked up talk among three PT-boats patrolling north of Savo. When one boat reported, "There go two big ones, but I don't know whose they are," Lee broke into the Cactus circuit again: "Refer your big boss about Ching Lee; Chinese, catchee? Call off your boys!" The PT-boat replied that he knew who Lee was and that he was not after him. In response to Lee's earlier request for information, Cactus replied that it had none.

Light cruiser *Sendai* had the van when her lookouts spotted "two enemy cruisers and four destroyers" north of Savo at 2210. Two destroyers were sent to look around the south side of Savo while *Sendai* and destroyer *Shikinami* attempted to close on the American column. Kondo, who was aboard heavy cruiser *Atago*, quickly deployed light cruiser *Nagara* and four destroyers as an advance force while all remaining warships were sent to support *Kirishima*.

The moon was setting behind the mountains around Cape Esperance when Lee came to a westerly heading south of Savo at 2252. Three minutes later, surface-search radars pinpointed *Sendai*. Admiral Lee held his fire for twenty-four long minutes as he sought additional targets and waited for the Japanese light cruiser (and her unperceived destroyer escort) to close range. Then, with destroyer *Gwin* firing salvoes of star shells, *Washington* and *South Dakota* opened fire. *Sendai* and *Shikinami* immediately reversed course and ran.

Minutes later, destroyer *Walke* made contact with destroyers

Aranami and *Uranami*, which had been dispatched earlier to scout south of Savo. Destroyers *Benham*, *Preston*, and *Walke* opened fire on both targets. *Aranami* was hit, but the Americans soon lost contact because the targets' radar images merged with Savo's profile.

Meanwhile, *Gwin*, the fourth destroyer in the American battle line, spotted light cruiser *Nagara* and her escort of four destroyers as they emerged from behind Savo. The American destroyer gamely opened fire alone upon the Japanese with torpedoes and her 5-inch guns.

Uranami and the injured *Aranami*, invisible to American radars, each fired a spread of torpedoes at 2330, and *Nagara* and her four escorts followed suit at 2335.

Capt Thomas Gatch, *South Dakota*'s skipper, saw *Aranami* erupt in flames that quickly spread down the length of the ship, and exclaimed to his navigator, "What a glorious sight!" But he immediately recanted, for at that very moment, *Walke* received numerous shell hits and fell off to port while her guncrews returned salvo for salvo.

Three hundred yards astern, *Benham* continued to fire her guns, but her captain sneered at the opportunity to fire torpedoes at what appeared to be only destroyers. *Preston*'s guns were right on *Nagara*, but she got more than she could give when her fire rooms were disabled and her after stack was toppled.

Then the Japanese torpedoes began surging in.

༄

Lt Jack Walsh, *Walke*'s communications officer, had had a feeling about this action. Though blooded at the Coral Sea, Walsh had never before taken the precautions he did this night, had never worn a steel helmet in action before, had never inflated his life belt before. When the torpedo that hit *Walke* blew off her bows and spewed burning fuel oil down the length of the portion that remained afloat, Walsh was bodily lifted from his position on the bridge and rammed into an angle iron on the overhead. The impact broke Walsh's fifth cervical vertebra. When Walsh came down, he came down hard, tearing ligaments in his left leg, shattering his left kneecap. As Walsh groped around the darkened deck for a hand-hold, he felt the mangled face of an officer who had worn no helmet this night.

Then an 8-inch shell from one of the heavy cruisers struck *Walke*'s pilothouse, only a dozen feet beneath Lt Jack Walsh's feet, and the entire steel surface beneath the injured communicator bobbed and rolled as though alive. When Walsh tasted a wet, sticky substance that had covered him, he was relieved to find it was fuel oil and not blood.

Benham also lost her bows to a torpedo. *Gwin* took a 4.7-inch shell in the aft engine room and an 8-incher through her fantail. The engine room was destroyed and all five men in it were killed by the release of high-pressure steam. The ship immediately slowed as her power was halved. She was running in a great circle because her hydraulic system to the rudder had been holed. A great explosion welled up from the depths beneath *Gwin* as she rocked across the wakes of other ships, breaking the shear pins on the ready torpedoes. One fish slid out of its tube and hit the weather-deck rail before plunging into the water. Then other torpedoes slid out of their tubes as the ship bobbed through yet more wakes.

While *Washington*'s powerful and numerous secondary batteries fired, her main turrets remained inactive while radarmen tried to sort through the profusion of targets and separate them from the confusing echoes of nearby land masses. *South Dakota*, trailing the flagship by nearly a mile, withheld all fire because Captain Gatch feared hitting friendly vessels. *South Dakota*'s main circuit breakers jumped out at 2333, closing down her surface and gunnery radars.

Uncertain that Lee's was the only American force in the vicinity, the Japanese were loath to commit all they had. As time passed without further sightings, however, the full potential of Japanese gunnery was readied. Even fleeing *Sendai* and *Shikinami* put about again in the hope of approaching the American column from the vulnerable rear.

All four of the American destroyers had been disabled by 2335, and *South Dakota*, which had yet to fire, was blind. Only *Washington* was fully capable of putting up a fight, and she had yet to be fired on.

Preston, which was burning from end to end, was abandoned at 2336. She rolled over ten minutes later.

Walke was nearly beneath the waves by 2342, when she was ordered abandoned. Lt Jack Walsh, her injured communicator, was on the ladder to the director deck, over the bridge, when the word arrived. As Walsh made his way to the nearest rail with another officer, he was amazed to see that *Walke*'s aft gun was still putting out rounds. The two officers were all set to leap when a rift in the smoke and flames revealed a 70-foot drop directly into a jagged shellhole in the destroyer's canted flank. "For God's sake," Walsh screamed, "don't jump!" At that instant, several men hurtled from above, directly into the hole.

Walsh beat off the flames that were blistering his arms and legs and painfully climbed over the side. Only then did he realize that he had earlier been blown clear out of his shoes. When he removed his helmet, he found that his encounter with the overhead had creased it down the center, turning it into a steel fedora. The ship was still sliding forward as survivors kicked aftward to reclaim rafts they had earlier thrown overboard. Shells were flying overhead, from every direction it seemed. And then *Walke* disappeared, subjecting her surviving crew to the ultimate cruelty. Her own ready depth charges exploded beneath the thrashing men. Jack Walsh watched shipmates stiffen and disappear as the incredible pressure ruptured their intestines, killing them in indescribable agony. Walsh survived. In addition to his other injuries, his lungs were damaged; he would be coughing blood for a month.

Benham limped clear without her bows. Only *Gwin* remained, putting out what gunfire she could.

Lee, in *Washington*, ordered his battleships to a new course at 2335 in the hope of passing the damaged destroyers. But *South Dakota* had to steer violently to avoid *Benham*. As *South Dakota* cleared the scene of destruction, she was bathed in scalding light by at least four large searchlights. Thankfully, her power had been fully restored only a minute earlier, and gunnery plotters were already on target. Secondary batteries opened in an instant, and the new fast battleship's 16-inch turrets swung to bear on what appeared to be a battleship and two cruisers. When at last *South Dakota*'s main batteries opened on *Sendai*, the flash from her after main turret set her own spotter plane afire. The concussion from the very next salvo blew the burning wreckage overboard.

Lee ordered the surviving destroyers to retire at 2348, then stalked the Japanese with the battleships alone. *South Dakota*'s abrupt course shift to avoid *Benham* had placed her right in the midst of the retiring *Nagara* force, and *Washington* was lost from view.

Word of *South Dakota*'s position was passed to Admiral Kondo, on *Atago*'s flag bridge, and he ordered all ready torpedoes—a total of thirty-four—fired at the American super-heavy. Then Kondo entered the fight with his main force, *Kirishima*, heavy cruisers *Atago* and *Takao*, and destroyers *Asagumo* and *Teruzuki*. *South Dakota* was first hit in her superstructure by Japanese batteries 5,000 yards off.

Still undetected some 8,000 yards astern *South Dakota*, *Washington* plotted the Japanese and, while the former acted as bait, cut loose. *Kirishima* sustained numerous 16-inch hits while *Washington*'s 5-inch batteries hit all five of Kondo's warships.

Asagumo launched torpedoes at *South Dakota* while the other Japanese warships maintained a rapid fire with their guns. The Japanese were so engrossed with *South Dakota* that *Washington* remained undetected until she pumped nine 16-inch and forty 5-inch shells into *Kirishima* alone, damaging the battleship's steering. *Atago* and *Takao* were hit by both American battleships.

South Dakota sustained severe damage. At least two 14-inch and thirty-five smaller shells struck her during the twenty-minute exchange. Communications were totally disrupted, and gunnery control sustained numerous casualties among key personnel. Fires were sweeping her superstructure when, at 2350, Captain Gatch ordered his navigator to steer clear of the fight.

Admiral Lee ordered *Washington* to the northwest in the hope of drawing the Japanese away from the American cripples. Then he circled once and beat a hasty retreat around Cape Esperance, loosely accompanied by the survivors of his task force.

Kondo pulled out just after midnight, November 15, leaving *Kirishima* and *Aranami* to be scuttled.

The first grey streaks of sunlight found RAdm Raizo Tanaka tiredly peering from destroyer *Hayashio*'s bridge at the nearby island that had claimed so many of his nation's best soldiers, sailors, and airmen.

As Tanaka's destroyer turned to run, the last four transports turned into the surf and beached themselves at Tassafaronga and Doma Cove. Within minutes, the surviving Nagoya Division infantrymen were streaming ashore just beyond the best range of the nearest American land-based artillery.

Indefatigable Maj Joe Sailer led the first of day-long strikes against the beached, bleeding transports and the supply dumps just back of the surf line. Additional Cactus aircraft bypassed the beached vessels and flew north to search for Japanese cripples, two of which were sunk in the Slot.

After participating in several strafing sorties in the morning and early afternoon, Capt Jim Jarman, the commander of 67th Pursuit, followed a hunch and returned to investigate an area where he had earlier seen the flotsam and jetsam of the night's naval contest. What he found at about 1430 were living sailors, most of the men who had survived the sinking of *Walke*, men who for fourteen hours had been feebly beating against the tide with their hands, men whose only hope was Jim Jarman and the ships and boats he called to rescue them, men who would have been driven ashore in enemy territory in a matter of a few hours. Jarman actually had to fire his .30-caliber machine guns across the bows of an American destroyer

447

to divert it from the pressing business of shelling the beached transports.

Lt Jack Walsh, one of less than sixty *Walke* survivors, was first picked up by a landing boat from Kukum, then transferred to the destroyer. He was taken below to a bunk in the chiefs' quarters, where the pain from his broken neck and kneecap did not really penetrate the shock of losing his ship and shipmates. The ordeal was not quite finished, for the rescue ship was bombed and strafed by three Japanese marauders. Five sailors, including three from *Walke*, were killed.

Bombing and strafing attacks continued through the day, reducing supply dumps and beached transports to rubble, extinguishing the last faint Japanese hope that anything of value might be salvaged from so thorough a defeat.

The Japanese had been beaten at Guadalcanal, and even they could no longer avoid that stark truth.

Epilogue

The campaign to win Guadalcanal ebbed and raged until February 9, 1943. But its outcome had been assured by the American Marines and Guardsmen who stood their ground at Alligator Creek and Bloody Ridge, by the aggressive Cactus aircrews over Henderson Field and the Slot, and by American sailors near Cape Esperance.

First Marine Division continued to spar with 17th Army until the first week in December 1942, when it was relieved by the U.S. Army's Americal Division and evacuated to Australia to sort itself out and piece itself back together.

Two U.S. Army divisions, and one of Marines, continued what became an essentially offensive campaign to the inevitable conclusion, fighting a slow, conventional battle of attrition, breakthrough, and pursuit. In the course of the latter, post-decisional, portion of the campaign, Sendai Division was destroyed and Nagoya Division was severely crippled. In fact, only 13,000 of more than 50,000 ground troops the Japanese committed to the land battle were saved in a secret evacuation during the first week of February 1943. It is incomprehensible, but true, that fully 9,000 Japanese soldiers—a staggering toll—died as a result of non-battle-related causes—malaria, dengue, other exotic diseases, and starvation.

Following its virtuoso performance during the mid-November crisis, Cactus Air was called upon less and less to defend its home base and the Lunga Perimeter and more and more to mount strikes against Japanese bases farther along the Slot—preparatory to contemplated Allied advances.

Raw statistics can be starkly revealing. In the six-month period beginning August 7, 1942, both navies lost twenty-six warships, and about equal tonnage at that. Neither had the ships to lose, certainly, but the Japanese would never be able to replace their losses while, in time, the awakening arsenals of America would. The Japanese naval air arm lost 600 carrier- and land-based aircrews, and these would never be replaced. The only essentially modern striking arm the Imperial Navy possessed—its air arm—had been defeated and, as such, the Imperial Navy—and the Empire itself—had been defeated.

Withal, the outcome of the Guadalcanal Campaign was less a positive feat of American arms than a negative feat of Japanese powers of comprehension. Japan neither understood nor accepted what she had at stake in the Eastern Solomons. While America's initial comprehension was on the fuzzy side, her commanders came to more important conclusions and resolves early enough to wrest victory from what had begun essentially as a gamble.

The commitment of 1st Marine Division, in August 1942, had been, truly, a last-ditch effort in the face of Japan's unprecedented successes in the Pacific and East Asia. Given a different outcome, that commitment would have been called criminal by an American public that hung on every word of news while it was happening, and by history.

The struggle by 1st Marine Division and its supports to save themselves—virtually an act of desperation—had been a whisker-splitting decision. An Allied victory in the Pacific became not only possible but inevitable as a by-product of that desperation, and given the differences between East and West. A decisive defeat at any point during the campaign would have destroyed America's by-then fragile resolve to wage an offensive war in the Pacific. The victory nearly did!

It would be a full year from the night Lewie Puller's thin battalion stood its ground near Bloody Ridge until U.S. armed forces achieved the mental set of potential victors. There is no saying what might have happened had Puller's battalion cracked, or Red Mike Edson's before it. What did happen, in the end, is their testament, the testament of every man who served there.

After seeing to the rehabilitation of 1st Marine Division, Archer Vandegrift assumed command of I Marine Amphibious Corps to oversee the initial stages of the Bougainville Campaign. He departed the Pacific in late 1943 to become the eighteenth Commandant of the Marine Corps upon the retirement of his mentor, LtGen Thomas Holcomb.

Roy Geiger succeeded his old friend, Vandegrift, as commander of I Marine Amphibious Corps. Following the death in action of the Tenth United States Army commander on Okinawa, Geiger became the only Marine and only aviator ever to command a full American field army in combat. He died of cancer in 1947, refusing to the last to retire from the service of his country.

Bill Halsey retained command of the South Pacific and formed Third United States Fleet, which he commanded as a five-star fleet admiral with characteristic aggressiveness until war's end.

The austere, brilliant Richmond Kelly Turner commanded the South Pacific (III) Amphibious Force well into 1943, then formed V Amphibious Force to support the Central Pacific offensive. It has been said of the curmudgeonly Turner that no other man could have forged, nor wielded, so perfect a weapon as the American amphibious capability. He died in 1961, aged seventy-five years.

Red Mike Edson was transferred to 2nd Marine Division and served as its chief of staff at Tarawa and assistant division commander at Saipan, where he far exceeded the performance normally expected of men in those positions. He retired with two stars in

1947, served the state of Vermont as commissioner of public safety, and died in 1955 at age fifty-eight by his own hand.

After spending two years in Washington following his relief as South Pacific aircraft commander, Slew McCain commanded the fast carriers during the final, triumphant year of the war he had spent his entire adult life preparing to fight. He barely survived that war, dying suddenly at age sixty-one in his own home on September 6, 1945, while en route from the Tokyo Bay surrender ceremonies to new duties in Washington.

Bill Whaling commanded 1st Marines on New Britain and won his star before Korea. A field soldier through and through, Whaling was not marked for high command, so retired from the Marine Corps in 1954 with his second star.

The acerbic, brilliant John Lucien Smith never again flew in combat, though he held various important staff and command positions until retiring from the Marine Corps as a full colonel in 1961. He died in 1972 at age fifty-seven by his own hand.

Pedro del Valle, the first Puerto Rican national to graduate from the U.S. Naval Academy, commanded 1st Marine Division at Okinawa and was retired with three stars after the war. He spent his declining years immersed in extreme right-wing and anti-Semitic politics, dying in 1978, aged eighty-four years.

Joe Foss, the hottest fighter pilot to emerge from Cactus Air, scored his twenty-sixth kill during his second tour at Guadalcanal in February 1943, thus tying Eddie Rickenbacker's World War I record. He was elected governor of his native South Dakota in 1954, and served two terms before going into private business. He attained flag rank as a member of the South Dakota Air National Guard.

Maj Joe Sailer, the late-arriving, incredibly skilled dive-bomber leader, died at the controls of his Dauntless on December 7, 1942, after aggressively pressing home his twenty-fifth dive-bombing attack in little more than a month. Ships' fire damaged the dive-bomber flown that day by the stocky, blond man who had left a good job with Sperry Rand to go on active duty in 1940, and a

Zero fighter finished him off before the unbelieving eyes of many of the men he had led so well.

Lt Smokey Stover returned home for leave and a new assignment following his departure with the last of Fighting-5 from Cactus. He served as a division leader aboard *Yorktown* and took part in the great Truk raid. On the first day of that raid, February 16, 1944, Stover was shot down just off the beach. He was seen getting into his life raft and, for over an hour, friends orbited overhead as the tide slowly carried him to the reef. He was never seen again—never ventured, as in boyhood dreams, outward to the stars.

Lew Walt earned Navy Crosses at Guadalcanal and New Britain. More than two decades later, he commanded all the Marines in Vietnam. He retired from the Marine Corps in 1971 after serving, with four stars, as assistant commandant.

Bill Hawkins was promoted major in October 1942, and shipped off the island to serve as quartermaster of a Navy cargo ship, which was sunk off Kukum on Hawkins's first trip back to the island. He subsequently served as quartermaster aboard Kelly Turner's flagship, which was tragically sunk by friendly PT-boats early in the New Georgia Campaign, in mid-1943. That ended Bill Hawkins's combat career, but he remained in the Marine Corps Reserve through the 1960s. Hawkins's brother, Bob, whom he last saw ashore during the Koro embarrassment, survived the loss of his ship at Savo, went into aviation, and was killed in the air late in the war.

Lewie Puller became a larger-than-life legend known as "Chesty." He served as Bill Whaling's exec with 1st Marines on New Britain, then commanded that regiment in the incredible, wasteful Peleliu fighting. He again commanded 1st Marines in Korea, at Inchon, Seoul, and the Chosin Reservoir, where he earned his fifth Navy Cross. Puller retired from the Marine Corps as a lieutenant general, having enlisted in 1917 as a private and having held every rank in between. No U.S. Marine has ever won more combat decorations than Chesty Puller.

Charlie Kelly, Puller's exec, remained on active duty after the war and eventually retired as a colonel. He underwent successful cancer surgery in 1979, but succumbed to a massive heart attack in 1982. And Frank Blakely, the 1st Regiment communicator who had married just before shipping out to the Pacific, succumbed to a long fight with cancer in 1984. They are but two from a long and growing list.

For a full generation, Marines of an age rightly or wrongly made claims to younger Marines and anyone who would listen that they had served at Guadalcanal "during the bad days." But the youngest of the veterans are long retired, and only faint echoes of their legend remain in a Marine Corps where now only a relative handful of active-duty Marines even weathered Vietnam.

And what of the tens of thousands of others who helped win Cactus? They served their hitches, won their war, learned their trades, earned their degrees, raised their families, and lived out the American dream they dreamed so vividly during those dark, dark days of their youth.

APPENDIX A

GROUND UNITS COMMAND LIST
August 7–November 14, 1942

FIRST MARINE DIVISION

Commanding General	MGen Alexander A. Vandegrift
Assistant Commander	BGen William H. Rupertus
Chief of Staff	Col William C. James (to Sept. 21)
	Col Gerald C. Thomas
Personnel	Col Robert C. Kilmartin, Jr. (to Sept. 21)
	Maj James C. Murray, Jr.
Intelligence	LtCol Frank B. Goettge (MIA, Aug. 12)
	LtCol Edmund J. Buckley
Operations	LtCol Gerald C. Thomas (to Sept. 21)
	LtCol Merrill B. Twining
Supply	LtCol Randolph McC. Pate (to Oct. 21)
	LtCol Raymond P. Coffman

1st Signal Company

CO	Maj Edward W. Snedeker

1st Amphibious Tractor Battalion

CO	Maj Walter C. Barr

1st Engineer Battalion
CO   Maj James G. Frazer (to Oct. 24)
                                   Maj Henry H. Crockett
1st Pioneer Battalion
CO   Col George B. Rowan (to Sept. 19)
                                   Maj Robert G. Ballance
1st Medical Battalion
CO   Cdr Don S. Knowlton, USN
1st Service Battalion
CO   LtCol Hawley C. Waterman
1st Tank Battalion (Forward Echelon)
CO   Maj Harvey S. Walseth
1st Special Weapons Battalion
CO   LtCol Robert B. Luckey (to Oct. 15)
                                   Maj Richard W. Wallace

1st MARINE REGIMENT

CO	Col Clifton B. Cates
1st Battalion	LtCol Lenard B. Cresswell
2nd Battalion	LtCol Edwin A. Pollock (to Sept. 25)
	LtCol William W. Stickney
3rd Battalion	LtCol William N. McKelvey, Jr.

5th MARINE REGIMENT

CO	Col Leroy P. Hunt (to Sept. 19)
	Col Merritt A. Edson
1st Battalion	LtCol William E. Maxwell (to Aug. 28)
	Maj Milton V. O'Connell (to Aug. 30)
	Maj Donald W. Fuller (to Oct. 11)
	Maj William K. Enright (to Oct. 23)
	Maj William P. Thyson (to Oct. 30)
	Maj William K. Enright
2nd Battalion	LtCol Harold E. Rosecrans (WIA, Sept. 11)
	Capt Joseph J. Dudkowski (to Sept. 17)
	Maj Walker A. Reaves (to Sept. 24)

	Capt Joseph J. Dudkowski (to Sept. 30)
	Maj David S. McDougal (WIA, Oct. 8)
	Maj Lewis W. Walt
3rd Battalion	LtCol Frederick C. Biebush (to Sept. 21)
	LtCol Robert O. Bowen

7th MARINE REGIMENT (from Sept. 18)

CO	Col James C. Webb (to Sept. 19)
	Col Amor L. Sims
1st Battalion	LtCol Lewis B. Puller (WIA, Nov. 8)
	Maj John C. Weber (to Nov. 12)
	Capt Charles W. Kelly, Jr.
2nd Battalion	LtCol Herman H. Hanneken
3rd Battalion	LtCol Edwin J. Farrell (to Sept. 21)
	LtCol William R. Williams

11th MARINE REGIMENT

CO	BGen Pedro A. del Valle
1st Battalion (from Sept. 18)	
	LtCol Joseph R. Knowlan (to Oct. 10)
	LtCol Manley L. Curry
2nd Battalion	LtCol Edward J. Hagen (to Oct. 19)
	Maj Forest C. Thompson (to Oct. 30)
	Maj Lewis A. Ennis (to Nov. 5)
	Maj Forest C. Thompson
3rd Battalion	LtCol James J. Keating
4th Battalion	*Not Committed*
5th Battalion	LtCol E. Hayden Price (to Oct. 30)
	Maj Noah P. Wood

ATTACHED GROUND UNITS

2nd MARINE REGIMENT

CO	Col John M. Arthur
1st Battalion	LtCol Robert E. Hill
2nd Battalion	LtCol Orin K. Pressley

3rd Battalion　　　　　　　　LtCol Robert G. Hunt

1st Battalion, 8th Marines (from Nov. 2)

CO　　　　　　　　　　　　LtCol Miles S. Newton

1st Battalion, 10th Marines (from Nov. 4)

CO　　　　　　　　　　　　LtCol Presley M. Rixey

3rd Battalion, 10th Marines

CO　　　　　　　　　　　　LtCol Manley L. Curry (to Oct. 17)

　　　　　　　　　　　　　　LtCol Donovan D. Sult

1st Raider Battalion (Aug. 7–Oct. 16)

CO　　　　　　　　　　　　LtCol Merritt A. Edson (to Sept. 20)

　　　　　　　　　　　　　　LtCol Samuel B. Griffith, II (WIA, Sept. 27)

　　　　　　　　　　　　　　Capt Ira J. Irwin

1st Parachute Battalion (Aug. 7–Sept. 18)

CO　　　　　　　　　　　　Maj Robert H. Williams (WIA, Aug. 7)

　　　　　　　　　　　　　　Maj Charles A. Miller (to Sept. 5)

　　　　　　　　　　　　　　Capt Harold L. Torgerson (to Sept. 8)

　　　　　　　　　　　　　　Maj Charles A. Miller (to Sept. 12)

　　　　　　　　　　　　　　Capt Harold L. Torgerson

3rd Defense Battalion

CO　　　　　　　　　　　　Col Robert H. Pepper

164th INFANTRY REGIMENT (U.S. Army) (from Oct. 13)

CO　　　　　　　　　　　　Col Bryant E. Moore

1st Battalion　　　　　　　LtCol Frank E. Richards

2nd Battalion　　　　　　　LtCol Arthur C. Timboe (to Nov. 10)

　　　　　　　　　　　　　　LtCol Ben J. Northridge

3rd Battalion　　　　　　　LtCol Robert K. Hall

6th Naval Construction Battalion (U.S. Navy) (from Sept. 1)

CO　　　　　　　　　　　　Cdr Joseph P. Blundon

Construction Unit (Base) 1 (U.S. Navy) (from Aug. 18)

CO　　　　　　　　　　　　Ens George K. Polk

APPENDIX B

AIR UNITS COMMAND LIST
(The Cactus Air Force)
August 20–November 14, 1942

FIRST MARINE AIRCRAFT WING (Forward Echelon)
(from Sept. 3)

Commanding General	BGen Roy S. Geiger
Chief of Staff	BGen Louis E. Woods
Personnel	LtCol Perry O. Parmelee
Intelligence	LtCol John C. Munn
Operations	Col Lawson H. M. Sanderson
Supply	Col Christian F. Schilt

MARINE AIR GROUP 14 (from Oct. 16)

CO	LtCol Albert D. Cooley

MARINE AIR GROUP 23 (Aug. 20–Nov. 4)

CO	Col William J. Wallace

MARINE AIR GROUP 25 (At Espiritu Santo) (from Sept. 3)

CO   Col Perry K. Smith

Marine Fighter Squadron 112 (from Nov. 2)
CO   Maj Paul J. Fontana

Marine Fighter Squadron 121 (from Oct. 2)
CO   Maj Leonard K. Davis

Marine Scout-Bomber Squadron 131 (from Nov. 11)
CO   LtCol Paul Moret

Marine Scout-Bomber Squadron 132 (from Nov. 1)
CO   Maj Joseph K. Sailer, Jr.

Marine Scout-Bomber Squadron 141 (from Sept. 23)
CO   Maj Gordon E. Bell (KIA, Oct. 14)
                                  1stLt Wortham S. Ashcroft (KIA, Nov. 8)
                                  1stLt Robert M. Patterson (to Nov. 11)
                                  2ndLt Walter R. Bartosh

Marine Scout-Bomber Squadron 142 (from Nov. 12)
CO   Maj Robert H. Richard

Marine Utility Squadron 152 (Transport)
CO   Maj Elmore W. Seeds

Marine Fighter Squadron 212 (from Oct. 17)
CO   LtCol Harold W. Bauer (MIA, Nov. 14)
                                  Maj Frederick R. Payne, Jr.

Marine Fighter Squadron 223 (Aug. 20–Oct. 16)
CO   Capt John L. Smith

Marine Fighter Squadron 224 (Aug. 30–Nov. 2)
CO   Maj Robert E. Galer

Marine Scout-Bomber Squadron 231 (Aug. 30–Nov. 14)
CO   Maj Leo R. Smith (to Sept. 18)
                                  Capt Ruben Iden (KIA, Sept. 20)
                                  Capt Elmer G. Glidden, Jr.

Marine Scout-Bomber Squadron 232 (Aug. 20–Nov. 2)
CO   Maj Richard C. Mangrum

Marine Observation Squadron 251 (from Aug. 19)
CO   LtCol John N. Hart (to Oct. 29)
                                  LtCol Charles H. Hayes

Marine Utility Squadron 253 (Transport) (from Sept. 3)
CO   Maj Harold A. Johnson (to Oct. 11)
        Maj Henry C. Lane

ARMY AIR FORCES UNITS

67th Pursuit Squadron (from Aug. 22)
CO   Capt Dale D. Brannon (WIA, Sept. 14)
        Capt James T. Jarman
11th Heavy Bombardment Group (At Espiritu Santo) (from Aug. 7)
CO   BGen La Verne G. Saunders

U.S. NAVY AIR UNITS

Enterprise Flight 300 (Aug. 24–Sept. 27)
CO   Lt Turner F. Caldwell, Jr.
Scouting Squadron 3 (Saratoga) (Sept. 6–Oct. 17)
CO   LCdr Louis J. Kirn
Fighting Squadron 5 (Saratoga) (Sept. 11–Oct. 16)
CO   LCdr Leroy C. Simpler
Torpedo Squadron 8 (Saratoga) (Sept. 13–Nov. 16)
CO   Lt Harold H. Larsen
Scouting Squadron 71 (Wasp) (Sept. 28–Nov. 7)
CO   LCdr John Eldridge, Jr. (KIA, Nov. 2)
Bombing Squadron 6 (Enterprise) (Oct. 14–Nov. 3)
CO   LCdr Ray Davis

BIBLIOGRAPHY

BOOKS

Belote, James H., and William N. Belote. *Titans of the Sea: The Development and Operations of Japanese and American Carrier Task Forces During World War II*. New York: Harper & Row, 1975.

Bulkley, Capt Robert J., Jr. *At Close Quarters*. Washington: Office of Naval History, 1962.

Cook, Capt Charles. *The Battle of Cape Esperance*. New York: Thomas W. Crowell Co., 1968.

Cooper, Harold. *Among Those Present: The Official Story of the Pacific Islands at War*. London: HM Printing Office, 1946.

Craven, Wesley F., and James Lea Cate, eds. *The Army Air Forces in World War II*, Vol. IV: *The Pacific: Guadalcanal to Saipan (August 1942–July 1944)*. Chicago: The University of Chicago Press, 1950.

Cronin, Francis D. *Under the Southern Cross: The Saga of the Americal Division*. Washington: Combat Forces Press, 1951.

Davis, Burke. *Marine!* Boston: Little, Brown & Co., 1962.

Feldt, Cdr Eric A. *The Coast Watchers.* New York: Oxford University Press, 1946.

Griffith, BGen Samuel B., II. *The Battle for Guadalcanal.* Philadelphia: J. B. Lippincott & Co., 1963.

Hailey, Foster. *Pacific Battle Line.* New York: MacMillan & Co., 1944.

Halsey, FAdm William F., Jr., and LCdr Julian Bryan. *Admiral Halsey's Story.* New York: Whittlesey House, 1947.

Hara, Capt Tameichi, with Fred Saito and Roger Pineau. *Japanese Destroyer Captain.* New York: Ballantine Books, 1961.

Hayashi, Saburo, and Alvin D. Coox. *Kogun: The Japanese Army in the Pacific War.* Quantico: Marine Corps Association, 1959.

Heinl, Col Robert D. *Soldiers of the Sea.* Annapolis: United States Naval Institute, 1962.

Hough, LtCol Frank O., Maj Verle E. Ludwig, and Henry I. Shaw. *U.S. Marine Corps Operations in World War II*, Vol. I: *Pearl Harbor to Guadalcanal.* Washington: U.S. Government Printing Office, 1958.

Isely, Jeter A., and Philip A. Crowl. *The U.S. Marines and Amphibious War.* Princeton: Princeton University Press, 1951.

Johnston, Richard W. *Follow Me: The Story of the Second Marine Division in World War II.* New York: Random House, 1948.

Leckie, Robert. *Helmet for My Pillow.* New York: Random House, 1962.

———. *Strong Men Armed.* New York: Random House, 1962.

———. *Challenge for The Pacific.* Garden City: Doubleday & Co., 1965.

Lord, Walter. *Lonely Vigil: Coastwatchers of the Solomons.* New York: Viking Press, 1977.

McMillan, George. *The Old Breed: A History of the First Marine Division in World War II.* Washington: Infantry Journal Press, 1949.

Merillat, Capt Herbert C. *The Island: A History of the Marines on Guadalcanal.* Boston: Houghton Mifflin & Co. and The Riverside Press, 1944.

Metcalf, Col Clyde H. *The Marine Corps Reader.* New York: G. P. Putnam & Sons, 1944.

Miller, John, Jr. *Guadalcanal: The First Offensive. The U.S. Army in World War II.* Washington: U.S. Government Printing Office, 1949.

Miller, Thomas G., Jr. *The Cactus Air Force.* New York: Harper & Row, 1969.

Morison, RAdm Samuel Eliot. *History of United States Naval Operations in World War II*, Vol. V: *The Struggle for Guadalcanal.* Boston: The Atlantic Monthly and Little, Brown & Co., 1962.

Newcomb, Richard F. *Savo!* New York: Holt, Rinehart & Winston, 1961.

Okumiya, Masatake, and Jiro Horikoshi. *Zero!: The Inside Story of Japan's Air War in the Pacific.* New York: E. P. Dutton & Co., 1956.

Potter, E. B. *Nimitz.* Annapolis: Naval Institute Press, 1976.

Pratt, Fletcher. *The Marines' War.* New York: William Sloane Associates, 1948.

Reeder, LtCol Russell P., Jr. *Fighting on Guadalcanal.* Washington: Department of the Army, 1943.

Roscoe, Theodore. *United States Destroyer Operations in World War II.* Annapolis: Naval Institute Press, 1953.

Sherrod, Robert. *History of Marine Corps Aviation in World War II.* Washington: Combat Forces Press, 1952.

Stafford, Cdr. Edward P. *The Big E: The Story of the USS Enterprise.* New York: Random House, 1962.

Stover, E. T., and Clark Reynolds. *The Saga of Smokey Stover.* Charleston: Tradd Street Press, 1978.

Toland, John. *The Rising Sun: The Decline and Fall of the Japanese Empire.* New York: Random House, 1970.

Tregaskis, Richard. *Guadalcanal Diary.* New York: Random House, 1943.

Vandegrift, Gen A. A., and Robert Asprey. *Once A Marine: The Memoirs of General A. A. Vandegrift, USMC.* New York: W. W. Norton & Co., 1964.

Williams, Mary R. *Chronology: 1941-1945. The U.S. Army in World War II.* Washington: U.S. Government Printing Office and Office of the Chief of Military History, 1950.

Zimmerman, Maj John. *The Guadalcanal Campaign.* Washington: U.S. Government Printing Office and Marine Corps Historical Branch, 1949.

PERIODICALS

Baglien, LtCol Samuel. "The Second Battle for Henderson Field." *Infantry Journal* (May 1944).

Baker, Col Warren P. "The Blackest Day of the War." *Marine Corps Gazette* (August 1984).

Cates, BGen Clifton B. "Battle of the Tenaru." *Marine Corps Gazette* (August 1943).

del Valle, BGen Pedro A. "Marine Field Artillery on Guadalcanal." *Field Artillery Journal* (October 1943).

Dieckmann, Edward A., Sr. "Manila John Basilone." *Marine Corps Gazette* (October 1963).

Gates, Thomas F. "Track of the Tomcatters: A History of VF-31, Part II: Fighting Six at Guadalcanal." *The Hook* (Winter 1984).

Hammel, Eric. "Guadalcanal: First Battle of the Matanikau." *Marine Corps Gazette* (August 1982).

———. "Gavutu." *Leatherneck* (November 1984).

———. "Bogies At Angels Twelve." *World War II* (May 1986).

———. "Stand At The Matanikau Sandspit." *Leatherneck* (October 1986).

———. "Black Tuesday." *Marine Corps Gazette* (November 1986).

Henderson, Col F. P., "Naval Gunfire Support in the Solomons, Part I: Guadalcanal." *Marine Corps Gazette* (March 1956).

Lundstrom, John B. "Saburo Sakai Over Guadalcanal." *Fighter Pilots in Aerial Combat* (Fall 1982, and Winter 1983).

Ohmae, Capt Toshikazu. "Japanese Commentary on Guadalcanal." *United States Naval Institute Proceedings* (Vol. 77).

Tanaka, RAdm Raizo. "Japan's Losing Struggle for Guadalcanal." *United States Naval Institute Proceedings* (Vol. 82).

INDEX

467

INDEX